CURSED LEGACY

FREDERIC SPOTTS

CURSED LEGACY

THE TRAGIC LIFE OF KLAUS MANN

YALE UNIVERSITY PRESS
NEW HAVEN AND LONDON

For information about this and other Yale University Press publications, please contact:

U.S. Office: sales.press@yale.edu   yalebooks.com
Europe Office: sales@yaleup.co.uk   yalebooks.co.uk

Typeset in Minion Pro by IDSUK (DataConnection) Ltd
Printed in Great Britain by TJ International Ltd, Padstow, Cornwall

Library of Congress Control Number: 2016932440

ISBN 978-0-300-21800-8

A catalogue record for this book is available from the British Library

10 9 8 7 6 5 4 3 2 1

But soon he knew himself the most unfit
Of men to herd with Man; with whom he held
Little in common; untaught to submit
His thoughts to others, though his soul was quell'd
In youth by his own thoughts; still uncompell'd,
He would not yield dominion of his mind
To spirits against whom his own rebell'd;
Proud though in desolation; which could find
A life within itself, to breathe without mankind.

Lord Byron

Contents

Illustrations

All illustrations courtesy of Literaturarchiv der Monacensia, Munich, except 2 © ullstein bild

Acknowledgements

However sincere, words of thanks generally lie cold on a page of acknowledgements. That said, let me express gratitude for help, advice and counsel in various ways I received from Candida Brazil, Ina Cooper, Sally Ciampa, Rachael Lonsdale, Anthea Morton-Saner, James Rogers and Ann Pellant.

I wish also to thank Monacensia, a branch of the Munich Stadtbibliotek, for access to their superb Klaus Mann archive. I am indebted to Duke University Libraries, Special Collections for letters of Carson McCullers and the Harry Ransom Center of the University of Texas at Austin for correspondence with McCullers, Sybille Bedford, Blanche Knopf, Ernst Morris and Carlton Lake.

Anyone interested in the life of Klaus Mann must feel admiration for Fredric Kroll who, assisted by Klaus Täubert, appears to have tracked down every surviving document pertaining to Klaus's life and work. He furthermore corresponded with or interviewed anyone with additional pertinent information. The results have been compiled in six volumes. Also indispensable is Michael Grunewald's *Klaus Mann 1906–1949: Eine Bibliographie*, listing everything Klaus wrote and got into print from 'Hamsters Ende' in 1916 when he was not yet six to *Der Wendepunkt* in 1952, altogether roughly a thousand items. Also valuable are two albums of photographs and text by Uwe Naumann: '*Ruhe gibt es nicht, bis zum Schluss*': *Klaus Mann (1906–1949)* (2001) and *Die Kinder der Manns: Ein Familienalbum* (2005).

This book would not be in print were it not for the confidence and support of Robert Baldock of Yale University Press, London.

Introduction

Klaus Mann was six times jinxed. A son of Thomas Mann. A homeless exile. A drug addict. A writer unable to publish in his native tongue. A not-so-gay gay. Someone haunted all his life by a fascination with death.

From the outbreak of the Great War when he was eight to the beginning of the Cold War when he was forty, he lived in a world of turmoil, fear, conflict and unspeakable atrocities. He witnessed the abdication of the Kaiser, the rise and fall of the Weimar Republic, the triumph of Hitler, emigration, war, occupation and the division of Europe. His life symbolized the plight of the European intellectual in the world created by Lenin, Stalin, Hitler, Mussolini, Franco and their lesser ilk.

'Every human life is at once unique and representative.' Klaus lived these words. Today he interests us both as an individual and as a European of the first half of the twentieth century. This is therefore the account not just of his life but of life as it was lived by tens of thousands of Germans and other nationalities made homeless because of their ideology, race or nationality. Klaus was the first to acknowledge that he was vastly better off than the great majority of exiles. But the problems he faced – statelessness, homelessness, loneliness, anxiety, dread of war, fear for his life – were the common lot. This is why he considered his novels and autobiographies, no less than his political writings, to be contributions to social history. And so they have come to be regarded.

Writing was what kept him going. It was the one unifying element in his discordant life. He lived for it and through it. He began at the age of six with a poem he gave his father one breakfast-time and then never stopped. But from early childhood he was torn between this irrepressible creative urge and equally irrepressible thoughts of extinction. Over and over again he turned to writing as an antidote to the attraction of death. 'I am reasonably well; I am trying to write' are the words he put down in a letter to his mother and sister Erika just hours before he died.

The signal mark of both Klaus's writings and his character is courage. The literary *enfant terrible* of the Weimar era, he dared to write the first gay play, the first gay novel and the first gay autobiography in Germany. And when the Nazis came to power, he was among the few who immediately took up a pen to fight them. His reward was to be blacklisted, to have his books burned in public squares around Germany, to be denounced as 'a dangerous half-Jew', and find himself deprived of his passport and citizenship.

Over the years Klaus published seven novels, a half-dozen plays, four biographies, three autobiographies and hundreds of stories, as well as an enormous number of essays, articles and reviews. With his sister Erika he further co-authored four works of nonfiction. Today he is perhaps best known as the author of *Mephisto*, a novel which, after scandalizing both the Nazi authorities and the postwar West German courts, became an unprecedented bestseller and was eventually turned into a prize-winning film.

After the war Klaus was almost forgotten. In 1933 he had rejected Hitler's Germany; after 1945 Adenauer's Germany rejected him. His works had been forbidden in Hitler's Germany; his works were forbidden for a time in Adenauer's Germany – or at least no publisher dared touch them. 'The public is not interested in the views of an émigré' are the approximate words of the West German courts in upholding a ban on *Mephisto* in 1971. Slandered as a disloyal renegade and Stalinist agent in the country of his birth and aspersed as a communist sex pervert in his adopted country of the United States, he died in France in 1949 as the ultimate homeless alien.

Perhaps it was fitting that his life ended there. Because it was in France where he was 'rediscovered'. *Visionaire, radical, courageux, engagé*, Klaus was the sort of figure who was bound to intrigue the French, who came to regard his life and works as essential to an understanding of the period. Even before 1933 several of his books had been published in Paris. And it was in Paris, after the war, where *Mephisto* first appeared, long before it was published in West Germany. However, it wasn't until 1979 that Klaus Mann's work saw a true renaissance, beginning with a sensational adaptation of *Mephisto* by Ariane Mnouchkine's Théâtre du Soleil. Then, one by one, his major fiction and nonfiction works, as well as his diaries and a variety of books about him, were translated, published and kept in print. When his autobiographical *Le Tournant* ('The Turning Point') was published in French in March 1985, it was an instant bestseller. An exhibition about his life organized by the Goethe Institute in Paris in 2002 ran for two years. In 2006, on the occasion of the hundredth anniversary of his birth, a symposium was held in Sanary-sur-Mer, his favourite refuge following his flight from the Third Reich.

By now a new generation of Germans, no longer complicit in the crimes of the past, had also discovered Klaus's writings and was fascinated. There was a sudden Klaus Mann revival, even the emergence of a Klaus Mann cult. Here was a person of whom they, as Germans, could be proud. The scandalous legal battle over *Mephisto*, the publication of his diary, letters, essays, journalism and fictional writings, along with the various documentary films about Klaus and his family, brought him vividly to public attention. He spoke to young Germans in a way his father did not. For his boldness in promoting understanding of homosexuals, the city of Frankfurt in September 1995 established Klaus-Mann-Platz in the city centre. Postwar fame came far too late, but it came.

Posthumous accounts of someone's life are often 'what-the-butler-saw'; a story viewed through a keyhole. No need to peek in Klaus's case; he flung open the door and, through his autobiographies, letters and the fictional writings that are to some extent allegories of his inner life, he invited the butler in. Although he destroyed a childhood diary, he started another in October 1931 and kept it until the end of his life. It was his best friend, from whom he withheld no secrets.

Still, diaries, letters and so on omit and conceal as much as they inform and reveal. For example, Klaus was perfectly frank about his sex life. But, even in the privacy of his diary, he found it almost impossible to discuss his relationship with his father, who despised, tormented and humiliated him. More than anything else Klaus craved Thomas's approval, and when this was denied him, he turned his frustration and anger inward, where it took shape in lifelong periods of depression, drug addiction and longing for death. Similarly, while his autobiographies paint a picture of someone content and productive, his diary sometimes reads like a verbal version of Munch's *The Scream*, revealing a man so desperately angst-ridden that he often had to dope himself to keep going and even then sometimes wanted to die. Thus writing his biography is much like trying to paint the portrait of ectoplasm, the obfusc and ethereal form never sits still.

'A cold grey blowy day, made memorable by the sight of a kingfisher . . .' So once wrote Virginia Woolf, adding, 'No biographer could possibly guess this important fact about my life in the late summer of 1926. Yet biographers pretend they know people.' To this her biographer and nephew Quentin Bell commented, 'They don't, or at least they ought not to. All that they can claim is that they know a little more than does the public at large . . .'

First Writings
1906–24

On a hill above the harbour at Cannes lies Le Grand-Jas, a large, pleasantly landscaped cemetery. Among those buried in the Protestant corner are Lord Brougham, the English peer who established Cannes as a famous resort; the actress Martine Carol; Peter Carl Fabergé, the jewellery designer; Picasso's first wife, Olga Khokhlova, along with his grandson Pablo-Luiz; the writer Prosper Mérimée; as well as the opera singer Lily Pons. And Klaus Mann. He died on the evening of 21 May 1949 at the age of forty-two. Biographic orthodoxy has it that he deliberately killed himself. Biographic orthodoxy errs.

'Where does the story begin?' Klaus asked himself when he came to write his autobiography, *The Turning Point*, in 1942. He was certain that it did not really start on 18 November 1906 at the family home on Franz Joseph Strasse 2 in Munich. His life had begun years, even centuries, earlier. He was a product, perhaps a victim, of remote adventures and forgotten passions. Was the restlessness in his blood, for example, the pirate tradition inherited from his father's Nordic ancestors? His compulsion to write: could that have been a trait from his mother's highly civilized family?

His father, Thomas, was of old Hanseatic gentry; his mother, Katia Pringsheim, came from a seriously wealthy and seriously cultivated family of Jews who had become Protestant a generation earlier. Klaus saw their marriage 'not as the meeting between two contrasting moods and races but rather the union of two beings mysteriously akin to one another in a protective alliance'. Katia's explanation was more limpid: 'I married only because I wanted children.'

And so she and Thomas were fruitful and multiplied. In 1905 the first child was born. To their disappointment it was a girl, whom they named Erika. The next year they were overjoyed when a boy, whom they called Klaus Heinrich Thomas, was born, guaranteeing the Mann dynastic name. He and Erika looked so much alike and were so emotionally close, they were known as 'the twins'; they dressed similarly and even celebrated their birthdays on the same date. Another son, Gottfried Angelus Thomas, followed in 1909, and a daughter, Monika, the year after. In 1918 Elisabeth Veronika arrived, and exactly a year later came Michael. They all had nicknames, which they used throughout their lives. Erika was Eri, Klaus was Eissi (also Aissi), Gottfried Angelus was replaced forever by Golo, Monika was Mönnle, Elisabeth was Medi and Michael was Bibi. The much-loved Pringsheim grandmother, Hedwig, was Offi, her husband, Alfred, Ofey. Katia, whose baptismal name was Katharina, was Mielein and Thomas was known as 'Der Zauberer' – 'The Magician' – having once dressed as one for a costume party. That was how Klaus always referred to him in his writing, never as 'Father' or 'Dad'.

What had Thomas and Katia brought into the world? With his customary exuberance, the literary journalist Marcel Reich-Ranicki called them 'the German Windsors', presumably meaning that, while some were respectable, a few scandalous and many controversial, they all effortlessly caught the public eye. 'What a strange family we are!' Klaus wrote in his diary on 3 July 1936. 'Books will be written about us.' And so they were. But the family's cultural influence went well beyond books. The Manns left a mark on Germany greater than that of any other family in the country's history, even the scandalous Wagners or the murderous Krupps.

Happy families are all alike; every unhappy family is unhappy in its own way, as has been famously said. This family's way to unhappiness can be summed up in two words: Thomas Mann. He was not simply a famous writer but an institution of almost mythical stature. For his children he was not just a *Vater* but an *Übervater*. In fact, he was even more than that. For reasons they themselves could never explain, he had the effect of a black hole, swallowing everything within its horizon. He exercised an inexplicable spell over them that each spent a lifetime trying, unsuccessfully, to exorcize.

Katia, however, never fell under this spell. To be sure, she had from the start reconciled herself to devoting her life to her family, taking charge of the household and attending to the children. Yet she was anything but a simple *hausfrau*. She was tough and she had a sharper mind than her husband – as he knew. But she overdid it in a *faux-naïf* comment late in her life, when she claimed, 'My husband and I never quarrelled and since the atmosphere was very harmonious, it was not unfavourable for the children.' The children knew better. Both parents were short tempered and their rows were painful. 'You never liked me and I did not like you either', Golo remembered Thomas once shouting at Katia. 'I writhed in silent agony. Their clashes caused me considerable sorrow.'

In everyday life Klaus summed up the children's relationship with their parents in two sentences: 'Mielein minds you losing your new gloves or being late at the dentist's. The Magician does not even know that you possess gloves or that your teeth require medical treatment.' Klaus described Katia as warm, understanding and always approachable. 'I could go to her to complain about critics, or to get a hundred marks or just simply to empty my heart. We all went to her, each of us with our cares, hopes and grievances.' Apart from at mealtimes, occasionally when he let them join him on his afternoon walk, or in the evening in his study when he read to them, the children hardly ever saw their father. He went once to visit them at bedtime when they were little, something so remarkable that Klaus remembered it as 'a rare event in itself!' Katia, however, was ever-present. 'Often in the evening when it was time to say goodnight', Klaus later reminisced, 'I felt a genuine, tremendous and sweet tenderness for my mother.' And Katia had a special place in her heart for Klaus.

Thomas, like other great writers, was a slave to his muse. He existed within the nutshell of his writing. Everything and everyone outside were little more than stage settings and supporting cast. He admitted no responsibility to anyone other than his reading public. Without exception and for the entirety of his life, family, friends, staff, in fact anyone with whom he came into contact, found him in varying degrees conceited, distant, self-absorbed and fonder of his dogs than of his children.

The first need of a writer is complete solitude and absolute silence. Klaus conveyed the aura of sanctity of his father's space: 'To enter his study while he is mysteriously occupied there would be as blasphemous as to invade a temple when a secret ceremony is taking place.' To which Golo added, 'We almost always had to keep quiet: in the morning because our father was working, in the afternoon because he read, then napped, and toward evening because he was again occupied with serious matters. And there would be a terrible outburst if we disturbed him, all the more hurtful because we almost never provoked him intentionally.' Even outdoors they had to be silent if they were near their father's study. 'At table as well, we usually kept quiet.'

'No one like me should have children', Thomas once wrote in his diary, and the children would have unanimously agreed. In old age, their recollections were dire. Even Klaus, who scrupulously avoided criticizing his father, described him as harsh, stiff and distant – 'always somewhat remote'. To which Golo added, 'Thomas Mann could be pleasant, but that was infrequent. When we were children there was no warm, cordial, relaxed feeling of trust.' In his letters and reminiscences he usually referred to his father impersonally as 'TM' or 'der Alte' ('the old man') and spoke of him without fondness and often with distaste. Most unfortunate of all was Michael. 'From the very beginning my father did not like him', Golo once wrote, 'because he did not even want to have him.' When asked by a friend later in life what his father was like, Michael replied, 'I didn't really know him.' Monika could not recall her father ever having a single conversation with her alone, and the cover of her little book of memoirs aptly shows them seated together and looking right past one another. 'It was as though I did not exist', she said in an interview. Elisabeth, admitted, 'I never spoke to him as equal-to-equal. In fact I can remember only one personal conversation and that was on his seventieth birthday when I was drunk.' She also remarked that when her father's diaries were published, she had no desire to know what they said. Monika flat refused to look at them, not out of indifference but in dread, she said, of learning what he wrote about her. It was just as well. When Michael read them, he was devastated to find that he was an accident and unwanted.

Speaking for everyone else who knew Thomas Mann, Golo described his father as 'incredibly vain'. But he was also cold. Somone once remarked that when he arrived, it was as though an iceberg entered the room. Thomas himself said he could count on the fingers of one hand everyone he addressed with the familiar 'du'.

In the Mann universe he was the sun and everything revolved around him. The earthly centre of this cosmos was his study, where he spent probably two-thirds of the day. Usually, he took a walk in the afternoon and, on returning, withdrew alone into the salon, where he would play the piano – usually *Tristan*. After dinner the children normally did not see him unless invited to his study.

But it was not just from indifference that the children suffered. Living with Thomas was somewhat like being billeted with one of the less genial Old Testament prophets. 'He has his little weaknesses and animosities which you must heed and respect ... To annoy or hurt your father is an exceedingly serious matter, although he never hits you', Klaus commented, quite untruthfully. According to Golo he did indeed thrash Klaus. On one occasion, probably in 1919, Klaus said something at family lunch that so enraged Thomas 'he rose up and beat him terribly. I believe all four of us children cried; I certainly did.' He added, 'I am nearly seventy-nine and I can still see the scene as though it happened yesterday.' And in fact mealtimes were always especially tense. Thomas was enraged if anyone so much as touched the food on his plate with his hands. 'Use the tip of your nose, if anything!' he would shout. 'Or your big toe.' Meals had an educational purpose, teaching the children that the world was a harsh and hostile place. During the Great War, when there was little food for the family, Thomas's plate was always full. On one occasion he gave some dates to Erika but none to the other children, explaining, 'It is just as well for you to get accustomed to injustice in life.'

The Mann household must at times have been the worst sort of tyranny, since it was impossible to know for certain what was right and what was wrong in the patriarch's view. 'You can never tell what he is going to notice and how he will react', Golo said. 'We had once loved our father almost as tenderly as our mother, but that changed during the war. He could still project an aura of kindness, but for the most part we experienced only silence, sternness, nervousness, or anger. I can remember all too well certain scenes at mealtimes, outbreaks of rage and brutality that were directed at my brother Klaus but brought tears to my own eyes.' To be sure, the *stalag* atmosphere must not be overdone. Thomas could on occasion be a lenient *père de famille*, as Klaus acknowledged. He was generous with money and hospitality. 'Sometimes our house looked very much like an informal country hotel ... bustling with intrigues and arguments, long-distance phone calls, flirtations and quarrels, people reciting poetry or perusing the timetable of the trans-European express trains, or just talking to each other that rapid gibberish that most of our friends picked up from the Mann family.' But Thomas's forbearance had narrow limits.

For the familial warmth that did not exist in his own home, Klaus had to look elsewhere. He found it in the family's neighbours – Bruno Walter, conductor of the Munich Opera, his wife Elsa and their two daughters, Gretel and Lotte. In their house he enjoyed relationships that were as easy as the one in his was difficult. A slight anecdote tells the story. On one occasion Klaus sang in the boys' chorus of his school in a performance of the *St Matthew Passion* that Walter directed. After the concert the conductor took the boy home in his grand official coach, with coachman and groom in blue livery. As Klaus alighted, Walter said to him jocularly, 'Without you the performance could not have taken place.' To jest like that was beyond Klaus's starchy father.

Klaus also remembered evenings he and Erika spent with the Walters when the conductor would sit at the piano, devoting an hour or two to explaining to them the structure and meaning of the opera they were soon to attend. Sometimes he would impersonate one or another of the characters. 'He played and talked and sang; he improvised, sparkled, elucidated; he made us laugh and weep . . . Everything was good and cozy . . . Our hilarity resounded throughout the house.' In none of Klaus's autobiographical writings is a similar passage to be found about life in his own home.

Yet, in its way, *chez* Mann was a marvellous place for young children. Fortunately they were numerous and bright and imaginative enough to create their own friendly universe, a private place that no one else was allowed to penetrate. They invented their own games and stories, created their own language, coined their own expressions, sang songs of their own composing, acted in plays they wrote, followed their own laws, observed their own taboos. In his autobiographies Klaus describes their fantasy world with great fondness. Not so Golo. Already drenched in gloom, he remembered those years very differently, writing in his 1931 diary, 'What a wretched childhood we had! . . . Being afraid of other children, of our parents, of school, melancholy evenings . . .'

As the eldest, Klaus and Erika were the supreme rulers of this domain. And emotionally they were so close they seemed virtually one. In a photo of them taken when they were aged around one and two, they look almost identical. 'Erika and I belonged together: our solidarity was absolute and indisputable ... The grown-ups as well as the kids had to accept us as an entity', is how Klaus described the relationship. In no time, however, it became apparent that Erika was the tougher, in some ways the more boyish, of the two.

Of the others, Klaus was especially fond of Golo, who was in awe of his elder brother. For Klaus, Golo was a trusted accomplice, a reliable ally, a patient listener, a friend ever ready to do whatever he was asked. In later years Golo admired his brother's courage and optimism, and envied his travels and adventures and active sex life. So strong was his devotion, even though he felt himself to be by nature a writer, he repressed the instinct 'because I did not want to trespass on my brother Klaus's preserve and had to wait for my father's death'.

Despite their confidence in one another, the two boys were already unlike. Klaus had imagination, was undisciplined, took risks and laughed in the face of propriety. Golo was conservative, cautious to the point of timidity and probably already suffered from the depression that later became serious. In life – as in family photos – he habitually retreated into the shadows. 'I had a melancholy disposition and did not expect much from life', he declared years later in a television interview. Very possibly this was explained by a wound he suffered in youth that clearly never healed. One day he had overheard Katia say to Erika and Klaus that of all the children *they* were her favourites. 'I actually heard her say this.' Although his father later came to respect and trust him – as he never did Klaus – Golo and Thomas were forever unreconciled, and many years later Golo shocked a TV audience when he said flatly he was actually glad when his father died. Then *he* felt free to write.

From an early age Monika was the outsider. The two exclusive alliances – Klaus and Erika, and Klaus and Golo – had taken shape, leaving no place for her. Her parents scarcely disguised their dislike for her; Katia described her as 'lazy and troublesome' and 'a thoroughly idle misfit'. Klaus was the only one in the family who was always friendly.

Because of the age difference, Elisabeth and Michael developed on their own. In her early years Elisabeth was Thomas's favourite child. 'For none of the earlier children did I feel what I feel for this one', he wrote to a friend after her birth in April 1918. Why this was so, he himself could not explain.

By contrast poor Michael was unexpected and undesired. As Thomas's diary revealed, Katia's pregnancy came as an unpleasant shock. They discussed an abortion – Katia had already had two – but time passed and eventually they had to abandon the idea. 'During his formative years he had no grounds for being grateful to Thomas Mann', Golo once said of his younger brother. One can believe it. When the child was still quite little, he was a gratuitous victim of his father's cruelty. As it happened, Michael was frightened of crucifixes. Thomas deliberately nailed one on the wall above his bed. Terrified, the lad hid under the blankets. When Katia complained, Thomas responded that this would teach the boy that life was hard. At the earliest age there took root a strong, life-long mutual dislike. It does not surprise that as a child Michael dreamed of having fistfights with his father and of being pricked with a needle. It also does not surprise that in later life he was violent, on occasion uncontrollably.

The exclusive intimacy of the Mann brood came at a terrible price. They grew up knowing scarcely any other children and even lacking a desire to meet any. Not until he was twelve did Klaus have contact outside his family circle. To be sure, several neighbourhood friends, Gretel and Lotte Walter, Ricky Hallgarten and Wilhelm Süskind, were eventually accepted, and a few intimate friendships developed in later years. But none of the Manns ever really fitted into conventional, or even conventionally unconventional, society. It is as though some tragic accident at an early age left them too hobbled to form solid, lasting friendships, never mind successful marriages. 'Loneliness on the outside, loneliness at home', Golo recalled in his memoirs. At boarding school at Salem between 1923 and 1927 his best friend was the nearby forest, where he frequently hiked. While a student at Heidelberg he even endured a period when 'for six weeks I spoke to no one but my landlady and the waitress at the restaurant'.

Still, it must be said that there were tremendous compensations for the relatively harsh life at home. The Mann household was cultivated and luxurious. In 1913 Thomas and Katia found a site on Poschinger Strasse in the Herzog Park area of Munich, not far from the Isar River, and there built a large, handsome villa. Thanks to the huge royalties from Thomas's novels, they were able to keep five servants and a chauffeur for their two cars, one American and one German. Summers were idyllic, spent at a house they had built at Bad Tölz in the Bavarian Alps in 1909. In his autobiographies

Klaus portrays life there as a paradise: 'Whenever I think "childhood", I think first of all of "Tölz". Recollections of those happy holidays were preserved in his *Kindernovelle* ('Children's Novella') of 1926.

In her memoirs Katia mentions some of the family's distinguished dinner guests – Hermann Hesse, Gerhart Hauptmann, Bruno Walter, Hugo von Hofmannsthal, André Gide, Frank Wedekind, Gustav Mahler, Wilhelm Furtwängler, as well as Hans Pfitzner, Max Liebermann and Stefan Zweig. 'We children', Klaus said, 'classified and judged the friends of our parents as if they had been comedians hired for our fun. None of them realized how mercilessly they were watched.' Because they told the best stories, guests from the theatrical world were their favourites. By far the person they liked most was Bruno Walter. And for the rest of his life he and Klaus remained the fondest of friends. As *Kapellmeister-Generalmusikdirektor* of the Munich Opera from 1913 to 1922 he had two seats reserved for himself and he often let Klaus and Erika occupy them. In no time Klaus found himself 'bewitched' by the opera. On one occasion when the Walter seats were not available, Klaus queued for ten hours for tickets to *The Magic Flute,* an opera he considered 'one of the finest and most curious things ever written'. His father's passion for Wagner, however, was one he emphatically did not share. *The Flying Dutchman* was the only one of The Master's works he in any way cared for. Perhaps the story of the lost wanderer, welcome in no port, already touched a deep chord.

With all the high-powered activity at home, Klaus and Erika saw no reason to attend school. That was not Katia's view. She enrolled them in what Klaus described as 'a rather dusty and pretentious little institution where the scions of Munich's "Upper Ten" were introduced to the mysteries of the alphabet and multiplication tables'. It meant neither big fun nor big trouble. Although Klaus's attitude can be gauged by his description of the teacher as 'a sour, elderly spinster and humorless freak', despite himself he no doubt received a solid primary education. As for his classmates, with very few exceptions, they never came close to being admitted to the Mann universe.

The outbreak of war in 1914 touched the Mann family in a variety of ways. Professional rivals, Thomas and his older brother Heinrich had also always been ideologically antipathetic. Heinrich was Francophile, bohemian and a man of the political left. Thomas was a *Kaisertreu* nationalist and an ultra-respectable burgher with a low regard for French culture. The war threw a stark light on these differences. Where Heinrich saw Prussian imperialism, Thomas saw the defence of German culture. The result was a bitter break; during the whole of the conflict the brothers did not meet or speak. Klaus was emphatically on his uncle's side – then and later – and in *The Turning Point* he made wicked fun of his father's jingoism. 'The deadly ecstasies of *Tristan und Isolde* became an argument in favor of Teutonic expansion and unrestricted submarine warfare.' However, in the Mann home the war was a non-subject.

The biggest family crisis of those years had nothing to do with the war. By some medical freak, in 1915 each of them, except Thomas, was serially struck down with appendicitis. In Klaus's case the rupture was so severe his doctors gave up hope for his life. Relatives in other cities discussed whether to attend his funeral and 'Klaus almost died' became a family legend. For two months he lay in the hospital recovering. Ever philosophical, the boy saw deep meaning in the experience, writing in *Kind dieser Zeit* ('Child of This Time'), the auto-biography of his early years, 'I believe it was of significance for my entire life that I was at that age so close to death. *Its shadow had visibly marked me . . .* The experience remained lodged in my subconscious.' He had cheated death on this occasion. But for the rest of his life he believed it was pursuing him.

The Manns were fortunate in not losing family members or close friends in a war during which well over a million of their countrymen perished. Klaus was eight when the conflict began and just twelve when it ended. By then he had some awareness of the larger world. This world had been shaken at Christmas 1917 when grandmother Pringsheim gave him a gift of Berta von Suttner's famous anti-war novel, *Put Down Your Weapons!* He later said that after reading it he began to question 'everything we were supposed to believe'.

Not so his father. Despite the continuing slaughter on the battlefront, he had no doubts about the rightness of the German cause. But he was in visible torment, as Klaus later described. 'This wartime father seems estranged and distant, essentially different from the father I had known before and after those years of struggle and bitterness. The paternal physiognomy that looms up when I recall that period seems devoid of the kindness and irony which both inseparably belong to his character. The face I visualize looks severe and sombre – a proud and nervous brow with sensitive temples and sunken cheeks.'

The war strained family finances. Some servants had to be let go. The country house at Bad Tölz was patriotically sold for war bonds. The children were taken out of their private school. After tutoring them at home for a time in Greek, Latin and mathematics, Katia decided in 1916 to send Klaus to a state school. Wilhelms-Gymnasium was by repute academically outstanding, but for the rest of his life Klaus had only bitter memories of it. Because of the 'gawky philistines who acted as teachers', a period of his life that should have been exciting was wasted. Worse than wasted. 'Even the most exciting drama, the sweetest poem, tarnished and turned hopelessly vapid when touched by their clumsy fingers.' Looking back, Klaus felt he owed nothing to 'the sleepy old Wilhelms-Gymnasium'. In these lines Klaus appears to have suffered a profound memory lapse. The school report for 1916–17 has fortunately survived and not only gives an entirely different picture but shows to what extent the child was father to the man.

'Mann, Klaus has neither interest nor talent in physical activities', it begins. 'He excels most other students in ability, intellectual curiosity, thirst for knowledge and active participation in class instruction.' Further, 'He excels all other students in independence of mind and creativity, both orally and in writing.' However, 'he is weak in subjects in the curriculum requiring detailed, persistent, concentrated and time-consuming dedication. By contrast he is very well read and independent in his judgements – as is evident in his nascent literary activity.' 'He is very respectful', it goes on, 'and for someone of his age very serious but also precocious, if overly self-confident.' The report notes in conclusion that 'his father, the writer Thomas Mann, has made no enquiries about his son, whose education is entirely the responsibility of his mother'. Much in Klaus's future could be plotted from these observations and judgements.

It was at the Wilhelms-Gymnasium that Klaus truly encountered the outside world for the first time. He did not like what he found. He hated the native Bavarians for what he considered their crass manners and uncouth dialect. And they bullied him; in their view he was a weakling and no better than a 'dirty Prussian'. But the underlying problem was not Bavarian provincialism. Klaus's interests were entirely intellectual and aesthetic; he enjoyed reading and writing poetry. He hated sports and other group activities. And there was a softness about him that was bound to antagonize schoolboy ruffians. It was in this formative period of his life that feelings of isolation, of having to survive in a hostile environment, took root and left him with a lasting sense of being an outsider. Years later, he remarked on 'the intrinsic law of my nature which prevents me from belonging to the enviable majority'.

These feelings of being different were greatly intensified by a growing awareness of his erotic attraction to other boys. Klaus said that his sexual awakening occurred when he was thirteen, and he was very frank about it. As he wrote in *Kind dieser Zeit*, he had up to then been 'completely uninterested in the "forbidden things" of adults. When suddenly this change occurred, I was completely unprepared'. Now he experienced 'real sexual life, with its initial humiliations and then the first, almost unbearably strong moments of joy'. On the surface everything went along as before at home and in school, but within him chaos reigned. He found himself leading a double life, he said, not out of dishonesty but because he was living in two worlds. 'No wonder my mother [and Erika] were deeply shocked when I carelessly allowed them to look in my diary – but actually it wasn't careless because I wanted to provoke them. No, they had never thought that of me, had never believed that I was so mixed up and cynical since I tried to appear so peaceful and sensible.'

The specific cause of this emotional *Sturm und Drang* was the passionate attraction he felt for a classmate during his last year at the Wilhelms-Gymnasium. 'Elmar had silky-smooth, short dark hair, canny but melancholy brown eyes and a smooth face.' Result, 'Suddenly a tremendous and merciless power took over my life.' Klaus thought of him when he went to bed at night; he thought of him when he awoke in the morning. So overwhelmed was he, he found his vocabulary inadequate to describe his feelings. Anything he wrote would profane the beauty and strength of his passion. In the classroom Klaus watched Elmar's every movement. He dreamed of their sitting together at the opera. He sent him poems – they were never acknowledged. In all their months together, they exchanged fewer than fifty words. For weeks he fantasized about how Elmar would respond if invited to the opera. When he at last found the courage to ask him, he was turned down cold. And so, at thirteen, he learned his first lesson in dealing with his homosexual feelings. The desire for friendship and an expression of affection risked being met with brutal, humiliating rejection.

For a born writer, everything is primal matter for a story – in this case one called 'Vorfrühling' ('Early Spring'), about an actor who falls in love with a fourteen-year-old boy named Elmar. Written at the end of Klaus's last year at the gymnasium, the work is unremarkable but daring in its public confession of homosexual sentiments. Provocatively, Klaus showed the text to his teacher. The response was predictable. Handing it back with open disgust, he commented coldly, 'If *that* is spring!' Again Klaus learned that society considered his deepest romantic feelings to be wicked, not to be spoken or written about.

'Why am I so different and in conflict with everything, at odds with my teachers and a stranger among other boys?' These are not Klaus's words but those of Tonio Kröger, from the eponymous, and largely autobiographical, novella that Thomas Mann had written three years before Klaus was born. Thomas had hated school and considered it worse than a waste of time, in later life echoing Klaus, 'School can destroy everything good.' There were other parallels between the youthful father and son. Both had fallen hopelessly in love with another boy; both had written poems confessing their love and in both cases the love was unrequited. In fact there are so many close parallels in the lives of the three that it might be said without outrageous exaggeration that Thomas Mann = Tonio Kröger = Klaus Mann. There was a big difference, however. Thomas surrendered to social respectability and disguised and sublimated his erotic feelings through writing. Klaus defied social convention, as well as the law of the land, and broadcast his erotic feelings in autobiography, fiction and everyday life. Thomas's novels avoid self-exposure through discretion; with Klaus discretion is flagrantly and contemptuously tossed aside. Thomas wrote about life; Klaus lived it. 'A bohemian with a guilty conscience' is how he once delicately characterized his father.

In plain text, Thomas, like three of his children – Erika, Klaus and Golo – was homosexual. Thomas's attraction to boys and young men was the great revelation of his diary when the surviving pages – 1918–21 and 1933–55 – were unsealed twenty years after his death. While it is impossible to form a full picture of this secret part of his life, there are clear hints in what survives.

In early 1918, for example, he complained about having slept poorly because of the erotic feelings aroused by that day observing some young soldiers in a park. And in an entry for 25 July 1920 he comments on a train trip back to Munich after a day in the country: 'Short conversation with the attractive young man in white trousers sitting next to me in third class. Gave me a lot of pleasure. It appears that I am done with women forever.' These are but two of many such remarks. Literati, who had up to then read the novels with eyes wide shut, now recognized that homoeroticism pervaded his fiction, and that fiction was the outlet for his repressed sexuality.

More surprising still, the diary revealed that Thomas's homoerotic feelings extended to his eldest son. This emerges from a series of entries which together build up a sort of pointillist picture. The first relevant remark, on 20 September 1918 when Klaus was twelve, relates that he went to his son's bedroom the night before and found him in a 'fantastic state of undress' and unable to explain what he was doing. 'Was he engaged in puberty games or was he sort of sleepwalking? . . . Perhaps both at the same time.' To which Thomas then added, 'Obviously someone like me "should" not bring children into the world.'

On the following Christmas Eve Thomas noted, 'I am really pleased to have such a beautiful boy as a son.' Similar comments followed throughout the succeeding months. 'Klaus with his short hair is pretty to look at', for example (24 May 1919). Certainly nothing wrong with any of that. But eventually the language became somewhat insinuative. 'To observe Eissi's transition from puberty to manhood is linked to wonderful feelings. His voice is changing now, his Adam's apple is developing, his bare legs are colossal, the direction of his drives is revolutionary' (26 April 1920). According to another entry, 'I made Klaus aware of my inclination with my caresses and by persuading him to be of good cheer' (25 May 1920). This was followed a few months later by, 'In love with Klaus these days.' On 5 July he wrote, 'Germ of a father-son novella – intellectual ferment.' There followed a few days after that a passing remark about 'Eissi, who at the moment enchants me' (11 July 1920). Two weeks later, 'Am enraptured with Eissi; frighteningly handsome in the bath. Find it very natural that I should be in love with my son' (25 July 1920). That night he added, 'Eissi lay reading in bed; his naked bronzed body left me unsettled.' Two days later, he recorded, 'Last night I read a novel of Eissi's filled with *Weltschmerz* and I commented on it while sitting on his bed and caressing him which, I believe, he enjoyed' (27 July 1920). One evening, after he and Klaus had gone cycling together, he described his son as 'delightful to see in his striped sailor suit', (13 August 1920). Several months after that he found his son masturbating: 'I heard some noise in the boys' room and came upon Eissi totally nude and up to some nonsense by Golo's bed. Deeply struck by his radiant, adolescent body; overwhelming' (17 October 1920).

What is to be made of all this? Katia caught on at a very early stage of their marriage that her husband was attracted to young men. So in time did the children. In a diary entry on 5 May 1934 Klaus noted in passing, as though it were thoroughly unremarkable, 'Dreamed about the Magician's secret gay life (relationship with Kruse) – Werner Kruse, a cabaret musician, was a friend of Erika and Klaus. Years later Golo commented, 'Naturally all of us also knew about his homosexual inclinations. I must have been very young to try to persuade myself he knew nothing about it. But he fought it to keep the family together; the family gave him the strength to maintain order in his life and a steady commitment which a shy boy could not give him from a distance.'

One of the gifts Klaus received on his twelfth birthday, on 18 November 1918, was a handsome notebook. He decided to use it to keep a diary. It opened dramatically, just as the *Kaiserreich* was collapsing. His first words recount the downfall of the Wittelsbach monarchy in Bavaria. 'Revolution! Revolution! Revolution! Military cars speed through the streets . . . It is all too laughable. And yet it is flattering to think that in a hundred years people will be talking about the Bavarian Revolution in the same way as the French Revolution.' According to other entries, 'we inspect a machine gun', 'no bread', 'city centre filled with soldiers'. When the Bavarian socialist republic was overthrown six months later, Klaus was disgusted by the violent repression that followed. The cheers of his reactionary schoolmates and teachers when the revolutionaries were executed in the school courtyard horrified him. 'One of them, a seventeen-year-old, refused to be blindfolded. The professor says such stubbornness proved how fanatic he was. But I think it was admirable.' For the school newspaper he was moved to write a short story making fun of the hysterical fear of the revolutionaries in Munich salons, and a little later even a brief drama called *Bavaria's Revolution*. All this in striking contrast to the views of his arch-conservative father. Clearly this boy, barely twelve years old, had a lively interest in the world around him and a courageous independence of thought.

As a result of his unhappy experiences at the Wilhelms-Gymnasium, Klaus resumed his solipsistic existence. From the age of six books were already his friend and refuge, initiating a lifetime of voracious, almost compulsive, reading. At the height of the Bavarian civil war his diary mentions that he risked walking down streets 'swarming with soldiers' to buy himself a copy of Gogol's *The Overcoat*. It was not long afterwards that he began reading a book a day. His selections were impressive. He may not have had a deep understanding of what he read in those years, but in a short time he came to have an acquaintance with the great masters of German literature and a fair array of others. And when he took an interest in an author, he read or browsed not just one book but the complete works – virtually all of Ibsen, Lessing, Schiller and Goethe, and the list went on. Nothing frightened him. Far from being too long, every book seemed too short. Although his father could not be bothered, Katia made suggestions. Eventually – inevitably – he was bold enough to sneak into Thomas's study and browse. He was caught and there was a terrible row.

A benefit for the children of living in this supremely literate family was to be regularly read to by their mother, father and grandmother. The range of their favourites was enormous – Gogol, Tolstoy and Dostoevsky, Shakespeare, Sir Walter Scott, Dickens and even Mark Twain. Above all, lots of Dickens. Offi, who had been a noted actress in her time, was a tremendous hit with the children. Not only did she read well, she would also impersonate the voices of the characters. So Sundays came to mean 'the Dickens hour' and for years to come Dickens and Sunday were associated in Klaus's mind. The ultimate, however, was being invited to be read to by Thomas in his smoky study. His father's favourites at the time were the Russians. 'We liked them, but we liked Dickens more', Klaus recalled.

'With the same enthusiasm that I read, so did I write', remembered Klaus, 'producing an ever-growing mountain of plays, poems and novels.' In a radio interview in 1966 Erika described how it all began. 'On his own and even before he could be conscious of having a father who was a writer, Klaus would spend the day making up stories which he would relate hours on end to Golo. At the age of five he began "dictating" them to me since I was six and could write a little.' Writing was therefore innate and not an impulse to imitate his father. 'He wrote the way other people breathe.' Or, as Klaus himself said, 'The drive was an end in itself'.

The first surviving example of Klaus's writing is a poem that he slipped under his father's table napkin at breakfast. Far from doggerel, it was, for a six-year-old, precocious in its understanding of how to handle words, rhyme and metre. His earliest plays, written around the same time, demonstrated an impressive familiarity with dramatic writing. One of them, 'Der gute Sohn' ('The Good Son'), hinted at the extent of his aspirations. He wrote on the title page, 'The Complete Works of Klaus Mann, Volume 1: Dramas'. In short order there followed poems as well as stories, novellas, ballads and more plays. They flowed, he said, as easily as pipe bubbles.

His debut as a story writer was made at the age of eleven, with rough drafts of 'Tragödie eines Knabens' ('Tragedy of a Lad'), about the suicide of a schoolboy. A year later there followed one entitled 'Wilhelm', and the year after that 'Heinrich Hollmann, Geschichte einer Jugend' ('Heinrich Hollmann, Story of a Youth'). As Klaus elucidated, 'The story of this Heinrich, by whom I meant myself and whom I characterize with a certain malice, is about a real moral problem – in fact, *the* moral problem par excellence: how man, as a spiritual-physical dichotomy, is pulled back and forth between sensual pleasure and higher devotion, how the animal in him vies with the god in him, the body with the mind.' He asked how they could be reconciled and his answer was that they cannot be. In the tale Hollmann is abandoned by his parents, mocked by his brother and flees to London, where he dies of drug addiction in the arms of a whore. Suicide, drugs, whores – morbid enough for someone his age, one would have thought. He made it darker still, however, by later claiming he could only foresee that he himself would end in sinful misery. 'I revelled in this thought and, while almost simultaneously attracted to the moral, was drawn to the morally degrading, the lost, the sinful, the decayed.' Here already emerged a theme of his mature writings – the association of sensuality and sex with ruin and death. It was a striking work for a boy of thirteen, and Klaus proudly gave the text to his father to read. The best Thomas could do was to correct the errors of grammar and spelling and, when he handed it back, to comment – no doubt untruthfully – that he 'had read it without reluctance'.

'I don't know how many notebooks I may have filled with dramatic sketches, lyrical outbursts, and narrative fantasies; it seems to me that my poetic outburst must have comprised more than a hundred "volumes" before I reached my fifteenth or sixteenth year.' There were love stories, mystery stories and historical dramas as well as novellas, essays, reviews and poetry. His only reader was the loyal Golo, who professed to be deeply impressed. Less impressed were the newspapers and publishers that were offered exclusive rights to one or another of these works of 'Natasha Huber'.

Klaus went too far when he ventured to launch himself publicly in two of the most notable publications in the country. His father was furious. 'Eissi has sent a story to *Simplissicimus*, an impossible one, of course, and intends to send another to the *Rundschau*', he complained to his diary. 'A folly from which he must be dissuaded.' But Klaus was undeterred by his father's disapproval and went on more furiously than ever. As the pile of unread masterpieces mounted, he sometimes presented one to some member of the family. A comedy he gave to Katia he had thought quite amusing. His father did not. At dinner he denounced the work as a case of 'tactlessness that only considerable youth could excuse'. Klaus was devastated. But prophets without honour at home are commonplace. So he sent a play to one of the biggest Munich theatres under the pseudonym Karl Trepitsch, generously offering to forego royalties. No response. Golo was then sent as the playwright's nephew, Fritz, to make enquiries. 'Where did I put that rubbish?' was the reader's response. He found it and handed it back, with the comment that Fritz's uncle should not trouble the theatre further. Not totally cast down by the rejection, Klaus commented, 'Well, at least he had not thrown it out.'

'It is almost incredible – and even in retrospect I cannot understand whatever was going on with me – that I could have written such rubbish that was so far from my own life', he remarked some years later. The reason was simple. As he confided to his diary just before dinner one evening when he was fourteen: 'Night falls, once again. Another night! How dull! I must, must, *must* become famous.' This could stand as the supreme impulse of his early years, if not his whole life. Not necessarily a famous writer. Just famous.

Like most children, only more so, the Mann kids loved make-believe. For a time, acting was their paramount interest. In January 1919 Klaus and Erika formed a theatre group which included Gretel and Lotte Walter and their close friend, Ricki Hallgarten. They started out modestly with performances of light, one-act plays and progressed to Lessing, Molière and Shakespeare. In the end the play-acting became more than childhood games. In fact Erika found the experience of playing in *Twelfth Night* so enthralling she decided then and there to become a professional actress.

The acting period coincided with a time of outlandish behaviour. Erika and Klaus had always been headstrong. But in their mid-teens they ran riot. Klaus devoted an entire chapter of *Kind dieser Zeit* to their antics. They started with petty thievery and progressed into moderately serious shop-lifting. Once, when their parents were away, they held a reception where all the refreshments – sausages, hams, fruit, liquors – had been stolen. Another stunt was playing tricks on old ladies. It also amused them to tell lies to anyone they met and to try to frighten people in the streets. But the *pièce de résistance* was mischievous phone calls. Erika was a genius at vocal mimicry; she could sound like an opera singer or a lady's maid or a Prussian official. Unwitting respondents found themselves invited to mythical dinner parties or other engagements. 'It looked as though we were on the point of really running wild', Klaus admitted. Did their antics simply reflect the *Zeitgeist*? Chaos was in the air. Germany itself was going wild. Suddenly no Kaiser, no colonies, no German Alsace-Lorraine, no fleet, no army, no generals, no decorations, no titles – and no social order. 'In the midst of emptiness and disintegration nothing seemed stable and worthwhile, except the lustful mystery of our own physical existence.'

In exasperation, Katia could think of nothing better than to deposit the two eldest children at the Bergschule, an experimental youth community not far from Frankfurt. Klaus seems to have liked the Spartan simplicity of the life, the coeducation and the method of instruction, which appears to have been nothing more than education *à la carte* – take what you want and ignore the rest. He even got along with his schoolmates and, as he wrote in *Kind dieser Zeit*, 'fell in love several times, though not with the consuming ardour as in the case of Elmar'. Meanwhile the woolly ideals of the teachers were leading to anarchic indiscipline and in July the school had to be closed. The time had not been wasted. While there Klaus had started writing what Golo considered his finest story, 'Die Jungen' ('Youth'). It was a period piece about the crisis of relations between the generations and the nihilism of youth, a subject on which Klaus was, at age fifteen, an authority.

Today Katia would probably be advised to medicate Klaus for attention deficit hyperactivity disorder. But in 1922 she knew of no alternative but to look for another school where he would fit in. She first took him to Salem, where Kurt Hahn and his benefactor, Prince Max of Baden, had just founded their famous, high-minded educational institution. After a long interview, Klaus was turned down – wisely. While acknowledging that he was intellectually advanced for his age, school officials found him arrogant and uninterested in accommodating himself to the real world, or Kurt Hahn's idea of it. In this they were right. Hahn wanted youth who could be molded to fit into the society of the *bien-pensants* of the time. Clearly Klaus was anything but promising material. Fortunately, however, there was an institution that encouraged individuality. Odenwald School was, in the words of an alumnus, 'a school for very talented, difficult children'. On both counts it should have been just the place for Klaus, and for a time it was. He liked the students, the teachers and the atmosphere. Excused from attending classes and other activities, he was allowed to spend the entire day on his own, walking, reading, writing and thinking, or just dreaming. He loved Odenwald and for a time thrived. Looking back ten years later, he remarked in a letter, 'It was in my fifteenth year that I began really and truly to live.'

But there was a problem. Although he made a few friends – including a girl named Eva whom he admired for taking him less seriously than he took himself – he fell in love with Uto, a slightly younger boy. So smitten was he that he wrote poems to him and once slipped him a note saying 'I love you'. But Uto was 'too naïve to recognize my hero-worship'. Cruelly disappointed in love, Klaus found the school hopelessly tarnished and decided he had to leave. In a letter to the headmaster, the much respected pedagogue Paul Geheeb, Klaus confided – prophetically – 'I don't belong here though admittedly where I would be *entirely* at home, God only knows. Wherever I live I shall be a stranger. A person of my type is always and everywhere lonely.'

When he wrote to Katia that he intended to leave school and return to Munich, she had little choice but to agree. She insisted, however, on hiring two tutors to prepare him for the *Abitur*, the examination taken at the end of secondary school education in Germany which opens the way to the sensible, conventional professions she wished for her children. Her hopes, however, were doomed to fail. Instinctively Klaus knew that his destiny lay elsewhere. He found his tutors intolerable, took to his bed and dispatched a letter to his father in his study declaring he had decided to go to Berlin and train to be a dancer – 'like Nijinsky'. Thomas humoured him, and in a day or two Klaus abandoned the idea. In the meantime the tutors were dismissed. So Klaus's formal education came to an end.

From his earliest years Klaus had been self-absorbed, effervescent, spontaneous, undisciplined, headstrong and downright reckless. He was also boundlessly curious, fizzing with ideas and energy, imaginative and wildly ambitious. He was both a dreamer and a dedicated, hard-working writer. And so he remained for the rest of his life. But from a young age there was also a pronounced dark side to his nature, a fascination with personal extinction. Golo recalled that one of his writings as a child was a play which concluded with the sentence, 'I believe she smiled as she jumped out the window.' 'Tragödie eines Knabens' was the first of a number of fictional stories in which the characters, like a later succession of friends and acquaintances, put an end to their lives.

A plaintive passage in *Kind dieser Zeit* described his ruminations at the time. 'Among all the pleasures of life I play again and again with the terrible and sweet idea of suicide. Regarding methods of suicide I firmly decided: the cord hangs on a strong hook in the storeroom; poison can be procured in one way or another; at night I could lie down in the snow, drink lots of schnapps beforehand and then go to sleep; or simply jump off the tower of the Frauenkirche, and splatter my brains on the sidewalk. How I longed to end it all precisely when everything is at its best and most exciting – that was the seventeen-year-old's most absurd and beautiful desire.'

It is difficult to know what to make of these ramblings. Morbid to be sure, but genuinely suicidal? To some extent Klaus's sentiments were in the long tradition of German youth. The tone had been set in 1774 with Goethe's famous *The Sorrows of Young Werther,* which is said to have prompted a wave of suicides modelled on Werther's violent end. Klaus in fact shared many of Werther's traits – he was high-strung, restless, disappointed in love and plagued by a sense of alienation. Did the melancholy come from a gene inherited from his father, whose two sisters, Carla and Julia, killed themselves and whose own works – *Buddenbrooks, The Magic Mountain, Doktor Faustus* and some of the stories – were obsessed with doom and death? Yet for all his praise of non-existence, Klaus was too fascinated with life to end it. He became instead a lifelong voyeur of death and suicide.

Now that he was free of school and completely on his own, Klaus would do only what he wanted to do. These were *les années folles* of European youth, and he was determined to experience as much of life and the world as possible as quickly as he could. The declaration of independence was promulgated in the summer of 1923 when he and Erika announced to their parents they wished to go on a walking tour of the Thuringian countryside. They had no intention of doing anything so respectable and boring, and secretly set off for Berlin. Here they discovered a totally new world, a world famously portrayed by George Grosz and Otto Dix. Klaus was overwhelmed. At last he was home!

In the 1920s the German capital was renowned as a lively homosexual centre. To Klaus it seemed like nirvana, or, as he described it, 'Sodom and Gomorrah in Prussian tempo'. He went to nightclubs and saw men dancing with men; he chatted with transvestites; he talked to prostitutes of all sexes. He was bewitched by the romanticism of the underworld: 'I was magnetized by the scum.' All of it together was so 'gorgeously corrupt' he could not bear to leave. So when his money ran out, he found a job in a cabaret reciting naughty ballads. His performance was a disaster from the first minute. 'It was a flop with a vengeance; it was the essence of non-success, the washout in its nightmarish extreme.' The next day he and Erika went back to Munich, but not before getting themselves briefed on the marvels of Thuringia – the Wartburg and other noble sites – to describe to their parents.

Not that Munich was completely without excitement. The monetary inflation that swept Germany in 1923 as a result of the war reparations dispute with France heightened the sense of anarchy. Money became so worthless that by the end of the year a single American dollar was worth four trillion marks. Nothing seemed to have value or make sense. That sort of chaos suited Klaus perfectly. 'Why should we be more stable than our currency?' he asked himself. If there was no currency stability, why should there be social stability, and if there was no social stability, the sky was the limit.

In the course of their sprees, Klaus, Erika and their narrow circle of friends found and adopted Theo, a young man who had made himself rich by gambling on the stock market. The more destructive the inflation and the crazier the tempo of life, the more splendid were his parties. After an evening at a nightclub financed by Theo, who almost passed out when the waiter presented the bill – three million five hundred thousand marks for each member of the party – they all retired to his apartment. There they spent the night. Dressed in colourful pajamas, they sang; Klaus recited; they boozed; they danced and painted their faces. The next morning they drove into the countryside and spent two or three days in Partenkirchen in a suite in one of the most elegant hotels in Germany – all paid for by Theo. At another party they put on their own cabaret-revue. One of the songs began, 'Perversion is good, my son. Perversion is fun, my son.' In another number, Klaus and Pamela Wedekind were dressed as nuns. 'That was how seventeen-year-olds enjoyed themselves.'

Understandably, Thomas and Katia were troubled by what they heard and observed. The family's reputation was at risk. 'With a patience I still admire, my father listened to all the nonsense that I spouted in our defence', Klaus admitted. However, relations between father and son eventually became so fraught he packed a bag and was headed to Berlin when Katia intercepted him. It was a not untypical teenage revolt. Or, as Klaus himself put it, 'Too young for the adult world, too unruly and difficult to live with my parents – looked at socially, I was an embarrassment.'

Not wanting to go to another school and unwanted at home, Klaus proposed withdrawing from society for a time and staying with his parents' acquaintance, Baron von Bernus, 'poet, alchemist and student of occultism', in his converted monastery near Heidelberg. Klaus described it as a spooky place run by a spooky couple engaged in, among other spooky things, sorcery, alchemy and metempsychosis. The Baron, he said, 'looked and acted precisely the way in which popular fancy wants a poet to behave and look – his face, pale, soft and flabby, but not without a certain dreamy energy, framed by a mane of rich, silky hair'. The Baroness believed, 'by no means a joke', that she was a reincarnation of a courtesan of Louis XIV. The Baron himself was previously a servant of Goethe's mother; another resident had once been Robespierre. But the zany inmates were irrelevant. The self-exile offered Klaus the solitude he needed to take his first serious steps toward a professional writing career.

There was an equally important reason he had chosen to stay with the Baron. Uto lived nearby. Klaus was determined to meet him and see whether they might yet become intimate friends. So they had long walks and long talks. But no intimacy. The two never saw one another after that, so Klaus never knew that his idol joined the Luftwaffe in 1939 and was shot down just before the end of the war.

As he neared the end of his teens Klaus was a youth in psychological, sexual and moral turmoil. He regarded sex as something not just to be experienced but to be understood – not easy in an era when sexual mores were changing overnight. 'We could hardly deviate from any ethical norm for the cogent reason there was none . . . Indeed, we deemed the old morality so definitely *passé* that we did not even bother attacking it any more.' But he foresaw the danger. The idolatry of the body was at the cost of reason and the intellect, and would become an end in itself. 'We sneered at the restrictions of absolute morality, but the coming barbarians would betray morals altogether for the sake of the racial doctrines.' Here he perceived, however dimly, the scarcely disguised homoeroticism and sadomasochism inherent in the up-and-coming political movement, the National Socialist German Workers' Party.

By the time Klaus left the Baron in the spring of 1924 he had written several articles and the partial draft of a book. Not only these. In February he had inaugurated his career as a professional writer with the publication of a short story, 'Die freie Schulgemeinde' ('The Free School Community'), in the mass-circulation Berlin newspaper *8-Uhr-Abendblatt*. In the following months the distinguished Berlin daily *Vossische Zeitung* brought out a number of his stories, including 'Nachmittag im Schloss' ('Afternoon in the Castle') in which he openly wrote about homosexual feelings.

In the meantime Erika decided to launch herself on the acting career that she was confident would make her a star. In September 1924 she left Munich for Berlin to study under Max Reinhardt. Some weeks later Klaus joined her. He had aspirations, too. He would become a noted author. Once installed, they felt they were living in heaven, even though heaven took the shape of two dreary little rooms in the dreary Uhlandstrasse. 'I can see it and smell it', Klaus wrote years later. 'It all comes back.' Though Klaus was not quite eighteen, adulthood now began.

CHAPTER 2

First Scandals
1924–28

'Yes, I had a job, or something like a job.'

In September 1924 Klaus was taken on by the popular Berlin daily *12-Uhr Mittagsblatt* as assistant theatre critic. Berliners loved going to plays and nearly forty theatres catered to their passion. Although he did not cover the most important ones, it was nonetheless quite an appointment. Of course, Klaus being Klaus, he pretended he did not take it all that seriously. 'I could not help feeling that this new position of mine was but another hoax to bamboozle the grown folks.' All the same he was conscientious enough to write more than thirty reviews in five months. He loved the work. It amused him to praise nobodies to the sky and to take the mickey out of distinguished actors. He enjoyed every minute of it and later wrote an amusing account of those days in *The Turning Point*.

At the same time Klaus continued writing an occasional piece for the *Vossische Zeitung* without causing remark. But in August he submitted two essays to the distinguished arts journal *Die Weltbühne* on the under-standing – admittedly somewhat ambiguous – they would be published anonymously. In the end the journal decided to identify the author and Klaus agreed. 'I was smart enough to gauge the opportunity, but too callow to sense the inherent danger.' He considered it 'the pivotal mistake' of his career. 'From now on I was labelled the precocious son of a distinguished father.' And from that problem many others followed. Were his writings accepted on their merits or because their author was a *Dichtersohn* – a great writer's son? Were they criticized because they were by a *Dichtersohn* and you could indirectly attack the *Dichter* by attacking the *Sohn*?

The relationship between father and son was touchy for another reason. Had Heinrich been Klaus's father, there would have been no problem. In his view there was space for both to pursue their careers and he had always encouraged his nephew. But Thomas wanted an exclusive personal copyright on the Mann name. Having a brother-writer was bad enough. A son-writer was just too much. Especially when the son's writing was a humiliation impossible to live down, much less forgive.

Despite all this Klaus had overnight achieved the ambition of his earliest youth. He was famous. He was talked about and written about. He was admired and despised. In any case, everything he wrote got into print and was conspicuously reviewed. That was all he cared about. Young though he was, he proved to be a veritable expert at self-promotion. Newspapers and publishers vied for his manuscripts. And he supplied them with a vengeance. 'Everything seemed so easy. People were interested in whatever I had to offer.' By March 1925 he had published thirty-one essays and critical reviews. In that year alone he wrote and performed in a play, saw his first book appear, travelled abroad for several months, returned to write his first novel, a little later brought out a collection of essays, all the while writing a miscellany of articles, including a fiftieth-birthday tribute to his father. In all, from then up to 1932 he would account for no fewer than four plays, three novels, three volumes of short stories, an autobiography, over one hundred essays, reviews and reports, two anthologies (one prose and one poetry), and, in collaboration with Erika, two travel books. No wonder Reich-Ranicki remarked, 'It is doubtful whether any other German writer began his career under such spectacular circumstances.'

Klaus's first book, *Vor dem Leben* ('Before Life'), published early in 1925, when he was only eighteen, comprised a number of short stories, some of which he had written while at the Odenwald School. Like his subsequent fiction, they were to a greater or lesser extent autobiographical. The stories, like many of his father's, were tinted with homoeroticism, death, sex, loneliness, even necrophilia. The notion that love, sex and death are somehow connected ran throughout. The collection was populated with lost youth, outcasts, deviants and the like. The centrepiece was the 'Kaspar Hauser Legends', about the adventures of a fifteen-year-old prince – Klaus was fifteen when he wrote them – who was a legendary and symbolic figure in the early nineteenth century, a mysterious, unwanted youth who made his way alone in a hostile world and who in the end was murdered. Klaus later said the story touched feelings too deep fully to understand. 'I read young Klaus's book with curiosity', Thomas commented to Erika. 'Much is quite remarkable. But the industrious lad has a "Magician complex" among other things.'

Thomas got his revenge in his own novella, *Unordnung und frühes Leid* ('Disorder and Early Sorrow'), which came out the following year. Usually referred to as a family portrait, it unveiled in frank terms his feelings toward his children. Thomas, alias Dr Cornelius, a history professor, lays his cards on the table. Of the six children, only Erika, 'a quite charming girl with a pleasing smile', and Elisabeth are portrayed sympathetically. Michael was denigrated as unsteady, nervous and at times violent, Monika as lazy. Klaus – Bert in the story – was skewered as someone 'who wanted to leave school as soon as possible and be either a dancer or a cabaret host or, providing it was in Cairo, a waiter'. Crude irony turned to malice when Bert was further described as someone who 'knows nothing, can do nothing and thinks only how to play the clown and lacks even the talent for that'. The father frankly admits he is ashamed of him. The story delighted the public, and Thomas delighted in his public readings of it in his visits around the country. Klaus was devastated. The offence was never forgiven.

Even if his father could not be counted among them, Klaus was not without friends and admirers. The encouragement he did not have from Thomas, he received from them. One was Stefan Zweig, who around this time wrote, 'Go ahead, young friend. There may be prejudices against you because of your famous parentage. Never mind. Say what you have to say! – it's quite a lot, if I am not mistaken. I expect a great deal from you. I want you to think of my expectations when you write your next book.' Some years later Klaus commented, 'I certainly did think of him. And it helped.'

Vor dem Leben was a notable success – if in sales more than reviews – and the royalties gave Klaus an opportunity to appease his curiosity about the world. Travel now became another compulsion and soon developed into a mania. The near-perpetual motion began in March 1925 when he collected the royalty check for his book and told his newspaper he was quitting. Accompanied by Wilhelm Süskind, his childhood friend from Munich, he headed to London. The visit was disappointing, though less because of London than because London was not Paris. So they cut the trip short and flew to France. Now he worried that his expectations were so high they might easily be dashed.

From the moment he arrived he was enthralled. 'The first day in Paris is now – as for centuries – a powerful, even overpowering experience', he wrote in a dispatch to his old newspaper. The light, the nacreous pallor of the buildings, the voices, the fountains, the parks, even the pissoirs – he loved it all. Sex, too. There was nothing furtive and squalid about it, as in Berlin. Legalized in 1791 and reaffirmed in the Napoleonic Code, homosexual relations were, as Klaus put it, 'treated with the perfect casualness that is the proof of real civilization'. Describing his impressions – both in articles and later in his two autobiographies *The Turning Point* and *Der Wendepunkt* – he was lyrical. For the first time he did not feel he was an outsider. A model of tolerance – that was France's supreme gift to him.

The visit to Paris only fed Klaus's wanderlust. The South of France beckoned. Enter Hans Feist, an old friend – twenty years older in fact – an art collector and a multi-lingual translator. He was also rich, gay and adored Klaus, an adoration that was not greatly reciprocated. When he proposed financing a trip around the Mediterranean, however, Klaus didn't hesitate. They began in Marseille. Klaus was fascinated, especially by the Vieux Port, Europe's most notorious den of wickedness. With its maze of alleys and tunnels, and what Klaus referred to as 'the blare and stink of massed, primitive vices', the old port catered to every sin known to man. North Africa was now irresistible. It did not disappoint – the Arabian landscape and intoxicating colours and smells of the towns enchanted him. The highlight of the trip was the interior of Tunisia with its exotic scenery and hypnotizing sounds. The low point was Italy. Palermo was boring, Naples 'depressingly dull' and Rome 'theatrical'. Everything about the country seemed hopelessly tainted by the sight of blackshirts and a ubiquitous veneer of fascism.

Refreshed from his travels, as soon as he was installed in his old room at home, Klaus worked ten hours a day and in no time gave birth to a play. It was called *Anja und Esther*. The drama takes place in what Klaus described as 'half ballet school, half sanatorium (with a touch of jail, brothel, and monastery)'. The four characters – Anja, Esther, Jacob and Caspar – were, in his words 'a bunch of forlorn youngsters . . . a little bit depraved and derelict'. All of them were madly in love with one another 'in the most tragic and mixed-up fashion'. The underlying theme, he said, was 'the destiny of man in general and our postwar generation in particular'. Phrased some- what more concretely, it was about young people's struggle to make sense of life and society in the wake of a lost war that destroyed the old, traditional social and political values. New mores had to be found and it would be for a new generation to find them. This would remain the principal theme of Klaus's fiction, no less than his nonfiction, in the years to come.

The very day he finished *Anja und Esther* he insisted on reading the text to a small family group after dinner in Thomas's study. 'Dismal silence.' Then, 'Strange. Very strange, indeed.' That was his father's comment. 'Rather on the morbid side' was his mother's. Unfamiliar with same-sex relationships, poor Aunt Lula was at sea. 'I must confess that I am some- what puzzled as to the relation between those two young ladies. Why are they so conspicuously fond of one another?'

When writing his play, Klaus had in mind for the female roles Erika and Pamela Wedekind, the daughter of Frank Wedekind, the noted playwright. By chance, one of Germany's up-and-coming young stars of the Hamburg theatre, Gustaf Gründgens, happened to see the book and enthusiastically volunteered to join the cast. Then the theatre management perceived the beauty of having a second actor named Mann on the bill, along with two daughters of famous writers, and recruited Klaus. The cast alone guaran- teed that the play would be at least a minor sensation. What went on during the rehearsals was a case of life imitating art. As if in a Feydeau bedroom comedy, there were fluctuating liaisons: Erika and Pamela; Gustaf and Klaus; Erika and Gustaf; and so on. Complicating matters, Klaus and Pamela had become engaged a year earlier, an engagement he described at the time as half serious and half spoof 'to horrify people'. Now Erika and Gustaf developed a liaison that, to her parents' dismay, eventually led to marriage.

Whatever is to be said against the play, it was an outstanding example of the expressionist mood of the early Weimar years, which took shape in the Bauhaus, non-objective painting, avant-garde film, twelve-tone music, but nowhere more than in theatre. Peter Gay conveyed the gist: 'Prolific and hostile – to the rules, to the audience, often to clarity – playwrights poured out plays eccentric in plot, staging, speech, characters, acting, and direction.' Beneath it all lay something more, as he further pointed out: 'There was one theme that pervades their work, the son's revolt against the father.'

Anja und Esther premiered in Munich on 20 October 1925 and opened in Hamburg two days later. The response in Munich Klaus described as one of 'chilly curiosity'. In Hamburg, where Klaus, Erika, Pamela and Gründgens appeared, the press had a field day. The headlines alone – 'Performance by Children of Famous Writers' – ensured that the shows would be sold out. The mass circulation *Berliner Illustrierte Zeitung* even made the event a national sensation by splashing 'the children's' photo – minus a rightly indignant Gründgens, who was literally cut out – on its cover with the caption '*Dichterkinder spielen Theater*' ('Writers' Children Play Theatre').

The spectacle – and that's what it really was – drew crowds wherever it was performed, not only in Germany but also in Vienna, Prague, Budapest and even sedate Rome. The reviews were good, bad and indifferent, but predominantly bad and sometimes atrocious. That it was widely damned as obscene, decadent and an affront to morals was exactly what its author intended. He revelled in the publicity. Bad notices were better than none, of course, and there were plenty. In Vienna Hugo von Hofmannsthal attended a performance and spoke nicely to Klaus during the intermission. That was enough to compensate for any amount of abuse. Everywhere young people flocked to see it. To be sure, he had let the enthusiasm and self-confidence of his precocious literary career run away with him and overtake his talent as a dramatist. Yet, at the very least, *Anja und Esther* was a daring social challenge. Early Weimar Germany was culturally as liberal as any country in Europe. But to present a play – the first in German theatre – about homosexual life was remarkable indeed.

The entire affair horrified Thomas. He felt his name was being exploited to promote an abomination. Attend a performance he would not. 'Ten horses couldn't drag me to the premiere', he wrote to an old friend. The work was an 'indescribably sick and corrupt little piece'. He had asked himself whether he should forbid it, and in the end decided, 'That would be ridiculous in today's world, which itself is nonsense'. 'Today's world' was shorthand for the huge generation gap that had opened up after 1918. It was in this opening that his son was forging a career. And, as Gründgens himself said, 'In Klaus Mann the younger generation has found its spokesman.'

Klaus freely admitted he at times confounded his father, whose fame was now greater than ever, following the publication in November 1924 of *The Magic Mountain*. 'The flamboyance with which my career began can be understood – and forgiven – only if one bears in mind the immensity of my father's fame. Having begun my career in his shadow, I wriggled and floundered and made myself rather conspicuous for fear of being totally overwhelmed . . . What I failed to realize was the amount of embarrassment my eccentricities caused my father.' A few years later, when he came to write *Kind dieser Zeit*, he defined the problem – which was the problem of his life. 'As I studied *The Magic Mountain* while it was bit by bit being written, and read his earlier works over and over, I wondered how I would ever be able to confront his solid block of achievement.' The answer was that of course he couldn't. Klaus had a subconscious solution to the dilemma, though. Repeatedly his diary in these years records dreams of Thomas's death, on occasion by suicide.

Intimacy, trust, understanding, friendship; of these there could obviously never be any. Klaus was so intimidated by his father that he was conditioned for the rest of his life to be submissive. So distant was the relationship that even in the privacy of his diary he never referred to him as 'Father' or 'Dad' but by an impersonal title, 'Zauberer' or 'Z', and in his letters by such downright baroque stylings as 'Lieber und verehrter Zauberer' and even 'Herr Zauberer, lieb und hochgeehrt'. Never was there an open break and never was there anything that could be called a relationship. Thomas never interfered, Klaus once said, but made his feelings known with 'a frown, a sorrowful smile, an apprehensive silence'. He then added the chilling comment, 'He never seemed to remember exactly with whom I lived, which book I was working on, or where I had been spending the time since he had last seen me.'

Klaus had returned from his Mediterranean adventure in May 1925 teeming with ideas. Even though occupied with getting *Anja und Esther* on stage, he could scarcely wait to write another book, his first novel. 'This time it had to be the real thing – the complete confession.' And so it was. Andreas, alias Klaus, is a clever young man, a painter, from a highly respectable family. He rebels against his bourgeois background, considers suicide and runs away to Berlin. There he becomes a dancer and lives in a demimonde of drugs and sex orgies. He falls in love with another man. 'Andreas gave himself entirely to this love, which he did not find aberrant. It never crossed his mind to lie to himself about it, to fight it as "degenerate" or as "sickness". Those words had as little to do with the truth as though they came from another world.'

Those words created genuine scandal. *Der fromme Tanz* ('The Devout Dance') was far more than Klaus's own public 'coming out'; it was the first openly gay novel in German literature and created a sensation. To say the least, it was a courageous work, all the more so for being written by a nineteen-year-old. Being homosexual never troubled Klaus. He was the way he was. He accepted it when a boy and lived his life without secrecy, a sense of inward guilt or outward shame. To be gay was no more perverted than to have blue eyes.

Such was far from the view of a notoriously stodgy German public. The very topic was taboo and the act itself punishable by imprisonment under Article 175 of the German criminal code. Enacted in 1871 with the establishment of the German Reich, the law was no dead letter. Even in the relatively liberal Weimar era, every year some five hundred men were sentenced to prison for up to four years for homosexual acts. Only a few noted figures dared publicly to praise the book and its author. One was the famous pioneer 'sexologist' Magnus Hirschfeld, who went so far as to maintain that the effect of the novel was not only to make homosexuality an acceptable social subject but even to encourage a change in the public attitude toward the law. Hirschfeld was wildly optimistic. Not until 1994 was the law formally abolished.

Just before *Der fromme Tanz* appeared in January 1926, Thomas published an essay, *Über die Ehe* ('On Marriage'), which condemned homosexual relations in terms that many decades later would have warmed the hearts of opponents of same-sex marriage. 'Homosexuality is free love and results in barrenness as well as lack of direction and responsibility', it began. More specifically, 'Its essence is dissipation, a gypsy life, frivolity'. Such 'sterile dissoluteness' is the very opposite of 'the fidelity and beauty of the ethically based and legally sanctioned bond between man and woman'. Given his acceptance of Erika's lesbian relationships and his own homosexual desires, it is easy to pass this off as straightforward hypocrisy. But, like German society, Thomas was deeply conventional. He had a façade to maintain and Klaus threatened to blow it apart. Under the circumstances the essay must be seen both as a pre-emptive attack on a gay novel and as a declaration of war against a gay son. Thomas's biographer, Klaus Harpprecht put it this way: 'Klaus did not conceal his homosexuality. He wrote about it; that was bad enough. He also lived it; that was worse. He lived dangerously but he lived – a challenge that Thomas found at times almost unbearable.'

Proving that he was not defenceless against his father, Klaus responded with a story about family relationships set against the background of the happy summer days at the family country home at Bad Tölz. He called it 'Kindernovelle' ('Children's Novella'). Using the same techniques as his father, he loosely modelled his fictional characters on members of the Mann family around 1916. Presumably by conscious intent, Klaus settled accounts with Thomas by killing him – that is, in the story the father is dead and, in commemoration, his death mask hangs on the wall of his widow's bedroom. The novella was published in October 1926. Reviews were friendly, and it not only sold well in Germany but was translated into French and into English for an American edition.

Kindernovelle was dedicated to René Crevel, the inspiration for the hero of the book. The two had met during Klaus's long sojourn in Paris in the spring of 1926 and there was an immediate mutual attraction – stronger on Klaus's part. Both had begun writing at the same early age. Both were homosexual. Both were fascinated by death. In fact, René was at the time writing a novel entitled *La Mort difficile*. Klaus admired him tremendously – he was one of the five or six friends he esteemed most in his life. However, Klaus found René frightening: 'Sometimes I was perplexed, even shocked, by the vehemence of his judgments.' Particularly dreadful to Klaus was the depth and obsession of his hatred of his mother, who was at the time quite ill. She wore black, so he dressed like an Apache; she hated foreigners, so he cultivated Germans, Russians and Chinese; she went to church, so he made jokes about Christianity; she was puritanical, so he taunted her with obscene stories.

René introduced Klaus to the great surrealist guru André Breton and some of the affiliates of his cenacle – Paul Éluard, Louis Aragon and Philippe Soupault. However, gurus and cenacles were not to his taste and, as he later wrote, 'My relations with Breton were cool and distant.' René was active in communist as well as Dadaist and surrealist circles and tried to reconcile his surrealism with his communism, and both with his homosexuality. Klaus had no patience with this sort of equivocation and in the end René himself fell victim to it. In the summer of 1935, on the eve of an anti-fascist conference he had helped to organize, he imitated the hero of *La Mort difficile* and took poison. The reason he gave could not have been simpler – 'I am disgusted with everything.' His farewell note illustrates the fundamental difference between the two friends. Whatever his problems, however hurt and depressed he may have been, however frustrated in love and work, however beguiled by the idea of death, Klaus did not lose his appetite for living. Which is another way of saying there was always another book to be written.

For someone with boundless curiosity about people and places, Paris in 1926 was paradise. And thanks to introductions and what he referred to as 'luncheon parties and gregarious evenings', Klaus made the acquaintance of some of the notable literary figures of the day – Jules Romains, André Maurois, Paul Valéry and Paul Morand, to mention a few. The men who meant most to him, however, were, not by chance, both writers and homosexuals.

The most important by far was André Gide. Thanks to an introduction through a mutual friend, the noted literary critic, E.R. Curtius, the two met over lunch in autumn 1926 at a modest brasserie near the Jardin du Luxembourg. Gide talked about his growing interest in German literature and in particular Goethe; Klaus, who by then had read all Gide's major novels, discussed his books. In no time Klaus came almost to worship Gide and loudly proclaimed him to be his guide and inspiration – 'like an older brother, a beloved friend'. He went on to explain, 'The encounter . . . helped me more than anything else to find the way, my way, to myself.' Gide had 'urged and encouraged me to become myself in a purer, more conscious and uncompromising way'. This was to some extent code. He was saying that Gide, a noted homosexual, gave him the confidence to live his life in the same way – not only defending but even praising homosexual relations.

And so what Klaus wanted from his father, he received from the Frenchman. 'He gave me self-assurance and the fortitude to endure life and to accept my own being with all its potentialities, dangers and dilemmas.' And Gide the writer? He was, Klaus affirmed, 'the most important contemporary author'. This was not the first time Klaus had slighted his father. Some years earlier he had let it be known that he preferred his uncle

Heinrich's works, though he was then candid enough to admit this was 'not to annoy my father but in order to prove my emancipation'. When he came to write *The Turning Point*, he acknowledged that complete liberation was impossible. His thinking was indelibly coloured by his father's writing – 'the very vocabulary', the 'death-bound romanticism', 'the colourful grandeur of his images', 'the fugue of his musical dialectics'.

It is always awkward to be friends with people who dislike one another. But Klaus successfully squared the circle, cordially admiring both Gide and Jean Cocteau, his other important French connection. Gide was a model, Cocteau was a mentor. When Klaus wrote to him, Cocteau at once invited him to his apartment in the rue d'Anjou, behind the Madeleine. He immediately took a shine to Klaus – a writer, young, gay and cosmopolitan – and the relationship seems to have been genuine and friendly from the start. When Klaus went to visit, Jean sealed the relationship by offering a pipe of opium with the reassuring aphorism, 'Liquor provokes paroxysms of folly; opium provokes paroxysms of wisdom.'

Klaus admired Jean enormously, once writing, 'Undoubtedly, he is one of the most gifted beings I have ever known and, perhaps, the most nearly perfect one.' Above all, he marvelled at the breadth of his creativity and his success at whatever he turned his hand to – novels, plays, drawings, poetry, short stories, songs, librettos for ballet and opera, prose essays, stage productions and more still. He envied this amazing expertise; in fact a friend later remarked that Klaus aspired to be 'the German Cocteau'. Jean encouraged Klaus's career in a number of important ways. In 1931 he arranged to have his biographical novel of Alexander the Great published in France and wrote an introduction in which he even went so far as to describe Klaus as 'one of my compatriots'. Later on, Klaus came to feel he had been too much beguiled by the surface glitter of Cocteau's life. But then and for some time to come, he was charmed.

There were any number of other French writers – Verlaine, Rimbaud, Huysmans, Radiguet, similarly outsiders and homosexuals – whom Klaus had admired since his youth. But among living writers, apart from Gide and Cocteau, it was the now largely forgotten novelist Julien Green whom Klaus was eager to meet. Given the 'sombre maturity' that Klaus sensed in his writings, he was surprised on their meeting to find someone who was 'young, handsome and alert', someone who might have been taken for a boulevardier had it not been for 'a strange sadness and sombre glow in his eyes'. It is difficult to understand how they could have connected – Klaus, guiltlessly, even defiantly gay; Green, devoutly Catholic and wallowing in a sense of guilt because of his sexual nature; Klaus, out in public, looking for sex; Green, achieving daily release by writing 'sexual jottings'.

What may have attracted him was Green's idealized vision of death. For the first time he felt he had met someone who shared, and even exceeded, his own grim view of life and looked forward to the solace that would be found when it came to an end. As Klaus wrote in *Der Wendepunkt*, 'I knew his books and loved them because they were so sad . . . He had no other theme, only pain and sadness; the great, heavy, utterly hopeless sadness of the unredeemed, unredeemable creature . . .' Baffled that someone so suave, so proper, so civilized could plumb the depths of human baseness in his books, Klaus ventured to ask him, 'How do you come upon your material?' The smug answer left Klaus understandably nonplussed. 'Never will I forget his mocking, amused smile, "But my dear friend. *I* am not the one who writes my novels. Someone else guides my hand. A stranger."'

Those spring and autumn months in France were a revelation to Klaus. Here he found a country – the only one in Europe, perhaps the world – where homosexuals could live their lives like everyone else, not just toler- ated but accepted as a matter of course. But of equal importance was Klaus's encounter with the wider world. Berlin and Munich were German; Paris was everything. Traces of his excitement were still evident when he came sixteen years later to write about the experience. 'Paris was swarming with foreigners of all races, colors, and social backgrounds. [It was] jammed with the motley crowd from Tokyo and Birmingham, Detroit and Tunisia, Rio de Janeiro and Hamburg, Shanghai, Stockholm and Kansas City. It was a veritable invasion of pleasure-seeking Babbitts, frustrated painters, stingy professors, flippant journalists, ladies of the monde or demi-monde, drunk- ards, scholars, art collectors, dressmakers, loafers, philosophers, criminals, millionaires, celebrities and nobodies.'

Practically overnight Klaus was transformed from a German into a European. From this moment on he was convinced the only way to preserve peace in Europe was for France and Germany to bring the poisonous rivalry between them to an end. To spread his views he wrote a long essay, later published as a pamphlet, 'Today and Tomorrow: The Situation of Young

European Intellectuals'. It was an amalgam of ideas extending from the pan-Europeanism of Richard von Coudenhove-Kalergi to the socialism of Ernst Bloch. The message was simple: 'We Europeans are members of a highly endangered society. Woe unto us, if we fail in our duty.' And the duty? To overcome the legacy of the war and traditional nationalist rivalries and encourage European cooperation. This was roughly what the two foreign ministers, Gustav Stresemann and Aristide Briand, were working toward at the time.

Klaus's real interest lay not in being a political missionary but in continuing his career as a creative entertainer. The result was *Revue zu Vieren* ('Four in Review'), a play he intended to be 'a light-hearted synthesis of religion, politics, eroticism and art'. In fact it was as much to keep together the dramatic quartet *Anja und Esther* as to convey another iconoclastic social message. Concocted in haste late in 1926, while he was rushing between Paris, Hamburg and Munich, the work was badly constructed and poorly written. In fact, as the cast soon discovered, the play was scarcely playable. Not surprisingly, during rehearsals relations among the actors frayed almost to breaking point.

The premiere in Leipzig in April 1927 was a fiasco that failed even to rise to the level of a *succès de scandale*. Though demoralized and rebellious, the cast went on to Berlin, where a disgusted Gründgens – in the face of Erika's threat to divorce him – finally walked out. Thanks to her unwavering support, Klaus persuaded his troupe to go on to engagements in Prague, Vienna and Budapest before they finally wound it up in Copenhagen. 'We were booed at by the Berliners, abused in Munich, applauded in Hamburg, and discussed as interesting freaks in Copenhagen', was how he summed up the response. 'We were sneered at by the critics, quarrelled with our agent, roared over our fan mail, and ruined our reputations.' Nevertheless, like a bit of flotsam in a flood, one line in the play survived the sunken drama: 'Everyone who is seventeen should shoot himself.'

The flop was all the greater because it was a Mann who flopped. Thomas was furious that Klaus had not used an alias. Literary criticism of Klaus's work, which had been rising for some time, now reached flood level. Anyone who enjoys public success must suffer public hurt. Early applause and early brickbats are part of being a star. Perhaps to some extent Klaus was his own worst enemy, at times giving an impression of being on a continuous, frivolous ego trip. But above all his avant-garde celebrity at the age of just twenty is what really galled critics. Here was a lad who needed to be taken down a peg or two. In no time Klaus could boast that he was despised by Siegfried Kracauer, Bertolt Brecht, Kurt Tucholsky, Walter Benjamin and Axel Eggebrecht – the leading literary critics of the time. One day he saw them sitting together in a café and remarked to his diary, 'A convention of my deadly enemies'.

The indictment was that Klaus amounted to nothing more than a literary lightweight whose work was contemptible. Eggebrecht dismissed him as 'the leader of a group of impotent but arrogant kids'. Tucholsky sneered at him as a showoff – 'Klaus sprained his right arm writing his hundredth publicity bulletin and will be unable to keep his speaking engagements in the weeks to come.' It was from this time to the end of his life that Klaus was derided less by the Nazis and the political right – which tended to ignore him – than by the left, the Social Democrats no less than the communists.

However legitimate some of the criticism, there was something ugly in the bullying and mean-spiritedness of his critics. Nicole Schaenzler devotes five pages of her biography of Klaus to examples of the abuse, often phrased in crude, locker-room argot. Brecht, rightly noted for the phrase 'sarcasm never failed', rather outdid himself in making great sport of Klaus's homosexuality, invented anal-erotic comparisons, derisively referred to him as 'Kläuschen' (little Klaus) and compared him to a 'breast-fed child' who 'plays in the rectum of his father'.

It was a hard lesson to learn, but Klaus learned it early. A few years later he wrote to his friend and fellow writer Erich Ebermayer, 'You simply must have strong nerves to stand up to the loathsome flood of hatred . . . It is very tiring to be so thoroughly hated – even when you understand the apparent reasons.' It is typical of Klaus that he never sought to get even, never played the game of tit for tat. He absorbed the punches and got on with his writing. In any case what was his offence? Did the iconoclastic Brecht feel outflanked by the even more iconoclastic Klaus Mann? Did they all perhaps fear that 'Kläuschen' – a homosexual! – left them in the shade as critics of the moral and social order? And while Klaus was being made fun of as a representative of a fatuous new generation, Thomas was being mocked by the same literary lefties as an old fogey who wrote anachronistic stories about a *passé* bourgeois world. The attacks ricocheted between father and son.

It was now that Pamela Wedekind told Klaus that their pseudo-engagement was definitely off. To the dismay of her friends she had decided to marry Carl Sternheim, a playwright twenty-eight years her elder. The break with Klaus had the further consequence of causing a rift with Erika. And Erika, although a remarkable success as an actress, was finding herself bored by the theatre. And bored with Gustaf Gründgens. That summer they formally separated. So a change of scene was called for. Why not go away, she wondered. Far away. To America perhaps? She broached the idea to Klaus, who jumped at it. That they had no money and spoke no English was no matter. They bought a book of English phrases which Erika memorized and could recite like a parrot. Klaus scrounged money from newspapers and publishers against promised reports. Dream became reality when he suddenly recalled having received an invitation from Horace Liveright and Donald Friede – New York publishers who had brought out *Kindernovelle* as *The Fifth Child* – to go to the United States and promote the American edition. The invitation had expired long ago, but Klaus brazenly cabled that he was now on his way and would be accompanied by his sister, the noted actress. And, oh, by the way, he and his sister were twins. The twins ruse was inspired, and on arriving in mid-October 1928 they found themselves marketed as 'The Literary Mann Twins'. As a headline in the *New York World* announced, 'Thomas Mann's Twin Children Arrive for American Tour'.

Realizing that the public's curiosity would be aroused because he was their father, Thomas lost no time in dissociating himself from their venture. No sooner were 'the twins' on the high seas than he told a Philadelphia newspaper, 'Personally, I have neither supported nor tried to hinder their journey. These children belong to a race who use the opportunities of world communication with more naïveté, daring and enterprise than their fathers had.'

On arriving, the twins were met at the dock by Friede, who had in the meantime arranged an extensive lecture tour for them. As he later wrote in his memoirs, 'It looked as if my plan was going to prove a brilliant one. Only a single detail had been overlooked, and when I met Klaus and Erika at the dock it was obviously too late to remedy this oversight on our part. We had neglected to ask them if they spoke English, and it turned out that they did not.' Fortunately Liveright was an affable man and in no time recovered from the shock. He showed them around New York and in the evenings took them to cocktail parties, an American novelty which they found all alike and all boring. Otto Kahn, the famous financier, showed them Wall Street. H.L. Mencken invited them to lunch at the Algonquin. They were delighted by the theatre and enchanted by the movies.

In the meantime a programme was worked out. Erika would open the event by reciting a talk she had memorized in English. Klaus would speak briefly on 'the situation of the new European generation'. Then Erika would conclude the occasion by reciting poems by Rilke, Brecht, Gottfried Benn and other modern German poets. Not surprisingly, Friede found there was little or no demand for lectures by a pair of German youngsters, even the offspring of a famous writer, who had little or nothing to say and could scarcely say it in English. Then, when Klaus tried to touch him for a 'loan', Friede had enough. To break the contract and get rid of them he handed over a check for $1,000 and wished them Godspeed on their return home. Home was the last place they had in mind. They thanked him, pocketed the money and headed for California – Hollywood, to be precise.

Naïve, daring and enterprising they certainly were, though also honest enough to consider themselves impostors. 'From the very beginning of our trip we could not help feeling that we duped the respectable folks, once again, by presenting ourselves as a couple of serious lecturers – without even speaking English.' Perhaps their age saved them. Klaus was a mere year beyond being a teenager, Erika only a year older than that. Though innocents abroad, they quickly became shrewd observers of places and people. They absorbed it all. The tall buildings of New York, the 'English charm' of Boston, the rough ways of Chicago, the anachronistic Germans of Milwaukee, the oppressive emptiness of Kansas, the splendour of the Grand Canyon, the urban chaos of Los Angeles. At the same time they were appalled by the vast gulf between blacks and whites, workers and employers, rich and poor. They never could quite get their heads around 'a callous system that allowed anyone to become president of the United States or to starve to death'. In its way it was titillating, they had to admit. 'There was something exciting and frightful about spending the afternoon with a bunch of penniless tramps and then rush home, to the Astor, and change clothes for an opulent dinner party.'

Klaus was only being candid when he characterized himself and Erika as 'callow vagabonds'. But they were also Manns. Wherever they went there was always someone – a devotee of their father, a member of the German community, a Rotarian or a bored society matron – to greet and entertain them. They were invited to Princeton, Harvard, Columbia, Bryn Mawr, Stanford, Loyola and Berkeley to speak to students and to meet professors. In Hollywood they were entertained by some of the leading actors and directors of the day. They attended football games and boxing matches, concerts and plays. They visited libraries, film studios, farms, hospitals, nightclubs, concert halls, speakeasies, oil wells, art museums and even a slaughterhouse. Their range of contacts extended from writers, bankers, painters and professors, to movie actors, journalists, Pullman porters and shoeshine boys. As they travelled they became ever less sightseers and ever more social critics.

They went from coast to coast three times, financed by lecture fees, newspaper contracts, parental subsidies, generous patrons and even strangers. But at the end of six months it was clear that the 'author-twin-industry', as Klaus called their escapade, had been milked dry. They were now in Hollywood where Klaus's secret dream of making a fortune as a scriptwriter and Erika's of becoming a famous movie star had both come to nothing. As usual they were broke. But to return home – or to go anywhere – was impossible until they could pay their two-month overdue hotel bill.

Perhaps it was their age or their sham innocence; whatever it was, they attracted benefactors wherever they went. So it was only to be expected that at a reception of the Friday Morning Club of Pasadena, a lady of a certain age should walk up to them and shyly present them with a bond worth $1,000. Once again, it was to be spent on a fare home. Once again, they went west.

Two weeks of sybaritic life on the beaches of Hawaii convinced them that paradise was boring. So on to Japan. Since Tokyo was still largely in ruins as a result of the 1923 earthquake, they took leisurely tours to Nara, Nikko and Kyoto. They were fascinated by Japanese theatre and charmed by the tea ceremony. They stayed in local inns, which they found uncomfortable, and ate Japanese food, which they found disgusting. Fully two months were spent in Tokyo – housed in Frank Lloyd Wright's magnificent Imperial Hotel – not as enchanted tourists but as disgruntled inmates, 'kept in that luxurious prison by the evil spell of our unpaid bill'. This time it was Klaus's indulgent German publisher, Samuel Fischer, who rescued them by commissioning a book about their travels. So, then on to Korea, Manchuria and across Siberia, which they found similar to but 'a hundred times more beautiful than the American plain states'.

From the first day of their visit, the Soviet Union left them perplexed and saddened. They had almost no contact with anyone and the people they passed on the street looked stolid and shabby. The Kremlin, the churches and narrow, winding streets of Moscow were fairly pleasant. But they observed enough to conclude that life in 'the proletarian dictatorship' was especially difficult for artists and intellectuals. All in all, the experience acted on Klaus as an inoculation against the blind pro-communism of many Western intellectuals in those years.

The Klaus Mann who returned in July 1928 from his trip around the globe was inevitably different from the one who had left. Although he was not quite twenty-two, he had seen enough of the world to have gained an entirely new perspective. When looked at from Kansas or Korea, he found that his life, his writings, even Europe, seemed small and almost irrelevant. But what struck him most forcibly was how little Americans and Europeans knew one another. Americans as a whole he liked – they were 'almost shockingly wholesome'. And the United States, itself? 'It was a rich and dynamic nation pregnant with infinite potentialities; but it was not ours. We remained Europeans.'

Not that he was happy about the state of Europe. Americans might be naïve and know little about the world beyond their shores, but Europeans were committing a huge mistake in feeling superior. 'A journey around the world is an effective lesson to cure any European of complacency.' Klaus returned convinced that Europe's dominance was finished. It had forfeited its right and lost its ability to run the world. If there were a revival of European nationalism, it would lead the continent to self-destruction. He was convinced all over again that the key to peace was an alliance between the two dominant powers in Europe, France and Germany. To spread this view, he wrote articles, reviewed books and gave lectures. In later years he reproached himself for his lack of passion. 'My fundamental error was that I ventured on those tremendous issues without having them in my heart and blood.' But who else was doing even that much?

CHAPTER 3

First Drugs
1929–32

Travel invariably unleashed an explosion of creative energy. And, as if any further encouragement to get down to work were needed, Klaus found on returning from his globetrotting that, despite the drubbing from critics and the public, his works were selling surprisingly well. *Kindernovelle* was a minor hit. *Der Fromme Tanz* and even the published text of *Revue zu Vieren* were not doing badly. Best of all, and testimony to his rising status as an author, Germany's most prestigious publishing house, S. Fischer – his father's publisher forsooth – offered him a contract to bring out all his fiction.

So the flood of works continued and at an even more feverish pace. 'I must write', he once said. 'Perhaps it would have been better to paint or dance or cultivate tulips, but there was no choice.' Writing was not only a vital psychological compulsion, it had become almost physical. 'The very act of writing has a soothing effect on my nervous system', he wrote in *The Turning Point*. So book after book, play after play, story after story, review after review, letter after letter, issued forth. There were anthologies, essay collections, even a film script. All of it to prove he existed – *j'écris, donc je suis*. The product was always interesting, usually clever, often original, sometimes daring, frequently controversial and occasionally a total failure. In these early years, *pour épater le bourgeois* was often his intent and almost as often the effect.

Klaus stood out from other contemporary writers not only because of his age but also on account of the sheer volume and variety of his work.

Volume implied speed, however, and speed implied haste and haste resulted in carelessness. His mind was as dazzling as a Catherine wheel, endlessly spewing out colour and fire. A reader can sense his excitement as he worked. He must have written almost as fast as he thought, putting down the first words that came to him without reflection or revision. Clarity, depth and precision were all too often victims of spontaneity – all the more remarkable because of his father's famously slow, meticulous mode of writing.

But he faced a problem that confronted no other author, and when he came to write *Kind dieser Zeit* he told the world all about it. 'The more contact I had with people, especially people in the literary world, the more clearly I became aware of the awkwardness and dangers of my situation. Without question my name and the fame of my father made my start easier. But within half a year the seeming advantages turned into disadvantages . . . It is remarkable how people scarcely took note of the disadvantages and made a huge to-do about the early advantages. The disadvantage, which no other German writer faced, was the prejudice people had toward me. I never found an unprejudiced reader. Not only the hostile ones but the friendly ones as well instinctively make a connection between whatever I write and my father's work. I am judged *as the son*. At the beginning I could have tried to avoid this awful problem by publishing under a pseudonym. But even if such a mask had been successful, would it have really been honest to have dealt with the bitterest problem of one's life by deception?' Klaus then went on to relate an anecdote about a woman who, on being introduced, said, 'Ah, in the shadow of a titan!' Though notoriously slow to anger, Klaus called down the wrath of God upon her and commented that all that was necessary to deepen the inferiority complex of the son of a famous man was to send him into the society of cretins. 'Useless to wish to have been born at a better time or to a better fate. You don't have any choice.' Such were his final, defiant words on the subject of his destiny as a writer.

In retrospect he admitted he had taken the bait thrown out by the press and the literary world, the bait being 'a shoddy halo which I confounded with fame'. The halo provoked sarcastic comments both about him and, since the two were paired, his father. Brecht led the pack: 'The whole world knows Klaus Mann, the son of Thomas Mann. By the way, who is Thomas Mann?' Then there was the caption of a caricature in the popular satirical weekly *Simplicissimus*. 'I am told, Father, that the son of a genius cannot be a genius himself. Therefore you are no genius.' At Christmas 1924 Thomas gave Klaus a copy of *The Magic Mountain* with his inscription, 'To my respected colleague – his promising father'. Klaus proudly showed the book to a friend, who informed a journalist, and very soon something as harmless as this droll dedication was turned against father and son and circulated throughout Germany and beyond.

Within a few weeks of returning to Munich from his round-the-world journey, Klaus was back on the road. First to the Salzburg Festival, where Bruno Walter was conducting a new production of *Cosi fan tutte*; then into the Austrian Alps, where he settled down with Erika and stitched together the reports he had sent various newspapers about their travels. The result was *Rundherum* ('All Around'). They had never intended it to be a serious travel book but, to their almost embarrassed surprise, such was its success that a second edition had to be published soon after the first. Later on Klaus wrote a chapter in *The Turning Point* with a rather franker and even more amusing account of their experiences.

As soon as *Rundherum* was out of the way, Klaus resumed his normal frenetic pace, lecturing, writing and contributing to anthologies. His next important work was a play, *Gegenüber von China* ('Across from China'). The story was about life among students at a small California college, based on conversations with American students. It gave an unsympathetic, but probably not inaccurate, picture of students at the time – callow and without intellectual interests, the boys preoccupied with girls and money, the girls preoccupied with finding a husband with money. Their aspirations went no further than to be in thirty years what their mothers and fathers then were. In writing the play Klaus said he intended to highlight the contrasts and similarities between young Americans and his own European generation. Done in a rush, it was one of his weakest works. 'I am afraid it was rather flimsy stuff, my dramatic treatise on American youth', he admitted. 'The satiric sidelights didn't amount to much, and the plot was clumsy. People were probably right when they reacted coolly.' 'Reacted coolly' was putting it mildly.

Never long discouraged, Klaus plodded ahead with a work he had begun earlier. It was a biographical novel about Alexander the Great. The topic, he later said, gave him more pleasure and also more pain than anything else he had written until then. He sometimes wondered, as he laboured on, whether he was equal to the challenge. Despite his damning words about his education at the Wilhelms-Gymnasium, he was apparently well grounded in the history of the ancient world and its literary sources.

There were several reasons for his choice of subject. Even though Klaus denied it, Alexander's being homosexual must have been a consideration. But what most interested him was presenting the life both as a political parable for contemporary Europe and as a fascinating adventure story. 'A centrifugal force – irrational and irresistible – seemed to impel Alexander away from the heart of Europe, outward, into the vastness of Asia. Awestruck and enchanted, I followed him on his manic venture.' But if Alexander was a conqueror, he was also a unifier. In Klaus's hands the biography had a political intent – to celebrate the utopian ideal of a peaceful empire. *Alexander* came out in December 1929, to mostly warm reviews. By some it was praised as his most serious, solid and best-written work to date, demonstrating that he had begun to develop his own style.

Some months after the appearance of *Alexander*, Erika and Klaus bought a car. It was a small Ford, which Klaus said appeared 'shaky and shabby but was more trustworthy than many a Mercedes limousine'. And so, in early April 1930, off they went together, with Erika at the wheel, on another mad expedition. This time they intended to travel by way of France and Spain to Morocco and then on to the Congo where they would take a ship to America – the venture to be largely financed by newspaper dispatches about their adventures. The *Dichterkinder* wheeze again.

The trip came to an abrupt end in Fez. There, one evening, their guide introduced them to hashish. They were delighted to make its acquaintance and, despite the guide's warning to be cautious, they could not get enough. After a time they became hysterical, shrieking with laughter at everything they saw, heard and said. That lasted an hour or so until they fell asleep. On waking up, they were trembling and delusional. The sound of frogs and crickets and the smell of plants were overpowering. One by one their arms fell off, then their legs, then their lips, then their heads, until finally what remained exploded into a thousand pieces. In the middle of the night they were delivered to a nearby French military hospital where they spent several days being detoxified. 'Never shall I be able to describe what it actually was like', Klaus wrote years later. 'It was insanity.

It was hell.' That brought to an end their third great travel adventure. Back in Munich at the end of May, Klaus immediately went to work on another book.

The hashish fiasco was by no means Klaus's first experience with drugs. Not without reason the 1920s are known as the 'sex, drugs and jazz era', and, ever precocious, Klaus had by the age of eighteen indulged – possibly introduced by his friends Hans Feist and Count Rudolf 'Jack' von Ripper. When he came to write *Der fromme Tanz* in 1925 he could use his broad knowledge of narcotics in telling the story. Scarcely a year after that Jean Cocteau had shared an opium pipe with him. Three years later he mentioned in a letter that he sometimes took morphine.

By the time he again began keeping a diary in 1931 Klaus was expert enough to make comparisons. 'Effects of cocaine not essentially different from those of morphine. The effects are milder and more calming. Morphine has a stronger physical effect and works faster. Cocaine affects the brain more, without physical euphoria. A more intense dizziness at the beginning.' After writing this entry, he went out with a friend and took a 'dose of "little sister" Eukodal.' As for opium, 'the effects of morphine are very similar, only milder, less medical'. In the end it was morphine in one form or another he preferred. In his novel *Treffpunkt im Unendlichen* ('Meeting Point in Infinity') one of the characters says, 'I don't take pure morphine. What I take is called Eukodal, "little sister Euka". We find it has a much better effect.'

What were the effects? Klaus's diary says very little. On one occasion, after taking a dose, he wrote, 'I read a bit of Kafka's *The Castle*; it opens magnificently. Had to lay my head down again and again, though, because of a slight euphoric queasiness.' At another time he commented, 'Injected euka myself. It went well – good and bad.' Klaus's intellectual curiosity led him to read up on the case of Thomas de Quincey and in May 1934 he wrote an essay on his *Confessions of an English Opium-Eater*. He concluded, as have literary and medical historians, that de Quincey was driven to opium for both medical and psychological reasons. In his own case Klaus believed the impulse was purely psychological, an antidote to an acute feeling of loneliness. So what had started as a casual pleasure gradually developed into a compulsion. Of the others in the family, Erika also indulged but never lost control.

Klaus was also in the grip of an older addiction: a compulsion to travel. Constant movement reflected a state of pathological restlessness that drove him ceaselessly from place to place in a flight from fears, frustrations and solitude – 'the different things that weigh on me', as he put it. Klaus's correspondence and diaries note almost continuous gyrations – at this period between Munich and Berlin, Paris and the Riviera, Vienna and various places in central Europe. He was well aware of the consequences. 'I ruined (and sometimes saved) relations, professional opportunities, studies and pleasures, by rushing away, just in order to move, to change, to remain alive.' In short, this was not simply travel; it was neurotic escape. 'I recall rooms – dozens, hundreds of them, scattered all over the continent. I spent my life in hotel rooms. Home meant to me the hospitality of my parents, or a room, somewhere, in a squalid inn or a grand caravansary.' So the pain-pleasure of travel and the pleasure-pain of writing were linked.

Klaus once composed a long, bittersweet poem about his vagabond life. With ironic hyperbole, he called it 'Greeting to the Twelve Hundredth Hotel Room'. In the words of the first few lines,

> Twelve hundredth hotel room, I greet you . . .
> My home for the last half-hour
> Home for two, three or fourteen days.
> Will you be friendly to me?
> Will I be allowed to rest?'

More than a hundred years before, Byron wrote lines explaining Klaus's situation better than he himself did:

> The race of life becomes a hopeless flight
>   To those who walk in darkness . . .
> But there are wanderers o'er Eternity
>   Whose bark drives on and on, and anchored ne'er shall be.

Klaus's writing routine almost rivalled his father's. 'My life was not without a certain regularity, almost monotonous, for all its erratic scurry', he remarked in *The Turning Point*. 'Almost never did I discontinue my work. When I arrived at a new resort, it was my first occupation to unpack and arrange, with nervous pedantry, the well-assorted desk equipment that I carried along in my bag.' The entry in his diary for 4 January 1935 mentions having with him photos of Katia, Erika, one or two intimate friends, as well as a drawing by Ricki and what he referred to as 'the classical childhood photo' of himself, Erika and Katia. Never one of Thomas. On occasion he travelled with a substantial reference library as well. 'During the time I was engaged in writing *Alexander*, my luggage was burdened with Aristotle, Xenophon, and Homer. I perused Babylonian legends at the Grand Hotel in Stockholm, Persian chronicles in a country house near Florence.'

On his way from the ill-fated visit to Morocco back to Munich at the end of May 1930, Klaus had stopped in Paris and called on Cocteau, whose novel *Les Enfants terribles* had just appeared to highly favourable reviews. The story, about two adolescents who live in a world of their own creating, was bound to appeal to Klaus. It appealed so much, in fact, that he asked Cocteau for the rights to adapt the work for theatre. Astonishingly – the novel itself had not yet been published in Germany – Cocteau agreed. While retaining Cocteau's basic plot, Klaus took a very free hand with his reworking of it. In the original, incest was marginal to the story; Klaus gave it importance, at least by insinuation. In the end the brother and sister achieve their longed-for union through a double suicide. When Cocteau learned of the text and its emphasis on incest he was livid, and in fact never forgave Klaus. *Geschwister* ('Brother and Sister') was written in five months and premiered, with an accomplished cast that included Erika, in Munich in November 1930, a few days before Klaus's twenty-fourth birthday.

If ever there was a play not for its time, *Geschwister* was it. The Weimar Republic was now in its death throes, following a Nazi victory in the September Reichstag election. Provocative themes were fast becoming taboo. At the premiere a terrific ruckus broke out during the first act and nearly brought the performance to an end. 'A noisy flop', was Klaus's accurate description of the critical response. In its review, the Nazi daily *Völkischer Beobachter* administered the worst cut of all: 'Were Klaus Mann not the son of Thomas Mann this play would certainly never have made it to the stage.' Since he thought it was good and because much of the criticism was unfair and politically motivated, Klaus felt the disappointment more than he did the failure of *Revue zu Vieren*. He swore he would never bring out another play under his own name. He kept his word. A subsequent drama, *Athen* ('Athens'), was written and published in 1932 under the pseudonym Vincenz Hofer. Ostensibly an intellectual dual between Socrates and Alcibiades, Klaus used the story as an anti-Nazi polemic. Despite his efforts, it was never performed in his lifetime.

Demonstrating that even humiliating failure could not repress his creative energy, Klaus now entered one of the most productive, if also one of the most frustrating, two years of his writing career. A few days after Christmas 1930, he and Erika travelled to the Riviera to collaborate on a book for a series, *Was nicht im Baedeker steht* ('What's Not in Baedeker'). Erika did much of the writing. Klaus, thanks to his frequent visits, knew the coast well and supplied the information. Henri Matisse contributed a few sketches. *Das Buch von der Riviera*, which can still be read with pleasure, was less about what to see than about where to stay, dine and even park your car. It displayed a different side of Klaus's character – lighthearted, joyous and as sunny as the Riviera itself. In retrospect, however, the book stands as a tragic period piece. In only a year or so the sunshine would go out of the authors' lives and the Riviera would be not a vacation site for German tourists but a place of exile for desperate German refugees.

Das Buch von der Riviera came out in spring 1931 and, despite the hard economic times, sold well. In the meantime, even before it was in print, a collection of Klaus's essays and reviews on literary subjects was published under the title *Auf der Suche nach einem Weg* ('In Search of a Way'). The articles, covering a vast range of subjects and including an equally broad range of people – Stefan George, Rilke, Hugo von Hofmannsthal, Raymond Radiguet, Oscar Wilde, Julien Green, Hemingway, Gottfried Benn, Virginia Woolf, Cocteau and Chagall among them – were a striking display of the breadth of Klaus's critical interests. Somehow he also found time to pursue the smouldering father-son literary war. 'Schauspieler in der Villa' ('Actor in the Villa'), about a meanspirited, authoritarian father, was such a clear and provocative response to Thomas's attack on him in the 1925 story 'Unordnung und frühes Leid' that he waited two years before seeking, unsuccessfully, to have it published.

It was that same summer, at the ripe age of twenty-four, that Klaus decided the world deserved his autobiography. He knew he had a remarkable story to tell and for once he intended to take his time in telling it. No sooner had he started, however, than the need for immediate gratification overtook him and he began another novel. Although working on the two books at the same time, he finished his novel in six months. *Treffpunkt im Unendlichen*, which appeared in January 1932, paints a picture of life among artists and intellectuals in Berlin and Paris at the end of the 1920s. It is, as Klaus explained, about the lives of young people pulled between longing and despair, political rebellion and flight from everyday life. It has four central themes that are linked to the author's own experiences – drugs, sex, love and suicide. The main characters, Sebastian and Sonya, bear many of the traits of Klaus and Erika, while Gregor Gregori, portrayed as an amoral careerist, was Klaus's ex-friend, Gustaf Gründgens. Underlying the story is a pervasive odour of alienation and loneliness that reflects its author's personal despondency at the time of writing. Samuel Fischer, Klaus's publisher, considered *Treffpunkt* his best work up to that time – his 'first real book' – and while some critics agreed, most did not. Klaus was familiar with such modernists as Joyce and Hemingway, and had been deeply impressed by Virginia Woolf, whose *Mrs Dalloway* he had reviewed a year earlier. Aware of their novel techniques, he had tried to develop a style of his own. He was generally felt to have failed.

Hermann Hesse did not like the book for other reasons. In a commentary published a year later, in May 1933, he condemned it for a gaffe caught neither by the author nor by his publisher. Early in the story one of the characters was said to be staying in room eleven of a hotel, while a little further along he was in room twelve. With that, Hesse complained, 'The whole book suddenly loses inner weight, responsibility, honesty and substance, all because of the damned number twelve.' To say the least, Hesse was being captious – the blunder was corrected in later printings – but the slip was a good example of Klaus's haste. It was also an illustration of the pleasure some critics took in catching him out.

Hesse's article also says a lot about the times. Published four months into the Third Reich, it was written to pass Nazi censorship. The problem was how to write a review of a book whose author's name could not be mentioned, because it appeared on the government's official blacklist, and whose works had just been banned and burned. A tricky problem simply resolved. 'Recently I read a new novel, the work of a talented young author, who has made a certain name for himself . . .' A novel without a name by an author without a name. In the end, who had disgraced himself more – Klaus for his carelessness or Hesse for truckling to Nazi censors with an idiotic review? Typically, Klaus took it all in stride. He knew Hesse fairly well – they had occasionally rambled through the streets of Paris together – and instead of being angry sent him a friendly letter thanking him for the 'fatherly critique' and expressing embarrassment for the slip-up.

Many years later the novel came to be regarded as a significant period piece, providing an incomparable picture of the German 'lost generation' in the waning days of the Weimar Republic and, as such, an important text for understanding the period. But at the time Klaus was crushed by the response to *Treffpunkt*. And the disaster of *Geschwister* still rankled. He reckoned he had found a new voice and been misunderstood by narrow-minded, vindictive critics who had it in for him. Depression, the other side of the coin of repressed anger, overwhelmed him. Now, for the first time, he lost confidence in himself. In one of the saddest lines he ever wrote, he confessed he could no longer believe in what he was doing: 'I sensed the innermost lack of substance and truth in everything I had accomplished.'

It was fortunate that around this time Klaus made a number of new and enduring friendships. One of these was with Christopher Isherwood. The two had met in Berlin around 1930 but did not come to know one another well until Christopher and his boyfriend, Heinz, fled from Berlin to Amsterdam in 1934. Though Klaus liked Christopher and remained a life-long friend, they were always separated by stark ideological differences. During the early 1930s Christopher was militantly left wing and even more militantly pacifist. Klaus had little time for either frivolous lefties or head-in-the-clouds pacifists but found Christopher personally so likeable that relations were never seriously strained. Above all, Klaus greatly respected his literary judgement and on occasion turned to him for help and advice.

Of an entirely different sort was Brian Howard. Years later Erika wrote of their encounter. 'We were very young when we first met him, my brother Klaus and I, and we struck up a friendship as only very young people can, instantly and forever.' Brian wrote to his mother, 'I have made a charming friend – a thing which happens so seldom. He is extremely charming, simple and sensitive.' To the literary critic Alan Pryce-Jones, Brian commented that Klaus was 'my find of the year – *delicious* person'. Though Klaus would never have referred to Brian, or anyone else, as 'delicious', he was equally fond of him, and their friendship deepened and endured over the years. Yet, despite the cordiality on both sides and the fact that both were unashamedly homosexual, it was an unlikely relationship. Klaus was the serious, almost ponderous, hard-working, insecure German; Brian one of the effervescent Bright Young Things of the London inter-war social scene, described by Evelyn Waugh – who used him as a model for Anthony Blanche in *Brideshead Revisited* – as 'mad, bad and dangerous to know'. It is impossible to imagine Klaus engaging in the wild bouts of drunkenness and sex that were a regular part of Brian's life. But while Brian appeared to be an orchidaceous dandy and flaneur – as indeed was the case – he was also intelligent, politically committed and courageous.

That summer Klaus took Brian to a Nazi rally in Munich. Brian could scarcely believe what he saw and heard. At that moment he became an outspoken and even violent anti-Nazi. Erika considered him 'probably the first Englishman to recognize the full immensity of the Nazi peril and to foresee, with shuddering horror, what was to come. While people like Klaus and myself could still laugh disdainfully at the Nazis, any mention of them put an end to gaiety as far as Brian was concerned.' Klaus invited him to family lunch at Poschinger Strasse – a memorable occasion for Brian, who was a great admirer of Thomas's novels – and they spent the summer of 1931 together on the shore of the Walchensee in southern Bavaria. Later on Brian proposed their sharing an apartment, but, both being hyper-itinerant, nothing came of it. Still, they took vacations together in places such as Sanary-sur-Mer and Sils Baselgia.

Several months after *Treffpunkt* appeared, Klaus finally finished *Kind dieser Zeit*, a history of the first eighteen years of his life. If George Orwell was right that a person who gives a good account of himself is probably lying, this autobiography must be considered generally honest. Klaus appeared almost gleeful in accounting for every rowdy, disreputable act he had ever committed. He also gave an inside picture, as it were, of the daily life in the household of a famous writer. And he did not hesitate to discuss his homosexual feelings. Where he flinched from telling the truth was about the relationship with his father. 'The father-son conflict was an issue for scarcely a year in my life. When I look back on it now, I find it the most irrelevant and uninteresting of all my problems.' Not then, not before, not after did Klaus go any further.

Throughout their lives both father and son shrank from open confrontation. Instead they joined in maintaining an impenetrable façade which would repress and conceal their differences, not only from the public but in a certain way from themselves. Thomas welcomed Klaus and his friends to the family home wherever in the world that was. He wrote his son long and friendly letters and Klaus responded in long and friendly letters. But their messages were like diplomatic exchanges between two distant monarchs. Byzantine politeness concealed true feelings.

It cannot have helped that Klaus grew up fast but then in some ways failed fully to mature, to cut the umbilical cord, to stand completely on his own. It was while he was staying with Baron von Bernus that he – and later the other children as well – was endowed with a monthly allowance that lasted to the end of his life. He never outgrew his dependence on his parents for money and a periodic home. It was Klaus's frank public homosexuality, however, that was the main cause of discord. That the son accepted his nature and acted on it was a constant torment for Thomas. The son suffered from being openly homosexual, the father from not being so.

Reich-Ranicki was close to the mark when he wrote of their relations, 'The son admired and respected his father. Love him he could not. But did he secretly hate him? The father disapproved of his son, despised him, in fact. Hate him he could not. But did he secretly fear him? To the son the father was a gigantic model by whom he felt crushed. To the father the son was a sinister caricature which terrified him.'

Kind dieser Zeit was well received and continues to be admired. No praise could have been warmer than that of the great cosmopolitan humanist of Weimar, Count Harry Kessler, who wrote in his diary, 'Klaus Mann's book, although strongly reflecting the influence of Proust and Rilke (and not at all his father's), is one of the most personal memoirs of recent times . . . *Kind dieser Zeit* is a really "significant" book, a book that *signifies* something, the book of the youngest generation about the last twenty years that I find perhaps the most congenial. I understand it better; it means more to *me* than do any of his father Thomas's or his uncle Heinrich's works.' The pity is that neither Klaus nor the public ever saw the comment. The autobiography was published in November 1932 and sold well – for a time. But Klaus was a man of no luck. Within three months Hitler was in power. That was the end of *Kind dieser Zeit*.

Klaus had dedicated the book to his and Erika's closest and oldest friend, Ricki Hallgarten. In *The Turning Point* Klaus described him as looking 'savage and delicate, somewhat like a neurotic gypsy . . . with black bushy eyebrows over a pair of violent eyes' – all of which is evident in photos. Ricki lived in his own tortured world, which he intended to escape from by suicide. 'It's a pity I'll have to do it', he would say. Hoping to establish himself as an artist, Ricki travelled to New York in 1927 to set up a studio. Typically refusing any money from his wealthy family, he supported himself as a dishwasher and flower shop delivery boy. Eventually doubting his talent for painting, Ricki returned to Munich after several years and fell into bouts of depression. Klaus and Erika did what they could to help. In the spring of 1931 Erika proposed entering a non-stop automobile race of ten thousand kilometres. Ricki went along with the idea, and they won. She also talked him into illustrating some of her books. As his psychological state worsened in the course of the following year, Klaus and Erika were so alarmed they turned to their mutual friend Annemarie Schwarzenbach – Miro, as they called her – to try to find some way of diverting him. Annemarie, from a rich, arch-conservative Swiss family, had met Klaus and Erika the year before in Berlin and lived just as fast a life as they did. Dressed in masculine clothes, she was an androgynous beauty who fascinated men and women equally. Though she had immediately fallen passionately in love with Erika – a passion not especially returned – she was at the same time one of Klaus's closest friends. Together the three of them proposed to Ricki to travel by car to Persia, a country Annemarie knew and loved. He readily fell in with the idea. 'It was lots of fun', Klaus later recalled. 'We tossed about with maps, piles of Baedeker guides, unpaid bills and farewell letters to our many friends. Ricki seemed as cheerful and thrilled as the rest of us.' The day before they were to leave, Ricki shot himself in the heart.

Klaus had great understanding for what Ricki had done. 'Out of selfishness and love we tried our very best to prevent him from doing what he was so terribly eager to do.' And in an obituary tribute, he sounded almost envious. 'Death, which once seemed so foreign to me, has become a more familiar region since so intimate a friend of my earthly life entrusted himself voluntarily to it. In a place where a friend is living one is somewhat at home before going there oneself.'

Suicide was an old acquaintance of Klaus's, going back to his early youth when he wrote 'Tragödie eines Knabens'. The idea of self-extinction figures in most of his subsequent fiction, in which there is usually at least one person who thinks of, attempts or commits suicide. In 1931 he wrote an article, 'Selbstmörder' ('Suicides'), about some of his friends 'who thought it nobler to give up than to carry on'. A few years later he had a long conversation about death with Julien Green which left a deep impression. 'He said it must be something splendid, the most beautiful moment, the great moment of departure from oneself.'

'I have lost more friends through suicide (including the less direct patterns of self-destruction) than through diseases, crimes, or accidents', Klaus wrote in *The Turning Point*. Some were persons of note – Franz von Hofmannsthal, Lili Schnitzler and the Parisian artist Jules Pascin. Some were total strangers, such as the young Swiss painter named Walser, whom Klaus had met at a café in Paris one grey winter afternoon. They talked about books and found they had many interests in common. On parting, Walser promised to meet the next day at the Café du Dôme when he would bring along some of his work. He did not show up and Klaus later found out why. 'He shot himself just a few hours after he told me life can be adorable, provided one has the strength and fortitude to bear it.' For himself, he thought it was better to persevere but, he added, 'with what bitter envy our gaze follows into the unknown those who have found the courage for the finest, most uncompromising of all gestures: freeing oneself of the burden'. This ambivalence – fascination with death while rejecting it – runs like a leitmotif through his life and his fictional writing.

It is possible Klaus had a mild case of manic depression. Beginning in his twenties, periods of exceptional excitability, boundless energy and great productivity were interrupted by sudden, precipitous descents into black despair and thoughts of death. The mood swings often bore no relation to the actual events of his life at the time. Things could go well or they could go badly. He valiantly withstood terrible emotional blows, suffering no more than 'normal' depression. Or he could be strolling along happily on a sunny day and suddenly sink into a black pit. Then he would long for death.

Yet this death had an unreal quality. Was it ever any more than a fist in the face of a God he never believed in?

To recover from the shock of Ricki's death, Klaus, Erika and Miro took off immediately for Venice. But it was no good. No happy faces are to be seen in the photos taken at the Lido. So they left, only to find a still greater disaster waiting for them when they returned to Germany. Political intrigues were threatening to open the way to Hitler's triumph. Staying in Munich was therefore unbearable. Again they fled, this time to Scandinavia. Why there? Because Klaus had a standing invitation to visit a friend.

Hans Aminoff was a young, wealthy, cultivated Finn of aristocratic origin whom Klaus had met in Paris in January 1932. They had quickly become intimate and Hans spent a short time with Klaus in Berlin and Munich. The romance had been brief but encouraging. When they parted, Hans invited Klaus to visit the family estate in Pekkala in western Finland. On the strength of this he, Erika and Annemarie left Munich in Erika's car in mid-July. Judging by Klaus's diary the visit was a happy occasion. The extended Aminoff family, along with friends who came and went, created an atmosphere of a cordial, somewhat chaotic house party. Hans and Klaus were often alone together and apparently there was a critical moment as they walked beside a nearby lake. It offered a perfect opportunity for Klaus to declare his feelings. He found he could not. Perhaps what he wanted was not marriage but a honeymoon. Whatever the reason for his reticence, he impulsively cut short the visit and went with Erika and Miro to tour northern Finland and Norway. Their only understanding was that Hans would soon come to Germany and they would be together again.

CHAPTER 4

Fleeing Hitler
1933

On the night of 30 January 1933 Klaus wrote in his diary, 'The news that Hitler is Reich chancellor. Horror. I never thought it possible.' In fact he and his family had thought it was possible. At least as early as mid-1931 they discussed having to flee. 'Serious talk about the necessity of leaving Germany. Appalling triumph of madness.' That was Klaus's entry for 25 May of that year. The following day, he added, 'Again long conversation with Mielein concerning exile. Is it inevitable?' On 19 November: 'Bruno Walter at dinner. (Discussion about Nazis. Possible governments, emigration.)' That was followed by six further entries, concluding in a remark about a dinner conversation on 14 December: 'Will it be necessary to leave Germany? Hitler's chances [of becoming] Reich President.'

These desperate thoughts were prompted by the outcome of the September 1930 Reichstag election. In a stunning surprise – not least of all to themselves – the Nazis had achieved a monumental electoral breakthrough, increasing their votes from eight hundred thousand to six and a half million, and the number of their Reichstag seats from twelve to one hundred and seven. The paradoxical effect of Hitler's victory was not to energize his opponents but to leave them dazed and immobilized. With the Manns, however, it was just the reverse. Heinrich had always been an outspoken defender of the Weimar Republic, and, after a wrenching internal struggle, Thomas had by now joined him. His passionate speech 'Von deutscher Republik' ('On the German Republic'), given in October 1922, announced his conversion from conservative nationalism to democratic republicanism. After the 1930 election he went beyond passive intellectual support for democracy and made a full-scale attack on National Socialism. 'Appeal to Reason', a justly famous address in Berlin on 17 October, denounced the murderous nature of Nazism and called for a broad alliance of democrats to defend the republic.

In his early years Klaus had been mostly absorbed writing fiction. 'Never before nor afterwards in my life have I been so intensely narrow-minded as during the period from my thirteenth until my seventeenth year.' Of how many boys is that not true? Still not yet a teenager he had followed with interest the brief establishment of a 'Bavarian Soviet Republic' and had sided with the revolutionaries. Later on he cycled through the poor areas of Munich, where he was appalled by the living conditions. So there were embers of a smoldering leftist social conscience. At that point, however, his opinions were more sentimental than political. In fact through most of the 1920s – and his own early twenties – he claimed he rarely saw a newspaper, and that when he did, it was usually to read the theatre column.

His indifference began to dissipate when he came across the writings of the American social reformers, Upton Sinclair and Sinclair Lewis, with whom he began to correspond. His tour of the United States had left him disgusted with the treatment of blacks and the conditions of the working class. But the social problems of America had no relevance to the political problems of Europe. These latter engaged him only in terms of a high-minded concern for the place of Europe in the world and for relations between Germany and France. About the repression of writers and the banning of films and plays that occurred in the waning days of the Weimar republic he said little or nothing.

Klaus later reproached himself for his detachment and failure to recognize the menace of Nazism earlier. 'I might have been a more efficient fighter if I had bothered to scrutinize the depth of the German psychosis. My illusions sprang from inadequate knowledge . . . I was not familiar with the Nazi frame of mind . . . I was bored and disgusted by them but not frightened enough.' He added cogently, 'Some sort of affinity to your antagonist seems indispensable to put up a good struggle.' He went on to say, 'I travelled about, lecturing on European culture, amusing myself (and sometimes, perhaps, my hearers) with flippancies ridiculing the Nazis.' But when it came to concrete political action – participating in political rallies or taking an active part in anti-fascist organizations – he held aloof. 'I spent more time in Paris or Villefranche than in Germany. I refused to have anything to do with the whole sordid mess.'

The whole sordid mess blew up in his face with the 1930 election. 'Anyone who was apathetic about politics yesterday was certainly shaken up by the Reichstag election.' These were words from 'What Kind of Future Do We Want?', a speech he delivered in Vienna several weeks after the election. With that he became one of one of the earliest and most vocal opponents of Nazism. Even before then he had openly eviscerated the pseudo-charismatic Ernst Jünger, whom Klaus accused of 'trying to sell us barbarism as a new ideology'. He warned, 'What makes him dangerous is that he can write; a mind with Jünger's fire can do a great deal of harm.'

As someone who had always considered himself representative of German youth, Klaus found it particularly galling that young people had voted in large numbers for Hitler and that Nazism was spreading especially fast in universities. But by no means just in universities. It was a profound shock to Klaus when his friend Stefan Zweig, stalwart pacifist democrat, published an article accepting the loud claim of fascists of the 1920s and 1930s, that democracy was ineffective and only dictatorship 'gets things done'. Were not young people engaged in 'a perhaps imprudent but fundamentally sound and acceptable revolt against the ineffectiveness of "high politics"?' Zweig asked. Klaus immediately countered with an open letter. 'As for myself I want to have nothing, nothing at all to do with this perverse kind of "radicalism". I cannot help preferring the slowness and uncertainty of the democratic process to the devastating swiftness of those dashing counter-revolutionaries.' He warned that passive acceptance of the illusions of fascism would lead to 'a new war and the downfall of European civilization'.

Klaus looked on aghast as he witnessed a growing number of mushy-headed Zweigs falling for the line that Hitler and his party represented a respectable 'conservative revolution'. To his horror he saw a link being forged between the world of intellectuals and the world of brownshirts. 'More and more of my friends began to wonder if the spirit of youth and revolution was not with the other side.' One by one the bards of Weimar democracy wavered. All too many succumbed. Klaus recalled a social reception at which he witnessed Germany's senior author – and eminent democrat – Gerhart Hauptmann, as he pondered aloud the rights and wrongs of Nazism. 'Hitler – after all – my dear friends! No hard feelings! Let's try to be. No, if you please, allow me. May I refill my glass? This champagne – very remarkable, indeed – that man Hitler, I mean. This champagne too, for that matter. German youth. Almost seven million votes. Those Germans, an incalculable nation – very mysterious indeed – cosmic impulses. As I tried to explain to my Jewish friends – this champagne! – German youth in its overflowing enthusiasm.' Klaus called Hauptmann 'the Hindenburg of German literature'.

But it was one of Klaus's less eminent friends who explained the appeal of Nazism more simply and concretely. Willi was a long-time, working-class bedmate in Berlin. He knew absolutely nothing except the weight of every boxer and the income of every movie star. He had no job, no home, no ambition; he was penniless, thoughtless and faithless. Klaus liked him for his 'tonic gaiety'. He also liked to tease him. Once he referred to Goethe as the famous general who led German troops to victory over the Chinese in the war of 1870. To which Willi answered that of course everyone knew that! Then one day Willi showed up in a stormtrooper uniform and explained why he had signed on: 'They are going to be the bosses and that's all there is to it.'

The possibility of the Nazis becoming the bosses grew with their triumph in the April 1932 provincial elections. 'Horrifying victory of lunacy', Klaus wrote in his diary. By now he and his family realized that the menace was real and present. An article Klaus published around this time provoked an open declaration of war. In response, *Völkische Beobachter* minced no words: 'The Mann family has become a scandal in Munich and must at an appropriate moment be liquidated.' The Mann family drew the appropriate conclusion. 'Extremely serious [discussion] of the necessity to emigrate.' Yet, like almost everyone else, the Manns still could not believe, *really* believe, that Hitler would ever come to power – a case of what Freud called 'knowing and not knowing'. Curiously, it was around the same time that Klaus found himself by chance one day sitting at a table next to Hitler in the Carlton Tea Room in Munich. There he was able to observe him and over-hear his conversation. 'It was a most unpleasant experience to have him so close to me, but at the same time it meant something like a relief. For I was positive he had no chance to conquer Germany.' As he later wrote, 'My mistake was not that I *under*estimated Schicklgruber but that I *over*estimated the German people.' Never was the catastrophe of January 1933 more concisely summed up.

The popular enthusiasm that accompanied Hitler's appointment as chancellor put Thomas in mind of the mood at the time of German entry into war in 1914 and he surmised that it would lead to a similarly bloody disaster. The next day, however, Klaus found him 'calmer than expected'. Bavaria itself was, for that matter, calmer than expected. It remained strangely unaffected, even though the Nazis were rapidly extending their power elsewhere. Anti-Nazis, who would have been arrested in other places, went about their lives in Munich in a normal way. On 1 February Thomas had his own Carlton Tea Room moment, confidently writing to friends, 'Though they may indeed be irrational, the German people are basically very intelligent.' In Bavaria the annual Fasching celebrations went ahead as usual and everyone had a good time. Or appeared to. Klaus described the mood as 'the fever of grim and feverish merriment'. People danced as the press was being muzzled. They went to masked balls while political parties were being disbanded. They went skiing when communists were being rounded up and imprisoned. They jammed cabaret performances as trade unions were being dissolved and their treasuries confiscated. But, contrary to the confident predictions of many, one event did not take place. Herr Hitler did not fall from power within six weeks.

Instead, as Klaus and millions of others looked on impotently, the Nazis step by step fastened their grip on the country. 'Great political tension', he wrote in his diary on 6 February. Then, quoting from one of his father's short stories: 'It is not going well, it is not going well, it most certainly is not going well.' Ten days later: 'Scarcely disguised dictatorship.' Heinrich fled to France on 20 February after waking up that morning to see that he had been denounced in the *Völkische Beobachter*. A week later a mad Dutch communist set the Reichstag on fire and Hitler seized the event to suspend civil liberties and effectively put an end to German democracy. The consequences for many of Klaus's friends were immediate. 'Conditions in Berlin indescribable. The last friends fleeing', he wrote in his diary. Within the space of a month, a democratically formed government had morphed into a totalitarian *coup d'état*.

While all this was going on, Thomas and Katia were on vacation in Switzerland following an exausting series of lectures on 'The Suffering and Greatness of Richard Wagner' in Amsterdam, Brussels and Paris. Monika was in Berlin and the two youngest children, Elisabeth and Michael, were in schools near Munich. Golo, who had just received his doctorate at Heidelberg under Karl Jaspers, was planning to spend the winter in Gottingen with his companion Kai. One morning he had the unsettling experience of answering his door to find two police officers demanding to know where he had been the night before, with whom he had been and whether he had passed out political pamphlets. Klaus and Erika were in Switzerland skiing. On arriving back in Munich on the evening of 12 March, they were warned by the family chauffeur, who they now realized had been working secretly for the Nazis, that they were in danger of arrest. Immediately they phoned their parents and told them in a guarded way not to return. After a day's hesitation they themselves decided to flee. Early on 13 March Erika drove in her car to join her parents. Klaus decided to take the night train to Paris. Diary jottings record his last melancholy hours in Germany. He wrote letters, dined with friends, listened to phonograph recordings of Strauss's *Salome* and Mahler's *Kindertotenlieder*, took a nap on the sofa, read Rilke's letters. 'Now unfortunately must pack; I don't want to leave; feelings of loneliness. Drank a cognac. Listened to more music recordings. To the station.' With him he took only two suitcases, his typewriter and an overcoat. Hitler could not last long and he expected to be back home in a few months.

Since it was fear of immediate arrest that drove the Manns away, their emigration was a shade less principled than Klaus and Thomas later maintained. 'The essential reason for exile, in our case, was irrefutably simple', Klaus wrote in *The Turning Point*. 'The truth is that we left voluntarily, or rather, that we were forced away by our own disgust, our horror and our forebodings. We left because we could not breathe the air in Nazi Germany.' This was the truth but not the whole truth. Monika remained in Berlin and Golo travelled in and out of the country for several months. As late as May he was urging his father and mother to return – which Klaus promptly denounced as '*bad* advice'. Meanwhile Thomas's lawyer was sounding out the authorities about a possible arrangement that would allow him to live in Munich. In a long letter published in the *Neue Zürcher Zeitung* in 1947,

Thomas said he could have gone back to Germany in 1933 but refused because the price was too high. That price was silence.

The Nazi authorities were also uncertain and confused in those early days. Reinhard Heydrich, Himmler's deputy, and the Munich Gestapo are said to have wanted to arrest Thomas, if not others in the family as well. Goebbels quashed any such notions. He recognized that Thomas would be a supreme cultural asset, on a level with Richard Strauss and Wilhelm Furtwängler, both of whom stayed. More than any other cultural figure, Thomas would burnish the national and international prestige of the Third Reich. So there was no chance of his being jailed.

The quibble over the ambiguity of the family's flight is worth mentioning if only to illustrate what a tremendous sacrifice it was for even such categorical opponents of Nazism as the Mann family to uproot themselves and give up everything except the clothes they were wearing – their homeland, their home, their friends, possessions, income, savings – and live as refugees. 'It is difficult to convey how profoundly shaken [Thomas] was by the emigration of 1933', Golo said. As long as possible Thomas had clung to wisps of hope that Bavaria would somehow be able to maintain a degree of autonomy, that Hitler was just one more chancellor pro tem, that the Nazis would soon be out and the nightmare over. Instead it was the Mann family that was out and their nightmare just beginning.

Kleiner Mann, Was Nun? ('Little Man, What Now?') – the title of Hans Fallada's famous novel of 1932 – was the question facing every German who fled after Hitler's takeover. A refugee may have saved his skin by escaping. But how was he to live; where was he to live; and what occupation could he find? The Manns were exceptionally, almost uniquely, well off in every way, but even they had no answers.

On arriving in Paris on the morning of 14 March 1933, Klaus was met by Bonzo, an old Parisian friend, who greeted him with the news that a mutual friend had been beaten up on the street in Berlin because he was 'Jewish, foreign and homosexual'. And so began exile.

Klaus's decision to go to Paris instead of Switzerland vexed his father but made clear that he intended to go right on leading the existence of an itinerate writer. His home for the moment was to be the Hotel Jacob, an inexpensive Left Bank hotel where he had stayed in the past. On the surface life at first continued along its usual agreeable course. In a typical day he might – as he did on 20 March – stroll along the grands boulevards, chat with an old German friend whom he passes on the street, buy a pair of eyeglasses to replace those he left on the train, stop for a Pernod at a café, spend an hour at the cinema, visit Cocteau for three hours and smoke a pipe or two, and then dine with a friend. But within a very short time, as he read with horror newspaper reports about the imprisonment and suicide of friends, about the Jewish boycotts, the closure of newspapers and journals, and the cancellation of concerts conducted by Bruno Walter and Otto Klemperer, he realized his life had changed forever.

At the same time he was also finding 'his' Paris a different place. In the early months of 1933 roughly one hundred thousand Germans are said to have fled to France. Most went on elsewhere, but at least twenty thousand were there at any one time. France was beginning to feel the effects of the worldwide depression, however, and with eight hundred thousand French unemployed, Germans were regarded not as unfortunate refugees but as highly unwelcome intruders. Klaus personally sensed the change of mood. Some assumed that, being German, he was a Nazi. Speaking German in public, he soon discovered, risked being insulted and even spat on. The great majority, however, found it incomprehensible – even suspicious – that a decent citizen would renounce his homeland. 'To give up your home, your friends, your career – everything! On account of what?' a Swiss acquaintance asked him when they happened to meet on the street. 'Because you have an animosity to Herr Hitler's nose. It is too silly for words.'

Here Klaus confronted one of the tragedies of the 1930s. On the one hand, most people outside Germany knew little and cared less about what Hitler was doing inside Germany. On the other, there was a widespread feeling, especially strong in political circles in Britain, that Germany had been badly treated by the Versailles Treaty and that Hitler was merely rectifying a wrong. The destruction of democracy and treatment of the Jews, well, that was Germany's own affair. For Klaus, combatting these notions was a daily agony. 'It was a tedious, ungrateful job, to warn a world that wished to be fooled.' And the world so wished. As he commented, 'British Tories and Labourites, French bureaucrats and professors, the powerful men from Wall Street and Detroit' were all willfully blind. 'They fawned upon the tyrant and sneered at his victims to boot.' In no time Klaus woke up to realize he was no longer a German writer living in Paris but one of those victims being sneered at.

Little man, *where* now? Paris and Prague – and, to a lesser extent, Vienna and Switzerland – were the main centres of German emigration. After several months in various places in Switzerland, Thomas, Katia and the two youngest children, along with Erika, spent the spring and summer on the Riviera, mostly at Sanary-sur-Mer, which was rapidly becoming a centre of refuge for German artists and writers. Courageously, Golo continued to go in and out of Germany, managing not only to spirit Thomas's inflammatory diaries out of their Poschinger Strasse hiding place but also to smuggle at least some of his savings – sixty thousand marks – from a German bank to the French embassy in Berlin where the money was dispatched by diplomatic bag to Paris. Having broken off his relations with Kai for political reasons, Golo left Germany at the end of May. Monika soon followed. Both ended up in Sanary.

Like most other writers, Klaus chose to stay in France. He had friends and professional contacts and some entrée into the publishing world. He was sure he would be able to earn his way. He might be taken on as a reader by the publisher Gallimard or by the *Nouvelle Revue Française*. Or he might write a French edition of *Kind dieser Zeit*. Perhaps he might set up an émigré publishing house. Another idea was to adapt *Athen* for the French stage. There seemed to be any number of promising possibilities. Alas, in no time he learned that no one wanted a German exile and none of his friends and contacts was inclined to help. So America beckoned. To the New York publisher of *Alexander* he wrote on 30 March, 'If you know of ANYTHING for Erika and me – any kind of literary work, in publishing, with a journal or at a university – please let me know.' A few weeks later he repeated his appeal to an old friend, the artist Eva Herrmann, an American resident. 'Cast your expressive eyes around and see if you can find a job, whether as lecturer, dramaturge, journalist, editor or whatever.' In the end he saw there was little alternative but to stay in France. And so he headed for Sanary.

Little man, *what* now? Almost overnight Klaus became a political writer. His realization that people outside Germany had no conception of the danger Hitler posed stirred in him a sense of mission. His aim was no longer to shock and entertain but to inform, warn and plead. He would be a political evangelist, making the public aware of the nature of Nazism and the threat it posed to Europe and the world, a threat recognized by shockingly few. He would do this by lecturing, writing and publishing.

At the same time, back in Berlin, the Nazis were busy creating their new Reich and erasing the old Germany. On 8 May they took their first step towards this end in the literary field by announcing a blacklist of one hundred and thirty-six writers whose works were to be banned. The names of both Klaus and his uncle Heinrich were on it, though, significantly, Thomas's wasn't. The list turned out to be the menu for the book burnings which began two days later in Berlin and then spread to thirty-four other university towns. Organized by students, the conflagration was modelled on the Wartburg Festival of 1817, when the Napoleonic Code and other 'un-German' works had been incinerated. In Berlin it took place in the centre, near the university. According to the procedure, someone would shout, 'I commit to the fire . . .' then one of the students would bellow the name of an author and into the flames he would toss a book. Roughly twenty-five thousand works were burned, including those of Heinrich and Klaus, though, contrary to widespread myth, none of Thomas's. 'Yesterday all my books in all German cities were publically burned, in Munich on the Königsplatz', Klaus wrote in his diary, adding, 'Barbarity to the point of infantilism. But I feel honoured.'

The young book-burners were bad enough. What sickened Klaus even more, though, was the betrayal of democratic ideals by mature artists and intellectuals whom he esteemed. For him the most painful case was the noted expressionist poet, Gottfried Benn, who happened to be a good friend of the Mann family and someone whose work Klaus had praised highly in published reviews. The Third Reich was scarcely three months old when Benn broadcast a speech pronouncing Nazism to be an admirable 'spiritual idea' and a great revolutionary force that would overcome 'political nihilism' through 'positive action'.

Klaus could scarcely believe the reports of what Benn had said. In a letter that was remarkable at the time and that became famous in postwar Germany, he wrote to express his shock. 'What could bring you – whose name is the very epitome of the highest standards and of fanatical purity – to place yourself at the disposition of those whose lack of standards is unexampled in European history and whose moral degradation the

world observes with disgust?' Who were the poet's admirers in the past? the
letter went on. Certainly not the Nazis. His admirers now lived in small
hotel rooms in Paris, Zurich and Prague. Among his old and close friends,
Heinrich Mann had fled and Thomas Mann was now an object of scorn
and insults. Klaus went on to note that for some time Benn had been
seeking intellectual refuge in German Romanticism and irrationality. 'At
present it seems almost an inevitable law that a strong leaning toward the
irrational leads to political reaction unless one is extremely careful. First
the great gesture against civilization. All of a sudden one arrives at the cult
of violence and then soon at Adolph Hitler.' For Klaus and many others,
Benn was one of the few they did not want to lose to Hitler. 'But in this
hour, anyone who wavers will never again be one of us', Klaus warned, and
concluded, 'Unless I am a bad prophet, your reward will be ingratitude and
mockery.'

To this eloquent challenge Benn replied not in a private letter but in a
radio broadcast from Berlin with the insulting title 'Answer to a Literary
Emigrant'. He remarked sarcastically that it was not for someone lolling
about on the Mediterranean coast to criticize loyal Germans who were
working hard to create a new state. Rationality was now passé, bankrupt.
History had always followed an irrational course. 'Irrationality meant being
creative. In this spirit a new biological type was developing in Germany. I
personally declare myself in favour of the new state because it is my nation
that is finding its way.' And in a verbal postscript, he added that no one in
Germany missed Klaus Mann.

Klaus was appalled and, like his father, was stung by the reference to
basking on the Riviera, wondering whether Benn was aware that were they
not living in hotel rooms in France, they would be rotting away in a concentration camp in Germany. With that one broadcast, Benn brought Klaus to
the forefront of the publicly committed Nazi opponents of the first hour.
Thirty years later, long after Klaus's death, Erika praised her brother's letter
as the first great manifesto of resistance. 'Klaus would be justly famous in
Germany had he, in the course of his whole life, written nothing more than
this letter to Gottfried Benn.' And Benn himself, in a memoir written in
1950, admitted that Klaus, 'who was then only twenty-seven', had understood the situation better than he himself at the age of forty-seven. Klaus's
prophecy that Benn would eventually fall out of favour came true in 1938

when he was expelled from the German Writers' Union and his works were banned.

At the time, however, the Benn episode was not at all to the liking of others in the Mann family. Facing the expropriation of everything – house, savings, even citizenship – Thomas was too rattled to do or say anything. Golo – who would have hesitated to leave a burning building – lapsed into passivity. The day after Hitler became chancellor, he wrote in his diary, 'I don't have the strength to get angry over this ridiculous Hitler nonsense.' He later added, 'Politically uncommitted, I left Germany at twenty-four with the feeling that I was in no way responsible for "our" defeat.' Now he warned his brother not to write or say anything that 'could cause the family's lovely home to be confiscated'. The patriarch himself was angered not only by the Benn affair but also by an aggressive speech Klaus gave on 9 June to the Exiled German Writers' Association in Paris. From this moment and for the next three years Thomas and his eldest son disagreed ever more strongly, not on the nature of National Socialism but on the correct public response to it. At this point the mere thought of not returning to Poschinger Strasse was so unbearable to Thomas he continued to hope that somehow a deal with the Nazis could be struck. Therefore, silence. Klaus had no intention of ever returning to a Germany that was Nazi. Therefore, open protest.

Certainly Klaus was no different from thousands of other émigrés in his foursquare opposition to Nazism. But he was virtually alone in devoting all his time and efforts to combatting it. Sooner and more clearly than others he recognized that Hitler intended war and that war for him was not just a means to an end but an end in itself. He also foresaw the annexation of Austria and Czechoslovakia. And sooner and more clearly he accepted the ugly fact that Hitler was genuinely popular with the German people and that they would follow wherever he took them.

Benn was all too typical of the German intellectuals who, now that Hitler was in power, could scarcely wait to jump on board the Nazi bandwagon. Among them were some of Klaus's oldest and closest friends. 'Letters reached me from Munich, Berlin, and other places, repeating, almost literally, the admonitions of my Swiss acquaintance on the street in Paris.' The most distressing came from his childhood friend and travel companion, Wilhelm Süskind. In condescending language he told Klaus how disappointed in him he was for being such an obtuse fanatic as to leave Germany. He should return and see at first hand what wonders Hitler was doing. 'Come back! Better today than tomorrow!'

Süskind was an intellectual version of Klaus's Berlin friend, Willi. A classic opportunist, he also signed up with the bosses at the first opportunity. In the grand redistribution of jobs following the Nazi takeover, he contrived to be appointed editor of *Die Literatur* – an old established literary journal that Klaus had contributed to – and oversaw its 'coordination', as it was called, into the Nazi propaganda machine. Overnight he also 'coordinated' himself, even to the extent – remarkable, to say the least, for a literary figure – of defending the book burnings. They were, he wrote to Klaus, 'basically well intentioned' though the choice of works might have been more careful. He himself would have excluded those of Arthur Schnitzler.

Klaus's hand trembled with rage as he wrote his reply. He said he could not bear to see the first issue of the Nazified *Die Literatur*, but someone had sent him a few pages and they were worse than he had feared. They included an article stating that Thomas Mann was the prototype of a decadent artist – a phrase that usually meant deserving to be banned. Klaus was sickened. 'Could you not at least have waited a little while?' The new educational system that Süskind praised, he went on, taught old reactionary Teutonic values and aggressive xenophobia. Simply stated, it was preparing youth for war. 'You will say I am being insulting', he wrote in conclusion; 'in fact I am sad, far more sad than angry.' The 'disloyal' were losing their citizenship, but who was really being disloyal?

In hurt tones, Süskind replied that he was offended by the 'polemical nature' of Klaus's letter. 'There is a wall of fog between us; we live in different circumstances.' As regards the book burnings, 'Accusations of [Nazi] barbarity do not help in the slightest.' He concluded, 'Come back, dear friend; we would talk it over and you would see that I am right. But you will not come, you will cut yourself off. You insist on being right.'

As if perfidy were not enough to bear, Klaus's self-esteem suffered a blow when Hans Aminoff abruptly cancelled his plans to visit. Although Klaus feared the relationship was in trouble, he was shocked to receive a letter in mid-June announcing his friend's engagement to a young Swedish painter. Klaus was devastated. But then so was Hans. In his letter he said he had been forced into the marriage by his family and the thought of ending his relationship with Klaus was more than he could bear. So Klaus went on dreaming of Hans; Hans continued to write and appeal for replies.

During the summer Klaus did a lot of soul-searching and finally sat down and told his diary about it. 'Throughout the day I think how unfair and sad it is that I am alone when I would be ready to –. [sic] I reflect upon all the failed and half-failed attempts. In some cases the problem was sexual. But even more bitter were the others where that was not a consideration (above all René and Hans Aminoff). Among the many others, since it was not a case of luck, the blame, the failure must be mine. An acknowledgement; seldom and ever more seldom do I feel any attraction to gays. To live a normal life with one of them would in the long term be impossible. But even this acknowledgement does not go far enough. There were cases where I could not go through with it. Even with Hans I must search for the failure in me. (I should never have left him that day by the lake.) I won't be able to get through the next half year if I continue to live like this. With all my strength I must try to find someone to help me get over Hans. I know he exists somewhere, perhaps is even waiting. Idiotic that I must think all this through. But you have to know what you are looking for.'

In practice Klaus settled for casual sex with mostly straight and bisexual men whom he met on the street and whom he often paid for sex, which then left him feeling ashamed. Over and over his diary records a first name or initial, or a simple word or phrase – 'sailor', 'a kid from Kufstein (Adonis)', or 'met Jan. Hotel. He is very sweet.' An entry about a visit to London in December 1932 tells a typical story. At the end of a frenetic day he went to the Turkish baths in Jermyn Street. There he spent an hour but saw 'nothing interesting' and so he made his way to Piccadilly Circus, where he found Jerry. He took him back to his hotel and they had sex 'paid for with 2 whiskies'. Occasionally there were longer-lasting casual relationships – such as with Willi in Berlin – but they never went much beyond quick sex. 'Since leaving Munich', he confided to his diary on 2 July, 'I have had love only by paying cash for it – sailors, masseurs, street boys. Except for two or three cases when I wanted something different (for example the Russian pianist), nothing came of it. The desire just wasn't there.' So the search continued. And the frustration went on.

Yet in the end what he really cared about, the centre of his life, was writing, pure and simple. And what could be better than writing an anti-Nazi book? So he decided to turn his hand to the story of Horst Wessel, the twenty-three-year-old stormtrooper who was killed in a brawl in 1930. Though the circumstances of his death – whether a quarrel over money or a whore – were never clear, the Nazis turned the affair into a huge cause célèbre. The lout himself was posthumously sanctified as a party martyr and the words he had composed for a Nazi marching song became known as the *Horst Wessel Lied*. As soon as Hitler was in power it was adopted as a party anthem. Provoked by two hagiographies that had just appeared, Klaus could not resist writing a bit of anti-Nazi propaganda through a debunking biography. Theoretically it was not a bad idea but, as friends warned him, in practice it was impossible. In no position to unearth reliable testimony or documents, when he got down to it he lapsed into crude polemics. In no time he realized the book was not working and dropped it. Then he found he could not let go. The fraudulence of Horst Wessel was symptomatic of the fraudulence of the Third Reich and had to be exposed. Salvaging some of the material, he wrote another version, only to find no German exile publisher wanted it.

Horst Wessel, book burnings, blacklists of writers, publications suppressed or 'coordinated', writers who 'coordinated' themselves or who were frightened into fleeing, the closing of art museums, the banning of certain composers and Jewish conductors, transforming Wagner and Nietzsche into proto-Nazis – all this demonstrated how German culture was being hijacked. Soon there would be two German cultures in direct competition with each other, and eventually only one. Countless German émigrés recognized the threat. Klaus was the only one who was determined to do something about it.

But what? Nothing came to him until one afternoon on 3 May when he was staying in Le Lavandou and ran into Annemarie Schwarzenbach. She broached the idea of bringing out an anti-Nazi journal. 'A marvellous opportunity. Let's hope', Klaus wrote in his diary that night. Within four days they had decided on a name – *Die Sammlung* ('The Collection') to convey the notion that it would be open to the entire range of anti-fascist views. It would be published in Zurich and financed by funds that Annemarie secured from her, presumably unknowing, parents. In his enthusiasm Klaus at once started contacting potential contributors and sponsors. Here for all to see was the Klaus that Golo described as 'naïve, courageous and optimistic'.

By lucky coincidence it was just at this time that Klaus met an old friend from his Berlin days. It was Fritz Landshoff, a publisher who had abandoned his Berlin firm and fled to Amsterdam almost immediately after Hitler came to power. In no time he had worked out an arrangement with the Dutch publisher Emanuel Querido to bring out the works of writers banned in Germany. Searching France for émigré authors, he had come to Le Lavandou to ask Klaus for the rights to all his books. Klaus readily agreed and took the occasion to mention his own project. Fritz was intrigued and promised to sound out Querido. A short time later Klaus noted in his diary, 'Another visit by Landshoff, thorough discussion about the journal – seems to be not without prospects – that would be the ideal solution.' Querido went along with the idea and ten days afterwards Klaus was invited to Amsterdam to sign a contract. With this, he had the publishing resources of Querido's firm behind him. For the next year Amsterdam was his home – not only a welcome place of refuge but also a city for which he almost immediately formed a strong and lasting affection.

Starting up the sort of journal Klaus had in mind would have been difficult at the best of times; 1933 was all too obviously the worst. Readership was bound to be limited, the financing dicey, contributions uncertain and opposition from across the Rhine tremendous. In the face of this, the determination and idealism on the part of all three partners was heroic. Emanuel Querido took the biggest gamble and later paid the biggest price. He and his wife were rounded up in 1942 and sent to a death camp.

The key to the smooth operation of the journal was the excellent relationship, both professional and personal, between Klaus and Fritz – paradoxically strengthened by the fact that both shared bouts of depression and periodic drug addiction. Klaus valued Fritz as a business colleague and loved him as a brother, referring to him in *Der Wendepunkt* as 'mein brüderlicher Freund' and his closest friend since the death of Ricki. In his memoir, *Amsterdam, Keizersgracht 333*, Fritz warmly reciprocated the feeling: 'Knowing Klaus was the greatest personal reward of my exile.'

While Klaus could depend on Querido to get the publication out, he alone was responsible for the contents. As editor-to-be he solicited articles, coped with piles of mail and edited cairns of manuscripts. Amazingly he managed to persuade André Gide and Aldous Huxley to join his uncle Heinrich as sponsors. With great effort he even cajoled his father to be listed as a contributor. And all the while he somehow managed to write anti-Nazi articles for an array of publications in Switzerland and Austria.

Landshoff recalled a typical day. Klaus would work in his room without a break until five in the afternoon and then go to the Querido office. He and Fritz might then roam around the city, chatting, have a drink at the Café Américain and later go to dinner. Afterwards there might be a film or concert. Sometimes they would go back to the pension where they were both staying and discuss the affairs of Querido. Or Klaus might read Fritz something he had written that day. Years later Golo commented, 'Klaus never lived so intensely, so excitedly, so actively, even indeed so happily, as in the early years of emigration.'

The friendship with Fritz encompassed the extended Mann family. Fritz and Thomas had a high regard for one another and Fritz was always a welcome visitor to the Mann home. He was particularly welcome to young Elisabeth, who later acknowledged that at the age of fifteen she had been deeply in love with him. At the time, he was in love with Erika. And Erika, while not reciprocating his feelings, eventually offered to marry him as a way of weaning him off drugs and away from thoughts of suicide. To her relief he declined.

Thomas's friendly feelings did not extend to the Querido publishing house. Just as Klaus and Fritz were getting started with *Die Sammlung*, Thomas finished work on the first volume of his new novel, *The Tales of Jacob*. Both Emmanuel Querido and Gottfried Bermann, who had taken over S. Fischer, Thomas's old publisher, badly wanted it. It would make Querido a major European publisher and it would keep Bermann in business in Germany. Klaus, like Erika, pressed him to take a stand. Begging him to place his new novel with Querido, Klaus wrote to his father, 'One does not entrust one's most precious possession to a country one has left in abhorrence. They will kill it.' He concluded firmly, 'I consider publication in this Germany to be a very serious mistake.' Typically, Thomas first agreed with his son, then did the opposite and gave the book to Bermann. His reason was simple. It would ensure sales in the more important market, the Third Reich.

By late August the first issue of *Die Sammlung* was ready to go to press. It was an amazing accomplishment. Hitler had been chancellor for scarcely six months and Klaus was already in a position to launch his anti-Nazi journal. Just as the publication was ready to go onto the newsstands, however, Klaus and Fritz took a good look at the contents and realized – somehow rather to their surprise – that there was a problem, a big one. Originally *Die Sammlung* was intended to be an exclusively literary publication and a few contributors had insisted on this. But in the mortal clash between democracy and totalitarianism in the Europe of the 1930s could there possibly be a literary journal that was not in some way political? By its very existence, by its aims, by its contributors, Klaus's journal would inevitably pose a direct challenge to Nazi ideology. *Die Sammlung*, not *Die Literatur* and its like, was to define German culture.

And so it came about that the leading article in the first issue was a stinging attack on Nazism by Heinrich Mann; in the same vein was an editorial by Klaus defining the purpose of the publication. 'The true, valid German literature cannot remain silent before the degradation of its people and the outrage it perpetrates on itself', it began. 'A literary periodical is not a political periodical . . . Nevertheless, today it will have a political mission. Its position must be unequivocal.' As publication day neared, both Landshoff and Klaus became increasingly nervous about Thomas's reaction. Since it had been difficult enough to persuade him to be a contributor, Klaus felt he should warn him that the initial issue would be 'not exactly bland' and could arouse controversy.

In dread of losing not only his home but also his homeland, Thomas was at this time a psychological wreck. 'If anyone lacks the qualities of a martyr, it is Thomas Mann', a friend said at the time. In material terms he faced having to give up everything that belonged to him except for the contents of the several suitcases he and Katia had taken with them on the lecture tour. He was so distraught he even tried briefly to convince himself that Nazism was perhaps, after all, simply a 'conservative revolution', and that he might yet be able to return to his home.

It is no surprise, then, that when *Die Sammlung* appeared on 1 September, it set off an explosion. Bermann was absolutely livid and virtually ordered Thomas to denounce his son's journal, since otherwise all his works would be banned in Germany. Unwilling to forsake the hope of returning to

Munich and wanting to keep his German readers – and the royalties that were a vital source of income – Thomas complied. In a telegram he knew would be made public, he announced, 'Must confirm that character first issue *Die Sammlung* not consistent with original programme.' This was not sufficient for Bermann, so a second telegram had to be more specific: 'My name to be deleted from list contributors.' Three other noted authors, Alfred Döblin, René Schickele and Stefan Zweig, issued statements that were even more grovelling.

Klaus was gobsmacked. 'Long letter from the Magician – the most painful sensation – his second telegram to Bermann, his dissociation from *Die Sammlung*, at the same time as that of Döblin and Schickele – very painful affair, sadness and confusion – and also a letter from Stefan Zweig – another cowardly back-down – misery – at first write rather sharply to Zweig – then long letters to Magician, Heinrich and Gide.'

'What is at issue in all this?' Klaus asked Zweig. 'It is so clear. None of the big names, none of those whose word at this critical time would have influence and weight will associate himself with those who fight. Heinrich Mann is almost the sole exception. Can you understand that I am devastated? Whom can we count on when all those we most trusted abandon us out of concern for the German [book] market?' Sales were, of course, the crucial issue for all of them. Zweig held the world record and he was determined to keep it. He was also, by nature, morally pusillanimous and very confused in his personal and professional lives. Despite their close friendship, Zweig's 1942 memoir, *Die Welt von Gestern* ('The World of Yesterday') never mentions Klaus's name, passes over in silence his early support for Hitler's 'conservative revolution' and says nothing about *Die Sammlung*. From 1933 until his suicide in 1942, Zweig refused to take a stand against Hitler.

For Thomas the affair provided an opportunity to vent his contempt for his son. In a furious letter he charged that the whole miserable business was Klaus's fault alone. He had violated his own guidelines. He and Heinrich put Thomas in 'a horrible position'. And not just himself; poor Schickele stood to lose the equivalent of a year's income. Sales of *The Tales of Jacob* had been endangered. And his book promised to be a 'far more stunning victory' over 'the rulers' – the word 'Nazi' was avoided – than 'a whole battery of polemics by émigrés'. Could Thomas really have believed that *Die*

Sammlung was nothing more than polemics by malcontented émigrés? Could he really have thought that his own books, by contrast, were in some way subversive when read in the Third Reich? Serious or not, he clung to this line of defence for some time to come. To kowtow, according to the dictionary, is 'to act in an obsequious manner, to show servile deference'. This well describes Thomas's behaviour. Nazi authorities in Berlin could not have been more pleased. That Klaus would be denounced by his own father was more than they could have hoped for. A memo from the Writers' Guild to the Propaganda Ministry gloated that Thomas Mann, whom they referred to as 'completely neutral toward National Socialist Germany', had 'thrown his son overboard'.

And so it was that the greatest testimony to the success of *Die Sammlung* came from the Nazis themselves. Of all exile publications, they considered Klaus's by far the most dangerous. 'The communist and Jewish literati who have fled from Germany are now trying to surround Germany with a wall of literary stink-gas from their crevice', commented *Die neue Literatur*, with typical Nazi delicatesse. Switching metaphors, it went on, 'The most dangerous of all these reptiles is without a doubt *Die Sammlung*, edited by the half-Jew Klaus Mann.'

In official circles, though, mere sarcasm was inadequate and a more muscular approach was proposed – kidnapping and assignment to a concentration camp no less. In a memo to Heinrich Himmler, Hanns Johst, a playwright and head of various Nazi writers' organizations, wrote, 'There is currently being published in Amsterdam a filthy émigré journal, *Die Sammlung* ... The publisher is the up-and-coming Klaus Mann, the offspring of Herr Thomas Mann. Since it is difficult to believe that this half-Jew will ever come over to our side and since we unfortunately cannot bring him to justice, I suggest we deal with this important matter by hostage-taking.' Johst asked, 'Would it not be possible to arrest Thomas Mann in his place? His intellectual output would not suffer from a little vacation in Dachau.' The letter gains added poignancy from the fact that Johst – the genuine author of the famous, usually misattributed line, 'Whenever I hear the word culture, I reach for my pistol' – had known and admired Thomas Mann in earlier years.

The Propaganda Ministry was jubilant, flaunting Thomas's public repudiation of *Die Sammlung* as his clear support for the Nazi state. It threatened any writer who contributed to *Die Sammlung* with a ban in the German book market. An official literary association warned that any contributor would be guilty of 'intellectual high treason', while a Berlin daily, the *Berliner Tageblatt*, published a 'Declaration against *Die Sammlung*' highlighting the statements by Thomas, Schikele and Döblin. When Zweig was asked by his publisher, Insel Verlag, to issue a second statement distancing himself even more explicitly from *Die Sammlung*, he promptly complied. A week later Robert Musil, author of the imperishable *Der Mann ohne Eigenschaften* ('The Man without Qualities'), wrote to Klaus resigning as a contributor. Revealing himself to be an author without qualities, he said writing for the publication was not worth the 'unforeseeable uncertainties'. 'Horrible', Klaus commented in his diary. 'And there is virtually nothing to be done about it.'

The whole affair had the additional effect of creating bad blood among the émigrés – wretches for whom Thomas felt little more than disdain, referring to them derisively as *Emigrantentum*, their publications as *Emigrantenpublizistik* and their criticism of the Nazis as so much *Emigrantenpolemik*. Who was this rabble that Thomas scorned? Partly it was Germany's intellectual elite. Hitler's coming to power set off the greatest exodus of intellectuals in history. Ten thousand, it is generally said, fled within the year. Noted writers defected virtually en bloc, almost all of them going sooner or later to the United States. The vast majority of the émigrés, however, were nobodies who were stuck. A long list of adjectives would be needed to describe their pathetic state and the fate that befell them after the fall of France.

A week after receiving Thomas's brutal letter, Klaus had lunch with his parents. Neither father nor son ever revealed what was said. Thomas's diary states simply, 'deterioration in the mood in the course of the afternoon'. Klaus's says even less: 'Tea in the little garden.' Evidently there was no real showdown. Nothing could have better exposed the profound cleft in Klaus's character than this episode. In the course of his twenty-seven years he had demonstrated his ability to stand up to his literary detractors, to the Nazis, to the communists, to homophobes, to depression, to loneliness, to the death of cherished friends, to expatriation, to crushing disappointments. But when it came to his father, it was almost as though he were under a spell. Not only was Klaus too psychologically paralyzed to defend himself, in his autobiographies and, with only one or two exceptions, in the privacy of his diary he could only praise his father.

It is revealing that even his fifteen-year-old sister Elisabeth noticed all this at the time and many decades later contrasted Erika's 'passion, aggressiveness and firmness' toward Thomas with her brother's submissiveness. 'Klaus did not ever have the same kind of intellectual violence. He also had strong convictions, he also felt betrayed when he did not get the support for his journal that he had hoped he would get. That was a bitter disappointment for him, but he never had the aggressiveness that Erika had, never.'

Even for Klaus, though, there was a limit, and that was reached with the perfidious Gottfried Bermann. After being stabbed in the back by his father, Klaus was then knifed in the front by his father's publisher. Bermann loathed Klaus and, not content to have lured Thomas away from Querido and *Die Sammlung*, he sought to bring about a complete break between father and son through what Klaus styled 'systematic defamation'. He badmouthed him in émigré circles and then invented stories that Klaus was badmouthing him. He even wrote to Thomas sneering at his son for publishing *Die Sammlung*, an activity in which Bermann held Klaus had not the slightest competence. And then, to justify his own and Thomas's truckling to Dr Goebbels, he commented, 'We must do what we can to avoid the worst.' Save what can be saved from the Nazis, was the favourite motto of the trimmers. Or, as Klaus Harpprecht has written, 'Here was the fatal formula that was used a thousand times in the twelve years to May 1945 – and after as well – in self-justification.'

Like many other writers and publishers, Bermann and Thomas allowed the Third Reich to use their prestige to prop up its cultural façade. Years later, after he himself finally made the break with the Nazis, Thomas pronounced anathemas on prominent German cultural figures who had continued, as he phrased it, 'producing culture in Germany while all the things we know of were taking place'. He went on, 'To do so meant palliating depravity, extenuating crime. Among the torments we suffered was the sight of German literature and art constantly serving as window-dressing for absolute monstrousness.' Powerful words, to be sure, but in reading them the word 'humbug' comes to mind.

For Klaus and Landshoff there seemed to be no end to the widening disaster. Querido itself was threatened and *Die Sammlung* immediately lost over a third of its subscribers. For both men it was a horrid blow. 'Dinner with Landshoff', Klaus wrote in his diary two weeks after the affair began. 'His depression. Then always the similarity with Ricki. Oh, *verloren*! Sadness, infectious. And now Zweig. Left in the lurch.' Several times the diary refers to suicide. 'Long discussion [with Landshoff] about suicide, the horror of life, etc. Once again terribly concerned about the similarity to Ricki.'

Klaus and *Die Sammlung* were not without their defenders. Romain Rolland, who had won the Nobel Prize for Literature in 1916, sent Klaus a fine message of support. The émigré press in Paris and Prague was appalled by what they considered to be Thomas's perfidy. The Austrian socialist *Arbeiter-Zeitung* jibed that Thomas and the others 'had committed not intellectual treason but treason to the intellect'. Thomas found this so insulting he replied that what he was accomplishing in Germany with his books was of greater importance than a venture to which he had 'from the very start attributed little real significance'. Open ridicule of Klaus and his work knew no restraint.

A cautious truce, if not peace and good will, ensued at the end of the year when the entire Mann family, joined by a few friends, gathered for Christmas at a house Thomas had rented in Küsnacht, near Zurich. They all made the best of a difficult time, though the occasion was anything but joyous. Katia and Thomas were still utterly disoriented by their home-less state. Klaus, with Landshoff in tow, came from Amsterdam and was still feeling bruised. Landshoff was in such a depression Thomas feared he might kill himself. Erika, now living with her parents, was exasperated with her father because of his treatment both of Klaus and herself. Monika was preoccupied with making plans to live in Florence to study piano with Luigi Dallapiccola. As usual, Golo, now reader in German at the École Normale Supérieure at Saint-Cloud, retreated into himself. At least Elisabeth and Michael were prospering. Golo had spirited Elisabeth out of her school on 2 April, the day before limits were imposed on exiting the country; Michael was on a school trip in Italy and did not return. He was now studying the violin and Elisabeth the piano at the Zurich Conservatory. Any holiday joy Klaus may have been feeling vanished on the second day of Christmas when his parents invited Gottfried Bermann to dinner. Disgusted, Klaus insisted on dining alone in his room.

CHAPTER 5

Homosexualities
1934–35

Like other German exiles, Klaus regarded his homeland as a country occupied by an alien force, one so alien it was impossible to believe that its presence could be more than a temporary phenomenon. He now entered a period when nightmare became waking reality and the alien occupation permanent. During these tumultuous years, there were many separate strands to his life, making a strictly chronological account impossible.

Shortly after returning to Amsterdam from Küsnacht in mid-January, Klaus wrote in his diary, 'Thoughts of death, very tempting. Will the situation here be tenable? I know no alternative.' As always, he turned to writing to save himself. At first it went well. Once installed in his pension, he plunged into work on another novel, this one drawing on recollections of his trip with Erika to Finland in July 1932. The impulse may have been quickened by a deeply affectionate letter he had received at Christmastime from Hans Aminoff – the first in a long while. Whatever the inspiration, the result was *Flucht in den Norden* ('Flight to the North').

Klaus's own summary of the plot went like this. Johanna, a young, German, middle-class woman who hates the Nazis, joins the underground and comes into contact with communists. She leaves her husband and flees to Finland, where she stays for a time with her student friend, Karin, and her brothers, Ragnar and Jens. Jens is close to the Finnish fascists and admires Nazi Germany; Ragnar passionately detests Nazism and associates the entire German population with it. He would like to see Germany wiped clean of Nazism and then strictly controlled by civilized states. Johanna rejects the notion that a whole nation is guilty and wants to work for a new, reformed Germany. She and Ragnar fall in love, and in her feelings for him, she is tempted to forswear her political commitment. Why should she give up her Nordic idyll? she thinks. And so arises the classic conflict between love and duty. She and Ragnar flee to the northernmost part of Finland – the end of the world – intending to abandon Europe. Suddenly she learns that her friend Bruno has been shot by the Gestapo while working in the underground in Germany. Reluctantly she decides she must obey her convictions. She leaves Ragnar and goes to Paris to join the conspirators.

'I wrote the novel with the greatest ease; all the characters and situations were waiting inside me. It wrote itself, and I took it down as if by dictation. The enchanting scenery through which the couple travel, the wide quiet lakes and forests of the far north, were all very familiar to me', Klaus explained. The description of the countryside and the people living there have been considered some of the best passages in the novel. Annemarie Schwarzenbach, 'a boyish girl', was the rough model for Johanna. The family was, of course, the Aminoffs, who gave the impression of being unruly and rather decadent. Johanna and Ragnar may be Klaus, pre- and post-Hitler – the former politically uninformed and uninvolved, the latter committed and active.

Throughout the work, as in most of his other fiction, there runs an undercurrent of futility and despair. Perhaps echoing Julien Green's words to him several years before, Ragnar says, 'Death cannot be bad. I believe now that death will more likely happen to us as a pleasant surprise.' To which Johanna replies, 'I often think I would rather die than anything else.' There are also passages of outspoken patriphobia. During the trip to the North Cape, Ragnar relates a dream about his mother's misery at the hands of her husband. ' "She suffered under him every day, every day he had a new atrocity ready for her ... That is why I hated my father," he said slowly, stressing every syllable.'

Klaus finished the novel in a mere three months, handing over the manuscript to Landshoff in April for publication by Querido in September. The text also appeared in sixty-five episodes in the German exile daily, *Pariser Tageblatt*. A translation was published by Gollancz in London and Knopf in the United States under the title *Journey into Freedom*. The critical reception was generally favourable and Klaus declared himself 'content with the literary echo'. From Thomas he received 'a lovely, long letter'. As if that were not enough, in 'the *Neue Zürcher* – a miracle! – a review with high praise', he noted in his diary. However, an unfavourable commentary in a social democratic émigré paper in Prague left an unpleasant taste. 'It really angers and offends me that these *stupid* attacks from the political left continue while the literary critics are delighted.' 'Delighted' was far from Hans Aminoff's reaction. He felt the family had been held up to fun. 'I am not angry', he wrote to Klaus, 'but I feel very upset, insulted and disappointed. *Fortunately* no one in the family beside Ingrid [Hans's wife] saw the book. It would have been terrible had my mother seen it.'

Flucht in den Norden was the first German 'exile novel'. And it was written with the authority of someone whose legal status, like that of other expatriates, was extremely dicey, leaving him liable to be extradited to Germany at any moment. Fortunately Dutch authorities were noted at the time for being accommodating to German exile writers. And on condition that he would strictly avoid political activity, they had issued him a residence permit and tolerated *Die Sammlung*. But pressure from across the Rhine was steadily increasing, and on 12 February Dutch police arrested a German novelist-playwright, Heinz Liepmann – one of the earliest concentration camp alumni – for a passage in his latest novel that Nazi authorities considered 'an insult to the head of state of a friendly state'. A Dutch court sentenced the writer to a month's imprisonment and subsequent deportation to Germany. Saved by an international outcry, he was instead banished to Belgium and from there he went on to France. In one of those surreal episodes that characterized these years, while Liebmann was languishing in prison, his latest play, *The Three Apple Trees*, was being performed every night in an Amsterdam theatre.

'And so it begins. A feeling of utter insecurity and paralysis', Klaus remarked to his diary. The Liepmann case came as a terrible shock to every German émigré, and especially to Klaus because it posed a threat not just to himself but to *Die Sammlung* as well. He was so rattled he even asked Fritz Landshoff whether they should think of fleeing, perhaps to South America. 'Nothing good is to be expected in Europe. The continent appears to be on the point of exploding.' Fritz was just as worried. With the Dutch government under remorseless German pressure, *Die Sammlung* and Querido itself were in danger. To minimize the risks, he postponed publication of a collection of Heinrich Mann's essays and instead devoted the entire next issue to uncontroversial Dutch writings.

Klaus and Fritz would have been more anxious still had they known that in Berlin on 10 April 1934 the Foreign Office and the Propaganda Ministry had started to compile a Liepmann-type dossier on Klaus, based on – in the words of the initial document – 'information that Thomas Mann had broken with his son Klaus Mann because Klaus Mann was publishing in Amsterdam the notorious monthly *Die Sammlung*. Thomas Mann has been completely neutral in his attitude toward the Third Reich.' The report could not forbear adding the titillating note, 'According to unconfirmed rumours there exist between brother and sister a more than normal brotherly-sisterly relationship. Klaus and Erika Mann are considered responsible for the misfortunes of the Thomas Mann family. Klaus Mann is author of the disgusting novel *Treffpunkt im Unendlichen*. His literary abilities are insignificant; he simply takes advantage of his father's name.'

The immediate threat facing Klaus was legal. Like other émigrés, he soon found himself in the predicament of an undocumented immigrant. On 2 April his passport had expired and German consulates were instructed to refuse to renew it. So, although he held a temporary Dutch residence permit, he otherwise had no valid identification and no authority to travel. He was trapped, dependent on the good will of Dutch authorities not to repatriate him to Germany. By this time these authorities had their own worries. When Klaus settled in Amsterdam on 15 June, some fifteen thousand Germans had by then fled to the Netherlands. They had been welcomed, or at least accepted, as temporary exiles. By now it was evident that the Third Reich was not going to collapse overnight and the émigrés were there to stay.

So when Klaus applied for a general travel document – a *Gunstpass* – the request was not warmly received. Discussions with the police sometimes took on the tone of hostile interrogations. He vented his frustration in a letter to H.G. Wells, president of the PEN club at the time, explaining why he could not accept an invitation to the meeting in Edinburgh in late June 1934. 'I have no passport', he wrote. 'I am no longer to be a German – for the time being. No other country is anxious to give a German refugee some document that would give him the right to travel. The German refugee must wait.' Not until the end of the month did he finally receive a pass, and then it was valid for only for six months. So he had to go through the same rigmarole again, this time being interviewed six times before a new pass was issued.

Klaus was already skating on thin political ice when he risked provoking an international incident. By the terms of the Versailles Treaty, the Saar region was to hold a plebiscite on 13 January 1935 on whether to remain an autonomous area administered by the League of Nations or be integrated into the Third Reich. For Hitler, victory was vital. No less was the opposite vital for Klaus. On 19 September he and his uncle Heinrich, along with a number of other prominent German writers, issued an open appeal to Saarlanders to vote to maintain the status quo. A month later, when he received an invitation to go to Saar to address a rally, Landshoff had to implore him not to attend: '*Under no circumstances* dare you go to Saarbrücken.' He would have been far from the first person to have been grabbed off the street by the Gestapo, bundled across the border and enrolled in a concentration camp. Although very tempted to go, Klaus took the advice.

So he remained in Amsterdam and instead wrote 'Krieg und Saar', an impassioned, not to say inflammatory, manifesto, published in *Neue Weltbühne* on 31 October and printed as a flyer smuggled into the area. Nazism, not Germany, was the issue, he insisted. 'When we went into emigration, we separated ourselves not from Germany but from National Socialism and its Führer.' To vote for continued autonomy would be to vote for that pre-Nazi Germany and against a war that was sure to result if Hitler was not stopped. Three days later in Berlin the Interior Ministry and the Foreign Office announced that Klaus and twenty-seven other 'traitors to the German community' had violated 'their obligation of loyalty to Reich and Volk' and were therefore stripped of their citizenship. In Klaus's case the action was specifically linked to his involvement in the Saar campaign. But what devastated him was less his expatriation than the disastrous outcome of the plebiscite ten days afterward in which Hitler won 90.8 per cent of the vote. 'That is our bitterest political defeat since January '33.'

He now found himself not only without a passport but also without a nationality. He had no doubt that Erika would soon find herself in similar legal limbo for her own anti-Nazi activities. And that leads to the story of *Pfeffermühle* ('Pepper Mill'), a political cabaret which Erika, Klaus, the noted actress Therese Giehse, and a young composer, Magnus Henning, had started in the last days of the Weimar Republic. Erika and Klaus wrote the texts of the songs and skits, Henning composed the music. To convey the sense of something mildly spicy, Thomas, so the story goes, proposed the name. Ten young Munich actors comprised the ensemble, with Erika the producer-director, chief lyricist, actress and mistress of cere-monies. The cabaret had opened on New Year's Day 1933 – exactly thirty days before Hitler was appointed chancellor – in a small pub near the Munich Hofbräuhaus, the famous Nazi hangout. It was an enormous success; even the Nazi daily, the *Völkischer Beobachter*, published a couple of favourable reviews, though Erika later suspected that the appeal was less the peppery political message than the personal popularity of some of the actors. To accommodate the growing audience, Erika decided to find a proper theatre. By the time that could be arranged, however, she and Klaus had fled Munich.

Pfeffermühle was, apart from a suitcase or two, all Erika had been able to take with her when she left. She revived it with the original cast in Zurich on 30 September, making it the first German-language theatre in exile. As in Munich, it was a huge success. Inevitably the cabaret sailed close to the political wind and Erika knew well that she had to avoid providing the German government with any opportunity to protest. Parable and meta-phor were her techniques; the word 'Germany', for example, was never used. So popular was the show that Swiss Nazi sympathizers were eventu-ally provoked to intervene with their fists. The riots began on 10 November. Six days later, James Schwarzenbach, the reactionary patriarch of the Schwarzenbach family and cousin of Annemarie, blew a loud whistle during a performance, which signalled rowdies to create mayhem inside the theatre. Outside a crowd bellowed anti-Semitic and anti-émigré slogans. Not yet content, Schwarzenbach sent a letter to the prestigious Swiss daily *Neue Zürcher Zeitung* accusing *Pfeffermühle* and Erika Mann, 'a former member of the German Communist party', of compromising the neutrality of Switzerland.

By then not only the performances but also the performers needed police protection. The ruckus continued until the *Neue Zürcher Zeitung* turned hostile, and several cantons, including Zurich, banned any further performances. By the end of 1934 Erika and her troupe had little choice but to leave. Unwelcome in Austria as well, they went on to Prague and later to the Low Countries, where they were again a big hit. Today, *Pfeffermühle* is of historical interest not only as the most renowned political cabaret ever but as an auspice of the relations between the Third Reich and its neighbours.

When Erika arrived in Amsterdam with her company in May 1935 she realized she was bound to be stripped of her citizenship very soon. Klaus was there editing *Die Sammlung* and they discussed the problem. By co-incidence, Christopher Isherwood and his German friend Heinz were staying in the same pension. 'Connect, only connect.' Klaus did, and came up with a wheeze to protect Erika legally. Having divorced Gründgens in January 1929, she was free to acquire foreign citizenship through marriage. Close at hand was the unmarried Isherwood. And so Klaus introduced the two. With an embarrassed smile, Erika is said to have asked, 'I have a some-what personal request: would you marry me?' A horrified Christopher politely declined, but offered to write on her behalf to his friend Wystan Auden, then a schoolmaster in England. No hesitancy there. He immedi-ately wired back, 'With pleasure.' So in mid-June Erika travelled to England to wed a person whom she had never seen and who did not know her name or, as he discovered at the ceremony, her date of birth. 'I didn't see her till the ceremony and perhaps I shall never see her again', the groom wrote to Stephen Spender. 'But she is very nice.' The wedding took place just in time. The following day, 16 June, Berlin announced its latest blacklist and Erika's name was on it. Klaus sent her a telegram welcoming her to 'The Legion of Honour of the III Reich'.

Not so easily solved were Klaus's personal problems. During the course of 1934 his life had again been ruffled by relationships that turned out as unhappily as previous ones. The most serious by far was with Wolfgang Hellmert, né Kohn, a less than stunningly successful exile actor and writer whom Klaus had first met in Paris in 1925. For reasons that Klaus's diary fails to make clear, he fell deeply in love with Hellmert and over the years they did the rounds in Paris, Berlin and Munich together. The two were extremely intimate in every way, even sharing a serious drug addiction. Eventually, in May 1934, Wolfgang was killed by it, leaving Klaus paralyzed with grief. 'WOLFGANG'S DEATH is in a certain sense more difficult to bear than all the others.' Two years later he was still mourning. Once he was suddenly flooded with recollections of their happiness together and poured out his heart to his diary. 'How powerful are the memories. How much I liked him! What close friends we were . . .' The simple thought of him evoked more vivid remembrances even than those of Ricki or any of his other earlier loves.

But nothing distracted Klaus long from events on the eastern side of the Rhine. Of course, the big guessing game was how much longer Hitler would hold on to power. Throughtout 1934 Klaus wavered, one day thinking Hitler was finished and the next day not. 'Hitler without question closer to collapse. What follows is unclear', he wrote in his final diary entry for 1934. Exactly a year afterward he noted in disappointment, 'And this Hitler still does not fall from power.' By the mid-1930s even the most optimistic émigrés were coming to accept that Hitler and his Third Reich were not about to vanish and they should make plans for a new life outside Germany. That was the shocking lesson of the outcome of the Saar plebiscite. The population of a democratic state had by 91 per cent freely chosen to give up its freedom and amalgamate itself with the Nazi Reich.

Klaus immediately recognized this meant that Hitler was so popular he would never be overthrown from within. 'No longer does the country have the strength to bring down the regime on its own', he wrote to Katia on 11 March. He further grasped that the plebiscite result legitimized Hitler's territorial demands on Austria and the Sudetenland. 'And then it will come to war, perhaps as early as in a half-year, perhaps not before three.' He was right; only his timing was slightly off. A bare week later Hitler, now confident of his position, nationally and internationally, introduced general military conscription as a first step in his long-term plan to destroy the Versailles Treaty by military means. Klaus's response was immediate: 'The WAR comes frighteningly closer.' Several weeks after that, he wondered when it would begin and whether Germany would win. 'Will it be followed by complete barbarism? Where will it lead?' Of one thing he was always certain. From the day Hitler became chancellor, Klaus was convinced he meant to take Europe into a military conflict. His diary for 1934 and 1935 is filled with entries speculating on the timing of such a struggle. One day he would think 'Hitler does not want war yet'. After reading newspapers the next day, however, he was not so sure. 'Were we – or are we – very close to war? Hitler must soon make his move.'

The Western democracies were failing to stand up to Hitler and Mussolini. Might the Soviet Union be a force, the only force, of opposition to the spread of fascism, Klaus wondered. The various crimes of Soviet communism were not well understood at the time. Knowledge of the starvation of the kulaks, the show trials, gulags and other horrors was only just filtering through. Desperate to find out what Russia was like, Klaus finagled an invitation to attend the First All-Union Congress of Soviet Writers in Moscow in August 1934. Once there, to avoid being branded a communist, he did his best to be inconspicuous to the point of declining to give a speech. Always elegant in manner and dress, however, he could not help but stand out among the workers, peasants and scruffy leftist intellectuals, as is evident from the photos of the event. Oskar Maria Graf, a friend and fellow traveller (in both senses of the expression), later remembered the impression Klaus left. 'He was the perfect picture of a young, cultivated man of the world, as neat as a peeled egg, insouciant, elegantly dressed, slim and trim, with an intelligent, well-bred face. His movements were nervous and his speech remarkably fast. Everything seemed a bit mannered. All in all there was about him something restless, over-intellectual and above all remarkably mature.'

The two-week conference was the usual Soviet propaganda jamboree, combining working sessions with sightseeing excursions. The Grand Old Man of Russian letters, Maxim Gorki, presided over the meetings and, in Klaus's words, 'whispered platitudes in a piping, pitiful voice'. The sessions impressed him as he observed how 'workers, soldiers and peasants [participated] with intelligent zeal in the discussions on modern poetry or the function of the theatre under socialism'. But the characterization of Western letters presented by the Russian speakers – passing off Proust as a symbol of a decadent bourgeoisie, for example, and dismissing Joyce as nothing more than a writer who 'examines a manure pile with a microscope' – he dismissed as so much Marxist hot air.

The official tours intended to display the wonders of Soviet society left Klaus cold. He was revolted by the conditions in a hospital. A tour of the Kremlin museum – where he considered the *objets d'art* more remarkable for their monetary value than their beauty – left him underwhelmed, as did the obligatory visit to a Moscow metro station and a tractor museum. In the end it was the aesthetic pleasures he derived on the side that gave him his only moments of real enjoyment: the Cézannes and van Goghs in Moscow and the whole of the collection in the Hermitage in Leningrad, which he visited twice. Is it surprising that the painting that moved him most was the one he considered Rembrandt's very greatest, *Return of the Prodigal Son.*

Klaus's response to the political background of the meetings is difficult to summarize. He was far from the only person in the early 1930s who had difficulty making out the nature of Soviet communism and clarifying his own thoughts about it. Certainly he sympathized with some of the aims and accomplishments of the system. But he was put off by what he referred to as 'the cult of official heroes, the nationalistic complacency and the rampant militarism' that permeated everything. Ultimately what most impressed him was what he referred to as 'the essential triviality of orthodox Marxism'. Although there was no one in the world whom he admired more than Gide, when he became a communist in 1934, Klaus dismissed it as 'the high-minded and naïve attempt of an aristocratic intelligence to coordinate his views and divinations to the scheme of an organized and collective effort'. For himself, he said, 'I could never embrace a gospel that promises salvation of the human race by virtue of an economic measure.'

There was another gospel he could not embrace. In March of that year the Russian government revoked the Leninist policy of toleration of homosexuals and enacted a Stalinist one of harsh repression. Then, on 23 May, *Pravda* published a statement by Maxim Gorki maintaining that in fascist countries homosexuality was allowed to thrive and corrupt young people, while in a country where the proletariat was in power, it was recognized to be a social crime and was severely punished. His dramatic conclusion was 'Root out homosexuality and fascism will disappear'.

By curious coincidence, at this very moment the Nazis were busy rooting out homosexuality in Germany in order to purify fascism. That is the story of the so-called 'Night of the Long Knives', when Hitler gave in to pressure from the military, industry and hardline Nazis to destroy the power of the unruly Stormtroops by killing its leaders. Since the head of the organization, Ernst Röhm, was a well-known homosexual, as were many of its members, it was convenient to maintain, as did Goebbels in a national radio address, that the purge was to rid the country of a clique of homosexual traitors.

Thomas's reaction to the issue was curious. Since Röhm had suddenly been condemned for sexual behaviour that was well known and accepted for years, he granted that the sex charge was merely a cover for political murder. Yet, at the same time, he regarded homosexuality as inherent in 'Kriegstum' and 'Deutschtum' – Teutonic words for bellicosity and chauvinism. These were also traits of German fascism. Echoing Gorki, he concluded that homosexuality was therefore inherent in Nazism.

All this Gorki, Röhm and Thomas Mann was too much for Klaus to bear in silence. He responded in a long essay originally entitled 'Die Linke und das "Laster"' ('The Left and "Debauchery"'), which was published as 'Homosexualität und Fascismus' in the German exile publication Europäische Hefte in early 1935.

The recent law in the Soviet Union severely punishing homosexuality, the article began, is contrary to what was to be expected of a socialist government. It defames and victimizes a small minority because of its sexual nature. The Russian press routinely labels homosexuals as 'murderers and pederasts' in the same way the Nazi press condemns 'traitors and Jews'. Yet a homosexual is simply a person, like Leonardo and Socrates, who has a propensity to prefer men over women. 'What should finally be grasped is that homosexuality is a love like any other, no better, no worse, with as many possibilities for the marvellous and affectionate, the melancholy, grotesque, beautiful or trivial as love between a man and a woman.' In many eras and many areas this love has been quite common; in others, people have considered it depraved.

The person who is exclusively homosexual was born so, the article went on, not seduced or evolved into it. Do people still believe that homosexuals comprise a unique and united group? This is a fallacy, partly arising from the notion of a 'third sex'. In reality there are homosexuals of all types, from decadent aesthetes to mercenary soldiers. Homosexuality was widespread in military societies, such as Sparta and Prussia, and in highly cultured ones, such as late Rome and the Renaissance, as well as in Paris and London at the turn of the century. Among them were a relatively large number of creative geniuses. The article concluded, 'In the Third Reich gays are regularly being rounded up and put in work camps or even castrated and executed. Outside Germany they are derided in the leftist press and the German émigré community. We are at the point where homosexuals are being made scapegoats on all sides. In any case homosexuality is not going to be "rooted out" and, if it were, it would leave civilization poorer.'

Such was the essence of the essay. Klaus had pondered for a long time whether to tackle the subject, was advised against it and had misgivings while working on it. 'But I am glad I wrote it', he said in a letter to a friend. 'The subject demands honest and serious treatment. Perhaps it would have been better had a "disinterested person" taken on the job. But no one came forward.' No one, indeed. At a time when gays were hated equally by fascists, capitalists, socialists and communists as well as by German émigrés and their press, Klaus was the only person in Europe willing to take a public stand. There was no praise for the article or the author's courage from his father, who commented in his diary that he found the essay 'problematic'. In fact Thomas was angered that a son of his was harping on a subject that was deeply 'problematic' to him for very personal reasons.

In the atmosphere of homophobia that raged in Germany in the wake of the Röhm affair, Klaus could not forbear wondering about the lot of such ex-friends as Erich Ebermayer and Gustaf Gründgens. He need not have worried. Ebermayer, while anything but a hardened Nazi, was thriving as a scriptwriter for UFA, Germany's great movie studio. 'Never again will I shake his hand', Klaus commented. Gründgens, he had heard, was in trouble. 'I would not want to be in his skin.' In the end the actor survived to prosper. Others were not so fortunate. It is said that the political murders and arrests that followed the Röhm purge set off such a general flight from the country that the Reichsbahn had to attach additional carriages to trains headed to Italy – so many that in one case, so the story goes, the train could not make it over the Goddard Pass.

On his way from Russia back to Amsterdam, Klaus decided, with the encouragement of Hans Aminoff but against the strong advice of Katia, Erika and Landshoff, to spend several days in Pekkala. Neither Hans nor Klaus seems ever to have been quite reconciled to a permanent break and both thought some sort of relationship might yet be worked out. So Klaus went. Hans introduced him to his wife and showed him their child. Klaus's diary tells the inevitable dénouement. 'The reunion. The problem with all reunions. The feeling of "can't go back", of "too late". Hans. The wife, the baby – he unchanged but with a bad cold. The experiment of his marriage. The extraordinary boredom which follows – went to the lake alone. The feeling of autumn. Return to the dark water. Once again, a tremendous wave of depression. Transience. How I sense the blessed sight of DEATH.' To which he added the next day: 'LONELINESS – I have the sense that "loneliness" and "transience" are the only reality. Numb with sadness.' As always, the old formula: love and death or, better, love or death.

Klaus returned to Amsterdam in a dismal mood. News of the suicide and arrest of friends and acquaintances sickened him. He could feel himself slipping further and further into permanent exile. Since Germany had now become Nazi Germany, he wondered in what sense he was still German or wished to be. 'Yes, it has come to that', he wrote in his diary. 'One is ashamed of being a German. I would sooner be a Rumanian. But that wouldn't stop my being German, unfortunately. (American – how glad I would be to be that!!)' So he found himself a native of a country that for him no longer existed.

In an effort to lift his depression, he took dope but it was no solace. 'I look without hope on what is coming.' In a letter to Katia several months later, he drew the conclusion: 'It is of course insane to remain in Europe. I would gladly get away.' So real seemed the Nazi threat during the summer and autumn of 1935 he and Erika began speculating about where to flee. It had to be remote. 'Perhaps the southern coast of Sicily. Ragusa?' By the end of the year Klaus was desperate. 'Our threatened lives. Threatened, poor, uncertain life . . . My great wish is to get myself out of all this. Next autumn, if circumstances don't change greatly – undoubtedly to another part of the world.'

Serendipity came to the rescue. On returning to Amsterdam from Küsnacht in January 1934, Klaus had attended a performance of the Concertgebouw Orchestra. Tchaikovsky's Fourth Symphony was the principal work. For Klaus it was love at first sound. The music touched something very deep. 'First two movements, quite beautiful but moved by it all', was his diary comment. So moved was he, he made up his mind then and there. 'Desire to write about Tchaikovsky (Tchaikovsky novel. A gay man).' Klaus was a true *mélomane* and here found an ideal topic – a person of interest in a field of interest.

The Manns were a musical family. Thomas might almost be termed a fanatic when it came to Wagner and took a serious interest in twelve-tone music. Monika, Elisabeth and Michael all trained to be professional musicians. Uncle Klaus Pringsheim was a composer and conductor. Klaus's own familiarity, broad rather than deep, extended from Haydn and Mozart to Mahler and Shostakovich. He formed his own judgments and was, for example, an admirer of Gershwin's *Porgy and Bess* long before it was considered a legitimate opera. He was also fond of *lieder*, and in his diary mentions taking a particular pleasure in those of Hugo Wolf. On one memorable occasion in Amsterdam in 1936 he attended an afternoon *lieder* concert by Marian Anderson, the famous black American singer, unwelcome as a performer in her own country. 'She sings *gloriously*', he wrote in his diary. 'The wonderful bell-like tones of her enormous voice. Händel, Schumann, Schubert, Sibelius and beautiful negro spirituals. I sat on the podium; it was fascinating to watch her face – her closed eyes, her gravity. Afterwards I spoke to her, her Finnish accompanist and her manager. She is charming.' Music, perhaps more than reading or drugs or sex, was the solace of Klaus's life.

Klaus loved Tchaikovsky's music, 'it speaks to me', he wrote. But he frankly acknowledged that he never overrated his rank as a composer. 'Obviously I know that the composer of such pleasantries as *The Nutcracker Suite* and the *1812 Overture* was no Beethoven. But then a Beethoven novel would almost inevitably turn out to be a pompous bore.' It was Tchaikovsky's tortured life that interested Klaus, and it interested him because in many respects it mirrored his own.

With all his other writing and responsibilities, it was not until the following November that he could give the idea further thought. It sat well. 'I wrote his story because I know all about him', he explained in *The Turning Point*. 'Only too intimately versed in his neurasthenic fixation, I could describe his aimless wanderings, the transient bliss of his elations, the unending anguish of his solitude. All I had to do was to articulate his own melodious confession – the gloomy message of his adagios, the frantic tempo of his prestos and his allegros. He was uprooted, disconnected; that's why I could write his story.' 'Even if there were no documents about the circumstances of his life and his traits of character,' Klaus wrote, 'the music told me enough. It was the writer's task simply to articulate his melodic confession, to put it into words.' Here Klaus was exploring the fascinating notion of reconstructing a composer's life – his emotional life, at least – from his music.

So in January 1935, exactly a full year after the inspirational concert, he signed a contract with Querido and on 13 March he wrote to Katia that he was about to begin work on his 'difficult novel'. This time it did not go well. In the case of Alexander the Great he had vague knowledge of the historical background. Now he needed grounding in music history and a minimal familiarity with musicology. He spent hours doing research in the Amsterdam library. For a time it all seemed too much for him. But on 17 March 1935 he noted in his diary, 'Tchaikovsky, perhaps I can yet bring it off.' So he plodded along, although what was a slow pace for him would have been breakneck for almost any other writer. And that at a time when he not only had responsibility for getting out *Die Sammlung* but was also contributing to various newspapers and journals, giving talks and maintaining a hectic social life – and all the while suffering bouts of depression. In spite of everything he finished the manuscript on 13 July, commenting in his diary, 'Tchaikovsky is an *autobiographical* book. Certainly my best. I hope its appearance does not coincide with a world war.' Several weeks later he turned over the manuscript to Landshoff for publication. Appropriately it was to be entitled *Symphonie Pathétique*. He later described it as his 'most beautiful and saddest book'.

A biographer of Tchaikovsky must deal with two mysteries: was the composer homosexual, and did he commit suicide? Like most biographers, Klaus was convinced he was gay. And in essence his novel is about the composer's resulting emotional suffering, which he associated with his own – being homosexual in a hostile society. As he later wrote in *Der Wendepunkt*, 'The particular form of love which was his destiny – I know it well, am well acquainted with the exhilaration and humiliation, the lingering anguish and the fleeting bliss, which accompanies this eros.' And then fell the lapidary, embittered conclusion – 'You cannot honour eros without becoming a pariah in our society as it is today. You cannot commit yourself to this form of love without incurring a mortal wound.' Like a ventriloquist, Klaus has his Tchaikovsky say 'I never loved when there was any hope or danger of its becoming serious, of my being tied, of my being loved in return and so committed'. This was the story of Klaus and Hans Aminoff and all those who went before and were to follow. In Klaus's case, then, there were two problems: the hatred of society and his own inability to establish a lasting relationship.

Going still further in identifying himself with the composer, Klaus argues that Tchaikovsky's story was essentially that of an artistic outsider. Derided by critics, disparaged by his contemporaries Brahms and Grieg, his music was rejected as a pastiche of the German by the French, as a pastiche of the French by the Germans, and as a pastiche of both by the Russians. He felt isolated and scorned. Everywhere in permanent exile. 'He was an émigré, not for political reasons but because he felt nowhere at home . . . And he suffered everywhere'.

The composer's life resonated with Klaus in other ways. Tchaikovsky felt rebuffed in what he most craved – appreciation by contemporary audiences, in Germany especially. In Klaus's case the audience was a father who was equally frugal with praise. And that led to the most devastating analogy of all. In assessing the composer's works, the biographer seems to be assessing his own. 'Most of it was certainly not very good; it generally did not come off and certainly did not reach the high, strict standards he aimed at. But perhaps there are, all the same, a few short pieces which will endure.'

The author of a biographical novel may take liberties, but some readers believed Klaus went too far in transferring his own loneliness, sense of homelessness and failure in relationships on to the composer. True, Tchaikovsky was sometimes depressed, lonely and hurt by professional rejection. However, he also received open recognition, including an honorary doctorate from Cambridge University. And while most critics and biographers acknowledged his homosexuality, they were not in agreement on how deeply it troubled him and to what extent it was expressed in his music. In the controversy over Tchaikovsky's death from cholera – by either accidentally or intentionally drinking polluted water – Klaus came down on the side of suicide. This may have been consistent with his personal belief that self-extinction can be the answer to suffering, but few shared his conclusion. Gay, an outsider, frustrated in love and labour, Klaus no doubt had an especially deep insight into his subject's life, but some concluded he almost turned a biographical novel into autobiography.

Needless to say, *Symphonie Pathétique* was proscribed in the Third Reich, not only because of its author but also because of its gay theme. In the German exile press and well beyond, it was warmly received. In no time it was published in translation in Czechoslovakia, Argentina and in Britain by Gollancz and years later in a number of other countries, including the United States. Uncle Heinrich, himself a much praised biographer of Henri IV, pronounced himself greatly impressed and sent Klaus a warm letter of congratulation. Enthusiasm was anything but the reaction of the critic whose praise Klaus most coveted. Thomas responded with what Klaus Harpprecht referred to as 'friendly reserve'.

In the summer of 1935, Klaus's much-loved child died after a lingering illness. The final issue of *Die Sammlung* appeared on 1 August. It had been a noble effort for the best of causes. The German government's efforts to suppress it were a measure of its success. But from the beginning it was probably based on optimism amounting to illusion. A publication of such rarefied intellectual quality was bound to have a limited readership, even in good times. Any chance it would prosper was undermined at the start by Thomas's ostentatious dissociation. Of the initial print run of three thousand copies, only two-thirds was sold, principally in the Netherlands, Austria and Switzerland, and circulation slipped steadily after that. In May 1934 the journal suffered another blow when the Austrian government gave in to German pressure and banned it. Klaus's appeals to Austrian diplomatic officials in The Hague as well as to friends in Vienna, Franz Werfel among them, achieved nothing. So he begged money from others and, like Landshoff, took no remuneration for himself. Annemarie Schwarzenbach and Lion Feuchtwanger, among others, did what they could to help. A special appeal enticed merely twenty-five new subscribers. By July it was clear the journal could not go on. The August issue was the last. What added to the pain was the knowledge of how much pleasure its death gave authorities in Berlin.

Even aside from the extraordinary conditions in which it was produced, *Die Sammlung* was an impressive publication. There were a few other exile journals, such as the *Neue Deutsche Blätter*, published by the Marxist Wieland Herzfelde in Prague, but none came close to achieving the intellectual distinction of *Die Sammlung*. In its short existence it offered an outlet for no fewer than three hundred writers across the spectrum – Marxist, socialist, and anarchist, as well as liberal, pacifist, conservative and apolitical. The contents included political and literary essays, poetry and stories, as well as excerpts from novels and biographies. Among contributors whose names are still familiar today were Benedetto Croce, Bertolt

Brecht, Max Brod, Jean Cocteau, Ernst Bloch, Alfred Döblin, Ilja Ehrenburg, Lion Feuchtwanger, Jean Giraudoux, Ernest Hemingway, Stefan Heym, Emil Ludwig, André Maurois, Robert Musil, Ortega y Gasset, Boris Pasternak, Romain Rolland, Joseph Roth, Count Carlo Sforza, Ignazio Silone, Julien Sorel, Stephen Spender, Ernst Toller and Arnold Zweig. Even Albert Einstein and Leon Trotsky contributed a short piece each. Hermann Hesse, Erich Maria Remarque and Franz Werfel were among the few notable holdouts. Klaus published not only German writers but also translations of works by French, Italian, English, Russian and Spanish authors. But it was not all high-minded literature; it also gave space to what he called 'anti-Nazi exposures, anti-Nazi satires and anti-Nazi statistics'.

Happily, *Die Sammlung* had a second life; in fact it underwent two resurrections when its collected articles were published in two volumes in East Germany in 1974 and in the Federal Republic in 1987. It sold out in no time.

Not long after he began writing *Symphonie Pathétique*, Klaus had made a promise to himself: 'Once it is done I will do a lot of travelling.' He kept his word and on 1 August, five days after correcting the page proofs, he headed for central Europe. Vienna was his first stop. There he met old friends and made new ones, including a 'film man' who was interested in making the Tchaikovsky novel into a movie. He went on to Brno, where he inspected the sights, spoke with German-Jewish émigrés, encountered several 'curious' Americans, went to a masseur 'without anything happening', met a professor who anticipated a German invasion in the spring and visited the battlefield at Austerlitz, the site of Napoleon's greatest victory. Then, while waiting for a Hungarian visa, he spent two weeks in Prague, where Erika's *Pfeffermühle* had recently begun performing.

In Budapest he stayed with acquaintances of his parents, the immensely wealthy Baron Lajos Hatvany and his third wife, Loli. This was the first of two visits to the Hungarian capital, which he described at the time as 'the most corrupt and frivolous city imaginable and undoubtedly one of the most amusing places on earth'. Social conditions, especially in the villages, he thought 'resembled those in France before 1789'. And Budapest, 'as far as tawdry elegance and sexy fun was concerned', exceeded even Berlin. For Klaus there was the added attraction of the baths, 'famed all over Europe for their salubrious wells and their loose morals'.

Klaus's nonstop activity was all the more remarkable in light of his appalling psychological condition. Drugs, dreams, depression and death pursued him like the Furies of Greek mythology, hardly giving him a moment's peace. And the further he settled into exile, the more he seemed to despair. His diary was a veritable databank of lamentations. 'Desperately sad. Feeling of loneliness. Desire to die.' And sometime later, '*Unbelievably* sad. Oh, why survive all this? In the evening I listen to [Mahler's] 'Kindertotenlieder' on the gramophone.' Such entries go on and on. Reading them coldly decades later is painful; living through those days had to have been hellish.

Even his sleep was tortured by nightmares so vivid they left him limp when he awoke. 'The whole day depressed and confused by horrible dreams during the night.' Dreams, the royal road to the subconscious, dredged up his most awful, repressed fears. Like a gruesome Walhalla, his nightmare world was inhabited by dead friends. One was Jack von Ripper, who, as he later found out, was tortured nearly to death by the Gestapo. There was even 'a cellar filled with the dead'. He found Erika there. She proposed that the two of them should go to Prague and poison themselves. 'Dreamed about being pursued by the Nazis – secret agents – kidnapped and taken to Germany, etc. – Uncle Heinrich, disguised with false beard, hides in an apartment. Betrayal by a loathsome woman. Struggle with a group of strong men who want to tie us up and spirit us across the border. Escape through a big apartment.' That was one diary entry. In another, 'A chloroform mask was put over my head because I wanted to warn my parents that war was coming.'

There was yet another type of dream, in a way more terrifying in that it revealed how Nazism infiltrated the minds of even its most stalwart opponents and bent them to willing submission. In the earliest of these – experienced within a few days of fleeing from Munich – he and Erika were lured by Hitler into a castle and arrested. Months later he dreamed he was sitting at a table with Göring and Goebbels and found that he got along quite well with Goebbels. That was troubling enough, but in another, four months after that, Thomas died and Elisabeth immediately decided to marry 'a young blond Nazi', a young, blond Nazi who insisted on holding hands with Klaus. In still another, Hitler showed up at Klaus's bedside. 'Hitler visited me in the hospital, charming and somewhat tough, so that I couldn't write anything bad about him any more.' He even dreamed that Katia divorced Thomas to save him problems resulting from her partly Jewish heritage.

Such dreams were neither uncommon nor inexplicable. Charlotte Beradt, a French anti-Nazi of the first hour, collected examples and after the war catalogued them in a book, *Rêver sous le IIIe Reich* ('Dreaming in the Third Reich'). On reading it, Bruno Bettelheim found himself shocked to realize how effectively the Nazis had murdered their enemies' sleep by forcing them to dream dreams showing that resistance was impossible and that safety lay only in submission and compliance.

To help him bear the pain he was constantly feeling, Klaus turned to his companion, drugs. Throughout these years he took increasing amounts, recording in his diary with a bookkeeper's care the name or nickname of the substance – Thunfish (tunafish), Thun, pantopon, Eukodal, Euko, cholera drops, heroin and opium. On occasion he noted simply 'gespritzt' (injected) or, most frequently, 'genommen' (took). Sometimes he felt better: 'Took heroin – it worked very nicely.' Sometimes not. 'Just a mild effect which helped but did not lift the depression.' These were the months when Klaus's drug-taking went from the more or less recreational to the seriously addictive.

Depression, drugs and longing for death reinforced one another. During the course of 1935 he was dosing on morphine or something similar every day and sometimes more than once – on 14 August four times. Back in Küsnacht in late August he made an unsuccessful attempt to quit. He was in particularly desperate shape during his three weeks in Budapest and the period that followed. 'The craving for drugs is scarcely to be separated from the desire for death', he recorded in his diary on 22 October. And a week after that he noted, 'Drugs . . . God help me, I had the feeling I could not have survived the night without them.' Katia and Erika did their best to help and persuaded him to consult Erich Katzenstein, a Zurich neurologist and family friend. After the meeting, Klaus wrote to him, saying he was resisting drugs as best he could but 'No doctor can save me from the various problems that weigh on me.' He added that if Katzenstein would read his Tchaikovsky biography, he would understand everything.

Finally, on 22 November, while in Küsnacht, he fell into the abyss. His diary tells the story: 'Evening. *Screamed* in sadness. Then uncontrollable weeping, as I have *never* known before, for a good half hour.' Katia called a doctor, who injected him with a sedative. Three days later, 'Once again screamed in sadness. How can I get through this? Dear God, how CAN I get through this? Ah, sweet death . . . Horrible night. It seems to me I can remember none so awful. Completely immobilized by depression, could not read, scarcely smoke. Ate nothing. Simply lay back and thought of death. Spent a few minutes with Erika. It is only withdrawal symptoms, she said. It is horrible that I must put her through this.'

Yet again it was writing that saved him. One turns the pages of his diary and reads with astonishment that on the morning after this horror, his thoughts were absorbed in an idea for a new book. Biographical novels never ceased to intrigue Klaus, and among other subjects he had recently thought about were Toulouse-Lautrec and Rimbaud. Now he was attracted by a biographical novel about Heinrich von Kleist. It is not difficult to understand why. Klaus admired him not as a great dramatist but as 'a symbol, a mythical event', the symbol and event being his suicide. As he said in *Der Wendepunkt*, 'The Kleist of my pantheon stands motionless, his revolver against his temple, his tragic forehead shining with the indescribable joy mentioned in his farewell letter. "The truth is that nothing on earth could help me" spoke the Kleist of my boyhood Olympus. "And so farewell." ' But the Kleist idea was soon dropped. Instead Klaus discussed with family members the notion of a 'family novel – the Pringsheim-Manns'. It is not hard to imagine Thomas's pure horror. Another thought was a work on 'the great utopian theme of a destroyed, anarchistic Europe in two hundred years'. Not long before the year's end, however, an old friend made a suggestion about a book that proved to be the road to notoriety and eventual fame.

CHAPTER 6

Lecturing to Americans
1936–37

On the morning of New Year's Day 1936, Klaus was sitting on the balcony of his room at a hotel in Davos. He was reading with admiration de Maupassant's *Bel-Ami*. The novel portrays the devious struggle of an unscrupulous young opportunist to reach the top of his profession. After a while Klaus put it aside and decided to go on a hike through the snow. Percolating in the back of his mind as he trudged along was the idea for a new book. This was a normal seasonal impulse. The beginning of a year usually found him brimming with energy and scarcely able to wait to start on something new. In 1929 it was *Rundherum*; in 1930, *Gegenüber von China*; 1931, *Das Buch von der Riviera*; 1932, *Treffpunkt im Unendlichen*; 1933, lyrics for *Pfeffermühle*; 1934, *Flucht in den Norden*; 1935, *Symphonie Pathétique*. This time, since politics trumped everything, he was thinking of an anti-Nazi novel in the guise of cultural satire.

The subject was timely. The paradox of a regime as barbaric as Hitler's Reich was that it gave supreme importance to culture. Hitler's primary interests lay in music and architecture. Göring and Goebbels were left to quarrel over the rest. The marshal managed to win control of the most important conglomeration of theatres, the Prussian state theatre system. This included the Berlin State Theatre and in 1934 he appointed Gustaf Gründgens to be its director. It was a strange choice. Here was someone who had not only performed in a scandalous play written by Klaus but had married into the notorious Mann family. He was also homosexual – Goebbels labelled him sarcastically 'a 175er', referring to the legal provision criminalizing homosexuality. And if all that were not damning enough, in Gründgens's youthful years he had been a supporter of communist causes. However, when Göring saw him as Mephistopheles in a spectacular performance of Goethe's *Faust, Part I*, he was so overwhelmed he forgave all. He offered him the most prestigious position in German theatre and, like the hero of *Bel-Ami*, Gründgens put aside his moral and political scruples and made his pact with the devil. To keep up appearances he had to marry the actress Marianne Hoppe. It is likely that few were fooled, and the rumour spread that above the matrimonial bed hung the epitaph of Simonides on the Spartans at Thermopylae: 'Here obedient to their laws we live.' The story cried out for fictional treatment.

It did not cry out to Klaus. His old friend, the novelist Hermann Kesten, however, thought it would be a perfect topic. In a letter on 15 November praising *Symphonie Pathétique*, he concluded, 'You should write a novel about a homosexual careerist in the Third Reich and there comes to mind Herr Staatsintendant Gründgens . . . A social satire.' Despite the encouragement from someone who was also an author and émigré, the idea still did not appeal. Not long afterward, Fritz Landshoff got wind of Kesten's suggestion and wrote to Klaus begging him to reconsider.

For over a month, Klaus pondered. He was not anxious to discredit his ex-friend and quondam brother-in-law. But reading de Maupassant's novel in the sharp Alpine air of that New Year's Day gave him the inspiration he needed to link Nazis, culture and personal ambition. So, despite lingering misgivings, he decided to follow his friends' proposal. Within a few days he had found a perfect title for what he referred to as his 'GG novel' – *Mephisto: Roman einer Karriere* ('Mephisto: Novel of a Career'). Gustaf Gründgens, alias GG, became Hendrik Höfgen, alias HH. If the double initials of both names, the umlauted vowels and the similar number of syllables did not make the protagonist's identity clear, Mephisto, alias Mephistopheles, clinched it.

Somehow writing did not come easily. Perhaps it was because it was a time when he was constantly oppressed by fear of war. Perhaps because he was back on drugs. Subconsciously he may have been frightened of the subject. In any case it was not until mid-March that he got down to work. Even then, he did not always know where he was taking the story or where the story was taking him. And how was he to handle Gründgen's homosexuality? It was no secret to anyone – except the general public. To expose him before the world could force Nazi authorities to sack him and perhaps despatch him to a concentration camp. Klaus disliked him but wished him no ill. On one occasion he told Landshoff how relieved he was to learn that a rumour of his arrest had been false. And how to handle the fact that his sister had been married to him? Nonetheless, when he read a draft chapter to Landshoff a few weeks later, he was much reassured by his praise and pressed on. By mid-April he had completed the first half of the book and allowed himself a vacation in the South of France. He started in Marseille, that 'most animated city in Europe', according to *Das Buch von der Riviera*. Then, to resume work on *Mephisto*, he moved on to Sanary.

Athough he felt lonely there, Klaus wrote swiftly, sometimes more than ten pages a day. His diary is unusually reticent, however, mentioning merely that he was helped by this or that work, such as de Maupassant's novel. A little later he commented, '*Mephisto* will be a cold, angry book. Perhaps it will have the sheen of hatred.' On 1 May he noted, 'About 8 pages more of chapter VIII.' Two days later he hit a psychological snag. 'I feel a certain resistance to the manuscript.' But he pressed on. 'Chapter IX. More than 10 pages. My impression of the whole is now better.' And then, 'Yesterday, 19 May – the *manuscript* of *Mephisto: Novel of a Career* was finished.' The text was serialized by the *Pariser Tageszeitung* beginning in June, and soon afterwards Querido published it in hardcover. Publication left a slight hangover. Klaus noted in his diary: 'Had a long and lively dream about Gustaf. (A bad conscience.)'

Mephisto portrays the rise of an ambition-consumed Hendrik Höfgen from a minor artists' theatre in Hamburg in 1926 to triumph as the leading actor-producer of the Third Reich. The crux of the story is the choice he has to make between integrity – political and moral, and opportunism – political and professional. He confronts the issue as soon as the Nazis come to power. In the winter of 1933, working in the film industry in Paris, he debates whether to break his ties with Germany and remain in exile, 'proud and voluntarily abandoning a country where the very air is contaminated'. How good he would feel about himself and what new purpose his life would have, he tells himself. His wife encourages him. 'She can be my good angel', he believes. But where there is an angel, there is also a devil. Eventually Höfgen decides to return to Germany. He is offered the role of Mephisto in

Faust, Part One. His performance is a triumph and he duly receives recognition and reward from the regime.

It is not just his politics but also his morals that are ambiguous. On the one hand he intervenes to save the life of an old communist friend in a concentration camp. On the other, when it becomes expedient, he jettisons Juliette, his mulatto mistress – 'Black Venus' – with whom he has been conducting a sadomasochistic affair. The black mistress episode was pure invention and Klaus was harshly criticized for it. It was not always understood, however, that the insertion of this 'perversion' was in fact a substitute for the 'perversion' of homosexuality, which would have left Gründgens at high risk of consignment to a concentration camp. Klaus had no desire to destroy the actor. *Mephisto* was in fact the only one of Klaus's novels that had no trace of homoeroticism.

Klaus supplied his own précis of his subject's character. 'Hendrik Höfgen – typecast as an elegant blackguard, murderer in evening dress, scheming courtier – sees nothing, hears nothing. He has nothing to do with the city of Berlin. Nothing but stages, film studios, dressing rooms, a few nightclubs, a few fashionable drawing rooms are real to him. Does he not feel the change in the seasons? Is he not aware that the years are passing – the last years of that Weimar Republic born amid so much hope and now so piteously expiring – the years 1930, 1931, 1932? The actor Höfgen lives from one first night to the next, from one film to another, his calendar composed of performance days and rehearsal days. He scarcely notices that the snow melts, that the trees and bushes are in bud or in full leaf, that there are flowers and earth and streams. Encapsulated by his ambition as in a prison cell, insatiable and tireless, always in a state of extreme hysterical tension, Hendrik embraces a destiny that seems to him exceptional but is in fact nothing but a vulgar arabesque at the edge of an enterprise doomed to collapse.'

It had been a tough book to write, but it reinforced Klaus's position as one of the most significant figures in the German exile world. Reviews at the time, limited to the small émigré press, generally praised it. Up to his usual backstabbing, Brecht did his best to prevent its even being reviewed. 'Old enmity never dies', Klaus wearily sighed. But from the beginning there was uncertainty. Was it biography or satire? Was its portrayal of artistic life in the Third Reich accurate or a caricature? Was Höfgen really Gründgens or simply a type? And if the story was biographical, was the book written out of hatred of the actor and envy of his success? When the *Pariser Tageszeitung* characterized the novel as a *roman-à-clef*, Landshoff feared legal action and prompted Klaus to issue a denial. 'This book is not about a specific person but rather the careerist, the intellectual who betrays his ideals', he wrote. 'Conceptually no novel can be purely polemical. The epical follows its own principles and laws. I had to try to change this type into a person, to turn this symbol into Hendrik Höfgen – a man of flesh and blood, with his weaknesses, his absurdities, frailties, ups and downs. I attempted to show how the Mephistophelian petit bourgeois had to become a traitor.'

A number of years later, in *The Turning Point*, Klaus looked at the question from a different angle. 'I visualize my ex-brother-in-law as the traitor par excellence, the macabre embodiment of corruption and cynicism . . . I thought it pertinent, indeed, necessary to expose and analyze the abject type of treacherous intellectual who prostitutes his talent for the sake of some tawdry fame and transitory wealth.' In his final word on the subject, when he came to write *Der Wendepunkt*, Klaus again stressed that his Höfgen was symbolic, not biographical. 'As an example I could just as easily have used someone else. My choice fell on Gründgens – not because I considered him especially bad (he was perhaps better than many another dignitary of the Third Reich) – but simply because I happened to know him quite well. Precisely because of our earlier closeness, his change, his fall were to me so fantastic, curious, incredible, amazing as to deserve a novel.'

Klaus frankly acknowledged that he had long despised his former friend, lover and brother-in-law without understanding the reason. In his diary for 24 December 1931, for example, he asked himself, 'Why do I think about him so much and with such strong antipathy? With Gregor Gregori I really should have been done with him.' It could not have been easy for Klaus to separate his personal repugnance from his treatment of the story as a parable of an artist's political opportunism. He admitted that the novel was written in '*schöpferischem Hass*' – creative hatred. It was an understandable scream of protest against the flourishing of artistic figures who collaborated while others, persecuted, impoverished and homeless, were lucky if they could just stay alive. Some four thousand actors and others in the theatre had fled Germany, accompanied by fifteen hundred writers and playwrights. Many of those not fortunate enough to get out died in concentration camps or committed suicide.

The most common criticism of *Mephisto* is that it unfairly portrays the conditions of life for an artist in the Third Reich by someone who had never lived there. Marcel Reich-Ranicki got himself so worked up on the point that he accused Klaus of turning Gründgens into 'a comic book villain'. But since there is no getting around the fact that the actor used his talents for the cultural glory of the Third Reich and prospered not only professionally but also personally, the novel continues to be widely praised and read. No physical blood on the actor's hands to be sure, but he shamelessly pandered to those whose were drenched in it.

Though *Mephisto* was banned in the Third Reich, Klaus sent Gründgens a copy. A few years later Gründgens made a film of the career of Friedemann Bach, son of Johann Sebastian, a composer who possessed the merest tincture of his father's genius and was a humiliating failure. Was this his revenge? It is difficult to think it was not. Did the German public make the connection? Did Klaus even know about the film? Friedemann Bach died lonely and in disgrace.

Ultimately *Mephisto* is a monument to Klaus's single-minded commitment to combatting Nazism. It was therefore all the more incomprehensible that his own father had refused year after year to take a public stand against the Third Reich. When an American Jewish novelist, Ludwig Lewisohn, appealed to Thomas to declare himself openly, he declined. 'If I told you what you wish to hear, my capital and property in Germany would be taken away from me tomorrow, my son would be arrested as a hostage, I do not know what would happen to my old parents-in-law, who are Jewish, no more of my books could be sold in Germany, and I do not know what the other consequences would be.' That was on 12 April 1933. There followed the disgraceful affair of *Die Sammlung* in September. Time passed. Again and again Klaus appealed to him to speak out, and again and again was rebuffed. By now, not in the hope of returning to his home but in order to avoid jeopardizing his sales in Germany and the adulation of his German readers, Thomas refused to say anything publicly that might antagonize the Nazi authorities. He buried himself in work on his new novel, *Joseph in Egypt*, and refused to face up to the issue.

Others did not. During Thomas's first visit to the United States in May–June 1934, the Jewish Rescue League again appealed for a clear statement. Again he demurred. He would do no more than send the organization a letter which in cautious terms approved its aims. Even so, the comment was picked up by the Nazi press and strongly condemned. Thomas cravenly apologized to Bermann for the lapse. Hectored all the while by Klaus and Erika, he debated with himself from time to time whether the moment might have come to make a public declaration that would 'deliver a blow that will be felt by the regime'. Invariably he decided to maintain his silence.

When he and Katia went on a lecture tour of Eastern Europe the following January, Thomas remained guarded. He lost no time in correcting an article in a minor Prague newspaper which slightly exaggerated his opposition to anti-Semitism. A short time later he was invited to give a talk at a meeting in Nice of the Permanent Committee of Letters and Arts of the League of Nations. With the encouragement of Bermann, he refused to speak or even attend the session and, though he submitted a paper, he would not permit it to be read. '*I could cry*', Klaus commented in his diary when he learned of this in a letter from Katia. The disagreement between father and son became deeper and deeper. In April 1935 Thomas let Bermann publish a book of essays. Klaus was appalled. 'How awful and how terrible that this should come out now *in Germany*.' While Thomas was travelling around Europe polishing his personal image, Klaus was in Barcelona attending a PEN meeting which approved a protest telegram he drafted on behalf of imprisoned German writers. Not long afterward it was Klaus, not Thomas, who spoke at the First International Writers' Congress for the Defence of Culture in Paris.

It is impossible to know how long Thomas would have gone on temporizing. But finally, after three years, his hand was forced by Leopold Schwarzschild, publisher of *Das Neue Tage-Buch*, an influential exile journal in Paris. Schwarzschild, a man inclined to inflammatory accusations, published an article on 11 January accusing Gottfried Bermann of having done a deal with Goebbels to establish a publishing house in Vienna that would serve the interests of the Third Reich. Infuriated, Bermann appealed to Thomas to defend him. Joined by Hermann Hesse and Annette Kolb, Thomas obligingly complied and in a letter to the *Neue Zürcher Zeitung* on 19 January asserted that the charges against Bermann were 'totally unjustified' and affirmed that he himself intended to continue publishing with him.

Although Klaus was at this time thoroughly immersed in *Mephisto*, immediately he saw the letter he telephoned Erika. 'I read her the shit in the *N.Z.Z.* She will write to the Magician', he noted in his diary. And write she did. In an incandescent letter she warned that it would be difficult for her even to 'be in your presence in the near future'. His defence of Bermann, she went on, marked the first occasion when he had ever defended anyone publicly – and that, after years of refusing to stand up for victims of the Nazis. Thanks to Bermann, she continued, 'this is now the second time – the first being in connection with *Die Sammlung* that you have stabbed in the back the entire émigré community and what it is doing . . . Your relationship with Dr Bermann and his publishing house are indestructible. You seem ready to make any sacrifice for it.' Thomas, then in Arosa with Katia, wrote back, begging her to be patient with him. Erika would have none of it. In a second letter she pointed out that Thomas had given his unwavering support to Bermann but had not only refused to stand behind *Pfeffermühle* when it was under attack in Switzerland but had also betrayed his own son by renouncing his association with *Die Sammlung*, an act which had caused more harm to Klaus than anything ever done by the Nazis. And Klaus? His diary records simply, 'A long letter from Erika – her letter to The Magician (especially good). For my part, wrote [Thomas] shorter, milder and more resigned.'

Schwarzschild did not let the matter rest. He taunted Thomas and his publisher as being no better than literary renegades. The only German cultural asset that had been saved from the Nazis was its literature, he maintained, and that was now collectively 'in emigration'. This sally in turn provoked the literary editor of the *Neue Zürcher Zeitung*, Eduard Korrodi, to make great fun of refugee writers. They were mostly Jews, he claimed, and therefore unrepresentative of German letters. As for the notion that German literature had 'emigrated', Thomas Mann demonstrated the fallacy of that claim.

Klaus's first impulse was to write a reply for a Paris émigré newspaper. Instead, joined by Landshoff, he sent a telegram appealing to his father now, at long last, to take a stand. 'Urgently request response to Korrodi's disastrous article in whatever way – this time it really is a question of life or death for us all.' By now Katia realized, if her husband did not, that the issue could no longer be parried and the time had come to speak out publicly. She drafted a letter which Thomas revised and sent. This essentially said that Nazi Germany had detached itself from the civilized world and that its anti-Semitism was ultimately directed not just against Jews but against everyone. The statement was published on 3 February, three years and four days after Hitler had come to power. The following December Thomas's German citizenship was revoked and his books were banned.

The episode well exposed the state of relations inside the Mann family. Katia was one of those formidable German wives – like Cosima Wagner in a sense – who enjoyed her husband's supreme confidence and who selflessly guided his affairs from the shadows. She counselled him on everything, drafted his speeches and letters, managed his business affairs, disposed in fact of everything so he could devote himself solely to his writing. The only other family member who counted was Erika. In a pregnant sentence written to her at the height of the Bermann imbroglio, Katia candidly said, 'You are, apart from me and Medi [Elisabeth], the only person to whom [his] heart really belongs.' And the other four? Golo stayed in the background and was ignored. Convictions he had, but act on them he would not. Like his father, he had little sympathy for émigrés and their affairs. He was convinced the Nazis were lodged so firmly in power that any political engagement – such as Klaus's anti-Nazi lectures and writings – was essentially pointless. Monika was, as usual, ignored when not despised; Elisabeth and Michael were too young to matter. If he was lucky, Klaus, like one of the family dogs, might occasionally get a pat on the head by his master but was regarded as an ill-disciplined nuisance. Too supine to stand up to Thomas and lacking his respect, Klaus had little or no influence within the family. He could shake his fist in Hitler's face but not in his father's.

Not that many public figures were shaking their fists in Hitler's face at the time. Even Churchill, who had said nice things about Mussolini over the years, still entertained hopes for the Führer until as late as 1936. Droves of refugees knew the score but none saw more clearly and warned more outspokenly than Klaus that Hitler was synonymous with war. 'THE WAR. Everyone *knows* it is coming – it is almost *entirely* inevitable – but they do not really believe it. (Similar to the way people think about death.)', he commented to his diary on 28 February. A few weeks after he wrote these words, Hitler ordered the German army into the Rhineland, taking one more step towards the conflict Klaus predicted. He also made another prediction – Hitler's next move would be to annex Austria. It was, two years later nearly to the day.

The spring and summer of 1936 were not a happy time for Klaus. Partly it was because of the emptiness at the core of his life – the emptiness of anyone without emotional attachments. The men he met gave him nothing. In one case less than nothing. During a brief visit to Toulon from Sanary one night, he went cruising in a park and was mugged by two hoods. He was beaten up, ran, was caught and mugged again. After robbing him of his wallet and his jacket, the thugs let him go. He went to the police, who took him to a hospital to be treated. A local newspaper learned of the incident and published a report, mercifully with all the vital facts wrong. Klaus was identified as 'Thomas Klau, German nationality, employee of the Hotel de Tour at Sanary'. His relief was palpable. 'Nothing would have given the Nazi press more pleasure than to have been able to report the [true] story.'

In the course of the summer Klaus found himself sinking into depression. His sleep was disturbed by terrible dreams; he was back on drugs; he was lonely. Death was a temptation, even a hope. 'But of course before that I should write something beautiful and moving', he wrote in his diary. 'And between me and the dark valley of the Promised Land – always, always, always my sister.' There was still more. He could see no future for himself. 'A liberal German writer had no chance in Europe, considering the present state and obvious trend of affairs.' But would it be better in the United States? He was not sure.

It so happened that Erika just then found herself upended. The peppery political message of *Pfeffermühle* had proved so popular in the Low Countries, in Amsterdam in particular, that the German embassy filed a stiff protest note. The Dutch authorities, whose overriding policy was one of strict neutrality, felt sufficiently intimidated to summon Erika and tell her the cabaret could continue but as a purely comedy routine, strictly avoiding anything remotely political. Without hesitation she politely turned down the proposal and decided to decamp to the New World, taking her troupe with her.

After thinking it over, Klaus decided to join her. Not long before, he had received an invitation from Alfred and Blanche Knopf, who had recently published *Journey into Freedom*. It had been an unanticipated success in the

United States and they wanted him to come to New York and give several talks. And so, on 18 September, he and Erika boarded the Dutch liner *Statendam*, almost exactly nine years since they had ventured forth as 'The Literary Mann Twins'. For Klaus the visit got off to a poor start when he was told on arrival that his topic was to be 'My Father and His Works' – than which no subject could have been better chosen to set his teeth on edge. He ignored the suggestion.

All in all he had a miserable time. A month after arriving he had a shock when the Knopfs – in the inscrutable way of publishers – declined to publish *Mephisto*. It did not help his mood when he read in newspapers that Gründgens's latest production in Berlin was a tremendous hit. His depression deepened. 'I ask myself, practically every hour of the day, whether DEATH, which is so close to my heart, will not be kind enough to take me to itself', he wrote in his diary a week after arriving in New York. The litany of sorrows continued. On his birthday on 18 November he commented, 'This last evening of my third decade. Tomorrow I shall be thirty. In all fervour I pray to God – who must exist – that it will not last much longer.' And a week later, 'This sadness, this depression is like physical pain. *It hurts.* I want to DIE. Because of overwhelming melancholy, unable to work.'

When he finally delivered his first talk, held at a synagogue on Long Island, the event did not go especially well. The very topic, 'Is Friendship between France and Germany possible?' was more than slightly off-key. It was Klaus's first lecture in English and both speaker and audience found it hard going. The audience was restless and Klaus found their questions 'idiotic'. The next lecture – 'Have German Intellectuals Failed?' – was given in German at the German-Jewish Club in Manhattan and was a success. This time the discussion was well informed and useful on both sides. The sessions he most enjoyed, however, were with students at two colleges, Smith and Sarah Lawrence. In what time he could find, he wrote reports on his impressions of America for newspapers in Paris, Basel, Prague and Amsterdam.

Inevitably, Christmas was a melancholy affair. Instead of the traditional festivities with family and friends at Küsnacht, he and Erika celebrated the holiday in her hotel room. They bought a little tree, exchanged a few modest gifts and ate cold roast chicken from a nearby delicatessen. Two weeks later, on 9 January, Klaus returned to Europe. The dockside farewell was despondent. Erika was in tears. Klaus was feeling miserable and later commented in his diary, 'A boundless feeling of sympathy, gentleness and the indestructible bond between my life and hers.'

In fact, the visit was a much greater disappointment for Erika. Pepper Mill premiered on 5 January and, in American theatrical parlance, it bombed. Her high hopes of introducing political cabaret to New York broke over its unfamiliarity to Americans, even to cosmopolitan New Yorkers. They grasped neither the medium nor the message. There were language problems, conceptual problems, acting problems, audience problems. The anti-fascist political message was lost on a country absorbed in its own economic difficulties and was, as Erika put it, 'not what I would call "Hitler conscious"'. After struggling for some weeks, she was sensible enough not to throw good money after bad. And so, after four years and more than a thousand performances, the show closed and the loyal troupe of friends disbanded. Erika remained in New York and decided to brush up her English and, like her brother, become a lecturer.

Klaus's talks had gone so well that when he left New York he had in his pocket a contract with a well-established lecture agent, William Feakins, to give a series of talks around the United States during the following autumn. The crossing back to Europe, despite some heavy seas, was enjoyable, some of the joy being provided by a young British sailor who had saved all his money and was travelling around the world in third class. On debarking at Le Havre early on 18 January 1937, Klaus took the boat train directly to Paris to see old friends. He had lunch with Gide, who told him about the difficulties with his new book criticizing the Soviet Union. He also went to see Cocteau, who gave him a copy of his latest work, *Mon premier voyage*. A few weeks later Klaus chanced to meet Hans Aminoff and his new friend, Holgar. They dined several times and went to a party together. Klaus described the encounter as 'painful'. Whatever remained of their relationship had by now vanished.

The meeting with Gide prompted Klaus to write a strong defence of Gide's new book – the famous apostate renunciation of his earlier praise of the Soviet Union, which had aroused the wrath of Stalinists everywhere. In supporting him in the article 'Streit um André Gide' ('The Controversy over André Gide') in *Die Neue Weltbühne* on 11 February, Klaus knew he would be roundly abused by the communists and the far left. 'But it is necessary, unavoidable.' His fiercest critic turned out to be his old friend Lion Feuchtwanger, the rich, German-Jewish, devout Stalinist émigré writer. Far more painful was the reaction of his uncle Heinrich, who never really forgave him for his article. The brouhaha over Gide coincided with the Moscow show trials and the two events together split German exiles into viciously opposing anti- and pro-communist camps. By April 1940 Klaus could write to a friend, 'Since October of last year I have had to part ways with my communist friends.'

Feeling unsettled during the early months of 1937 and having no concrete idea for a new book, Klaus decided to visit his family in Küsnacht. On arriving on 25 February he had a terrible shock. His father had agreed to be co-founder and co-editor of a new bi-monthly publication, *Mass und Wert*, which followed the lines of *Die Sammlung* in terms of its contributors and intellectual intent. Considering that he had two years of experience in organizing, managing and editing *Die Sammlung*, Klaus would have been the obvious person to have edited the new journal. But not only had he been left in the dark, he had been completely left out. As if that were not enough, the managing editor, Ferdinand Lion, one of Thomas's old cronies, let Klaus know he considered him an intellectual lightweight whose writings would not be welcome. Grinding his face further into the dust, Lion made it clear that he considered Golo a writer of distinction who would have a role to play. If Thomas's withdrawal from *Die Sammlung* was sabotage, here was flagrant aggression, a deliberate display of antipathy, a brutal rejection of his eldest son.

At long last, all the cuts and barbs, all the years of indignities and hostility finally got to Klaus and he exploded – to his diary. 'I again feel very strongly and not without bitterness The Magician's utter *coldness* toward me. Whether sympathetic or petulant (in a very strange way "irritated" by the existence of a son) *never* interested, *never* in a serious way concerned about me. His general lack of interest in human beings is especially strong toward me. There is a straight line from the out-and-out superficiality – because of lack of interest – of the character sketch of me in "Unordnung [und frühes Leid]" down to the situation where he flat out forgets me in connection with the new publication. It is the same with my friends (Fritz Landshoff at the moment) . . . Pleasant comments, as occasionally, for example, on *Flucht in den Norden* or *Mephisto* are *no* proof to the contrary. He writes just as pleasantly to total strangers. A mixture of highly intelligent, almost kindly conciliation – and icy cold. All this is especially emphatic when it concerns me. I am not mistaken.'

Of course he was not. In his own diary around this time, Thomas made several corresponding entries proving Klaus's point. 'The boy is morally and intellectually not intact', reads one of them. 'Tolerates no authority and asserts the right not to do so.' Eventually Klaus decided to talk to Katia. She showed no sympathy and replied coolly that Thomas was 'irritated with members of the family who write – especially Heinrich but me as well'. Clearly she had no intention of trying to bring together father and son. Her devotion to Thomas was absolute; she would unconditionally side with him and was content to see her unhappy family remain unhappy in its own neurotic way. Outsiders quickly caught on. Golo once overheard Wystan Auden say, 'A novelist's son is always a nuisance; he is like a character in one of his novels that has taken physical form.' To which Golo commented, 'Naturally Klaus felt the same.' Christopher Lazare, a young American art historian and friend in later years, elaborated. 'What hurt Klaus so much was his father's veiled contempt, which was evident in so many of Thomas Mann's literary portraits – Goethe's son in *Lotte* and in many of the short stories. In his father's eyes he was only material for irony, satire and disappointment.' As usual, Klaus absorbed the pain and turned it against himself, where it took form in depression. Thus continued the usual pattern – rejection, depression, drugs, depression.

In the end his lack of involvement in *Mass und Wert* did him no harm. The journal failed to achieve the international character of *Die Sammlung*, both in terms of writers and content. Not only did it fail to establish itself, it quickly proved to be such a burden that Thomas wished he had never been involved. To distinguish it from *Die Sammlung*, he had emphasized in the first issue that the publication was dedicated to 'an autonomous, apolitical art'. This from the same person who after the war condemned those who thought they were making art when they were in fact turning a blind eye to the real world and providing camouflage for crime. The final issue appeared in October 1940.

Perhaps it was an effort to rebound from his latest humiliations, or perhaps it was simply his usual ceaseless prowl for new subjects; in either case Klaus was now brimming over with ideas. One was to write a 'refugee novel'. In early March he sketched out a few thoughts which he shared with his father. When this did not find a good reception, he put it aside. Not long afterward it suddenly occurred to him to write another biographical novel, this one about Ludwig II of Bavaria. 'Excited to do a Ludwig novella', he commented to his diary on 14 March. 'Sixty pages. Analysis of Romanticism, eros, ecstasy, downfall. The end in Lake Starnberg. It could be a lot of fun.'

The topic touched deep sentimental feelings. Like his father, Klaus never ceased to be homesick for Bavaria. In his autobiographies he wrote of it as a sort of utopia. And, like all good Bavarians, he considered Ludwig a hero. 'His prodigious castles – monumental whims scattered all over Bavaria – belonged to the mythic landscape of my childhood', he later commented in *The Turning Point*. 'He remained alive in my heart. The iridescent twilight in which his drama is bathed never ceased to captivate my fancy. In fact it was quite a relief to delve into the poetic ambiguities of King Ludwig's legend.'

Ambiguities were many in Ludwig's story, not to mention homosexuality and suggestions of vile conspiracies. Ludwig II, 'the Fairy-Tale King', also known as 'the Mad King' and 'the Swan King', was deposed on 10 June 1886 following a dubious claim of mental incapacity. Confined to Schloss Berg on Lake Starnberg, he was found, drowned, three days later. It smelled of a *coup d'état*. Klaus was fascinated, and while at Küsnacht began reading about the subject. Lacking access to original German souces, he had to depend on what could be found in Switzerland – works such as Fritz Linde's *Ich, der König* and Carl Friedrich Glasenapp's classic biography of Richard Wagner. 'The material excites me.'

For Klaus, however, two nascent books were not nearly enough to occupy him. His visit to the United States, albeit brief, had left him in a buoyant mood about the role he hoped America would play in the future. So he decided to go round Europe giving what he described as a 'rhapsodic speech' entitled 'Hoffnung auf Amerika', which he rendered into English as 'America – Token of Hope'. After a few appearances in the Low Countries and Switzerland, he set out on 13 April and for the next month gave his pep talk in Vienna, Prague and other Czech cities. Everywhere he had large and sympathetic audiences. Sympathetic perhaps, but the Viennese found it hard to believe there was much to be hopeful about. Klaus agreed. 'One promenade through the streets sufficed to convince any clear-sighted person of Austria's doom and imminent disaster.'

Austria may have been in bad shape, but Klaus's condition was even worse. By the spring of 1937 his addiction to heroin, morphine and Eukodal had reached a frightening level. At times he vented his despair in plaintive – and untranslatable – scribblings in his diary. Now his professional life was being affected. On a number of occasions he broke out in nervous sweats while giving a speech. He made spasmodic efforts to stop and was very proud when he managed to stay off drugs for the better part of a day. But he would start again and then feel guilty and depressed. What is astonishing, almost inexplicable, is Klaus's ability in this condition to stand up to a truly punishing schedule of meetings and lectures. Everywhere he went he met friends, went to dinners, gave interviews. On 5 May he even had a full, hour-long discussion about European politics with the president of Czechoslovakia, Edvard Beneš. A week later he travelled to Budapest to visit the Hatvanys. By now he was obviously in such bad shape the baron recognized he needed professional help. On 27 May Klaus agreed to enter the Siesta Sanatorium in Budapest. An old hand at living in small rooms, albeit without bars on the windows, as this one had, he immediately erected his altar of photographs – Erika, Katia, Ricki, Gide – and made himself at home. From a distance he could hear the howls of patients. 'A right melancholy comedy, all this.' He was attended by three doctors and several nurses and was pleased with himself when they told him he was standing up well to the initial phase of the treatment. His principal doctor was Robert Klopstock, a young German émigré with literary interests. The physician had treated Franz Kafka for tuberculosis and it was in his arms that the writer is said to have died. He immediately attempted to probe the reason for Klaus's addiction. 'Klopstock asks me *why* I have been taking morphine. I answer simply, "because I would like to die ('Todestrieb')". Everyone to whom I felt attached and who felt attracted to me wants (or wanted) to die. (Erika is perhaps the *one* big exception. But at what cost? Who knows what it costs her.) How will I go on living *without* this dangerous balm.' So went the diary entry of 28 May.

Within a few days he found it almost impossible to sleep and was swept away by uncontrollable bouts of weeping. 'A pleasure that is NOT.' The famous line in Goethe's *Faust*, 'Entbehren sollst du, sollst entbehren' – 'deny yourself, you must deny yourself', ran continuously through his head. Then he slept nonstop for two days. Once aroused he worked a bit on Ludwig and let Katia know the treatment had gone exceptionally well. Only three days had been really terrible, he told her, and those had now almost receded from memory. He concluded with words that his mother could not have found completely reassuring: 'In the foreseeable future I shall certainly *not* start again – perhaps *much* later sometime. Why should anyone reach 80? But first I want to write a few good things.'

From Thomas he received a letter offering not friendly encouragement but cold remonstrance. 'You have seen many of your friends ruined by it [morphine], but you probably paid them no attention', ran one sentence. It was not a letter a thoughtful father would have sent to an ill son; the son responded – to himself, of course – with exasperation. 'I *pay no* attention to those who want DEATH? Just ask yourself how desperate they were and how they dealt with this horribly burdensome life. To seek death is not contemptible but wise.' It was on that note that, in the middle of June, he pronounced himself 'entirely healthy' and on 21 June left Budapest for Vienna. Before going, he read Klopstock a piece he had written on Kafka while in the sanatorium.

Throughout this period Klaus's diary mentions over and over the name Thomas Quinn Curtiss. The two had been introduced by Baron Hatvany shortly after Klaus's arrival in Budapest. Curtiss, nine years younger, had been studying film and theatre in Vienna and Moscow, where he claimed to have been a pupil of Sergei Eisenstein. He then landed in Budapest in the hope of making a movie there. Klaus immediately fell in love with him, commenting to his diary, 'The luck and mystery of a first meeting. His hysteria, sadness, intelligence, gentleness, sensuality, his smile, his moans, eyes, lips, expression, voice.' Klaus was in no doubt that his feelings for Curtiss helped him get through the detoxification ordeal as well as he did. In his diary he referred to him as 'Curtiss-darling' and 'Curtiss-dear' and eventually a nickname of his own invention, 'Tomski'. Almost every day Tomski had visited the sanatorium and was always 'a comfort and delight'. Over and over during his treatment Klaus referred to Curtiss as his lifeline, his final hope. More than a month after their first acquaintance, he felt 'still very happy with Curtiss – happier than I should have thought possible'.

But recurrently welling up in the back of his mind, like the curse motif in Wagner's *Ring*, were dark misgivings. 'Shall I love dear Th. C. enough? I pray that I can love him enough. So much strength is needed *really* to love. I am afraid of losing interest. And he – he loves death even more than me.' Although vexed by doubts, when the time came for Klaus to leave the sanatorium, all was well and they travelled together happily for the remainder of the summer. Klaus took him to all the places he loved – to Annemarie Schwarzenbach's vacation house in the Swiss Alps; to the family home in Küsnacht; to Paris and Amsterdam; and even to Bandol and Sanary on the Riviera. For a time the relationship went smoothly. 'I was happy. I could work again.' But he could never quite rid himself of nagging worries, not only about Curtiss's feelings but equally his own. And inevitably there were strains. As he once complained to his diary, 'Sad about Tomski who almost never comes back before 3 o'clock, so I see very little of him. *Alone.*' But he always forgave all.

Erika remained Erika, his mainstay, the one he could always rely on. But she now had romances of her own with several men who were fervently in love with her. These affairs began not long after she and Klaus had arrived in New York in September 1936. There they stayed at the Bedford Hotel on East Fortieth Street in Manhattan, a hotel managed by a German couple who made it a refuge for German émigrés. Among these was Martin Gumpert, a physician and writer from Berlin. He became a close friend of Klaus, to whom he supplied drugs, and an even closer friend of Erika's, to whom he provided sex. In the course of her very active social life, Erika met other men as well. Maurice Wertheim, a wealthy, enlightened, American investment banker, was one. He wanted desperately to marry her and Erika seriously considered it. They would have made an interesting couple. But the not entirely disinterested Gumpert and several other friends talked her out of it. So for the next several years Klaus had his Tomski and Erika her Martin. While there was no overt change in the relations between brother and sister, they were moving apart.

Klaus's travel with Tomski would not have been possible without the great good fortune of acquiring foreign citizenship and a passport to go with it. Ever since the expiration of his German passport in April 1934 and his loss of German citizenship the following November, Klaus found it difficult and at times impossible to travel. More than that, being stateless, as he was for nearly three years, he was vulnerable to imprisonment or extradition. So it was an enormous relief when the problem was solved almost by magic.

The man wielding the wand was Edvard Beneš. He was a highly cultivated man and, out of his enormous respect for Thomas and the entire Mann family, he offered them all Czech citizenship. Thomas took his oath at the Czech consulate in Zurich on 19 November 1936 and Klaus his on 25 March 1937. A few days later he picked up his passport. 'Now I have it', he exulted. 'Valid for five years.' Well, not quite five. When Czechoslovakia was extinguished two years later at Munich, Klaus found himself once more stateless and without a valid passport.

While at the sanatorium Klaus had laboured as best he could on his Ludwig biography and by the time he left Budapest he had little more to write. On 29 June he and Curtiss arrived at Annemarie's house at Sils Baselgia, where he hoped to finish the text in short order. His diary entry for the day was gloomy. 'Slight depression. Feeling of hopelessness both regarding my work and Curtiss. If I really try I should be able to make it.' Work did not go especially well, however. The weather was dreary and cold. More to the point, the subject was not well suited to a recovering drug addict with psychological problems. He struggled on and finished a holograph text by 10 July. Like most authors, he had difficulty finding a good title. Then there suddenly flashed into his memory Ludwig's incarceration in Schloss Berg, which reminded him of his own 'incarceration' in a room with a barred window in the Siesta Sanatorium. Hence, *Vergittertes Fenster* ('Barred Window'). A month later he made the final corrections and dedicated the book to Curtiss. 'I like this sad romance', he commented in his diary. '(Autobiographical just as strong as in Tchaikovsky).' In mid-September he corrected the proofs and received printed copies on 16 November. He was greatly pleased. And so were reviewers. The exiled cinéaste Max Ophüls was so impressed he proposed to make a film of it, dropping the idea only when the war broke out.

Klaus's Ludwig was 'not the charming fairy-tale prince and picturesque Lohengrin idealised by his people and praised by the Parisian Symbolists', as he wrote in *Der Wendepunkt*. 'He was a man lost, victim of secret intrigues and his own hubris, the psychopath, the martyr, a prince of passion, more like Oscar Wilde than a Wagnarian hero.' Below the surface of the story were two subtexts – an appeal for toleration of homosexuals and a hostility to Wagner, who was his father's best-liked composer and therefore Klaus's least. In his commentary on Klaus's writings, Peter Hoffer has argued that

'*Vergittertes Fenster* is, in many respects, an innovative work of considerable artistic merit . . . and should be ranked among Klaus Mann's best short works'.

Klaus had a genius for compartmentalizing the various elements of his life. He could be happy and productive, writing books and essays, travelling and giving lectures, and yet around the same time he might suddenly descend into despair and the miseries of drug addiction. And that is what now happened. A reversion to drugs coincided with turbulence in his love life. The curse motif could not be avoided. Tomski was often 'rather crass, unmannerly, obstinate' and suffered from 'an infantile need for luxury'. While insisting he was as attached to him as ever, Klaus was forced to admit '*he* already loves me a lot less than before, at the beginning in Budapest . . . The great, beautiful gentleness is no longer there.'

Klaus had more important matters on his mind, however. For all the pleasure he took in *Vergittertes Fenster*, he came to feel that the subject was escapist. Ludwig was a morbid fairy-tale prince; Hitler was reality. Americans still had no idea what a menace he was. Klaus would make it his mission to wake them up. So he boarded the French Line *Champlain* on 18 September to take up the lecture tour around the United States that Feakins had arranged. He prepared talks on a number of topics, which he varied according to his audience: 'Germany and the World', 'A Family against Dictatorship', 'After Hitler – What?', 'My Father and His Work', 'Germany Yesterday – Germany Tomorrow'. With these he, as he put it, 'harangued' the low-brow Elks club of Buffalo, the liberal intelligentsia in New England, the Quakers in Philadelphia (who offered him a choice of milk or water with his meagre meal), the Rotarians in Des Moines, students at Cornell and Duke, Jews in Chicago, society ladies in Richmond and Kalamazoo, teachers in San Diego and the highbrows of San Francisco. Almost wherever he spoke he was given a warm reception. His diary mentions overfilled auditoriums, lively discussions, cordial social events and large dinner parties in his honour. Feakins was so pleased he extended the tour by two months.

Lecturing was a dog's life. He would rush from an evening talk to the train station, spend an uncomfortable night in a stuffy Pullman car, arrive at an unearthly morning hour in another city, check into a hotel, go off to a lunch, then attend a reception which was followed by a dinner and, after giving his speech, return to his hotel for the night and leave early the next morning for another engagement. It was tough and boring and involved lots of travel, little sleep and even less pleasure. Not often, but occasionally, he grumbled. He became sick to death of 'these Pullman cars, these dining cars, these railway station drug stores'. And he could never quite get over a near sense of agoraphobia induced by the seeming infinity of the American Midwest. But without a doubt he learned vastly more about average Americans than other exiles. And this made him realize how wide the Atlantic was – how different the political tradition and practices, how different the way of life and way of thinking. What impelled him to continue was a sense of mission to do all he could to awaken Americans to the situation in Europe. Did his audiences learn anything from him? They listened attentively, but, while he was careful never to appear critical, he rather doubted that he left much of a dent in their ignorance about Europe, their indifference to the dictators or their blind isolationism.

After weeks of ceaseless travel Klaus felt he deserved a holiday and decided there was no better place to spend the end of the year than in the omnipresent sunshine of California. On 20 December, accompanied by Curtiss, he arrived in Hollywood. As always 'holiday' was for Klaus a relative term. In the days after his arrival he had lunch successively with Billy Wilder, Ernst Lubitsch and Fritz Lang. He attended a Christmas party at David Selznick's studio and was taken by George Kukor to the shooting of a scene for *Gone with the Wind*. For Tomski, the visit was a god-sent opportunity to scout around for a career in film. Only Christmas Day itself was a disappointment. No one had thought to invite them, and they were lonely. Klaus passed the time by writing a letter to Erika and the first three pages of an article, 'Return to Hollywood'. They took a walk and in the evening went to see the pre-release of the new Disney film *Snow White*, which Klaus found 'charming'.

Klaus was at a New Year's Eve party given by Vicki Baum when 1937 came to an end. Afterwards he once again used the final diary entry to jot down a year-end balance. It was brief this time. Positive: Tomski. Bitter: the two drug treatments. Exhausting: travel. Work: a lot of essays and plans for new books. Writing: *Vergittertes Fenster*. 'I am really pleased with it.' Outlook: 'Year of war, year before war?'

CHAPTER 7

Stalin's Agent
1938–39

'Catastrophic' was the last word Klaus wrote in his 1937 diary. It was a prediction, in a word, of political disasters on the way. These were painfully obvious to Klaus but still not to the Americans. So, like a tireless Sisyphus, he decided to give the political boulder one more push. He would stay in the United States and continue to try to educate Americans on the realities of what was going on in Europe and how Nazism could eventually engulf them as well. As soon as he persuaded Feakins to finance another round of talks, he set off.

He began on 7 January in San Francisco with a lunch and a radio broadcast lecture to the Commonwealth Club on 'Germany and the World'. Then it was on to San Diego, Des Moines, Chicago and finally Montreal, where he was the guest of honour at a lunch given by the Canadian PEN club. By the end of the month he was in New York at the Bedford.

The trip was a success. Once again, wherever he appeared he was warmly received, and with some pride he wrote in his diary of the packed auditoriums, welcoming receptions and praise for his talk. 'Went well', 'long discussion', read most entries, if occasionally marred by 'the usual stupid questions'. One businessman so admired his speech he had his secretary immediately type up a copy.

The lecture tour concluded, on 13 February Klaus boarded the *Ile de France* to return to Europe. He had with him two contracts, one with Feakins for yet another series of talks to be undertaken in the autumn, and a second one for a book on which he would collaborate with Erika.

The latter was the result of his efforts in the previous November sounding out the Boston publishing house Houghton Mifflin for a book about noted Germans and Austrians who had fled into exile. The editors liked the idea – liked it so much, in fact, they wanted to get the book out as quickly as possible. *Escape to Life: German Culture in Exile* was to be the title.

The crossing was uneventful, if not very pleasant. The only entertainment was a kitschy film starring 'this ghastly little Shirley Temple'. Even less entertaining were reports in the ship's newspaper about a deepening crisis in German-Austrian relations. After a brief sojourn in Amsterdam to see Landshoff, Klaus arrived in Paris early on the morning of 12 March, at the very moment, several hundred miles away, when German troops were arriving in Austria to incorporate that country into Hitler's Grossdeutsches Reich. The news left Klaus devastated. 'The events of the past few days are probably the most awful that have taken place in Europe since 1918', he wrote in his diary. 'The enormous, almost insane brutality on the one side and the total lethargy on the other . . . Europe's darkest hour. The nightmarish triumph of iniquity.' The acquiescence of the British and French to this gross violation of the Versailles Treaty left him in despair.

The Austrian debacle coincided with other events that battered Klaus almost as though they were physical blows. Chief of these were the continued advances of fascism, not only by Germany in central Europe but also by Italy in Africa and Franco in Spain. At the same time the Moscow show trials put the Soviet Union, Hitler's sole opponent, beyond the pale as an ally. For Klaus personally the result was a first-class depression. After six months of abstention, he had gradually begun taking drugs again and by now was once more in the grip of addiction. He was so desperate to be numbed one night, he spent hours wandering around Montmartre searching for a dealer. Finally, at four a.m., he had to wake Thea Sternheim, an old friend from his Berlin days, to get a hit. His psychological state can be gauged from a scarcely coherent diary entry penned around six that morning. 'LIFE – my work – Tomski – Europe's downfall – confusion and clarity. I want to express it all. Dark hour –. Reading, writing, thinking, suffering, vomiting.'

No drug could make Hitler go away, however. And with his redrawing of the map of Europe, it was clear to Klaus that he must return to Küsnacht as quickly as possible to discuss the family's future. He arrived on 18 March and found Golo waiting for him at the Zurich station. From that moment they talked about nothing else. '*What should we do?*' Klaus wrote in his diary that evening. 'Leave immediately for America? Will the parents and Erika stay there? Closing up everything here?' The uncertainty was compounded by the absence of both Erika, who was still in New York, and of Thomas and Katia, who had arrived in the United States just as Klaus had returned to Europe.

Thomas was committed to a demanding schedule of appointments – giving lectures and receiving honours – and was not due to return until mid-July. However, even in far-off America the Anschluss left him in no doubt about what to do. Frightened that Switzerland might suffer the same fate as Austria, he and Katia decided within week to emigrate to the United States. To initiate the formal procedure, it was necessary to enter the country from elsewhere and file an application at the border. So on 2 May they travelled to Toronto and executed an official application. In the meantime Thomas's great patron, Agnes Meyer, arranged for Princeton University to offer him an honorary professorship for the following autumn with the sole obligation to give three lectures a year and hold seminars on *The Magic Mountain* and Goethe's *Faust*. The ever-competent Katia ventured to Princeton in June and found a handsome house around the corner from Albert Einstein.

Even at six thousand miles distance, Thomas could give his son the heebie-jeebies. Late in March Klaus learned that his parents had reached Los Angeles – which he took to mean Hollywood – and intended to spend the spring and summer there. Had he been seen on a stage at this point, he would have made an outstanding Othello. 'It appears highly likely that The Magician will bring off a really big deal in Hollywood. My reaction, which surprises even me and is really dumb (I must admit) is dominated by envy and pointless hurt. He triumphs wherever he goes. Shall *I* ever get out from under his shadow? Will my strength last so long? In a word, "great men" should certainly not have sons.'

The exasperation and self-confessed resentment are easy to understand. His father was invited everywhere, welcomed everywhere, honoured everywhere. Klaus felt he was by comparison at best a mealtime entertainer. Long before his father, he had been in Hollywood, had met any number of film producers and had made any number of proposals for a movie of one or another of his novels, all without success. At the same time he had been the one travelling coast to coast warning Americans about Nazism. Now it looked as though he was to be shoved aside by his upstart father. He felt bitter.

But Klaus faced a more immediate problem. By the time he had reached Küsnacht from Paris, he was a physical wreck. The drugs he had persuaded himself were helpful to his writing were instead ruining him. On the advice of Dr Katzenstein, the Zurich neurologist he had consulted in November 1935, he decided to have treatment at a private Zurich clinic run by a Swiss psychiatrist, Ludwig Binswanger, founder of a therapy he called '*dasein analysis*' aka 'anthropological psychiatry'. No one outside the family was to know; 'officially' Klaus was in Paris. 'I do not think it will be so difficult this time to say farewell to this sweet fish', he told himself – 'fish' being his old private slang for drugs. 'It has been giving me more trouble than pleasure recently and it has *not* helped my work; on the contrary it has made me sleepy and nauseated. And yet I will never forget it. They were such *beautiful* hours.'

After what he referred to as a 'brief interrogation' by Binswanger, Klaus was given a series of small injections of an opium derivative called pantopon, a medication designed to block craving and reduce the suffering of withdrawal. These left him increasingly weak and tired, and in the late afternoon of the second day he suffered what he described as a 'total collapse', 'helpless weeping and great pain'. The fourth day was worse. 'Went through hell. TEARS. Despair . . . Diarrhea. Freezing. Misery. *Tears.*' At the next stage he spent much of the time dozing and sleeping. Amazingly, he read a great deal, as always, and wrote an astonishing number of letters, among them to Lion Feuchtwanger, Bruno Walter, Emil Ludwig, Feakins, Erika and, of course, Tomski. 'Ah, if only Tomski were here' became a refrain.

Like Klopstock before him, Binswanger straightaway tried to probe the reasons for Klaus's addiction. And straightaway the discussion led nowhere. According to Klaus's diary notes of their meeting on the second day, 'Binswanger wants to know WHY this addiction? Longing for the earth, for MOTHER? DEATH? DESIRE? (Political affairs are hardly an explanation – in *my* case and in Wolfgang [Hellmert]'s case since it began before then.) Dissatisfaction with sexuality (= castration complex?). But I did it often with Tomski. WHY? The thought of Tomski, painful, bitter and sweet.' The comments for day six read, 'My thoughts are clearer – problems also clearer . . . The shadow of René, Ricki, Gerts. But I am stronger than *all* of them and yet not strong enough. The desire to succumb is too deep in me. What can a Binswanger do about that?' Asked years later why he thought his brother was periodically addicted, Golo said, 'I do not know. I never discussed "why" with him. In any case he would not have given an answer.'

Klaus left the clinic at the end of a week. But before then Binswanger made a final attempt. 'Discussion of the family. Aunt Carla, etc. Suicide complex and drugs. Death and mother-fixation. Erika's role as mother substitute. It doesn't really take me further.' It did not take him any further because he did not want to follow. What is astonishing is that someone with such intense intellectual curiosity should be so lacking in curiosity about his own psychiatric state. Perhaps a clue may be found in *The Turning Point*, in which Klaus fantasized a lighthearted exchange between Freud and Marx, concluding with Freud's remark, 'What we teach is true. But it is not the whole truth. We lie when we claim to possess the clue to ultimate wisdom.' Here was a key element in Klaus's philosophy – no one or no institution could claim ultimate wisdom.

But people with neuroses can stumble through life successfully just like those with chronic illnesses. It does not amaze, then, that by the third week of April Klaus was writing, 'Drugs. I use them cynically and am vexed about it. Must it, will it soon start again? I want to live and work with Tomski.' What does amaze is that for once he took responsibility and cut back his doses of Eukodal. But then there was a relapse. He fled to Katzenstein for encouragement. A stiff lecture is what he got. 'No addict *ever* says the truth when it concerns his addiction', he was told. To this he commented to his diary, 'I didn't breathe one word in contradiction.' Somehow something clicked and he now successfully came off drugs.

During the course of 1937, several publications had asked Klaus to go to Spain to report on the civil war. He was tempted. It would be a dramatic way to die. A *Heldentod*! On reflection he decided a hero's death could wait until he finished his biography of Ludwig. Now, a year later, in mid-March 1938, the editor of the *Pariser Tageszeitung* repeated the proposal, and this time Klaus accepted. By chance Erika arrived from New York just then and insisted on going along. 'We both wanted to see the apocalyptic actuality of a volcanic outburst. We realized that what was happening in Spain was but a bloody prologue, a sort of mortally serious rehearsal of what might be in store for the world at large.' So to the consternation of their parents and friends, they set off on 20 June. First stop was Paris where with difficulty they managed to secure visas and entry documents to Spain. Klaus was exhilarated. 'I don't really *want* death now. I am not afraid; but [I intend] to write some more or less good stuff, before going away.' The next day they took the train to Perpignan on the border and from there took several car journeys, reaching Barcelona on 24 June.

In all they spent three weeks in Spain. After several days in Barcelona, Klaus filed his first report, 'Barcelona Is Calm'. Then they ventured to the front line at the Ebro River. It was here that what turned out to be the longest and bloodiest battle of the civil war had just commenced. In *Escape to Life*, published in 1939, he described at some length his observations. From the front line they found their way with great difficulty to Valencia. En route from there to Madrid several days later, they had the unnerving experience of sharing their car with a near-skeleton of a man who was actively dying of typhus. They were in Madrid for only a day and a half, but that was enough to leave an indelible impression. In an article 'The Miracle of Madrid' for the *Pariser Tageszeitung*, Klaus described the fearlessness of everyone in the face of starvation and bombardment. What he saw there, he said, 'I shall never forget in my entire life'.

Returning to Valencia, he and Erika experienced daily life in a city near the front and under periodic bombardment. Since it was now surrounded by Franco's forces, they had to be evacuated by sea. Thanks to her British passport, Erika got out on a British destroyer. Klaus escaped on a British freighter, not by submarine, as reports reaching his parents claimed. The journey back to Barcelona he described as 'un voyage infernal' of thirty hours in intense heat with nothing to eat or drink. Arriving half dead, he had to trudge from the dock to a hotel. Following a brief stay, he and Erika left Barcelona on 14 July and, by way of Paris, reached Küsnacht a week later. Waiting for them were their parents, just back from their long tour of the United States, as well as all their brothers and sisters. There were not to be many more family reunions.

It would have been nearly impossible for anyone to have accomplished more than Klaus and Erika during those three weeks in Spain. 'We made friends with soldiers, officers, political instructors. We interviewed working women, poets, homeless children, nurses, government officials, mothers whose sons had been killed, fugitives from Guernica (Catholic priests among them), truck drivers, invalids, pilots.' They also met Alvarez del Vayo, the foreign minister, along with the defence minister and several generals. At lunches and dinners they ran into any number of old acquaintances from Germany, including several prominent German members of the Comintern. Even though by the end of 1937 the original euphoric revolutionary enthusiasm had dissipated, Klaus and Erika still sensed it.

Klaus filed a dozen newspaper reports about these experiences, made several broadcasts and used them to write a chapter in *Escape to Life*. As war-tourists they could not have been expected to understand, much less master, the impenetrable complexities of loyalist politics – the splintered factions of the left, the murderous persecution of political enemies, the reign of terror instituted by the communists. They were not much helped by having fallen into the hands – in Erika's case, into the bed – of General Hans Kahle. Kahle, a German veteran of the Great War, was a communist and a commandant in the communist-controlled International Brigades. But Klaus was never fooled, later describing the communists as a 'mendacious and unscrupulous' lot who slandered anyone who disagreed with them. When he came to write *The Turning Point* a few years later, he admitted 'I didn't have a good time in Spain, naturally'. The suffering, the destruction, the hunger had been hard enough to take. Worse still, he and Erika had left Spain fearing the Republican cause was lost.

Once back in Küsnacht on 21 July, Klaus could not wait to get down to work. While his father was in his study labouring on his long-gestated historical novel, *Lotte in Weimar,* Klaus was up in his room in a frenzy unusual even for him. For the *Pariser Tageszeitung* he produced an article a day in a series called 'Spanisches Tagebuch' ('Spanish Diary'). For the *National-Zeitung* of Basle, he wrote 'Junge Dichter in Spanien' ('Young Poets in Spain'). At the same time he was contributing articles to the *Nation*, the *Washington Post* and a number of other American publications. Somehow he managed to finish the whole section on culture in the Third Reich for *Escape to Life*. He astonished even himself. 'How remarkably simple it is for me to write! It seems to go as easily as others find breathing.' Later he added, 'Writing is the only thing that is really natural to me.'

The halcyon days came to an end as soon as Katia, Thomas and Erika returned from Sils Baselgia. The atmosphere in the house on Schiedhaldenstrasse immediately went from cloudy to dark and stormy. Father and son got on one another's nerves in a big way. In a rare outburst Klaus expressed – but only to his diary of course – his utter exasperation. 'A series of annoying little things confirm my old feeling that I cannot live with The Magician under the same roof for very long.' Three days later, when Uncle Heinrich came to visit, Klaus was appalled at his appearance. 'Very old, almost senile. We talk a bit about Monika, for whom he feels a lot of sympathy, human feeling. The Magician is often gratuitously cruel to him.' Klaus added, 'But to whom isn't he the same?'

On 30 August packers arrived to prepare the furniture and effects for shipment to Princeton. To Klaus it felt like 'a small death'. In fact it was not small. It was one thing to move two hundred miles from Munich to Zurich; only a line on the map separated the two places, which were culturally and linguistically and in almost every other way identical. It was another to cross an ocean and plunge into a vast country that was different in almost every respect. This time it was not simply moving but ripping up roots, leaving behind friends and abandoning a whole way of life. In a superficial way Klaus knew the United States very well. But how would he feel living there? He wasn't at all sure. He shared his fears with his diary. 'Deep despondency, unlike any for a long time. A paralyzing sense of gloom.'

The Manns left Küsnacht and arrived in Paris on 11 September. It was not a happy time to be there. The press was filled with reports of the horrors being committed against Jews in Vienna and in other places in Austria. The chatter Klaus heard at cafés was all about the imminence of war, though he still doubted the moment had arrived. The French seemed increasingly suspicious and even hostile toward émigrés. Everyone was waiting for Hitler's next speech and his next move. In that atmosphere the family set sail for New York, Katia and Thomas along with Elisabeth on the *New Amsterdam* and the others on the *Champlain*.

While the sea was calm throughout the voyage, Europe and Klaus were not. Two days out, he read in the ship's newspaper that Chamberlain had flown to Bad Godesberg to meet Hitler and propose a settlement of the German demand for Czechoslovakia to cede the Sudetenland. He could scarcely contain his fury. 'The cold sacrifice of the Czech Republic. One more success for Hitler. Blackmail.'

He landed in New York early on 25 September. On disembarking, he was interviewed by the *New York Herald Tribune* and, after checking into the Bedford, immediately looked up old friends. One of them was his pal Jack von Ripper, who had fled to New York and become a surprisingly successful minor painter. Later in the afternoon Klaus attended a huge rally organized by a 'Save Czechoslovakia Committee' in Madison Square Garden. There were twelve thousand attendees and one of the most roundly cheered speakers was his father who, virtually within hours of arriving in the United States as a refugee, had in effect become the de facto leader of German opposition to Germany. Actually, Thomas had staked out this claim seven months earlier on his arrival in America on 21 February. Asked by reporters at the dockside whether he had found it difficult to go into exile, the *New York Times* quoted him as replying, 'It is hard to bear. But what makes it easier is the realization of the poisoned atmosphere in Germany. That makes it easier because it's actually no loss. I carry my German culture in me. Where I am, there is Germany.'

It was a good answer. But in some ears it must have sounded impossibly arrogant. The ears were those of exiled German writers unknown in America, which was 99.9 per cent of them; being unknown, they were effectively mute. Opera singers, conductors, musicians, film producers, even actors generally encountered a friendly and often enthusiastic reception. Not so authors. Worse, their trade was not transferable. Unable to write and sometimes even to speak English, not to mention lacking the fame of Thomas Mann, they found themselves out of place, out of work, helpless, ignored and generally unwelcome.

Writing in his diary in his still far from perfect English, Klaus cogently laid out the problems facing displaced authors. 'The dilemma which confronts the writer of our time who is an exile from fascism has no historic parallel. Plato, Dante, Heine did produce great works in exile. Yet aside from their native genius, they had the psychological incentive which comes from being singled out as an exceptional instance. They were thus endowed with the role of representative men outside their native ground. The unprecedented fascist strategy of forcing a mass exodus of its writers, artists and thinkers has not only deprived the exiles of their field of action at home but of their distinctive role as well. The resulting complex of their social and psychological *dislocation* has had an important bearing on their art.'

With no income, no possibility of being published, virtually no possibility of finding jobs as writers – apart from the lucky few who were taken on temporarily as screenwriters in Hollywood – the wretches took what work they could find. Lacking the language, they were isolated from Americans, fell back upon themselves, bickered and quarrelled, all the while suffering massive culture shock. For some it was too much. Ernst Toller, Stefan Zweig and Zweig's wife killed themselves. Others, such as Heinrich Mann, sank into psychological and financial misery. At the end of the war most left the ruins of a career in the United States and returned to the physical ruins of Europe.

In the meantime a political tempest was gathering. Europe was poised between peace and war. What resulted was a faux peace when, on 30 September, Chamberlain and Daladier ventured to Munich and agreed to the dismemberment of Czechoslovakia. On hearing the news, Einstein said it was the worst day of his life. Thomas called it 'a crushing blow to democracy'. Klaus considered it the most calamitous event since Hitler came to power. '*Profound political depression*', his diary reads. 'The betrayal by the democracies. Their total degradation. Hopes vanish. Bleakness sets in. Tried to work; distracted and tired . . . The dirty liaison Hitler-Chamberlain.'

In the epilogue to *Escape to Life,* which he was then still working on, Klaus argued in essence, as did Churchill and others, that the Munich agreement would only lead to war on more favourable terms for Hitler. For days and days he was so depressed his compulsion to write abandoned him. Even the weather contributed to the gloom by depositing an unseasonably cold rain. And there was also a very personal aspect to the Czech tragedy since the Manns, except for Erika, were all Czech citizens. On the family's behalf Thomas sent Beneš a telegram of commiseration. But commiseration did not produce valid passports, and when Germany seized what remained of Czechoslovakia the following March, most of the family again found themselves stateless. Thomas and Katia were safe, having already applied for American citizenship. But Klaus was in the United States on a visitor's visa of limited duration. His only option was to lie low and stay out of sight of the authorities.

If there had been such a thing as a misery monitor and Klaus had owned one, he would no doubt have found that it registered roughly equal results for his feelings about Czechoslovakia and those about Curtiss. His friend's spectre had been haunting him. His worries were pitiable and incessant. In fact Tomski was not doing well either. His world was in ruins. Hollywood had been a bust. Worse than a bust, it had been a humiliation. In disgust he had fled for Mexico City where he sat bankrupt, bitter and bewildered. When he finally wrote, he explained that he did not have the funds to travel to New York. Klaus persuaded Katia to send him the money. Tomski thanked him coldly, but even then was silent about returning. Weeks went by and finally his patience was coming to an end. On 3 November he was introduced to a young Russian, Ury Cabell, 'un petit sauvage russe' with 'la tête faunesque de Nijinskij'. He was not Curtiss and he might not have been terribly bright but he was fun and he was – Klaus's highest qualification – gentle. He would do. In any case Curtiss, 'this crazy fool', was becoming intolerable. 'I am fed up.'

'And then suddenly Tomski was there, dressed in a yellow cowboy jacket.' Their first encounters did not go well. Klaus was frightened by him. He had a nervous way of speaking and went on endlessly about his loathing of Hollywood and the Jews who controlled it. His anti-Semitism reached such loony heights it put Klaus in mind of the craziness of Louis-Ferdinand Céline. Soon their discussions became arguments and the arguments, when about the Jews, became ugly. Klaus found Tomski's rants so compulsive as to verge on illness.

Klaus had other concerns. One of these was to help organize an exhibition at the New York World's Fair of 1939 that would stand in opposition to the official German – Nazi – pavilion. The idea was to display a German culture unsullied by Nazism. It was to be called 'The Other Germany' and would isolate Goethe's Germany from Hitler's. His father didn't think much of the idea. When Klaus raised it with Einstein, he ran into a wall. Klaus had always found the physicist, with his 'beautiful, big head', very likeable but 'strangely stubborn and childlike, if also humorous'. And stubborn he now was. 'Anything German never interested me', was his response. Klaus nonetheless persevered, and even when he was in Los Angeles at year's end, he discussed the proposal with members of the German film colony. Their minds were on other things, however. Finally Hitler settled the matter by deciding the Third Reich should not be represented at the fair – the only major country to absent itself. With that, 'The Other Germany' lost its point. What the episode showed was that Klaus was fighting a two-front war – on one side against Nazism, on the other against the lethargy and self-absorption of the exile community.

It was now late November and time to start on the lecture circuit again. Klaus had given only one talk since arriving in New York in September. It was at the Authors' Club and had been a hit. The new series began with a joint performance at Columbia University with Erika, who had become an accomplished speaker herself. On 28 November he left for the West Coast. Once again he faced the discomfort of travel, the bilious meals – 'strawberry cup, celery and olives; roast chicken; bricks of ice cream', according to one surviving menu – and loneliness. The fees, which ranged from $150 to an occasional $300, were good for those times but scarcely compensated. The tour felt like déjà vu – Portland Oregon, Chicago, St Paul, San Francisco, Fresno, Los Angeles, Kansas City and back to New York in time for family Christmas. In the early months of 1939 he resumed, now to Memphis, Toledo, Chicago, Toronto, Cincinnati, culminating in a joint performance with Erika at Carnegie Hall in New York on 15 April. While he was careful never to criticize the United States, his message was always the same – Wake up America; Hitler is a menace and must be resisted.

On 18 November Klaus had celebrated his thirty-second birthday. Over the years he had lived through so much, had succeeded at so much and had failed at so much that it was always difficult to realize how young he still was. He was so self-deprecatory that any satisfaction he found in his achievements was usually somehow tarnished. Even when he did achieve something he knew was good – the publication of *Die Sammlung*, for example – initial success usually ended in humiliating failure. A man of no luck; that seemed to him to be his destiny. His life constantly hovered between exuberant high spirits and despairing entreaties to join the dead. The ambivalence was evident in his sotto voce comment to his diary on this birthday, 'A feeling of melancholy satisfaction that I have travelled as far as I have'. For him the race of life was a hopeless flight. Whatever he did, there was always his father's fame to mock him.

For Klaus, lecturing – in reality political evangelism – was more duty than pleasure. Pleasure was writing, and in every free moment he wrote.

But for the first time even he admitted he was overdoing it. To keep up his energy he had started taking fairly large doses of Benzedrine – an amphetamine popular in artistic and intellectual circles at the time. 'Not without danger', he confessed to his diary. Holed up at the Bedford or with his parents in Princeton, he was simultaneously turning out articles for a variety of periodicals – the *Atlantic*, the *Nation* and the *Washington Post* among them – while putting the finishing touches to *Escape to Life* as well as what he referred to as his 'émigré novel', *Der Vulkan* ('The Volcano').

The idea for the novel had first come to him in early May 1936. 'Suddenly think of my next book. Perhaps it will be my most beautiful. Entirely frank, shamelessly lyrical, irreverent, despairing.' Excited though he was, he was uncharacteristically slow in getting down to work and did not begin until the following February. A month later, now back in Küsnacht, he read what he had written to family members. The reaction was not favourable, so he decided to go no further for the moment and concentrate on King Ludwig's story. Not until June 1938 did he finally start again. For nearly two years, while travelling and lecturing, he took it up whenever he had a free moment.

The topic, the tragic life of émigrés, was one that had troubled him from the time he had arrived in France in 1933 and found that Germans were considered unwelcome refugees. While he himself had the means to survive comfortably, most others did not. The sad and shabby lives to which they were reduced was the topic of the first thing he wrote in exile, a short story in December 1933 called 'Letztes Gespräch' ('Last Conversation'). Although Thomas typically did not think much of the story, when published in *Die Sammlung* in February, it had an excellent response. That year's Nobel Laureate, Roger Martin du Gard, whom Klaus had known during his visits to Paris in 1926, wrote a warm letter of praise.

The events in *Der Vulkan* take place between April 1933 and January 1939 in various places of refuge – Paris, Vienna, Prague, Amsterdam, Zurich and the United States. The fictional pendant to *Escape to Life*, it tells the stories of typical exiles who have lost everything, are legally stateless, live in constant fear of arrest and deportation and how they survive, or fail to survive. There are, roughly, two themes, very generally corresponding to the two sides of Klaus's character – the depressive and self-destructive, and the dynamic and utopian. On the one hand, the symbolism of the volcano, the ever-present threat of a malevolent destructive natural force that knows no mercy. And on the other, a positive, idealistic vision of how a new society might be constructed. The ultimate aim, then, was not just the defeat of fascism and the liberation of Germany. 'The trials and sacrifices of the emigration were a prelude – indeed, almost a precondition – to the establishment of "the kingdom of heaven on earth".'

This book about exiles was not the sort of book about exiles that pleased many exiles. Unlike other fictional works on the subject, *Der Vulkan* is not just about respectable people but also about drug addicts, homosexuals, anarchists and other social detritus. As such, Uwe Naumann observed, this aspect of the book was not only an affront to the middle class but equally to socialists and communists. 'In practically no other work in the exile literature are social and political outsiders – usually dismissed as social freaks – treated with such understanding and sympathy as in Klaus Mann's *Vulkan*.'

Klaus finished the novel on 18 February and took the manuscript to the pier where the *Aquitania* was tied up and dispatched it to Fritz Landshoff in Amsterdam. It had been quite a slog. Never before had any book cost him so much effort and time. The book was published by Querido in early May 1939. Typically, Klaus argued with himself about whether it was any good. Some years later, when he came to write *Der Wendepunkt*, the most he would say was 'my best work, perhaps'. But at the time he belittled it, observing the cold truth that power, not ideas, was what counted in the end. As he wrote memorably of both it and *Escape to Life*, 'Neither effort was adequate to resuscitate one of Hitler's victims; nor could my prose save anybody from the claws of the Gestapo or melt the callous heart of democratic consuls. A consul is a much more important man than a novelist. For the novelist can only immortalize the suffering of his fellow men, while the consul is in a position to shorten it by means of a stamp in a passport.'

Of the three most highly regarded 'émigré novels' – Lion Feuchtwanger's *Exil* (1940), Anna Seghers's *Transit* (1944) and *Der Vulkan* – Klaus's has been considered the best and is the only one still in print in German and other languages. Reviews were uniformly good. One of the the most favourable was by the competition. Feuchtwanger praised it as by far Klaus's finest work and said it placed him in the first rank of German writers. Even Thomas pronounced himself impressed. His diary shows that he read it slowly and with care. On 22 July he wrote to his son from the Netherlands, where he and Katia were vacationing, and commented he had read the book 'with emotion and amusement, pleasure and satisfaction and was more than once moved'. But he could not resist adding a malicious jab. 'For a long time they did not take you seriously, regarding you as "a sonny boy" and "windbag". There is nothing I could do about it. But it can now no longer be contested that you can achieve more than most others – hence my satisfaction in reading it.'

Which hurt more, the gratuitous sting or the backhanded compliment? Klaus had no doubt. 'Your letter which arrived this morning is such a beautiful, comforting and encouraging gift that I want to reply right away and thank you . . . You write that the good parts of *Vulkan* gave you satisfaction. And satisfaction is certainly the right word to describe my feelings on receiving your epistle.' Then, referring to the fact that Thomas was at the head of the list of those who had pronounced him to be a 'sonny boy' and a 'windbag', he went on to write, 'If it is a satisfaction to the father to see the son prove himself to some extent successful before the world, so the son, in turn, feels satisfaction in proving to the "great eye of the father" that he is more than a mere "sonny boy and windbag". That is even more the case since the father's view was at times of a rather skeptical and derisory nature.' Never before or after did he so frankly address his father.

But once again Klaus was a man of no luck. Out of a print run of three thousand, only three hundred copies were sold. He had assumed that, among the thousands of refugees strewn around Europe, there would be many to whom the book would speak personally. Instead he found, as he put it, that the volcano never erupted. Perhaps by the summer of 1939 few émigrés cared to read about a Moloch that was about to swallow them. *Der Vulkan* also aroused no interest in the United States. When he proposed an American edition to Houghton Mifflin, he was turned down, the argument being that the novel covered much the same territory as *Escape to Life*. Lunch with Alfred Knopf – 'a barbaric gentleman but this time relatively affable and civilized' – led nowhere. A call upon Bennett Cerf of Random House proved equally futile. It is easy to understand Klaus's bitterness. A few appreciative notices in return for years of hard labour.

To make matters worse, Erika's *School for Barbarians: Education Under the Nazis* came out around the same time, both in English and in German. Within a matter of a few months it sold forty thousand copies. Of course it could not have hurt that her father wrote an introduction which was prominently advertised on the jacket. Klaus can only have felt a pang of jealousy. Suddenly Erika threatened to become the better known of the *Dichterkinder* in America. Already in the early nineteen thirties she had published several admired children's books, which Ricki Hallgarten had illustrated. Now it appeared she was becoming a serious writer.

It is impossible not to sympathize with Klaus's bitterness over the failure of *Der Vulkan*. 'I see everything very darkly – personally, in terms of career, everything', he commented to his diary. 'No one wants to know anything about Vulkan. *How tired I am*. I await my death the way a child looks forward to a vacation.' It was at this very moment that he was shattered by another blow – news of the suicide of a close and admired friend, Ernst Toller. The two had known one another since the mid-1920s and when Toller landed in New York in 1936, he and Klaus travelled in the same left literary circles. As time passed Klaus noticed that Toller was increasingly distraught. His wife had left him and he was impoverished, having donated all his money to help Spanish refugees. On 12 May Klaus and he went together to Washington to attend a lunch at the White House arranged by Eleanor Roosevelt for members of PEN. Ten days later Toller hanged himself in his hotel room. Klaus gave the eulogy at the funeral service and soon afterwards published moving articles in *Die Neue Weltbüne* and the *New Republic* about their final day together. In his diary he wrote, 'He *needed* fame – to compensate for so much.' The tragedy was a page out of *Der Vulkan*. Even more stricken was Fritz Landshoff. He and Toller had shared an apartment in Berlin in the 1920s and remained extremely close. Depressive at the best of times, Fritz was so distressed for several days that either Klaus or Erika stayed with him around the clock in order to prevent his suicide.

In the meantime *Escape to Life* had finally been published. The theme, neatly stated on the title page, quoted the popular American journalist, Dorothy Thompson, 'Practically everybody who in world opinion had stood for what was currently called German culture prior to 1933 is now a refugee.' The book was the first and for a long time the only one describing cultural life in the Third Reich and the background of the mass emigration. In essence it was a who's who of émigrés from the world of music, literature, painting, science and so on – a good many of whom had at one time or another been guests at Poschinger Strasse and were known personally to the authors. The book highlighted the rupture that had occurred in the lives and careers of some of Germany's most eminent figures and at the same time showed what a windfall their presence was for the United States. To get it out in a hurry, they wrote in German, which was then translated.

The work was very favourably reviewed in the important American dailies and weeklies, though in Klaus's judgement without great depth of understanding. It sold sufficiently well to warrant reprinting soon after-wards and was a posthumous success as well. A German edition – in the original German text – was published in 1991 and came to be regarded as an important work about the country's cultural history.

While Klaus wrote most of *Escape to Life*, a more genuine joint venture was *The Other Germany*. Probably a remnant of the project for the alterna-tive pavilion at the World's Fair, it was essentially a trawl through German literature and history with the intent of salvaging German culture and showing that fascism was not grounded in the German character. The book was by no means profound but it was precocious in anticipating one of the most fervent postwar debates in academic circles, particularly in Britain. Was all German history simply a march in lock-step from Frederick Barbarossa and Frederick the Great via Bismarck to Hitler? Was the year 1933 a break or fulfilment? All the while Klaus was going on with his writing. Thanks to Benzedrine by day and sleeping pills by night, nothing stemmed the flow. There were book reviews and essays, commentaries and factual reports. He penned an anti-Nazi 'Appeal to Writers in the Third Reich', which was smuggled into Germany. Casual reading only sparked ideas for still other articles. In the course of this and the previous year he wrote nearly one hundred pieces.

Yet there was a void in Klaus's life that even writing could not fill. Despite a good number of close friends – though many were now lost in Europe – he continued to lead a life of emotional solitude. He was not domesticated. He could not take care of himself. He lived in a hotel room rather than an apartment and had all his meals out. He earned money from his writing and talks but always spent more than he made and was dependent on his parents. Occasionally he stayed a few days in Princeton but, no doubt because of his father's antipathy, never remained long. Now, as in the past, he was at home nowhere and everywhere. In America he was in a country that was not his and in a society whose way of life he did not share. In the summer of 1939 these feelings were particularly strong, bolstered by the usual postnatal emptiness that followed finishing a book. His diary continued to be punctuated by thoughts of a better life in death. The most dramatic entry was made on 27 March. 'Strange. At the moment I am not actually unhappy. Yet the almost continuous thought of death is all that makes life bearable. I *can* and *do not want* to live very long. Sometime I will seek death through the gruesome roundabout way of drugs. That will not be "weakness". I will want it.' Here, once again, emerges the mysterious 'death idea', a longing for extinction that existed independent of the circumstances of his daily life.

His unloving love life did not help. Relations with Curtiss were changing. Klaus was becoming less emotionally dependent at a time when Tomski was becoming steadily more irritable, sullen and contentious. The misunderstandings, spats and hurt feelings were as constant as the reconciliations. By July Klaus had had enough and decided to run away to California with Ury. He bought an old Buick which Ury, with considerable effort, learned more or less to drive. Klaus found his friend neither exciting nor especially intelligent, but he was likeable, and the trip went well enough. They arrived in Beverly Hills on 26 July. Klaus rented a small house that delighted him and there they spent the better part of two months.

Klaus quickly fell in with the formidable German exile community of Los Angeles and, to judge by his diary, lived in a social whirl. On arriving he went to a meeting of the Anti-Nazi League of Los Angeles, followed by a reception at the Brown Derby, was then visited by his neighbour Vicky Baum, gave a highly successful dinner party prepared by Ury, attended a large luncheon for Hollywood notables, dined with Aldous Huxley, attended a dinner party hosted by George Cukor and 'his three little boyfriends' and chatted with Billy Wilder, who apologized for having made an anti-Soviet film. He also went with Fritz Lang – 'stately, well tanned with monocle and girlfriend' – to a studio to record a programme to be transmitted to Germany. Such were a few of the highlights of his first week or two.

Always uppermost in his mind were developments in Europe, and to keep up with them he regularly looked at as many as five newspapers a day. Purchasing a new notepad for his diary he wrote on the first page, 'I scarcely dare to begin writing in a new notebook, to record such horrible things that will have occurred by the time I finish it. A murderous time. The volcano is erupting. My face and hair are already singed.' From the moment he started to keep a diary again in October 1931, the entries had been little more than a catalogue of horrors, as Hitler rose to dominance, first in Germany and then in Europe, while the democracies looked on helplessly, if not with indifference. Their folly had eaten into his soul. To him the issues, political and moral, were so clear, and the lessons of recent history so obvious, that only the willingly blind, deaf and dumb did not grasp them.

By now his political nerves were so frayed it took only one false word, even by friends, to send him into a rage. When Gumpert speculated that skilful diplomacy might succeed in detaching Italy from the Axis and align the country with Britain, Klaus cut off the discussion. 'Not a true word.' As always Golo's attitude was to look on passively as matters took their course. And when Klaus argued that German émigrés should play a role in the reconstruction of a postwar Germany and his brother disagreed, he was so overcome with anger he broke down and cried in frustration when he returned home.

But no one exasperated him more than Wystan Auden and Christopher Isherwood. When the two had arrived in New York on 28 January 1939 on the *Champlain*, Erika and Klaus were on the quarantine launch to greet them. Having left Britain at a time when war threatened, both were widely criticized in literary circles at home. Evelyn Waugh famously mocked them in his novel *Put Out More Flags*, referring to them as 'Parsnip and Pimpernel'.

Klaus disdained them not because he thought they were cowards but because he considered them fools who had not a clue about the gravity of the danger. On one occasion he was so infuriated by their pacifism and their 'British insolence combined with their "Marxist" arrogance' he told himself, 'Both are very talented. But I don't want to have anything more to do with them.' A few weeks later he ran into them at a small party also attended by Nancy Mitford and her husband Peter Rodd. Again he was disgusted. The views of these 'young British leftists is thoroughly addled by their hatred of British imperialism. They are against a war because they "do not want to defend the Empire" – as if *that* is what is at stake.'

To burn his bridges and guarantee he could never return to Britain, Christopher hatched a ruse. Not long after arriving in the United States he outspokenly condemned the 'war propaganda' of Klaus and Erika so that his words would find their way into the London press and he could not go back even if he later wanted to. He succeeded. In November 1939 his remarks were quoted in the *Daily Express* and set off a wave of public indignation. And indeed he did not return until well after the end of the war.

With Auden the differences went deeper. Klaus admired him as a poet and for a short time liked him as a person. But there had quickly developed a mutual antipathy. Within six months he was writing in his diary, 'Between Auden and me no serious contact is any longer possible.' Klaus found him intellectually mushy, a man whose confusions encompassed war, politics, religion and sex. Wystan was in fact a self-hating homosexual who referred to gays as buggers, queers and perverts. He considered gay sex not simply indecent but sinful and even sick – he had once tried to be 'cured' of it through psychoanalysis. All this Klaus simply laughed off. But what really got under his skin was Wystan's indifference to the Nazi menace and more broadly to the responsibility of the artist and intellectual in political affairs.

Certainly Wystan did not share Shelley's belief that poets are 'the unacknowledged legislators of the world', but then he didn't like Shelley's verses either. 'Writers understand nothing about politics', he said to Klaus. 'They should concern themselves with the hereafter, the real.' To Klaus this was head-in-the-sand nonsense. The future, 'the real', would be determined by political events. Auden had a very strange concept of morals if he thought they had no relevance to what went on in the world. His line, 'Everything that lives is Holy' earned the derisory repost, 'For example, Heinrich Himmler'.

Then on 23 August the real world brutally intervened. Like millions of others, Klaus was blindsided by reports of the German-Soviet non-aggression pact. At first it appeared too incredible to believe. Finally it sank in. No longer was there any ideological division between fascists and anti-fascists. 'On what basis are we now expected to fight after this brutal destruction of the Popular Front in the Russian interest?' Anti-fascist unity had been destroyed. 'Entre nous', he remarked, as though it were a secret between himself and his diary, 'an orthodox Marxist Germany would be for me almost as intolerable as the current one.' Once again he recalled René Crevel's final words, 'Je suis dégoûté de *tout*.' Uncle Heinrich was so uprooted by the accord he withdrew from sight for a time and then managed to defend Soviet policy as a defensive manoeuvre. Thomas was travelling in

Sweden and could not make anything of it. But to Klaus it was clear that war was the only way to destroy Hitler and his Reich.

The outbreak of the Second World War found Klaus in Santa Monica. After predicting it ever since Hitler came to power, he was now overwhelmed. He stayed up until one in the morning to hear Hitler's speech to the Reichstag and then wrote in English in his diary, 'This is his end' and underlined the words. The local German colony greeted the news with a tremendous sense of relief. 'We all felt', Klaus commented, 'an almost eerie euphoria, as if some terrible weight had been lifted, some long illness overcome.' He noted that in the larger world there was no enthusiasm for war on either side. In Berlin the public reacted with marked silence. 'Empty streets. No cheers.' Although he did not think the conflict would last long, he felt he must participate in some way. 'But how? Return to Europe? Patience. Wait on developments.'

From the time of his earliest contacts with *l'Amérique profonde*, Klaus was all too aware that its citizens had little or no interest in what went on outside the United States. Separated from the rest of the world by two huge oceans, most Americans felt a smug superiority to those pesky, quarrelling Europeans. They believed they had saved France and Britain in 1918; now they were again expected, in the popular phrase of the period, to 'pull England's chestnuts out of the fire'. They wanted nothing to do with it.

After years of carefully avoiding any criticism of the United States – except when it came to its puritanical attitude toward alcohol – Klaus finally lost his patience. 'These Americans', he commented on the eve of the war, 'are so happy and calm as if nothing unusual is going on.' When Roosevelt, whom he almost deified, addressed a 'peace appeal' to Hitler and Mussolini on 15 April asking for an assurance they would not attack their neighbours, Klaus was appalled. It was utterly naïve, it was terribly dangerous. 'Whatever did he have in mind? Back to the Munich methods? As if the promises of thugs are worth anything at all. The whole thing is irrelevant and disturbing.' When the president announced at the outbreak of hostilities that the United States would be neutral, he was disappointed but not surprised.

The estrangement arose not just out of differing views of international affairs. Like most German exiles, Klaus never really felt at home in the United Sates. He once said a foreigner living in France could never become French but a foreigner in America could become American. Eventually he found this was not true, at least in his case. Europe, France in particular, remained his natural home. It was where friends were. The way of life was one he knew and liked. The United States remained foreign, he had very few close friends and he was unaware that there was any way of life to like or dislike. 'Why don't Americans know how to live?' he once asked himself. He never made fun of the people, either in the great cities or in the small hick towns he visited, but he had very little in common with them. Of American urban life, he commented simply, 'Everything very, very sad.'

This was the country where he spent the last months of 1939 lecturing – he had signed up for another tour after finding the royalties for his various books inadequate. The first stop was the small Washington coastal town of Everett, the second the even smaller Yakima, after which he went on to Colorado to visit the exotic Indian village of Pueblo. In all three places he gave his talk 'After Hitler – What?' It is difficult to imagine what the topic may have meant to the Indians of Pueblo – or for that matter to the apple-growers of Yakima or the dock-workers of Everett. He was fascinated by his brief time in Pueblo. Particularly intriguing were two illiterate Indian squaws – 'beautiful, dignified and anachronistic'. In the end he was as pessimistic as usual. 'Even the type of literary endeavour directly related to current events seems remote and irrelevant in view of the rough, impe-rative realities which require action, not analysis.'

No sooner was he launched on his lecture circuit than he found himself the object of a gratuitous and malicious attack by a number of right-wing German émigrés. The principal instigator was Julius Epstein, a red-baiting journalist who years later appropriately ended up at the Hoover Institution. The ostensible issue was the Molotov-Ribbentrop agreement. Not long after its signature, Epstein asked a number of exiles, including both Thomas and Klaus Mann, whether they were for or against the accord. The question was a trap – those in favour were considered *ipso facto* communists – and Klaus fell into it. Replying well but unwisely, he maintained the matter was too complex to permit a simplistic, yes-or-no response. That provided an opening for an anonymous article in Leopold Schwarzschild's *Das Neue Tage-Buch* on 28 October claiming that Klaus was 'a Soviet agent' and had been promoting communist objectives since his youth.

Stalin would have had to be really desperate to recruit the likes of Klaus Mann as a secret agent. The denunciation was all the more shocking for having been published by Schwarzschild, with whom Klaus had always had good relations and whom he had praised to the heavens as an outstanding journalist in *Escape to Life*. What worried him was not just the accusation, preposterous as it was, but the threat that it could result in his deportation. He immediately sent the journal a letter denying that he was a communist, much less a Soviet operative, or that he had ever accepted money from communists. Schwarzschild refused to publish the statement and further refused to explain why he refused. The anonymous letter-writer Klaus suspected to be Willi Schlamm, an ex-communist and now an anti-communist zealot whose German surname appropriately means 'mud'. Inevitably the mud splattered and Klaus had to waste hours responding to the claim. 'Is that the price for the efforts of seven years?' he wondered. Eventually Schlamm was able to convince Klaus that he was not the culprit and in time even the recalcitrant Schwarzschild apologized, though only privately. Finally in early January 1940 Klaus sent an emphatic denial to Gerhart Seger, editor of the *Neue Volkszeitung* of New York, who published it shortly afterward. Clearly Klaus was the victim of a personal vendetta. But why and by whom? For the moment he succeeded in defending himself, but only for the moment.

On 18 November Klaus penned a sombre entry in his diary. 'My birthday, 33 years old. It is fine with me – and yet again *somewhat* melancholy since almost no one cares.' Tomski had gone to Cuba with a boyfriend. To Klaus it seemed that the relationship was winding down. 'The end of a love affair. I tried too hard. He is more distant from me than ever.'

The Mann family was scattered. Monika was in London with Jenö Lányi, a Hungarian art historian, whom she had met in Florence in 1936. They had been living together in Vienna and barely got out before the Germans marched in. With Klaus's encouragement they married in London. Frightened by the Blitz, they were waiting for sea passage to the United States. Michael and Gret Moser, who had also married not long before, were in London, living in the same house and waiting to leave. Michael was very loath to go. If he was not sure he would like the United States, he was damned sure he did not want to be near his father, as he frankly wrote to Katia. Golo was in Zurich editing *Mass und Wert*. Erika was living in New York.

Elisabeth was with her parents in Princeton and on Thanksgiving Day married Giuseppe Antonio Borgese, a passionately anti-fascist professor of literature at the University of Chicago. Since the hatchet-faced groom was only seven years younger than his father-in-law, a year older than his mother-in-law and thirty-six years older than his bride, the perplexed family did not quite know what to make of the match. In fact Elisabeth did not know either. 'No, I didn't know him', she later said. 'I only knew his books. But that was enough for me.' Another participant in the unhappy Mann family saga, Elisabeth was in all likelihood marrying to escape from home. Despite being her father's favourite, she grew up without any sense of self-worth. She considered herself less attractive than Erika and less intelligent than her brothers. For a time she was bulimic. Photos of her show a girl who looked and dressed like a tomboy. She tried to work through the problem by devoting herself single-mindedly to studying piano with a view to becoming a concert pianist. This had been the focus of her years in Munich and Zurich. Her other mode of liberation was marriage.

Klaus cast his usual benevolent eye on the affair. He found 'Borgi' pleasant but quirky. As he joked to Golo, he had come to the great discovery that behind all the problems of the world lay the evil genius of the pope. During the ceremony Medi seemed, as Klaus phrased it, 'rather happy'. Presumably as a result of losing his much-loved Elisabeth to someone he did not quite trust, Thomas went to pieces and sobbed throughout the proceedings. When the newlyweds left for Chicago, Thomas and Katia were home entirely alone for the first time since Erika was born.

Despite his tribulations, Klaus's life was settling down. The past two years had been a period of relative calm. Though he had taken a lot of Benzedrine, he was now off drugs. And while he periodically still talked about death, somehow his appeals to heaven lacked conviction. He travelled and wrote frenetically. He had a few homosexual friends but, having been left impotent by Benzedrine, his sex life was limited to casual encounters in the baths or hotel rooms. It cannot be said that Klaus was ever really content or that there was much in his life that was solid. But he was formidably productive, and that for the moment gave him solace.

1 Klaus aged twelve. 'I read almost a book a day – Geman Romantics and stories by Björn, Björnson, Shakespeare, Grillparzer's diary, Faust, Hamsun, Mörike, Dehmel, Walter Scott, Ibsen and Hauptmann' (*Kind dieser Zeit*).

2 The Mann family on vacation
at Hiddensee on the Baltic Sea,
summer 1924: Katia, Monika,
Michael, Elisabeth, Thomas, Klaus
and Erika.

3 Pamela Wedekind and Klaus at
the time of their 'engagement' in
summer 1924. Pamela was having
an affair with Erika and Klaus with
Gustaf Gründgens. The caricature
was drawn by their close friend
Thea (Mopsa) Sternheim.

4 The cast of *Anja und Esther*, October 1925: (from left) Gustaf Grundgrens, Erika, Pamela Wedekind and Klaus. 'The theatre was a lot of fun – the intrigues, the tension and triumphs of acting life. It was amusing and interesting to experience it all' (*Der Wendepunkt*).

5 The Mann family at tea in the garden at Poschinger Strasse in 1927: Monika, Michael, Golo, Katia, Thomas, Elisabeth, Erika and Klaus.

Twin Geniuses Follow in Father's Footsteps

Erica and Klaus Mann.

6 The 'Twin Geniuses' in America. 'The Literary Mann Twins' as portrayed in a New York newspaper on 27 February 1928 at the outset of their ten-month journey around the world.

7 Klaus and Erika in the late 1920s. For all their emotional closeness, Erika played no role in Klaus's professional life as publisher, essayist, political commentator, lecturer and arts critic.

8 After destroying a childhood diary, Klaus began on 9 October 1931 to keep a new daily record of his thoughts and activities. To the left is the first page of the new diary, and below, some of the notebooks and pocket diaries in which he subsequently wrote his notes.

9 Klaus with Annemarie Schwarzenbach (far left) and the painter Sonja Sekula (centre), *c.* 1935. Annemarie suffered periodically from severe depression and morphine addiction. Irrepressibly adventurous, she travelled frequently around Europe, the Middle East and the United States. In the summer of 1939 she purchased a Ford convertible and drove from Geneva to Istanbul, Tehran, Kabul and ultimately Turkmenistan.

DISTINGUISHED SON OF A NOTED FAMILY

KLAUS MANN

Novelist

Editor

Playwright

offers for this season's lecture subjects

AFTER HITLER—WHAT?
A FAMILY AGAINST A DICTATORSHIP
MY FATHER AND HIS WORK
THE TWO GERMANYS
SCHOOL OF HUMANITY
(Democracy and the Youth)
GERMANY YESTERDAY—GERMANY TOMORROW

[Mr. Mann will be glad to speak on a suggested
  literary subject if notified far enough in advance]

Exclusive Management
WILLIAM B. FEAKINS, INC.

500 Fifth Avenue
New York

Vista del Arroyo
Pasadena

10 Advertisement for a lecture tour in America, 1937. Determined to do whatever he could to awaken Americans to the menace of Nazism, Klaus crisscrossed the United States for three years giving public lectures.

11 Erika, Klaus and General Hans Kahle, a commander in the International Brigades in Spain during the civil war, 1938. Klaus later wrote articles about his observations for a variety of European and American publications.

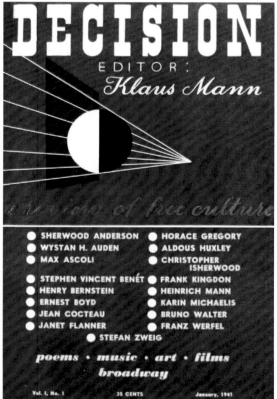

12 Thomas, Lotte Lehmann, Klaus, Erika, and Bruno, Elsa and Lotte Walter. 'Went with the Walters to visit Lotte Lehmann in her highly unusual mountain home above Santa Barbara' (Diary, 23 August 1940).

13 The high intellectual standard of *Decision* is evident in the names of the contributors to the first issue in January 1941 alone. The journal was also an outlet for Klaus's highly regarded professional criticism in art, music and film.

14 A page from an FBI report, 18 June 1942, identifying Klaus as a 'Communist [who] is openly aiding [the] Communist Party in [the] US', a sexual pervert, a sympathizer with 'the Communist cause' and, like Erika, a person who did not 'believe in marriage'. This is one of over two hundred such reports in his FBI files.

15 Thomas Quinn Curtiss in 1944. During the war Curtiss served in the American army under the Allied command in Europe and later with the air force. After military service, he settled in Paris where he was theatre critic for the *New York Herald Tribune*, writing also for the *New York Times* and *Vogue*.

16 Klaus at the ruined Poschinger Strasse family villa, in a conversation with a destitute squatter on 10 May 1945.

17 Klaus with Fritz Landshoff and his wife Rini in 1945. Even before the end of the war Klaus was in discussions with Fritz about getting *Mephisto* published in Germany.

18 Klaus concluded his military career as a correspondent of the American army newspaper *Stars and Stripes*, travelling throughout Germany as well as Austria and Czechoslovakia.

19 On 2 May, before checking into the Clinique St Luc, Klaus was photographed at a studio in Cannes. He was not pleased with the resulting images.

20 Announcement of Ariane Mnouchkine's 1979 theatrical adaptation of *Mephisto*. After opening in Paris, it appeared also in Lyon, Rome, Berlin, Munich and several other venues in Belgium and France. In all, 160,000 spectators attended the play.

CHAPTER 8

Farewell to Germany
1940–41

On 1 January *Time* magazine anointed Hitler its 'Man of the Year' for 1938. There was good cause. By then he had undone the Versailles Treaty and gone on to effect the biggest reordering of Europe since the Congress of Vienna in 1815. Britain and France were in a trance. The Americans had their isolationist heads buried even more firmly in the sand after the Republican gains in the 1938 congressional election. Then the war began and Hitler became master of Europe. Now not even the most optimistic émigré could harbour any hope of seeing his homeland again. If no homeland then no nationality and if no nationality then no native language. For a writer it was like having your hands cut off.

With considerable bitterness Klaus addressed the issue in *The Turning Point*. 'How about an author who happens to have no home? An uprooted vagabond whose name has been forgotten in the country from which he comes and is not established as yet in the land that shelters him now?' What these deracinated itinerates faced was not simply surrendering their cultural heritage but even giving up their very language. Translations, then? These were possible only for the most noted writers and more often than not with unhappy results, as Thomas could testify. So what should they do?

Klaus laid out the alternatives bluntly. 'The innermost substance of my emotional and intellectual life is, and will always remain, indissolubly tied to the German language. To renounce my language – the only possession I cherished – seemed more of a sacrifice than I could possibly bear.' But that way lay silence. The dire sales fiasco of *Der Vulkan* proved that there was effectively no market for books in German outside the Third Reich – and after 1939 outside the Third Reich meant simply Switzerland.

He drew the obvious conclusion, one of the very few German émigré authors to do so. 'The writer must not cling with stubborn nostalgia to his mother tongue [because] it becomes nonsensical to produce German books for which there would be no readers.' Instead he must 'find a new vocabulary, a new set of rhythms and devices, a new medium to articulate his sorrows and emotions, his protests, and his prayers'. And so, with typical daring, he decided 'to take a chance, to make an effort to venture into a new style'. It was a horrible wrench and it is difficult not to feel sympathy for him when around this time he chanced to see a copy of *Mass und Wert* that included his review of Gide's published diary. He looked at it 'with sadness', he said. 'The last thing I wrote in German. How much richer was my style there. Must I lose the only thing I ever possessed – my language?'

Klaus's first venture into English was a jaunty work to be called *Distinguished Visitors*. It would compile what he called the 'sad-grotesque stories' of noted visitors to the United States during the century. He had a lot of fun with the characters, which included, among others, Rimbaud and Verlaine, Baudelaire, Nijinsky, Wilde and Duse as well as Tchaikovsky, Chateaubriand and Trotsky. He began on New Year's Day and for almost nine months toiled away.

As it turned out, his practical challenge was less one of digesting a vast amount of material, though that was tough enough, than of writing his stories in an English that was sufficiently polished to be published. He was by now speaking fluently, if with an accent, but composition proved rough going. He later referred to his 'battle over the English language' in which he had to fight to conquer every word, idiom and sentence. For a time he had someone to help, but the helper turned out to be less than no help because she 'helped' so much that 'what results is hardly any more by me'. So he soldiered on alone, occasionally showing his work to one or other friend. When he gave a draft chapter to Curtiss for comment, the response was so brutal, he nearly cried in frustration.

In the end he prevailed. True, his English never achieved the sophistication of his German. But it was completely fluent and displayed humour and irony. The vocabulary was generally excellent, marred only by an occasional slip: 'hearers' instead of 'listeners', 'efficacy' rather than 'efficiency' and such. In all, it was the prose of a highly skilled native. Even his harshest critic, his father, seemed genuinely impressed.

Finally, on 14 August, Klaus was able to write to Hermann Kesten to say the manuscript was finished. He had counted on Houghton Mifflin's publishing it since they had reacted favourably when the idea was originally broached. To his shock, they turned it down. As did Random House. As did others. With some reason. He may have enjoyed writing it and conceptually it was intriguing. But the research was inadequate, the composition was careless, and two chapters remained unfinished. Considering the effort he had put into the venture, it was testimony to his emotional stability at the time that he was able to take in his stride a rejection that in earlier years would have crushed him. Sadly, he did not live to know what happened to his manuscript. Never published in the English he struggled to master, it had to wait until 1992, when a German-language translation was brought out with the title, *Distinguished Visitors: der amerikanische Traum*.

While learning English, Klaus was unlearning his native tongue. He confessed to a growing aversion even to reading books in German. 'I have a few – by Döblin, Feuchtwanger – but throughout the entire summer I did not read a single page.' He asked himself, 'Can it be that Hitler has polluted the language of Nietzsche and Hölderlin?' Of course that is precisely what was happening. There were new meanings, new words, forbidden words, words whose meanings could not be translated because of the political context. Not only did he stop reading German, he stopped writing it even privately, apart from an occasional letter. Eventually, in mid-March 1942, he began keeping his diary in English.

Antipathy to the language was matched by antagonism to the country. He realized this after giving a talk in mid-March in the small town of Hornell in northern New York. 'The Two Germanies' was the title. As he asked himself, 'To be honest, does it interest me at all any longer?? This "exile" has gone on for 7 years. Germany has become more and more foreign, distant, boring, even if still worrisome.' He now realized his night-mare had become reality. 'Germany' was now the Third Reich. Did he care any longer? He discovered he did not. 'Let them all go to hell, these philo-sophizing sadists and hysterical gangsters. *Germany makes me want to vomit.*' Would he ever go back? He doubted it. Either the world would be his home or he would be homeless. There would be no tenth year of exile.

'Exile has reached its end', he assured himself. Not only that. 'Eventually I will be alienated from all my old acquaintances or indeed with all Germans. That would be all right with me.' No longer German, not yet American. 'Again and again the oppressive feeling of being *totally* adrift and isolated – in *every* respect.'

Trouble with Germans, trouble with language, trouble with publishers. 'Trouble all around', Klaus complained to his diary on 18 February. 'Untold sadness. The wish to die is physical. The feeling of loneliness is like a frost. Everything is dissolving, breaking up . . . Tomski is also sinking into loneliness. Erika has her mind on other things because of her successes, travel, activities and her ties to Gumpert. How long ago Anja und Esther! How she has grown. No estrangement from me but step by step distancing herself. I often think I am Pygmalion. What would she be without me? What am I without her?' Then, addressing her rhetorically, he went on, 'You can't just leave me, but you know that. The nights when we cried; the days which brought us together – do you forget? Nothing forgotten. "Every eye must weep alone" – beautiful words from Auden's latest volume.'

As old friends fell away, Klaus took what fleeting consolation he could from drifters he found on the street. A few were more than simple overnighters. One was Buddie, someone he had met earlier in the year. Naïve and trusting as ever, Klaus had been intrigued, regarding him almost as an ethnological curiosity. 'Cute little scoundrel, Buddie. His fantastic life. His infantile, generous extravagance. Some people gave him $10. He spent half of it on a bottle of champagne.' In no time he was passing the night in Klaus's apartment. One evening Buddie showed up with a friend and together they went to Harlem, bought marijuana and cocaine, returned and spent the night getting stoned. Klaus reacted with almost clinical delight, finding the experience 'terribly interesting' as an example of how 'primitives' respond to drugs. Not long afterward Buddie appeared with 'cousin Jim'; both were drunk out of their minds. Jim's face was swollen and covered with blood; he had a knife cut above the ear. At this point the two started to blackmail Klaus for money, threatening to report him to the police as a drug dealer. The threats and demands for money continued for several weeks. He gave them all he could.

Klaus used the affair for a story in which Buddie became 'Speed', a vagrant who blackmails a Viennese refugee for money to buy drugs. Still uncertain about his English, he sent the text to Christopher Isherwood who found little to correct and was impressed with the story itself. 'The character of Speed', he told Klaus, 'is certainly one of the best things you've ever written.' Klaus was enormously pleased. 'So it will be dedicated to him.' Like *Distinguished Visitors*, 'Speed' was also not published in his lifetime. Only in 1990 did it get into print when it was brought out with fourteen other stories written between 1926 and 1943 as *Speed: Die Erzählungen aus dem Exil* ('Speed: Stories from Exile'). They are heavily based on Klaus's personal life – nostalgia for a happy childhood; adventures in the steamy world of cabarets, bars and saunas; the miseries of exile, homosexuality and drugs – almost everything reeking of disillusionment and despair.

The day he finished 'Speed', Klaus complained about 'the strange feeling of being "unemployed" for the first time in a long while'. The strange feeling did not last. Less than three weeks later he was at work on a new story, 'Le dernier cri'. Finished by mid-December, it appeared in *Esquire* the following May, his sole English-language short story published in his lifetime.

All the while he was weighed down by the awful incubus of a Europe destroying itself. If a single year were to be pinpointed as marking the complete end of Europe's dominance in the world, 1940 would be that year. With the advance of fascism and its lust for war, Klaus could see this calamitous finale taking place before his very eyes. The crushing of the Spanish Republic, the Russian attack on Finland, the German invasion of Denmark, Norway and the Low Countries – it was all beyond belief. Then the ultimate nightmare, the French surrender. 'France is dead – long live France!' he wrote in his diary on 26 June. For a time he could not take it in. He likened it to the death of an intimate friend. 'What is worst is not the defeat but the betrayal – Laval et al. The Duke of Windsor intriguing in Madrid. And here, Lindbergh? Mr Ford?' The way things were going he even wondered whether Lindbergh might end up in the White House.

And in fact the Wehrmacht and Luftwaffe were everywhere victorious. '*Deutschland siegt an allen Fronten*', a jubilant banner draped on the Eiffel Tower proclaimed. 'It makes you literally sick to see Nazi soldiers being photographed grinning in front of the Eiffel Tower. They smile at French girls. Some smile back. Oh, ma pauvre France!' The horror of it all followed him like a shadow. '*Hours* of doubt, despair and scepticism. Hours of *weariness* and *supine lethargy*. All of us have experienced them.' He found himself in never-ending amazement that the world revolved as usual, that somehow the sun shone, flowers bloomed and birds chirped as though nothing in the world was amiss.

There were no flowers blooming in the lives of the tens of thousands of refugees who had fled to France for safety and, now trapped, faced deportation to concentration camps. To escape they had first to secure permission to leave France, difficult enough, and then permission to enter the United States, far more difficult. 'Now the news from our people in France pours in – only too much of it', Klaus wrote in his diary on 12 July. 'Desperate cries for help – that is to say, for visas to the United States. They cable from everywhere – from Nice, Marseille. Vichy, Perpignan, Casablanca. Others are already in comparative safety, in Portugal. Others in the absolute security of death. New wave of suicides.' No one really cared about them. No one except a small number of Americans who organized themselves to help. This was, above all, the story of Frank Kingdon and Varian Fry and the Emergency Rescue Committee of New York, which eventually succeeded in assisting more than two thousand people to get away.

Among those lost in the chaos of the French capitulation and at risk of being handed over to the Gestapo were Golo, Heinrich and his wife, Nelly Kröger. 'No news of them', according to Klaus's diary as late as 17 July. Desperately worried, Thomas appealed to Agnes Meyer to help. She used all her Washington connections to do what she could, which was not much. The last the family had heard from Golo was while he was serving, as a Czech refugee, in the French army as an ambulance driver. After the surrender he was interned by the French as an alien. He escaped, was caught, was interned again and talked his way out of the camp, but still faced the risk of being discovered and deported to Germany. Heinrich, being nearly seventy, was not at first interned but, as a Mann, was in acute danger. Eventually he managed to make his way with Nelly from Nice to Marseille where he put himself in the hands of Varian Fry. A short time afterwards they were joined by Golo. Fry arranged to smuggle the three of them out, along with Alma Mahler and Franz Werfel. After making their way by foot across the Pyrenees – anything but easy for Heinrich, who was not in the best of health – they went by car to Barcelona. From there they flew – on a Lufthansa flight – to Lisbon. With great difficulty they arranged passage on a ship that left on 3 October. When they arrived in New York ten days later, Thomas, Katia and Klaus were at the pier to greet them.

Not so lucky were some of Klaus's friends and acquaintances who did not make it and committed suicide in the attempt. One of the notable cases was Walter Benjamin – noted philosopher, and also noted for being hostile to Klaus. 'I never really liked him', Klaus commented. 'But nonetheless –. It is appalling. It is *appalling*.'

Thomas, Katia, Erika and Klaus were central in the efforts on the American side to identify refugees who should be helped to escape. It was inevitable that Thomas would be involved. Commenting on his status with German exiles, Herbert Marcuse remarked in his autobiography, 'During his American exile, Thomas Mann occupied a role he never sought – Kaiser of all German émigrés, especially writers. Everything was expected of him, he was thanked for everything, he was held responsible for everything . . . It was the opinion of everyone that nothing worked without him.' Consequently it was he who had the horrible responsibility of deciding who should be helped. Erika drew up a list based on suggestions by the family and friends. It was a miserable business, their decisions essentially amounting to the difference between rescue and death. Those on the Mann's list received, if technically possible, an emergency visa. The others had little or no chance of surviving. Money was also needed and Thomas even indulged in that very American phenomenon, the fundraiser. A party he hosted collected $4,500 for the Emergency Rescue Committee. Since it generally cost $300 to get someone out of France, the thirty guests in effect helped to save fifteen stranded writers.

Unfortunately the thirty donors were exceptional. Most Americans, including President Roosevelt, sat on their hands, indifferent to the danger. And what was that danger? Klaus defined it. 'What we are now living through is nothing less than the decisive battle over the spiritual destiny of our planet. The furious attack of totalitarian barbarism is not directed solely – or even primarily – against certain racial minorities or political parties; it is against culture pure and simple.' It was beyond his comprehension that the American isolationists could not see that. Worse still were European friends such as Christopher Isherwood and Wystan Auden, who knew the world but refused to understand the need to resist Hitler by military force.

So when Klaus and Christopher met in July 1940, during Klaus's visit to his parents in California, there was an inevitable confrontation. Christopher recorded in his diary, 'I tried to explain my position and asked Klaus what he thought I should do. He said that I should "make a definite statement" in support of the Allies ... I answered that, even if I believed this, I would hesitate to make propaganda, at a safe distance of six thousand miles, encouraging other people to get killed in my place.' To this Klaus responded that, while he personally could not kill anyone, 'pacifism couldn't possibly be applied in every case: if you let Nazis kill everyone, you allowed civilization to be destroyed. I [Christopher] quoted Aldous's argument that civilization dies anyhow of blood poisoning the moment it takes up its enemies' weapons and exchanges crime for crime.'

Klaus rejected this feeble casuistry. 'Long conversation with C.I. this afternoon', he noted in his diary. 'I find it difficult to follow him in the absolute pacifism to which he now adheres. Since the disaster of Munich and the fall of the Spanish republic, the issue – war or peace? – has no relevance anymore. The democracies forfeited peace when they tried to collaborate with Hitlerism, which is the essence of war.' He added, 'What began in September 1939 is by no means another martial adventure but a desperate effort to prevent the spirit of war from conquering the world. How can a genuine pacifist disapprove of a struggle designed and destined to save pacifism?' Christopher had no answer and instead evaded the issue by remarking, 'Klaus looks very tired. He is paler, fatter and has a bald patch like a tonsure on the crown of his head. He chain-smokes nervously. But, as always, there is something very attractive and even stimulating about him. He isn't a despairing loafer, like so many of the others. He's always on the alert, always working. He has energy and courage. He says he has started writing in English. He speaks very fluently nowadays.'

Klaus and Christopher parted as friends. With Wystan there was a complete break. Humphrey Carpenter, one of Wystan's biographers, believed that his pacifist stance was partly provoked by 'the strength of the anti-Nazi cry' and the 'almost hysterical tone' of Erika and Klaus, whom Wystan considered 'virulent on the subject of Hitler and the war'. The disagreement had the effect of opening a family rift. Golo almost worshipped Wystan and, like him, adopted a quietist position of letting the juggernaut roll on without resistance. Erika strongly agreed with Klaus. Her relations with Wystan were a casualty.

During a visit to the Mann family in California at the end of 1941 the differences came to a head at the lunch table. One can easily picture the scene as the Manns dined with someone who dismissed their views on Hitler and the war as 'almost hysterical' and 'virulent'. To add to the offence Wystan made the risible comment that Klaus was wasting his life in New York, pretending too much and achieving too little. For his part Wystan was put out because he was left with the impression that the family resented his fame as a poet and did not like his partner because he was Jewish. He left them without any desire to return, and they obligingly reciprocated by hoping never to see him again.

It did not quite end there, though. During a visit to London in the summer of 1942 Erika publically denounced her husband's pacifism. 'Erika Mann does not attempt to defend or condone him', the *Evening Standard* quoted her in an interview. 'She just cannot understand his "pseudo-detachment".' The pseudo-detachment came to an abrupt stop in the spring of 1945 when the pacifist poet suddenly decided – now that the war was over – to volunteer for the American army. Thanks to high-powered connections in Washington he was endowed with the rank of major and left for Europe in April to participate in a strategic bombing survey. His appearance on the streets of London in an American army major's uniform did not go over well with the British public. 'I would never have made such a miscalculation', Isherwood remarked.

The nonsense spouted by the non-interventionists reinforced Klaus's wish somehow to be directly involved in the war. 'Once again stubborn, sad, strong preoccupation with the thought of going to Europe to make myself available. But TO WHOM and FOR WHAT?' In any event he was stuck. He had no passport and no prospects. Erika had both. The BBC had offered her a job broadcasting to Germany. She hesitated, debated and finally accepted. Klaus and a few friends saw her off at the airport on 23 August. Returning home – the family was living in Princeton at the time – Klaus wrote in his diary, 'I can't put together all the thoughts that confuse my heart. Envy – pride – sadness – feeling of being stalled.' Flying by way of Lisbon, Erika arrived in London just in time for the Blitz. Her telegrams were brief and rare. 'Safe so far' was the not wildly reassuring message her desperately worried family received on 22 September. A month later she arrived safely home. Even then she and Klaus had little contact. 'We see each other but seldom. It's not my fault; *she* rushes around like mad.' By now neither Klaus nor Erika could disguise the fact from themselves that their relationship was becoming more distant. The trip to London was not the cause but the evidence.

Not so fortunate in her transatlantic travel was poor Monika – in the family it was always 'poor Monika'. On 13 September she and Jenö – the only one of his three brothers-in-law of whom Klaus was fond – boarded the *City of Benares*, a British passenger ship sailing from Liverpool to Montreal with four hundred adults and ninety-two children being evacuated to escape the Blitz. On 18 September at a minute past midnight the ship was torpedoed on the high seas by a German submarine.

Monika later described what happened. 'It all took place in a quarter of an hour. The explosion, the initial order, the panic, the plunge into the depths, the chaos on the burning ship, our cries, our silence . . . We seemed to fall to the bottom of the sea . . . When we surfaced, we shouted to one another as best we could, we had swallowed fuel oil and were exhausted and looking for something to hold onto. We called to one another; I heard his voice three times and then no more . . . And then there were bodies floating all around me and black night and huge waves; the waves covered me entirely, they came toward me like black mountains. There were dead children, dead from shock and cold. They floated like dolls. Then pouring rain and then moonlight, and now the children floating on the black waves in the moonlight.' For twenty hours she drifted, clinging to a small open boat, until at four in the afternoon a British warship arrived, picked up the survivors and took them to Scotland.

Only nineteen children and one hundred and forty adults had survived. When Monika was finally united with her family on 28 October, she was still a nervous wreck. Klaus, the one person in the family invariably friendly to her, was appalled by the change in her physical appearance. She looked, he thought, as if she had been transformed into 'an aged spinster'. In his diary Thomas wrote, 'poor, little widow'. Both Klaus and Erika memorialized her tragedy – Klaus in a play, *The Dead Don't Care*, which incorporated Monika's first-hand account, and Erika in her novel, *A Gang of Ten*, about the children. After the war the submarine commander was put on trial by a war crimes court. He refused to apologize or express regret, arguing that he had no way of knowing children were on board.

Klaus never suffered bombs or torpedoes. But staying in America was agonizing in its own way. Almost daily he had to listen to outrageous remarks by social acquaintances. At a reception one evening a left-Catholic professor and Hannah Tillich, wife of the noted theologian, both spent the evening mouthing passionate anti-British sentiments. 'Chamberlain is more dangerous than Hitler.' 'England's victory would mean the victory of reaction.' Such were among their comments. On another occasion – and there were many more – he was subjected to, as he described it, 'a fatal combination of neo-communist slogans and egoistic-hypocritical American isolationism – an imperialist war, etc.' Even following a lecture he gave at the New School in New York – a centre for refugee German intellectuals – he heard bitter attacks on Britain. Later that day he attended a meeting of the German Writers' Association. They all talked past one another and none of them made sense. He resigned.

From Curtiss as well he endured a constant dose of Anglophobia and just about every other phobia. At the time of Trotsky's assassination in 1940 Klaus got up and left a restaurant when Curtiss launched a diatribe against Vice President Wallace, regretting that he also had not been killed by a stab in the head with an ice pick. Roosevelt, whom he considered as bad as Hitler, was the principal target of what Klaus described as 'obsessive, manic loathing, repeated over and over again with monotonous vehemence'. 'It is impossible to discuss any American political issue with you,' Curtiss once complained, 'because you go on about Hitler. When Roosevelt's dirty work is completed, even you may see how closely his present policy resembles that of the Führer . . . It is so clearly a political opportunity to send undesirables to a concentration camp.' After Roosevelt introduced conscription in 1940, Curtiss predicted that he 'would Hitlerize America overnight'. Adding to the mystery of this obnoxious fellow, he decided that summer to join the National Guard. When Klaus asked him why, he said it was 'because those tiresome Teutons have a morbid penchant for guns.'

The continuing isolationism in America, along with a widespread irrational hatred of Roosevelt, were all the more worrying because of the steady successes of the Wehrmacht. These were now so stunning that Klaus even began to wonder whether it might be necessary to flee yet again. 'If America allows Hitler to triumph – that is, continues stupidly to refuse Britain essential help – how will matters unfold? Will it be possible to remain here much longer? And where to go this time? The Magician speaks – not without a certain amused curiosity – of Tokyo or Peking.' Judging by his own diary, The Magician was anything but amused. 'From America *nothing* is to be expected. The question is whether it is humanly possible for England to hold out. If not then in this country a fascist revolution or possibly a bitter civil war can be expected.' Such was the world in the summer of 1940 when those such as the Mann family, having fled their homeland to live in Switzerland and having left there for exile in the United States, now considered fleeing to Asia.

It could be said that throughout 1940 Klaus lived parallel lives, one as an author and the other, once again, as an editor. Against the background of a world turned upside down, Klaus found that writing fiction, much as he enjoyed it, was not satisfying. He had always insisted that writers and artists had no choice but to be politically engaged. 'The more dramatic and imminent the catastrophe becomes, the more important is the job of the anti-fascist writer, especially the German anti-fascist writer', he had said in 1938. 'Now above all and more than ever we must prove to the world that there is "another Germany".' *Escape to Life* and *The Other Germany* had grown out of this conviction. So it was that towards the end of 1939 he began mulling over the idea of putting out a journal in which cultural figures could speak out. As he wrote to Golo, 'Yes, political-literary (more the latter than the former); yes indeed, a monthly by damn! – but of course in English.'

To say that his family and friends reacted with dismay would be a drastic understatement. 'Erika did not even bother to read a resumé. Landshoff avoids talking about it', he complained to his diary. Thomas and Katia warned him that this was not the time to attempt something so clearly risky. Who would support it financially and otherwise? The reactions left Klaus deeply hurt. 'How can you manage when you are so alone? So alone – how can you manage?' Who was right? Those who said culture should be put aside for the duration, or Klaus, who maintained that this was precisely the moment to keep the cultural flag flying? He hesitated. But like all dreamers, he was not to be deterred. Hard facts may be hard facts but the dreamer knows dreams can come true.

Not until 26 June 1940 does his diary mention the idea again. 'More and more taken up with the project of a new literary review. I have a hunch that it is precisely this I ought to venture on, at this crucial point – the foundation of a truly cosmopolitan magazine devoted to creative writing and the discussion of all great, timely issues. Something on a much larger scale and infinitely more exciting than *Die Sammlung* used to be. I cannot help feeling that an international forum of this particular type could have a significant function, here and now.'

His point was that culture was not a pretty ornament decorating life but an essential part of a nation's substance. And the war was not just over territory but over ideas as well. Ideas do not know national borders, so there had to be an interchange between European and American intellectuals. 'The most distinguished representatives of European literature are doomed to perish unless they have contact with the vigour and youth of American literature.'

Despite the fact that he was a complete outsider in the American and British literary worlds, Klaus had striking success in assembling a group of outstanding contributors. Recruiting them took him on what amounted to an anthropological field trip. One of the first specimens he encountered was the hugely cantankerous H.G. Wells, whom he found to be hugely cantankerous. 'I felt a sense of antipathy at the first glance (probably mutual). The small senile little mouth; his look is cold, grim and veiled. Unspeakably vain. Not under any circumstances would he condescend to have any dealings with so preposterous an exercise. Complains about everything and everyone. Regarding the English who have fled here, "They've made a mistake; they will never return to England." About all his fellow writers – Huxley, "what a fool", good old Stefan Zweig, "utterly despicable". Furious at The Magician. Constantly tried to provoke me with his fathomless hatred of everything German. Germany obviously must be dismembered, left powerless and totally disarmed (on this I agree with him). But also in passing he let it slip that culturally Germany had never achieved anything even on a level with Kipling. I reply, "You forget to mention the most ridiculous German delusion – that they possess anything one might possibly call music." All in all what a *nasty* old creature. But he had refined manners. A very fine aromatic tea he served with old-fashioned politesse – in pauses between two insulting remarks.'

Far different but rather delicate was his meeting with Aldous Huxley, whom he had known for several years. 'Tea with the Huxleys. Aldous in brilliant shape. Much less timid and intimidating than he used to be. His delightful malice, now banished from his philosophy, still animates his conversation. It pops out, most amusingly, when he describes his experiences in the film studios.' But Huxley's pacifism was a block between them. Klaus took care. 'We avoid any reference to the political situation, according to an unspoken agreement.'

No argument over pacifism with Noël Coward – gung-ho producer of the super-patriotic film *In Which We Serve* – whom Klaus had met several times socially and now wanted to enlist. 'Went to see Noël Coward, who seems to be really interested in the project. His colossal vanity is softened, even made likeable, by a really delightful charm and politesse. He was very proud of his extremely elegant figure and visible lack of a paunch.' Even more was Klaus charmed by Somerset Maugham, who offered him an essay on the prose style of Edmund Burke. 'The nicest person, Somerset Maugham. A clever and quiescent small man. Charming. Inhibitions. His peculiar stutter. He is also the best speaker at a banquet for Heinrich [Mann] and Werfel.'

Eventually Klaus's talent search took him to, in the words of his diary, 'the strange house in Brooklyn where George Davis has settled and fitted out'. 'Strange house' was putting it mildly. And, as a promiscuous gay who was mentoring America's most famous female stripteaser, George himself was not exactly the conventional bourgeois. Klaus had met him in Paris in November 1932 and they dined at Brasserie Lipp. George very proudly presented Klaus with a copy of his highly praised first novel, *The Opening of a Door*. They talked, Klaus about Cocteau and George about American literature. In October 1936 they met again in New York when Klaus sought him out at *Harper's Bazaar*, where he had just become a brilliant fiction editor. Brilliant but anarchic. In September 1940 he was sacked, ran off to Brooklyn, where he rented a ramshackle brownstone at 7 Middagh Street and moved in with his bi-sexual protégé, Carson McCullers. To help finance the venture they invited Wystan Auden and his companion Chester Kallman to join them. Eventually they took in the striptease vedette Gypsy Rose Lee, whom George was helping to write her mystery novel, *The G-String Murders*. Louis MacNeice, Benjamin Britten,

Peter Pears, Paul and Jane Bowles and Golo Mann also lived there at one time or another.

Klaus described the scene of his first visit. 'George in a blue-red plaid shirt which he wears like a kaftan over his trousers in the rude-oriental fashion. All around, a chaos of furniture, papers, lamps, colors, junk. He showed me the whole wonderful establishment – the apartment of Wystan whom I see for a few minutes with Chester, also the rooms of Carson McCullers who later arrives from the theatre with her mother. What a novel could be written about all this! George's engagement with the popular Broadway star Gypsy [Rose Lee]. McCullers, consumed by her talent, her consumption and her ridiculous love of Miro.' The scene was a bit over-powering even to the blasé Klaus Mann, who noted that Carson was in love with Annemarie Schwarzenbach, who was in love with Erika, who was married to Wystan, who lived with Chester, who was in love with Chester. What a novel indeed. For once he did not try to write it.

At their first meeting in June, Klaus had not known quite what to make of Carson, then only twenty-three but already an admired writer. 'Made a strange, new acquaintance, author of *The Heart Is A Lonely Hunter*, along with her equally strange husband, just arrived from the South', he had commented to his diary on 15 June. 'Strange, primitive, naïve and simple creature. Possibly very talented', he added. When Klaus introduced her to Annemarie, Carson was bowled over. 'She had a face that I knew would haunt me for the rest of my life.' Although the passion was not shared – Annemarie did not think well of her novel and had her own problematic affair going on at the time with another woman – Carson was besotted, so much so her husband eventually left her. A year later, when her new novel, *Reflections in a Golden Eye*, appeared, Annemarie found it had been dedicated to her.

As time passed, the establishment – which Anaïs Nin christened 'February House' since many of the communards had a birthday that month – became ever more fantastic. At one point the denizens briefly included – in addition to the resident cats – an organ grinder, his wife and two children, plus trained dogs and a chimpanzee. Not surprisingly, 7 Middagh Street became *the* social address for the trendiest clerisy who flocked to Brooklyn. Sometimes as many as a hundred are said to have dropped in on an evening. Although he knew most of them and liked some of them, Klaus found the whole arrangement outlandish and referred to the place alliteratively as '*das unheimliche Heim*', 'the creepy house'. One evening he arrived to behold George, totally naked with a cigarette in his mouth, playing the piano. Carson was lying on the floor sipping a gallon of sherry. Then Wystan entered and, in his best English schoolmaster manner, announced dinner. It would have been on such an occasion that Klaus went home and wrote in his diary in English, 'What a weird set-up, altogether.'

Even so, he and Erika often took the subway out to Brooklyn to discuss his publication. Although Klaus kept no diary between 28 January 1941 and 19 March 1942 – the period when the journal was taking shape – there is no doubt that conversations at February House were important. He recruited a number of its habitués for his board of editorial advisors and a few as contributors.

One of the denizens of 7 Middagh Street was Janet Flanner, who had been Paris correspondent of the *New Yorker* before the fall of France. On returning to the United States she had been so intrigued by Klaus, Erika and the entire Mann family that she spent eighteen months writing 'Goethe in Hollywood', a two-part 'profile' of Thomas Mann which was published in December 1941. While by no means unfriendly, the text contained errors and characterizations that infuriated its subject.

It also contained a passage suggesting that Flanner lived in some fantasyland. 'Klaus and Erika', she wrote, 'have cut the widest swath of all the Mann children, are the most traveled, and have been the most talked about, the most sought after, and the busiest sister-and-brother émigré unit here or in Europe.' On and on she went, claiming that in Paris they had been 'in the Cocteau group' and had harboured 'an almost guilty filial admiration' for their father's 'international rival, André Gide'. The article concluded, 'Klaus and Erika always know everybody everywhere and are always active in whatever country they may find themselves. In America, they are considered to have the German-émigré situation well in hand. Among the refugees here there is a standing joke that unless you are O.K.'d by Klaus and Erika you aren't a real refugee.'

Klaus was not amused, not because of her over-heated imagination but for a sentence which was a dagger in the heart. 'Klaus, the most distrait and disarming of the Manns', Flanner had written, 'has since his youth been an enthusiastic writer in that minor way that fate imposes on the sons of major writers'. When an offended Klaus met her soon afterwards at a Christmas party, she explained that in referring to him as a 'minor writer' she had simply meant he was not in the same category as a T.S. Eliot. She claimed she failed to understand what had caused offence and, needless to say, Klaus forgave her. While Janet respected Klaus in some ways, she found him egotistical and hard to get along with.

This was by no means the view of others. During these middle years of exile it was more often affection and sympathy, even compassion, that he evoked. And from no one did he receive more than from Carson McCullers. From the first, she genuinely respected his writing and was fond of him personally. At the same time she was sensitive enough to realize that he was in some ways insecure and badly needed an occasional pat on the back. As she once wrote to him, 'You should be proud of yourself. I want to be your friend, Klaus, and for us to keep in touch with each other – even if only remotely.' In a subsequent letter she remarked reassuringly, 'I miss you and think of you often' – a sentiment repeated in later correspondence. Once, sensing he was completely jaded, she did her best to reassure him, writing to him during the war, 'You are brilliantly gifted, and I believe that almost anything is possible to you. It will be fascinating to see what you will do after these war years.' She added, 'I value our friendship more, perhaps, than you realize.' Here she put her finger on the nub of a problem – his inability to believe that anyone could love him. But then he did not feel lovable.

Another sympathetic friend of those years was the clever young novelist Frederic Prokosch. Klaus and Erika had met him in October 1927 during their first American tour and had stayed in touch. Ten years on, he and Klaus met again in New York and, according to Prokosch's biographer, began 'a passionate friendship'. Just how passionate it was is not clear from Klaus's diary. But he made no secret of his admiration for Frederic as a novelist and as a skilled translator of Hölderlin's poems. In *The Turning Point* he wrote of him with great affection as a person of exceptional flair and imagination. In a nice touch he recalled that Frederic had been envious of his impending trip to Asia back in 1928. 'I went there and he didn't. Yet he saw more of it than I did.'

The admiration was reciprocated. Prokosch had a high regard for *The Devout Dance* and valued Klaus as a friend. 'I liked Klaus because of his impetuous but apprehensive form of idealism ... There was something very touching and pathetic about Klaus. He wrote his memoirs in *The Turning Point* but they barely scratched the surface . . . He was the child of a disintegrating era in Germany and his childlike idealism was doomed from the beginning. I was deeply devoted to Klaus but I felt disconcerted by him, as one might by a child who is showing symptoms of somnambulism. I knew that the day would come when Klaus would say goodbye and stumble into everlasting darkness.'

Klaus left a similar impression on yet another friend of those days, David Diamond, then in the early years of his successful career as a composer. When it came to music David was surprised to find that Klaus's knowledge was sufficiently professional that he could actually enjoy their exchanges. On one occasion he listened with fascination to a discussion between Klaus and Artur Rodzinski during a rehearsal of the American première of Shostakovich's Seventh Symphony. Once in a while he would tag along when Bruno Walter visited Elisabeth Schumann and sit in on one of her vocal coaching sessions. But even on such casual occasions what struck David was that Klaus was always rather withdrawn and seemingly on guard. Although Klaus did his best to repress his feelings, he could not, as David put it, conceal darkness from showing on his face and in his nervous movements. Sensing that something was troubling him, he tried several times to draw him out. 'Sometimes I would like to take Klaus in my arms', he once said to Carson, 'and ask him why he is so despairing.' To this she replied that it would be pointless. He was too controlled, his defences were too entrenched. Many years later David told Fredric Kroll that his overall recollection of Klaus was one of 'a wandering, poor soul'.

Be that as it may, it is hard to think that a somnambulist and wandering poor soul would have ventured to take on an enterprise as gigantic as getting a publication started from scratch. But, as Klaus proved over and over, he had grit. As a life-long book addict, he knew his way around the literary-cultural world on both sides of the Atlantic. As a result he had a good sense for who would be right for his journal. And of course he had the benefit of advice from the literati at February House. Gradually he put together a remarkable mix of sponsors and contributors and an equally remarkable mix of nationalities. The Board of Editorial Advisors speaks for itself. Among the members were Sherwood Anderson, Wysten Auden, Stephen Vincent Benét, Jean Cocteau, Aldous Huxley, Christopher

Isherwood, Heinrich Mann, Bruno Walter, Franz Werfel and Stefan Zweig. Austrian, English, French, German and American. There had never been anything like it.

When it came to the degrading business of funding, however, Klaus ran into the same problems as anyone else trying to launch a new venture. He spent months travelling around the country, touching a tycoon here and a wealthy widow there. He began early in July in Washington, where he called on Archibald MacLeish, Librarian of Congress, Michael Huxley, Secretary at the British embassy, and an official of the Czech Legation to ask for their support. It was a foolish move. It would have compromised the editorial independence of the journal and made it into a propaganda sheet. Predictably he was turned down flat. 'Worn out and somewhat depressed after a long, busy day', he noted in his diary. 'Maybe it is the "official" atmosphere of the capital that renders even the intellectuals so diplomatic and noncommittal.'

It was not the Washington atmosphere. The problem was just as acute in New York. There, William Paley, the go-getting head of CBS radio, refused to help, using the phony excuse – as did a number of others – that he would sooner use the money to save German refugees. In September Klaus ventured to San Francisco where he saw 'a lot of people – potential contributors, advisors, readers, promoters, angels and enemies'. Curtiss contributed but told Klaus that his request had put at risk their friendship – this from someone who in the past had been completely dependent on Klaus's generosity. Although he accumulated more promises than cash, somehow by November he had scraped together just enough to go ahead. Once the journal got going, he told himself, all would be well.

Before that happy time, however, he found himself at the base of a mountain of challenges. One of them threatened to scuttle the whole project and himself with it. To establish a business and to publish, he needed legal authority. This was awkward since he was not a legal resident, had not applied for naturalization and therefore faced extradition. Somehow he managed to arrange an audience with the attorney general in Washington. His diary entry for 17 November reports the result. '8 hours in the train for a 10-minute conversation with Francis Biddle in the Department of Justice. Now I will finally get this damned work permit.' Then a further difficulty arose. Because he was legally an alien, he could not earn any income. So that issue had to be fudged. Finally the moment arrived when he could begin setting up an office and recruiting staff. An advertisement in the *New York Times* for a business manager brought forth no fewer than a hundred responses. As with most new publications, finding a good title proved difficult and, from a not very inspiring list, he eventually chose *Decision. A Review of Free Culture.*

And so, as Klaus commented, 'Amazingly it materializes. There is something called "Decision, Inc," with officers, office and a bank account. The secretary looks the way a real secretary should look and apparently fails to notice that I don't look like a boss.' Klaus could never take the measure of his accomplishments. On this occasion he remarked, 'Curiously, I can't help feeling surprised when any proposition of mine is taken seriously by "the grown-ups". In this respect my attitude has hardly changed since the Zwölf-Uhr Mittagsblatt. When I was eighteen it tickled me to impersonate a theatrical critic. I never stopped wondering whether or not the printers would actually bother to set in type what I had written down. And, later, when my own plays were produced, it seemed funny and flattering that veritable actors should go out of their way to memorize my lines. This time it is a magazine.' Even when confronted by success, Klaus could not quite believe it. It was a contradiction that lent a sense of unreality in his mind to whatever he did.

He was therefore pleasantly surprised when articles began trickling in. The first came from Bruno Walter and Aldous Huxley. Then one arrived from William Carlos Williams and another from Sherwood Anderson. 'I had scarcely believed that Sherwood Anderson would really give us a story. He didn't actually commit himself when I went to see him a couple of weeks ago. Now he has come through with an enchanting tale.' Judging by the contributors, American literati welcomed an outlet of this sort. The names alone were eminent enough to ensure attention.

It is difficult to credit how Klaus managed to lay the foundation for *Decision* and simultaneously write two books (*Distinguished Visitors* and *The Turning Point*), several major articles, 'Speed' and an introduction to an American edition of Kafka's *Amerika*, while giving occasional talks and recording broadcasts to Germany. And to do all this while struggling to learn English composition. The amount of correspondence in connection with *Decision* was huge and there were endless lunches and meetings to discuss ideas and decide on contributors. At night he often attended the theatre and concerts, went to the cinema and occasionally picked up some young man on the street to take back to his hotel.

By the end of September, with a staff, a raft of articles and a bit of money, Klaus believed he should go ahead. Others, including his parents, did not. 'Some friends keep warning me to postpone the start until I have really solid backing. But I don't want to wait. Now is the time for this venture.' He reckoned that the expenses would be less than predicted and funding would flow once the publication 'had proved itself'. On 20 December the galleys of the first issue arrived and, as a *coup d'envoi*, on 7 January he and Erika hosted a cocktail party for one hundred and fifty guests. Three days later five thousand copies of the first issue of *Decision* were on the newsstands. He was pleased with it, and it sold fairly well. 'All in all I am *happy* that I undertook this adventure, risky and burdensome as it is. It was the right thing to do.' As far as can be gauged, the critical reception was on the whole highly positive. Even Thomas had strong words of praise. In a letter to Carl Sandburg, he commented, 'It seems to me that so far there has been in America no medium like *Decision*, for even the purely literary monthlies, like *Harper's* and the *Atlantic Monthly*, remain within a more conventional, circulation-conscious form.'

He was right. There were a number of good literary monthlies in the United States in the interwar period, even though many of the smaller ones did not make it through the depression. *Decision* was unique in being international in its contributors and content. It was the only outlet for European exiles, and the only one offering Americans a European perspective. All in all its pages provided an unrivalled insight into the intellectual mood of the period. It counted among its writers, including members of the board, Jean-Paul Sartre, Henry Bernstein, Jules Romains, Pierre Lazareff, Eudora Welty, Thomas Mann, Upton Sinclair, E. M. Forster, Carson McCullers and the exiled Czech president Edvard Beneš. Marianne Moore, Bertolt Brecht, Cecil Day Lewis and Stephen Spender contributed poems; Erich von Stroheim wrote on film; Bruno Walter on music; David Diamond on film music. *Decision* also published for the first time in America Virginia Woolf's *Moments of Being*.

If it is true that good deeds never go unpunished, Klaus's *Decision* demonstrates the point. Far from being overestimated, its expenses had been drastically underestimated. Circulation did not rise much above two thousand copies. By the time the third issue came out Klaus realized that to get his journal on a solid financial footing he would need at least $20,000. He had no idea where to find this sum. The problem had not arisen with *Die Sammlung* since publication expenses had been assumed by Querido. Klaus had no more native business sense than businessmen had native aesthetic sensibility. And in the hard-boiled American business world Klaus's aura alone – that of a somewhat oddball foreigner with a strange accent and idealistic dreams – would not have inspired confidence.

There can be no question that Klaus was totally dedicated. He started early in the morning and stayed until late. 'I work at least ten hours a day, or actually sixteen, taking into consideration all the lunch appointments and cocktail parties to keep the thing afloat', he wrote to Katia. But after a time the managerial side spiralled out of control and he became increasingly disorganized. Out of bed at the crack of noon, he rarely appeared in his office before two. As one of his editorial assistants, Lloyd Frankenberg, commented, 'Klaus goes to all those cocktail parties. Somebody talks a good article to him and he invites him to write it. Then when it comes in, it turns out to be unusable. So he pops it in a file marked 'accepted' and forgets all about it.' Manuscripts piled up unread, correspondence went unanswered. Printers phoned demanding payment. Irate agents and contributors called wanting to know what had become of their submissions. Matters went from bad to worse and by the end of the year Klaus was on the emotional edge. Another editorial assistant, Richard Plant, later remarked that Klaus was at this time the most nervous man he had ever met. 'He spoke too fast. He constantly fluttered around, then suddenly lurched for the telephone, then sat down and would groan, "I feel horrible" and then ramble on about something quite different. It was as though he was continuously being cranked up by some fidgety machine, completely out of control. I never knew how he ever managed just to stay seated and write.'

Klaus received little or no sympathy from his family, who considered it reckless of him ever to have gone ahead with his project and wanted the venture to be ended as soon as possible. Nonetheless, Erika wrote to Thomas warning him that an 'I told you so' attitude could easily propel Klaus into a complete breakdown. But neither she nor anyone else in the family was inclined to bail him out. To be sure, Thomas himself was in some financial difficulty because of the expenses of a house he was having constructed in Pacific Palisades. Perhaps thinking of his responsibility in the failure of *Die Sammlung*, however, and realizing that the death of *Decision* would mean the incorporeal, if not corporeal, death of his son, he tried his best to help. If he could not contribute money, he could take advantage of his contacts to lead Klaus to people who had it.

Negotiating a peace treaty could scarcely have been more convoluted than the dickering and paltering Klaus and Thomas had to engage in over the following weeks. Soon they found that they faced an Alphonse and Gaston routine – donors would donate only when other donors donated first. Even then most reneged. A meanspirited Agnes Meyer, so generous with Thomas, was not good for a single penny.

The worst of the lot was Alfred Strelsin, a New York industrialist and arts patron whose pastime was hobnobbing with cultural figures of note. When Klaus called on him on 9 April in his splendid apartment over-looking Central Park, Strelsin offered to provide the $20,000 Klaus needed. But there was a proviso. The editor's name had to be Thomas rather than Klaus Mann. The reaction of both can be surmised. Thomas told his diary 'absolutely not' and Klaus wrote to his father that it was a straight-out insult. Nonetheless they pondered how they could meet the condition in other ways. Thomas might be appointed 'editorial advisor' and contribute three or four editorials a year. Or he and Carl Sandburg might be 'joint patrons'. Klaus called on Strelsin two weeks later to discuss various proposals, only to find that the 'vulgar Croesus', as Klaus called him, would recognize Thomas alone as his valid interlocutor. In California on business a little later, Strelsin called on the Manns not once but twice, taking lunch from them and, to Thomas's annoyance, overstaying his visit. In the end he did not contribute anything. This was all too typical. Klaus was bitter. 'How cruel and capricious are the rich. As soon as they realize you are interested in their cash, they lose interest in you and in what they used to call "our common cause".' Dr Goebbels treated his intellectuals far better, he grumbled to himself. In a way he was right.

By the end of April everyone sensed that *Decision* was in terminal decline. Everyone except Klaus. On 2 May he hosted a cocktail party for all the rich and famous he could think of, believing they would outdo one another in pledging money. Not only did the event produce no money, it riled people whom he should not have riled. 'Social gatherings are certainly very pleasant affairs, but your present plight is a business plight', Max Ascoli lectured him sternly. Ascoli, an Italian political refugee married to a wealthy American, wanted *Decision* to succeed and was in a position to help, but he made Klaus crawl. And crawl he did. 'I felt very strongly that my conduct the other day in your studio may not have been exactly *comme il faut*', Klaus apologized. To Katia, however, he wrote, 'The Mephistophelian old pimp keeps me wriggling and before he will honour his repeated promises he sets down all sorts of hard and contrived conditions.' By the end of the month the situation was so desperate Klaus had no choice. On 28 May he went to Ascoli's office at the New School and flat out begged. He left with a cheque for $1,500, barely enough to get out the June issue.

On that very day, however, he sighted what he thought could be the long-hoped-for *deus ex machina* that would solve all his financial problems. It was in fact a *deus ex Chicago*, in the form of Marshall Field III, Eton and Oxford, investment banker, publisher, racehorse owner/breeder, philanthropist and heir to the fortune of a prominent Chicago family. Thanks to Thomas's good offices, Field wired Klaus that he would see him to discuss his journal. The meeting went so well Klaus felt emboldened to raise the ante and said he needed $25,000. Field's response was encouraging. He would be good for at least part of that sum but wanted to think on it. Privately Klaus reckoned that if Field would contribute at least five thousand, Ascoli would probably come in for a similar amount and *Decision* would be out of the woods, or at least partway out. On 17 June, however, the *deus* turned out to be an Icarus whose wings of wax melted at the critical moment, sending him crashing down. 'I am afraid you will be very disappointed', Klaus read in a letter from him on that day, 'but after having consulted with some of my advisors on this subject, I have decided I should not risk any money on *Decision* magazine.'

That was the end. Klaus had hinted to Erika sometime earlier that if *Decision* failed, he would commit suicide. Now he meant to keep his word. He sat down and wrote a five-page mock newspaper obituary with the headline, 'Son of Famous Novelist Commits Suicide as Magazine Fails'. The text was an unrestrained malediction against America. *Decision* was not a failure as a literary publication – far from it. It was a failure for financial reasons. 'One of the richest men in this country, Mr. Marshall Field, promised me – I swear that he *promised* me! – a considerable amount of money: at least a part, as he said, of the $20,000 needed.' Max Ascoli, whom he referred to as 'an Italian sociologist with a Mephistophelian mask in place of a human face and a wealthy wife in place of any talent', had treated him as 'a contemptible beggar'. Strelsin, 'an illiterate businessman from Rumania or Poland', merely feigned interest in culture.

Klaus acknowledged receiving encouragement from writers such as Max Lerner, Upton Sinclair and Louis Fischer. But overwhelmingly he had been cut, humiliated, betrayed. 'I went through an inferno of insults and disappointments.' And from whom? Rich Americans. 'I have seen their true face. They are callous and snobbish and selfish; paralyzed by their vanity, haunted by their mania for making money.' And that led to his ultimate target, the society from which they sprang. 'The America that Walt Whitman visualized and praised as "*the* indissoluble continent", "the divine, magnetic lands" has utterly failed to come into actual being.'

Thomas himself was hardly less bitter, later writing to his old friend Erich Kahler, 'When I think of all that I did, how I humiliated myself, how many rebuffs I received in an effort to save Klaus's *Decision*, which really deserved to survive and to which he was devoted! No use.'

After writing his 'obituary', Klaus swallowed sleeping tablets and lay down on his bed, presumably to die. When Christopher Lazare, now on the *Decision* staff, went by chance to Klaus's hotel room that evening, he found him lying on his bed asleep. He roused him so easily the apparent overdose could have been nothing more than a heavy measure, the first of a number of similarly failed 'suicide attempts' designed to satisfy honour by seeming to be genuine.

So refreshed was Klaus the next day, he decided even now not to give up. Once again he passed around the hat, begging donations from family, friends, strangers and even a few enemies, like Gottfried Bermann, with whom he had not exchanged a word in years. David Diamond not only collected money, he also gave Klaus all the royalties he had earned for a composition of background music for a film. Klaus's eyes must have popped when he opened his mail one day to find a cheque for $1,000 from a partially repentant Marshall Field. With a few other contributions he had enough to get out one last issue, a number largely devoted to occupied France. '*La douce France* bleeds and writhes – wounded, degraded, polluted, burdened with guilt and pain', were his final words in the final issue. On 29 December he wrote to Muriel Rukeyser, one of his closest assistants at *Decision*, 'Rien *à faire*. I am through. Or rather, *Decision* is . . . I am worn out and sad. I give up.'

CHAPTER 9

A New Identity
1942

The final issue of *Decision* appeared in February 1942. The journal had lasted only a year. Klaus was profoundly bitter. 'I have invested more love and labour in this thing than in any other venture before. It was all in vain.' Then he added, 'Not in vain perhaps; for I don't think *Decision* an actual failure. But it has to remain a fragment, for want of some thousand dollars. It was never given a chance.'

Klaus was right. He had brought forth a first-rate periodical and one that spoke to the intellectual needs of the time. It was a scandal that the paltry funds necessary to keep it going could not be found, money that would have been chicken-feed to countless rich Americans. To be sure, he had not been hardheaded enough at the outset. That was his impulsive, impatient side. He erred in thinking that because it should be, it could be. He was beguiled by the potential. But the fiasco ultimately reflects badly not on Klaus but on American lack of interest in a serious cultural magazine of international scope.

The point becomes vividly clear when the fortunes of *Decision* are compared to those of *Horizon*, an almost identical sort of publication established in London in December 1939 by the literary critic Cyril Connolly. In fundamental ways the journals were alike. Both were the inspiration of one man, both started from scratch, and both had generally similar aims – to make some effort, however modest, to provide the public, however limited, with some cultural sustenance in wartime. Otherwise the differences were enormous. Connolly was a well-established literary figure in an incestuous society of writers who knew, or knew of, one another. Klaus was almost entirely unknown and had to search far and wide across a vast continent for contacts and contributors. Unlike Klaus, who managed entirely on his own, Connolly had the help of Stephen Spender as assistant editor and, above all, Peter Watson as financial godfather. Watson was an enormously wealthy English art collector and philanthropist who unstintingly bankrolled the publication for its entire existence. Connolly never had money worries and had no need to occupy Klaus's quadruple role of office manager, editor, fundraiser and treasurer. That was the crucial difference in the destiny of the two journals.

There were other, if less important, contrasts. Although both men were sophisticated cosmopolites, *Horizon* was essentially English, *Decision* was international. Unlike Klaus, Connolly wanted to ignore the war as much as possible and concentrate on literature and art, and even to be entertaining. The two men themselves could scarcely have been more different. With an insouciance typical of his social class, Connolly rarely appeared in his office before noon and then withdrew to the Café Royal for a long lunch. In the week after Dunkirk, he relaxed in a cottage in Devon, worrying about his supply of champagne and cognac from France. Three thousand miles away and wild with despair, Klaus was worried to distraction about how to help writers and artists escape from France.

The history of *Horizon* refutes the argument made by Thomas and others that this was not the moment to bring out an intellectual publication. For Britain, no year since 1066 was as menacing as 1940 – the year of Dunkirk, the Blitz and the Battle of Britain. So Klaus reasonably asked himself at the time, 'If a venture of this type has a fighting chance in war-torn, beleaguered England, why should it not succeed in this neutral country?' In fact it was when he saw the first issue of *Horizon* that he was encouraged to forge ahead.

The initial print run of *Horizon* was a thousand copies. In a relatively short time it became so popular its circulation rose to ten thousand and never fell far below that figure. Ironically, its very success was almost its undoing, which Klaus had a curious role in preventing. As newsprint became increasingly scarce after the fall of Norway, *Horizon* risked losing its paper ration, thereby forcing its closure. Within the British government the most powerful argument for keeping it going was the favourable publicity it was receiving in the United States. And Klaus was primarily responsible. In a seven-page commentary in the March 1941 issue of *Decision,* he not only extolled *Horizon* as the finest of British cultural journals but went on to appeal to authorities in London to increase the number of copies authorized for export. He even called on *Decision* readers to petition the British embassy in Washington. So well did this suit the embassy's public relations programme in America, Klaus was invited to Washington to consult.

His support paralleled Connolly's own appeals to the British government to such an extent it might be thought they had colluded. In fact Connolly was not even aware of the *Decision* article until after it had appeared. On hearing about it – possibly through Erika – he wrote Klaus a cordial letter. 'I don't know what you said but I would like to thank you very much for it and to say how much we are all looking forward to seeing it.' He then went on, 'It is a very great pleasure for us to be known in America and the ideals of *Decision* are much closer to us than are a great many activities here.' He then added, in a masterpiece of ill-judged, if innocent, encouragement, 'There is so much advice I would like to give you about the horrors of editing – you will find everyone seems to let you down.'

Klaus never really recovered from the dashing of his dream. Golo later said that it left him bowed but not broken. He erred. Klaus was both bowed and broken. The demise of *Decision* was the worst blow he ever suffered. His self-confidence was demolished. He felt reduced to nothing, a reject without prospects or even hopes. The two wellsprings of his life – love and work – had run dry. There had never been much love in his life and now there was no work. His identity was so inseparable from his writing that just when the one seemed gone, he lost the other.

That was not all. He was now bankrupt. Worse than bankrupt. He had personally assumed all the debts of the journal and creditors were demanding repayment. To help relieve some of the burden he cleaned out his files and sold the lot to Yale University – legal documents, draft articles, poems, and correspondence with Auden, Gide, Huxley, Isherwood, Heinrich and Thomas Mann, William Carlos Williams and Stephan Zweig, as well as the proofs of an article by Vladimir Nabokov, 'Soviet Literature 1940'.

The structure of Klaus's life virtually fell apart after that. Failure leaves a stench which can be smelled at a long distance. He began finding he was shunned, no longer asked to give lectures, participate in meetings or even to attend them. Manuscripts were rejected, contracts cancelled. Fewer and fewer social invitations arrived. And, worst of all, his links both to the American intellectual world and to German exiles were broken. He had always been an outsider and now the full force of his isolation hit him. His parents kept a distance and even Erika had no idea of his state.

When sorrows come, they come not single spies but in battalions, as Klaus's diary for 11 June testifies. 'Feeling indescribably low. Everything goes wrong. Fed up with life as I was never before. Hankering for death like a thirsty man for a gulp of water. Yesterday Lee Keedick informed me bluntly that he does not wish to handle my lectures. *Threshold* magazine notified me that they are not interested in my review of *Mud on the Stars*. (The editor, Irwin Ross, was so pleased and humble just a year ago when I let him contribute to *Decision* and paid him an especially nice fee.) This morning *Story* magazine returned 'African Romance' (the hashish story). Erika writes me, in a roundabout way, as nicely as possible, that my visit to California seems not advisable "under the circumstances". I don't know what to do. No place to go. Nothing to look forward to. Blackout.'

When even your family spurns you, you are bound to fall into an abyss of loneliness, and there is no loneliness lonelier than being alone in a big city. 'I suppose this is the most lonely summer I've ever experienced', he wrote in his diary on 10 August. Over the years travel, writing and lecturing had been substitutes of a sort. And he had a multitude of friends and acquaintances. Above all Erika had always been there for him. Now even she was gone. And Landshoff. Once, in a particularly filthy mood, Klaus told himself his old friend would sooner let him commit suicide than help him *in extremis*. Even old affections turned cold. He discovered this one day when, of all people, Hans Aminoff turned up in New York in the company of a new, young boyfriend. They dined in a small French restaurant where the accordion music and atmosphere made Klaus so nostalgic for Paris and his life there that the evening was ruined, and he left the restaurant despondent. Between him and Aminoff he found there were no feelings at all.

Klaus's sex life, such as it was, only reinforced his isolation. The bars around Times Square offered a sexual buffet. But he was apparently shy and usually waited for someone to approach him. When that did not happen he would roam around parks and street corners, sometimes only chatting with down-and-out vagabonds whom he might help out by offering a friendly word or a little money. When he found someone to take back to his hotel, as often as not the encounter was a fiasco. A 'soldat inconnu' he picked up told him, when they got down to it, 'he did that sort of thing once and didn't like it'. Klaus gave him a few dollars and sent him on his way. 'I am left alone and cry like crazy.' On another occasion he met a young man, 'a bit too effeminate but with beautiful eyes'. They went to his room. 'Nothing happened, he left and I was alone.' Another experience was all too typical. 'There was this little fellow in a cafeteria on 42nd street – he attracts me because he is happy, simple and nice-looking and because he really *needs* someone in these terrible times. He asks me to return at 4 in the morning. I spend two hours at the baths. I return and there he is with an ugly old man and disappears with him. I have been duped, once again. I go with another guy to a small hotel on 2nd Avenue. Before even beginning anything, I find him disgusting, drunk and effeminate. I leave without even touching him. There I am, alone.' *Pars pro toto.*

To be sure, Klaus did sometimes find a sympathetic character for more than overnight. Gerry was one. 'He tells me how much he likes literature – particularly the classics. "I read quite a few things by Shakespeare – 'The Raven', for example."' Then there was Frank from Arizona. A likeable young fellow, he had had a hard life and was uneducated but had aspirations. He told Klaus 'he wanted to see a play by that Swedish fellow Eipsen'. Erika was appalled by his low-brow friends. But Klaus never looked down on them; on the contrary, he was intrigued by his 'American boys' and sometimes thought of writing a cycle of novels about them. 'But that would be too provocative', he decided, and for the time and place it would have been. Desperate as the encounters were, through them Klaus learned about a slice of American life that probably no other émigré writer ever came close to knowing.

Now and then he developed a genuine feeling for someone – Johnny Fletcher, for example. Johnny was a Wozzeck character, someone who never had a chance in life and was destined at birth for the trash heap of society. He and Klaus had met in 1942, just after the turn of the year, and hit it off right away. They were total opposites, which probably explains the mutual appeal. Many nights when Klaus was in despair, Johnny was the only one to comfort him. In June, however, he suddenly announced he had to go to Texas and left Klaus utterly dejected. 'I shall not forget the evening of his departure when he made for the bus in the blue overalls of mine, with $10 and a bottle of rye. May God bless him. I am fond of him.' Yet again Klaus had been too trusting. Johnny did not go to Texas; he went to Long Island. When he phoned from there, Klaus could not find it in himself to be angry and was merely annoyed on learning they were so close but could not meet. A week later he ran into him on Times Square. He looked so down and out Klaus felt sorry for him. 'I really care about him', he wrote in his diary that night.

By now he knew that Johnny had given him not just friendship but syphilis. A few days later the two had dinner together and in a shocking diary entry Klaus subsequently wrote, 'He is – and remains, *malgré tout* – the only person I see more or less regularly without any tension or tiresome misunderstandings coming up. He is simple and good. I am afraid I like him more rather than less, since he has given "it" to me. Feeling like a woman towards the man who made her pregnant. I bear the germ of death, thanks to him. Is that nothing to be grateful for?'

Klaus's relationship with Curtiss was toxic in a different way. Almost from the beginning there had been, psychologically speaking, a sado-masochistic taint to the association. A typical diary note – this one in March 1939 – describes Tomski as 'appalling, drunk, infuriated, hysterical but at the same time very tender and nice'. By the early 1940s this had evolved into a classic example of battered person syndrome, in which the abuser alternates kindness with cruelty, leaving the partner feeling responsible and therefore guilty and depressed, but too passive to sever ties. This was evident in several entries in Klaus's diary during a three-week period in May–June 1942, a time when Klaus's self-esteem was at zero and he was particularly vulnerable to emotional assault.

After being angry at something Klaus had said or done, Curtiss froze him out for weeks. Taking the blame on himself, Klaus commented, 'How inadequate my feeling for him must have been that I have to atone so long and in so painful a manner.' When they finally met again, the usual emotional seesaw followed. 'Better today than it was last night, when his attitude exasperated and hurt me to the limits of the endurable. (My own fault, I suppose. He is the way he is.)' Two days later he wrote, 'After dinner

I went to see Tomski – full of the most affectionate feelings and more willing than ever to get along with him. However, he launched into one of his political tirades – raving against England, FDR, the war, etc. His obvious, if unwitting, purpose in doing so was to hurt and depress me, which he accomplished only too well.'

Around this time Curtiss found a new boyfriend, but far from being resentful, Klaus was congratulatory. 'Tomski's romance progresses well, which is for me a certain relief. Total lack of jealousy. I only want to see *him* happy.' On that same day, however, Klaus recorded that they had had another 'endless, rather violent dispute' – typically, Curtiss blamed this on Klaus's 'persecution mania'. Klaus sadly remarked, 'Yes, I am afraid that problem child of mine will never cease to intrigue me. What a disconcerting blend of loyalty and cruelty in his attitude toward me ... And still he is unable to make any gesture that could possibly comfort or encourage me. Somehow he fails to realize that I am a human being, after all. To him, I am an *institution*, rather than a friend. How could I otherwise explain his appalling lack of delicacy in his conduct? I was so pleased to find that old booklet on the *Burgtheater* which I gave him as a birthday gift. The price of $5 means more of a sacrifice to me than $50 to him. He hardly looked at the thing. Left it here with me. Didn't even ask after it when he dropped in last night.' Just as in his relationship with his father, Klaus was psychologically too soft either to stand up to Curtiss or to part company with him.

Bereft of true friends, rejected by his father, devastated by the failure of *Decision* and without professional prospects, Klaus reckoned he had reached the end. The game was over. He would throw in his hand. The Klaus Mann who all his life had been a free spirit, rebellious, creative, adventurous and defiantly unconventional, now decided almost literally overnight to surrender his autonomy, his individuality even, and amalgamate himself with the mass. He would enlist in the American army. 'For the first time in my life, I want to belong to the rank and file. I am avid for subordination – hankering for anonymity.' As if to convince himself, he repeated the sentiment some weeks later. 'Yes, I want to give up my privacy and to become a private.'

Nothing could have been more natural than for someone who felt humiliated and embittered to retreat into a corner and lick his wounds. Nor was it unnatural to feel a masochistic desire for self-punishment because of failure. But Klaus went further. In joining the army he was volunteering for a form of imprisonment. He would deliver himself into the hands of others. He who had always acted with abandon would no longer make decisions. It was a willing abasement that brings to mind the dramatic example of T. E. Lawrence – colonel, war hero, 'uncrowned king of the Arabs', advisor at the Paris Peace Conference in 1919 – who created a sensation in December 1922 by changing his name and becoming a private soldier. For whatever reason, what he wanted was escape, self-effacement, a new identity – 'to forget and be forgotten', in Lawrence's own words.

In Klaus's case, submission was followed by another humiliation. The army rejected him for medical reasons. The cure for syphilis in those pre-penicillin days was slow and terrible. Fortunately, Martin Gumpert was there to help him through it. He began treatment on 4 June, injecting Klaus with an arsenic compound called Salvarsan, the only known remedy. Not since his drug treatment years before had Klaus suffered so. For commiseration he phoned George Davis, who had gone through the same regimen. 'It would be difficult, if not impossible', he wrote in his diary and no doubt said to Davis, 'to describe the ups and downs, the paroxysms of despair, relative confidence and apathy I passed through, from the day Gumpert told me about my disease. Several nights very close to suicide. It seems kind of foolish that I failed to go through with it, after all. It is exclusively the thoughts of Erika and Mielein that prevented me. And yet I may hurt them more by staying alive than I may have done than by dying.' Military authorities were informed by the FBI later on that Klaus had received thirteen arsenical and thirty-nine heavy metal injections.

Even when cured, his induction was put off. 'I am impatient to get into the army, as though the American uniform were a talisman against the evil ghosts haunting and harassing me.' What he did not know was that he had been denounced in an anonymous letter, similar in content to the article published in the *Neue Tage-Buch* in October 1939, as having been a Soviet spy ever since his youth. The letter, sent to the American embassy in London in May 1941, asserted that both Klaus and Erika were 'very active agents of the Comintern'. It continued, 'They were very active in Berlin before Hitler came to power' (Klaus would have been barely out of his teens at that point). 'Klaus Mann', it went on, 'was an active agent of Stalin in Paris, for many years.' *Decision*, it said, was a 'camouflaged Communist propaganda-instrument'. The pen pal explained, 'The first thing these Soviet propagandists do is secure highly unsuspected [*sic*] international personalities, who sign their appeals and declarations in the launching-period of their publication. In this case, besides a number of prominent American people unsuspected of Communist connections, they also obtained the name of Beneš, President of the Czechoslovak Government in London.'

The perpetrator of this 'information', it later emerged, was in fact Walther Schevenels, a Belgian anti-communist fanatic who had fled to Britain in 1940 and became an important official in the International Federation of Trade Unions. His accusations were so far fetched it is difficult to avoid suspecting that Schevenels himself was a Soviet operative whose mission was to destroy the reputations of prominent anti-communist leftists. In any case, the charges flew in the face of Klaus's public record as one of the most outspoken defenders of André Gide's dramatic attack on the Soviet Union in 1936. And what sort of espionage could he and Erika possibly have been engaged in? However, the hysterical red scare in the United States was just beginning and unsupported rumour trumped even the most common sense. Domestic intelligence agencies used all the powers they were given – and some that they were not – to spy on people who were politically defenceless, irrelevant from a security standpoint and targeted for all the wrong reasons. But they needed something to get their teeth into. So Schevenels's allegations were raw meat to the FBI which, under J. Edgar Hoover's gimlet eye, promptly set off on the chase.

Klaus's case was anything but unique. Among the American population as a whole the mere presence of foreigners had triggered an old, notorious strain of paranoia and xenophobia. Every refugee fell under suspicion. The scrutiny of German intellectual figures – *grosso modo* on the soft left – was particularly aggressive. Einstein, the whole Mann family, virtually the entire German colony in Los Angeles – novelists, actors and directors – were among countless others who were regarded as actual or potential security risks.

What had begun in September 1940 as a routine investigation of Klaus's application for naturalization got hot as a result of Schevenels's letter and then became entangled a year later in his application to join the army. By now the charges had broadened. An FBI informant testified that 'Klaus Mann, Erika Mann Auden, her husband Auden and his collaborator

Christopher Isherwood are all sexual perverts and the most morally corrupt individuals he has ever seen . . . Informant further advised that Klaus Mann is definitely a Communist.' To these revelations another exile added that 'it was an open secret' in Germany that Klaus and Erika had had incestuous relations and that this had been the subject of one of their father's novels. And as if that were still not enough to whet their prurient appetites, the gumshoes stumbled on to the fact that Klaus had for a time supported the German-American Relief Committee, an organization founded by several communist exiles to help anti-Nazis escape from Germany.

In short, a communist sex pervert! Klaus was an FBI agent's dream. If the suspicions were validated, Klaus would not merely have been rejected for citizenship and military service, he would have faced deportation. This danger was far from hypothetical. In June 1942, Immigration and Naturalization Service lawyers found there were legal grounds to expel him and were on the point of doing so. Only at the last minute was the action forestalled as a result of the intervention of someone in the executive branch, though a claim that this someone was Roosevelt himself is unlikely.

The investigations were conducted by the FBI, the Immigration and Naturalization Service and Military Intelligence, whose agents behaved like characters who might have risen out of the world of Franz Kafka, the Keystone Kops or Monty Python. Eventually they produced more than two hundred pages of reports based on stalking, snooping, telephone taps, interviews, newspaper articles and mail intercepts. The range of informants and interviewees extended from postmen, police, the staff of the Bedford, close friends, parents and their friends, neighbours and neighbours' servants, and even people who knew Klaus only by name, if that. Though his diary and letters make no mention of it, he must have been aware that he was being investigated.

The Bedford was an obvious target and the staff were only too flattered to be asked to participate in cloak-and-dagger high jinks. One of them – disguised as 'Confidential Agent T3' – attested that 'subject occupies room 1403 which faces the front of the hotel and is the fifth window in front from the east side of the building'. With that information the sleuths were able to observe the goings-on from the outside as well as the inside. And so they did. Ever on the qui-vive, T3 would on occasion 'telephonically advise' the FBI when someone arrived. Many of the visitors were characterized as

'long-hairs' – long hair at that time in America being prima facie evidence
of perversion of some sort. Agents were quick to note that when guests went
to room 1403 at night, the lights were soon afterward turned off. Removing
any remaining doubt about hanky-panky, they learned from another hotel
employee that there was only a single bed in the room. Ergo . . .

Klaus was of course followed and, to ensure that the right person was
being tracked, the stalker was informed that his prey had a nose that was
'sharp', a face that was 'oval' and a mouth that was 'medium'. On one occasion, 28 May 1942, he was followed to a doctor's office which, according to
the sleuth, he entered 'at 12:32 p.m. at which time he was wearing a gray
suit, no hat, horn-rimmed glasses and brown shoes. He left the doctor's
office at 12:47 p.m. and took a Lexington Avenue subway to 86th Street. At
this point he left the subway and walked over to Geiger's Restaurant at 206
East 86th Street and made a purchase of some pastry. It was 1:06 p.m. at this
time. He thereafter returned to the Lexington Avenue subway and took an
express train to Grand Central Station . . .' And on the report went.

The Los Angeles FBI office carried the investigation to the family home
in Pacific Palisades. There an agent interrogated a postman who 'stated that
Klaus Mann had received mail at his father's address and that he had a
discussion with Klaus Mann as to where the mailbox should be placed at
the Thomas Mann residence'. Actually he had spoken to Golo. Equally
informative was an interview with the maid at a neighbour's house. 'The
Negro domestic servant at 449 North Rockingham recalls that the Mann
family lived at 449 North Rockingham during the summer of 1940, but had
no further information.'

Of course *Decision* also came under scrutiny. Sources variously described it as 'communistic', 'subtly communistic' and 'in no way communistic'. Agent T5 'advised that there was a decadent culture behind the
magazine which was obvious from its contents', while another interviewee
maintained that the contents were 'essentially Teutonic in their thoughts
and expressions'. No one in the Bureau ever claimed to have laid eyes on a
single issue.

Klaus's finances were meticulously raked over. From 'informants' – hotel
staff again – agents learned that he had an outstanding bill at the Bedford
of $500. They grilled Klaus himself on his own income as well as his
father's. Questions about paying taxes on his royalties, such as they were, he

successfully parried. He could truthfully say that Thomas was his principal source of funds. Sex, politics, money. No aspect of his life was left unexamined and there seems to have been no deadline on clearing him. For Klaus, in the summer of 1942 this meant that his applications for military service and citizenship were indefinitely stalled. All the same he applied for a job with the Office of War Information, a propaganda outfit created to undermine German morale. Needless to say he was turned down, even though Erika was at the time working for the agency.

He had no alternative but to while away the time, and whiling away time for him, even in his dire mood, meant writing. In fact he had only just finished one of his major works, his second autobiography, *The Turning Point*. He had begun it on 11 August the previous year and laboured on through the long, miserable summer as *Decision* was in its death throes. That he somehow managed to edit a journal, hunt for money to keep it going and at the same time to write a book – in English – speaks for how hard he could work.

Klaus had all his life been searching for himself, wondering who he was, where he had been and where he was going. He was introspective by nature, and an important aim of his diary had been to record his confessions. Following the failure of *Decision*, he touched bottom. He was stripped bare. 'I don't want to lie anymore. I am fed up with all disguises and contrivances. Whom should I try to please or impress? I am alone. I am free. I possess nothing nor do I wish to possess anything. Whatever I may have owned has been taken from me – even the language I used to consider mine.'

It was in this mood he had started work on *The Turning Point*, and just before putting pen to paper, he wrote in his diary, as though he were counselling himself, 'To tell the truth, the whole truth, and nothing but the truth. To tell my own story.' The entry continued, 'To tell the story of an intellectual in the period from 1920 to 1940 – a character who spent the best time of his life in a social and spiritual vacuum, striving for a true community but never finding it, disconnected, restless, wandering, haunted by those solemn abstractions in which nobody else believes – civilization, progress, liberty. To tell the story of a German who wanted to be a European, of a European who wanted to be a citizen of the world.'

The Turning Point, like all autobiography, is a broth of fact seasoned with a bit of *suppressio veri* and a touch of *suggestio falsi*. It is as though the author has poured the story of his life through a sieve and strained out the loneliness, hurt, anger, agonies, sexual frustration, longing for death and the like. He is frank about his own failings – his self-obsession, rebellious-ness, compulsive nonconformity and desire for quick fame, along with the disorderliness of his life. He is extremely guarded, however, about his family. The words about his father, while not affectionate, are admiring. Thomas emerges as distant and preoccupied rather than harsh or unloving, though heartily exasperated at times by his son's bohemian life.

The text, written with sophistication and humour – and not a little of his father's irony – shows that Klaus was one of the very few German exile writers to master the English language. Paradoxically the book was published by his old nemesis Gottfried Bermann, who had moved the old firm S. Fischer from Berlin to Vienna, then to Stockholm and, after merging with Querido, finally to New York in 1940.

The Turning Point concludes with what amounts to a virtual political testament. The argument was simple. Nationalism is the original sin. It inevitably leads to war. The founder of civilization was the first person to throw an epithet rather than a spear at his enemy – the point Freud made in his *Civilization and Its Discontents*, a book Klaus read only several years later. This was the cornerstone of his political credo and all his hopes for a postwar world order. 'I am not interested in countries and their spheres of influence. All I believe in is the indivisible, universal civilization to be created by man where one will be at everywhere or nowhere.' A first crucial step towards this 'universal civilization' was Franco-German reconciliation. That ideal broadened into the dream of the new world order that he hoped would emerge after the war. It would be a place where nationalism and national boundaries would effectively vanish. Eventually he came to ask himself, 'Shall I ever live in Germany again? I don't think so. Or rather, the question has lost its relevance as far as I am concerned. I have gone far – too far, indeed, to go back. You can't go home again nor can you find a new home. The world will be your home or you will be homeless, disconnected, doomed.'

Just at that point America entered the war. Turning the European conflict into a global battle for unconditional surrender would, Klaus believed, cause a moral brutalization of society. The combatants would accept no limits on their actions and out of this mayhem would come

saturation bombing of cities, war crimes and mass murder. As a consequence, moral destruction would lead to physical destruction, which would
lead to further moral destruction. 'How often I am *paralyzed* by the infinite
sadness of the war', he wrote in his diary on 22 March. 'The fact that it *had*
to be is so overwhelmingly depressing that it requires almost superhuman
(or inhuman!) callousness to remain duly interested in the war.'

This view hardened in him, despite his outstanding application to join
the army. While visiting his family in California that summer, the issue of
the mass destruction of German cities was mentioned at Sunday lunch.
Going back to his youth, mealtimes were dangerous; one false word could
provoke Thomas to explode. Several times in his diary Klaus mentions that
when he and his father were alone at a meal, remarks were strictly limited
to trivialities. But on family occasions, the conversation was not always
guarded. This Sunday, 26 July, was one of them.

In the spring of 1942 the RAF began its terror bombing of German
cities. Thomas's birthplace, Lübeck – though a cultural centre of no military
significance – was the first victim. Thomas defended the conduct of the war
and believed the German people were getting what they deserved. When he
saw photos of the ruins of his old family home and the neighbourhood he
knew well from his youth, he consoled himself with the thought that the
people of Lübeck had in 1933 been among the most devout Nazis. 'To keep
things in perspective', he said, after a devastating raid on Cologne, 'you
must think of Prague and Poland, must think of Guernica, of Rotterdam. It
is a bitter necessity.' As the bombings went on, he asked himself, 'What
atonement will destiny bring? It can never be too terrible.'

By now Klaus found such talk unbearable. So on this occasion he took
issue with his father, saying something to the effect that to fight the war like
Nazis was to risk becoming Nazis. His comment enraged Thomas to the
extent that he unleashed such a stream of abuse that Klaus fled from the
table. When he did not appear at meals the next day, Thomas told the family
he was sorry for having lost his temper but then went on again to vent so
much hostility toward his son that Erika stormed from the room in fury.
Whether Klaus ever manifested himself again was a matter of indifference
to Thomas. But Erika's defection devastated him. As his diary records, 'Ill.
Monday and Tuesday in bed, taking only soup.' The whole sorry episode
was then repeated between Klaus and Golo. All of which went to prove,

once again, that the unhappy Mann family remained unhappy in its own special way.

In reality the differences between father and son were not all that great. Klaus recognized the need for military force and Thomas keenly felt the horror of the destruction. There were, moreover, other issues on which Klaus and Thomas were in heated agreement. About now both were becoming disillusioned with the United States. Never could Klaus comprehend the indifference of the American public to the larger world, its failure to take the measure of the Nazi threat and its apathy towards the desperate situation of Britain after the fall of France – indeed, the outright Anglophobia he encountered at almost every turn. That attitude changed once America was in the war but was replaced by the rise of anti-communist hysteria, which seemed almost to make communism rather than Nazism the great enemy. More worrying still was the failure of anyone in the country to think about the shape of a postwar world. 'I don't see any reason to hope that America will live up to her tremendous mission', he wrote in his unfinished novel, *The Last Decision*. 'What I see is smugness and ignorance, greed and vanity.'

So in April 1942, when Roosevelt announced 'A War for Survival', Klaus was alarmed. The president appeared to look forward not to the end of nationalism but to a slightly revised version of the old system of nation-states and their spheres of influence. As a German, Klaus was the first to recognize that when power was in the hands of a political zealot, the results were bound to be disastrous. And behold, there suddenly appeared Henry Luce who, through his magazines *Time* and *Life*, began advocating, if not predicting, a postwar world dominated by a messianic America. In a long-winded editorial in *Life*, he essentially argued that the United States should run the world for the good of the world. Hence the twentieth century would become 'the first great American century'. Klaus had had more than enough of that hubristic nationalism from Hitler. 'If I have to make up my mind between the lugubrious prophesies of Dr Paul Joseph Goebbels and Henry Luce's dashing vision of an "American Century", I prefer – suicide.' He went on, 'This century is not the Germanic Century nor is it the American Century nor the Century of the Soviet Union. It is the century to prepare the birth of the indivisible, universal civilization.' This was utterly illusionary of course and anything but what that century turned into.

Nonetheless, Klaus's ideals – a rejuvenation of democracy, the suppression of nationalism, the creation of federal relationships among nations – became the same goals that animated Schumann, Adenauer and de Gasperi after the war and that led to the foundation of the European Union.

Klaus finished *The Turning Point* on 28 May. A few weeks later he went alone to see Noël Coward's recent comedy *Blithe Spirit*, a spoof about the supernatural. So delighted was he, he immediately thought of developing similar ideas of his own for a short story to be entitled 'Ghost Story'. Scarcely had he started work when on 19 June he received a concrete offer from a small New York publisher, Creative Age, to bring out a brief work on André Gide, a project he had had in mind for years. Around the same time Katia finally took pity on him and sent money for the train fare to Pacific Palisades. And it is there that he wrote – at his usual supersonic speed – the main part of the book. Complete by early October, it was published the following year.

Klaus returned to New York on 28 August just as *The Turning Point* appeared in print. A copy reached the family in early September. In a telegram signed 'YOUR DEAR ONES' but no doubt written by Erika, they expressed their delight. 'WHOLE FAMILY READING FRANTICALLY. DAD DEEPLY CAPTIVATED. MIELEIN CONFUSED AND TOUCHED BY SPLENDID MONUMENT WHICH SHOULD BRING CREATOR AS MUCH GLORY AS IT BRINGS HER HONOUR. E[rika]. GREATLY SURPRISED, MOVED AND AFFECTED. EVERYBODY WISHING LUCK AND SENDING LOVE.'

The book, written in a hurry and almost as a pastime – not to mention at a miserable period of his life – was quite different from *Kind dieser Zeit* and after the war he rewrote it. Whatever its shortcomings, it was a fascinating story, well and ironically told. He had reason to be content with the reception. Bermann was delighted and on 7 October wrote to Thomas, 'The *N.Y. Times, Herald Tribune, World Telegram, Chicago Daily News* and many others have published excellent reviews. We hope to have good sales during the next week.' In a comment on his writing style, the reviewer for the *New York Herald Tribune* remarked, 'Were it not for an occasional slang phrase dropped awkwardly into its formal prose or for a slightly German flavor to its transcendentalism, *The Turning Point* might have been written by any American writer who spent the '20s in Paris and returned home to social consciousness and the front against Fascism.'

But that was not the review Klaus cared about. Muriel Rukeyser described Klaus's mood on the Day of Judgement. 'He longed for the letter from his father. I was there when it arrived; that letter meant more to Klaus Mann than can be said; he read it in a moving, suspended moment of all the mixed feelings that can be found in the autobiography itself.'

Thomas pronounced judgement in his usual logorrhoeic style. 'It is an unusually charming, sensitively warm-hearted, accomplished and personally candid book.' He praised the writing style as so fluent and skilled, he couldn't help wondering who the translator was. 'We old folks can be content with the impression we left.' The words about Katia, he added, could not have been more affectionately filial. She herself saw the book as her trophy. The chapter 'Olympus', he said, was the *pièce de résistance*. He was touched by Klaus's recollection of a scene in his youth when he was leaving home and turned back to see his father waving goodbye. In commenting in his diary on the favourable response of friends and book reviewers, with not a word does Klaus refer to his father.

In addition to the good reviews in the dailies and the weekly journals, Klaus received any number of laudatory letters from persons of note. But the work failed to make the breakthrough into the American literary world that he and Bermann had hoped. Neither did it catch public attention. The United States was now at war and the life of an émigré writer held little interest for the American public. Only several hundred copies were sold. To add to the humiliation, Franz Werfel's vomitous novel, *The Song of Bernadette*, published at the same time, was a runaway bestseller. Yet again a man of no luck.

Klaus returned to New York on 2 September and two days later appeared for his induction into the army. After a very thorough examination, he was both accepted and rejected. He was declared eligible but his entry was put off for six months. He didn't realize, he said, how arduous it would be to get into this 'exclusive club'. An application to join the branch of military intelligence preparing for the postwar occupation of Germany was turned down. He did his best to cheer himself up. '6 months will pass quickly. Or, more accurately, 4 months and 28 days.'

Time did not pass quickly. The weeks that followed were a calvary. A person who all his life, as photographs show, had been meticulous about his appearance, was always well and expensively dressed and carefully coiffed, was now so impoverished he was nearly reduced to the level of a bum. The awful shadow of indignity was not even lifted by the favourable reception of *The Turning Point*. 'Encouraging', he told his diary, 'but my pleasure is considerably spoiled by the constant, humiliating, almost unbearable lack of money. Completely broke for days. ... Haunted by the suicide idea.' Penury and death were the twin themes that dominated his life during the ensuing months. Did his financial situation justify 'making this final gesture', he asked himself over and over. 'I consider it unbearably humiliating that I have to go about like a Parnassian simply because I don't have the cash to get myself a haircut. *Tomorrow will be another* day without a proper meal and the need to think over for a long time whether I can afford both to ride the subway *and* to buy a newspaper. I would have gone hungry yesterday and today had Johnny not taken my brown suit to the pawn shop.' When Carson McCullers interrupted these lamentations by phoning to praise *The Turning Point*, Klaus found the conversation wearisome. 'I feel like an actor who plays a part when I talk to people.' When she rang off, thoughts of suicide returned.

Emotional suffering and physical suffering reinforced one another. 'Passed the morning till noon without anything to eat, of course', runs a typical diary passage. 'My total capital is 65 cents.' Faced with a choice between food and art, he chose art and spent much of the sum on a visit to the newly opened Guggenheim Art Collection, which he wanted to write an article about. Hunger did not impair his aesthetic judgement and most of the works he found disappointing. 'Apart from a marvelous de Chirico (Pink Tower) and one sad and lovely Chagall, there was little to admire. The few Picassos did not amount to much and the Max Ernsts even less.'

From the museum he walked to Gumpert's office for an injection and then to a cafeteria for lunch. The meal cost thirty cents, leaving him five, 'which I treasure'. That afternoon Curtiss phoned and offered to take him to dinner at seven. 'So I postpone my suicide.' But then he called again to say he couldn't meet until ten. Klaus was starving and in despair when Johnny arrived. 'Realizing I am broke and hungry, he insists on my coming with him to Thompson's where he spends his last penny to buy me something to eat. I am infinitely grateful for this simple gesture and I will not forget it.' And indeed he did not forget that night. When they returned to the Bedford, a military officer was waiting for Johnny and arrested him.

Klaus was in a state of shock when Curtiss finally phoned to say he was with friends and could not keep their date after all. It was the last straw. 'This is obviously the right moment. I decide not to lose time anymore but to do "it" quickly. I get a hot bath ready and take the little knife – the one I bought several weeks ago for this particular purpose. I try to cut the artery on my right wrist. But the knife is not as sharp as I expected; besides it is kind of dirty – the knife, I mean, and not the whole affair. It hurts – not badly but unpleasantly. I begin to bleed. I stop – scared, I suppose. As I wonder whether I ought to try it again, the phone rings – Christopher [Lazare] wants to have drinks with me.' That was the end of the 'suicide attempt' that day. The two spent the rest of the night drinking. When Lazare belaboured him for having been taken in by Johnny – 'a pathological liar' – Klaus replied simply, 'All I can answer is that Johnny is a good guy and was always decent to me and that I like him.'

Klaus awoke the next morning unable to think of anything but death. In the course of the day he planned his funeral. 'No speeches, please! no music! no flowers! no lies.' He would die tired and sad but without bitterness. 'It's just that I can't stand life anymore.' He added in scarcely legible scratching in his diary, 'My last wish is that John Fletcher, Cell 19, [will be] decently treated.' Johnny, he had learned, was to be court-martialled as a deserter. 'A hard blow.'

Some hours later, at one a.m., Klaus made another attempt, equally half-hearted, to slit his wrists. A half-hour after that Johnny's girlfriend, Helen, turned up at the hotel where she introduced herself as Johnny's wife. 'After having sobbed a little, she tells me her whole biography. The orphanage, the misery, the disease, mental collapse. Home for derelict girls. On the street again. Johnny, misery and love.' Helen left at three. Hearing the account of her tragic life and her now thwarted love for Johnny, Klaus was so deeply moved he suddenly felt that his own problems were in comparison not so tragic after all. He fell asleep. On waking five hours later he found he was possessed by one thought. 'I shall try to live again. The visit of that poor little creature, Helen, was saddening; but it somehow helped me regain my equilibrium.'

'Writers are not people exactly', says a character in F. Scott Fitzgerald's novel *The Last Tycoon*. He might have had Klaus in mind. The contradiction in his life – creativity versus oblivion – was never more blatant than now and in the months to come. Utterly impoverished, syphilitic, trapped in destructive relationships, more isolated than ever, ignored by his family, depressed to the point of feeling suicidal, he at the same time craved doing what he most loved to do. So with his enormous powers of concentration, he went on writing as though his life were as peaceful and regulated as his father's. After finishing *The Turning Point* at the end of May, he immediately started work on his long-planned biographical study of Gide. As if that were not enough he agreed to a joint project with Hermann Kesten to be published by Gottfried Bermann. It was to be an anthology of essays by no fewer than a hundred and forty-one European writers from twenty-one countries. Although Klaus was not excited about the topic, they finished it in the course of several months. It was published with the title *Heart of Europe: An Anthology of Creative Writing in Europe 1920–1940.*

Work did not stop there. Not only did he give the odd talk, in the two final months of the year he also wrote no fewer than six review-essays: 'Virginia Woolf's Posthumous Essays', 'M. André Maurois's Reminiscences of Pre-Vichy France', 'Germany's Generals – Villains and Victims of this War', 'Klaus Mann Gaily Reports Family's Prodigious Reading', 'Memories of Free France: Exhortation to Her Conquerers' and 'Dorothy Thompson Speaks to Her German Friend, Hans'. It was the piece about Virginia Woolf, one of his favourite authors, that interested him most. Her suicide in 1941 had deepened his fascination with her life and work and it is likely that one of the essays under review, 'The Death of the Moth' – the first published after her death – spoke directly to him as a metaphor for his own situation. In the story, a moth, wishing to realize its instinct and fly, wears itself out in the attempt to escape through the window and dies. 'Oh yes, he seemed to say, death is stronger than I am.'

It was now December. The American army needed men so badly recruiting officials were not fussy about whom they took into the ranks. After another medical check-up, Klaus was officially accepted on 14 December and inducted just before the end of the year.

CHAPTER 10

'Misplaced'
1943

Klaus began his military career not on a rifle range learning to kill but in the infirmary at Fort Dix in New Jersey, where doctors made sure he was cured of the pox. Finally, on 2 February 1943, he was shipped to Camp Robinson in Arkansas for basic training. And so began the rocambolesque adventures and misadventures familiar to probably every recruit in every army in history. From now on his life was at the whim of invisible forces. He might be transferred from one unit to another without any apparent reason. Or he might be assigned to do technical work for which he had no qualification. Alternatively, he might be so massively overqualified his superiors had no idea what to do with him.

Basic training was above all a levelling experience. Klaus came from one end of the social and intellectual scale, his fellow recruits – mostly Brooklynite manual workers of Italian descent – from the other. To be sure, he'd had years of contact with uneducated young guys from the street, and he may have seen his army buddies as so many Franks, Gerrys and Johnnys. But now he lived among them as an equal. He dressed like them, ate the same army chow in a communal mess hall, slept on a narrow cot in a barracks without any privacy and waited for hours in long queues, sometimes without reason. He peeled tons of potatoes, mopped acres of latrine floors and retrieved bushels of cigarette butts from the camp grounds. When he travelled by rail it was no longer in a Pullman sleeping car but sitting upright in an uncomfortable, overcrowded, un-airconditioned troop train that was invariably many hours late.

Military life above all demands mindless conformity. With his strange accent and manner, Klaus had no hope of being a typical soldier. He tried, but the cultural gulf was too vast. Happily, the other recruits seem to have accepted him with good humour. Not so some of the professional non-coms who saw it as their responsibility to humiliate this brainy, upper-class foreigner. Klaus never expected to be given special treatment because of his age or background but even less did he anticipate being punished for it. And if he hoped for once in his life to escape the shadow of his father, he was disappointed. 'Don't think you will have any privileges just because you are the son of Thomas Mann', he was brutally told by one training sergeant within a few days of arriving in camp. And with that *Liebesgruss* he was dispatched to the kitchen to work from five in the morning until ten that night.

For Klaus, military life was not just normal martial initiation, it was also a crash course in Americanization. Thanks to his lecture tours, he already knew the country geographically at first hand better than other German émigrés – and most Americans for that matter. And like no other exile he had ventured into small-town, middle America in remote parts of the Midwest and the northern Pacific coast. But he didn't know Americans. Giving a talk and then attending a dinner with the Kiwanis Club or speaking to the solid burghers of a small town in Kansas was not the same as rubbing shoulders with undereducated plumbers, car mechanics and farmhands who would probably have had difficulty pointing to Germany on a map. He had wanted to lose himself in the mass and was now succeeding magnificently.

With little or nothing in common, Klaus and the other recruits had little or nothing to talk about. He told them about his travels and his writings, but that only isolated him further. Even though they did not have much to say to one another, he was fascinated to hear their street slang and GI jargon, and made long lists of phrases which he translated into conventional English. Latrine graffiti also intrigued him; he even admitted to being 'unduly fascinated' by it, but more often than not found it revolting. In the barracks the predominant topic of conversation, inevitable among twenty-somethings with raging hormones, was sex. This was not a subject Klaus could participate in. To appear to be one of the boys, however, he decided at least to imitate them by tacking a photo of a sweetheart on the wall by his bed. Where to find one? The fascinating but boyish-looking

Annemarie Schwarzenbach would scarcely do. Eventually he thought of Lotte Walter. He needed a picture, he wrote to her, 'for two reasons: a. I would *really* like to have one and b. I would like to impress my barracks buddies with a beautiful girlfriend. So send me one that is terribly seductive, with naked shoulders, a sexy look and so on.'

It would almost be possible to write a sketch of the course of his basic training without knowing any of the actual facts. Klaus being Klaus and the military being the military, in broad outline the relationship was easily predictable. To begin with, nothing could staunch the flow of his reading and writing. It began during the long, miserable ride to Arkansas and continued throughout the months that followed. Contemporary novels, classic German poetry, dramas, nonfiction – everything he could beg, buy or borrow – were his cherished companions. He even found time to write book reviews, mostly for the *Chicago Sun*'s 'Book Week'. In no time his barrack-mates, a good many of whom had probably never read a book, referred to him as 'the professor', in a way intended as a term of respect but one that set him still further apart. Nonetheless, the nomination inspired him to write a short story, never published, called 'The Monk', about a common soldier who was incompetent in almost everything military – the classic outsider. Yet far from looking down on his mates, in a drastic excess of naïveté, Klaus tried to educate them. To awaken them to the glories of modern poetry, he read them some lines by, of all poets, T.S. Eliot. He recorded the result. 'It don't make no sense', they said. 'Sounds kind of cute, though. Like music or something.' Evidently they did not dislike it. Good-natured mutual incomprehension roughly summed up the relationship between Klaus and his fellow recruits.

At the same time, the army being the army, he was almost immediately found to be less than a model soldier. 'I don't give a damn how many books you've written', a sergeant hollered at him shortly after his arrival. 'If your rifle is not clean tonight, you will spend the next four weekends on KP, buddy. I'll teach you a lesson. Think you're sophisticated, huh? Want to be a wise guy? This is the army, buddy.'

Training started a week after arriving at boot camp and apart from a few staccato words – 'marching', 'saluting', 'rifle practice', 'machine gun practice', 'night problems', 'mortar' – his diary says remarkably little about his life during those early months. By the end of the day he was totally exhausted.

And anyway what was there to say? Learning to fire a rifle was almost beyond him and in a letter to Katia he complained, 'The drills are especially *difficult* for me; I just can't get anywhere with rifle practice.' He consoled himself with the thought that his father had never learned to typewrite.

Few men are cut out to be warriors and Klaus was not one of those few. He was roughly twice the age of most other recruits and, since he had always disliked sports and any type of physical exertion, he was far from muscle-toned. It is easy to imagine how tough it was for him and how he must have tested the patience of his instructors. Some of them Klaus found 'detestable and sadistic'. Sergeant Merritt, a direct superior, had an equally baleful opinion of him. In an official report he declared that Klaus was 'irregular in his work in basic training, required frequent correction on minor matters, often left the company area just prior to formation of the company, was inattentive to instructions, seemed absent-minded or preoccupied with other matters, was a fanatic on books with little horse-sense and whose only influence on the other trainees was through his lack of discipline'.

What he did not record in his diary Klaus reported to Erika in a long letter on 14 February, giving his own sad commentary on his first two weeks. 'I am certainly not the best soldier in the company. The exercise is rather hard for me and the long marches leave me really tired and weaponry is beyond me. You well know my manual incompetence. The football players make fun of me. My accent is strange, I read books and am even said to have written several. Nobody sniggers but they smile and call me "the professor". That is meant as good-natured irony – not unfriendly, in fact with a certain humorous respect. Would European soldiers treat me with equal tact and tolerance? The average American may be less well educated and more naïve than the average European but this very naïvete makes him friendlier and more generous. I felt more isolated and lonely among the boys at the Wilhelms-Gymnasium than I do among the GIs.'

But relations would always be distant, the letter went on to say. 'It is better not to attempt to talk about anything serious. And that almost never happens. The main topic is girls. When by chance no one has a story about his girl or a photo to show, then the army is criticized. The thing to do is to hate and sneer at everything military. Yet it is considered an obligation to serve and be a good trooper. It is taken for granted that America will win the war but they have no idea what issues and circumstances led to it. Those who think about it – and there are very few – believe that the United States was pushed into a war with Hitler by selfish, cynical England. Recently a very well-done film, *What We Are Fighting For*, was shown. Everyone had to see it and could have learned a lot from it. A well-done film and required viewing. And the reaction of the men? They shrug. Just propaganda. Nothing can shake this sceptical ignorance. Concentration camps? Gestapo terror? Invasion of neighbouring countries? Violation of agreements? Mass murder? Plans for taking over the world? The response – grins and shrugs. "That's just propaganda." They consider Hitler and Mussolini harmless clowns whose antics they find amusing. The Nuremberg party rallies – "a pretty good show", the book burnings – "a lot of fun".

Klaus's diary for 1943 almost leaves the impression that, in his own mind at least, military life was a pastime while writing and other activities were his principal occupation. Obviously the impression is wrong, but the extent to which he continued to read, write reviews and give talks is astonishing. By the social standards prevailing at Camp Robinson and the nearby state capital, Little Rock, Klaus was a veritable celebrity. He was invited to dinner by the local gentry. And both the Chamber of Commerce of Little Rock and the camp's social centre arranged for him to give an occasional talk. One topic – 'From the European Literary Scene to American Army Life', comparing the self-discipline of the writer to the regimen of military life – was interesting but could not have meant much to his audiences. On the other hand 'Family against a Dictatorship' always went over well.

Out of what undoubtedly seemed another world, there arrived in the post one day a copy of *André Gide and the Crisis of Modern Thought*. What his emotions were, Klaus did not tell his diary. But he had reason to be pleased. The reviews, and there were many, were predominantly very favourable and from old friends he received warm letters. One of the warmest came from one of the oldest, Bruno Walter. 'So that your mind is not totally occupied with sounds of battle, military strategy, tactics, ballistics and other earthly things, perhaps you would like to be reminded of gentler things. I wanted to tell you that I am in the middle of your book about André Gide and am deeply interested, indeed gripped by your compassionate and perceptive portrayal. It seems to me the best of yours that I have read. It is inconceivable to me how you can manage to find time to write such a concise book – excuse the bald comparison – on the bridge between literature and soldiering.' For Thomas the subject was obviously sensitive since Klaus had long ago openly declared Gide to be his literary ideal. In a neutral-polite letter, Thomas praised his son's knowledge of his subject and remarked that Gide could have found no better American champion.

The subject himself did not like the book – far from the first biographee to be unhappy with his biographer. But the sad fact is Gide never had a very high regard for his admirer and it cannot be said he was as kind to him as he could have been. He was well aware of Klaus's adoration and agreed to have lunch a number of times with him. To that extent he was polite. But he was never genuinely friendly. At times Klaus could be obtuse and only slowly caught on. So instead of taking the coolness silently to heart, he naïvely wrote to Gide, remarking that 'our relationship is more distant than I would so much like it to be'. He was terribly hurt when Gide's journals were published in 1939 and he read an entry in which Gide commented that he scarcely knew Klaus – despite having first met him thirteen years previously. When Klaus's monograph appeared, the old man wrote a warm letter of praise and thanks. But a few years later he remarked to his German friend, E.R. Curtius, that the work was 'a confused mixture of absurd judgements, imprecise or badly understood facts'. That was bad enough, but then he added he did not think very highly of its author. The failure to establish a genuine friendship with Gide was one of the greatest sadnesses of his life, so sad he could not admit it to himself, though he must have known it was true. Lacking both a father and an ersatz father was more than he could bear.

Quite unintentionally *Gide* provoked an unprecedented row between Thomas and Agnes Meyer, one in fact that nearly led to a break. Agnes intensely disliked the Mann children, especially Klaus and Erika. Although she had not read Klaus's book, she had read about it. And what she read about it was that Klaus had referred to her ex-lover Paul Claudel – the French playwright and Catholic rival of the Protestant Gide – as a Catholic fascist and Vichy collaborator. She was enraged and wrote to Thomas, casting aspersions not only on the book but on Klaus's purported failure to serve in the armed forces. She further derided Erika's lecturing and war reporting as frivolous.

Thomas replied in one of the angriest letters he ever wrote. 'I have suffered bitterly and long from your having nothing but feelings of scorn and rejection of my children ... If only you knew how long I sat there, [your] letter in hand, shaking my head.' He went on, 'Erika's lecture work ... her stay in England at the time of the worst blitz – to you all that was nothing but mischief-making.' As for Klaus, 'Although he was thirty-six years old and a totally untrained intellectual, he went through the harsh *basic training* with the willpower of enthusiasm. With humorously paternal pride I reported this to you. You sent not a word of appreciation or congratulation.' With respect to *Gide*, he went on, 'I must defend a talented, hardworking and courageous son against what I consider the unjust charge that he made unseemly statements about a great poet who, moreover, is your friend.' The letter continued at great length about his sense of hurt and concluded, 'I bid you a heartfelt farewell.' For Klaus at least there was a happy postscript. *Gide* sold so well it earned him enough to pay off his $500 outstanding bill at the Bedford.

What was uppermost in Klaus's mind at that moment, however, was not his father's neurotic patron, whom he shrugged off, but his blatant confrontation with racial discrimination. This was an issue that had troubled him at the time of his first visit to the United States in 1927. Now it hit him head on. From the War of 1812 until the Korean War, the American military was racially segregated and prejudice against blacks was vehement. One day he witnessed a white recruit refuse to salute a black officer and was deeply shocked. That night, thinking he might like to write about the problem sometime, he sat up in bed and jotted down some thoughts. 'Only since I have lived in the "deep south" have I come to see the problem in its urgency and bitterness. Of the four men in my tent one comes from Alabama. His name is Johnny and he is a really nice person, barely twenty years old. Soft in appearance and character. But you should hear him on the subject of the "f------ niggers". No Nazi could be worse. I believe that Alabama Johnny would die of starvation rather than sit down at a table with a negro. Rather sleep in the rain than in a room with a negro. "Those bastards stink."'

Klaus's notes went on: 'It is in the army that segregation becomes an intolerable scandal. Can you believe it? We never come into contact with our black buddies. Negro troops are stationed in Camp Robinson. But they live alone in a separate area of the camp, a sort of black ghetto with their own church, their own cinema, and their own PX. The bus to Little Rock has a special section for "colored people". If these people are good enough to fight and die for our country, then they can't be too bad for our service club. What must these people make of this war? The question, *what are we fighting for*, can't be easy for these people to answer. But it will soon be light outside, the trumpets will sound reveille. We have bayonet practice this morning and this afternoon a twelve-kilometre walk. You cannot conceive how heavy a fully-packed knapsack is when you have to trudge three or four hours. And if I can't go any further, my Alabama Johnny will take pity and carry it for a time.'

It was not just American racism Klaus witnessed but, for the first time since leaving Germany in 1933, overt anti-Semitism. During weekend leave in New York he returned to the Bedford, where the doorman took him aside. So many Jews, he said, were officers, it was time people like Klaus should be made one too. Not long afterward, back at camp, he witnessed a drunken sergeant setting about a trooper named Alfred Wolf. 'You are a Jew, one of those refugees. Whenever I see a Jew, I want to beat him up', and he proceeded to do just that.

Klaus finished basic training at the end of March and summed up the experience in a few sentences. 'They have taught me how to march and how to fire a rifle. I have learned to pack a haversack and to read a map and to execute the terrible motion of running a bayonet into an enemy's body. I am trained in the basic gestures and tactics of warfare in this murderous century.' In at least one respect training was imperfect. Evidently still unsure of the difference between fatigues and dress uniform, poor Klaus committed a grave sartorial solecism and for five days suffered the consequences – in the words of his diary, 'confined to barracks because of "mixed uniform"'.

But in the end all was well. The officers at Camp Robinson recognized that Klaus was supremely unsuited for a combat role and would be of greatest value in some area of military intelligence. So it came about that he was sent to Camp Ritchie in Maryland, near Washington, which had been established some months earlier as a Military Intelligence training school. There he was assigned to a psychological warfare unit, which was to interview prisoners of war and find ways to break down enemy morale on the battlefront. It had the cover name First Mobile Radio Broadcasting Company and was a good place for him. When he arrived at the base on

5 April he immediately felt at home. Half the personnel were German and a good many of them friends or acquaintances. English, he found, was rarely to be heard. Throughout the month the unit waited to be shipped to Europe and, while waiting, Klaus was promoted directly from private to staff sergeant – a big jump, but not quite to the lieutenancy for which his father had hoped.

In the meantime Klaus's application for naturalization had finally been approved and on 30 April he travelled to Baltimore for the swearing-in ceremony. Nemesis was waiting. She took shape as a judge who, a few minutes before the event, called Klaus aside and said he had received information which made his naturalization impossible. Further investigation was necessary and in the meantime he could not leave the country. The next day his unit boarded a boat for Casablanca. His diary reads, 'Disappointment, confusion, discussions. Depression.'

What information had been brought to the judge's attention? According to the archives of the FBI and Military Intelligence, the old story had been resurrected that Klaus was a secret communist agent and notorious pervert. The chief assassins in this latest *Rufmord* were Gerhart Seger and Rudolf Katz plus a few other German exiles who came out of the same right-wing social democratic labour movement circles as Walther Schevenels – he who had accused Klaus and Erika of being Cominform agents. Seger, who in January 1940 had published Klaus's denial of being a Soviet spy, was now only too happy to stick in the knife. In the words of an FBI report, '[Seger] considers Klaus Mann, whom he knows well, to be a shallow and degenerate man. He added that practically everyone shares the same opinion of Subject, even Thomas Mann, his father. He claimed that when visiting Thomas Mann in California in 1941 he asked him if he had ever read Subject's books, and Thomas Mann had replied, "No, it is difficult enough to have him as a son"' – Thomas's diary makes no mention of such a remark. Seger went on to tell the FBI that Klaus 'has exhibited strong totalitarian beliefs, and his magazine, *Decision*, had certainly shown an undercurrent of Communistic influence in its editorial policy'. Katz then added, as if in a game of 'Can You Top That?', 'He knew Subject well and considers him to be a 100 per cent fellow traveler.' The FBI investigator assured his agency that the accusers were 'reliable and well-informed'.

Not so those who told a different story. They were treated to interviews that took on an overtly belligerent tone and their testimony was labelled 'not objective'. Fritz Landshoff, for example, was questioned at great length, especially about Klaus's view of the Molotov–Ribbentrop pact. His favourable comments did not suit the interrogator and so they were dismissed as 'unreliable'. Most blatant was the interrogation of Thomas Curtiss. To help it along, the agent gave him a lead on how to answer his questions – 'He is pro-Communist, isn't he?' 'How did you account for people getting the impression that Mann was a pro-Communist and in part used the magazine to promulgate his Communist beliefs?' 'You had no indication whatever that he is homosexual?' And, 'He used to entertain a lot of soldiers in his room, didn't he?' The inquiry was particularly farcical since the investigators should have known from secret agent T3 that Curtiss himself was the most regular visitor to room 1403 at the Bedford hotel.

Klaus's sex life was delved into with salacious fascination. Here again Katz and Seger did their best to bring him into disgrace. Katz told the FBI that it was common knowledge that Klaus 'had engaged in all forms of moral degeneracy'. Seger, according to the report, 'confirmed this, adding that he had himself been thoroughly shocked by the sensuality of one of Subject's books which obviously dealt with his private life and that of his sister, Erika, adding that it was quite understandable why the work had never been translated into English'. This particular canard harked back to the rumour propagated in 1936 in Goebbels's propaganda apparatus suggesting that Klaus and Erika had had incestuous relations. In any case the work to which Katz and Seger referred was not by Klaus but by his father. It was the Wagner-inspired novella, *The Blood of the Walsungs*, written a year before Erika's birth. However, the FBI was only too pleased by what it heard and made no attempt to verify it.

Why did Schevenels, Epstein, Seger, Katz and their friends want to destroy Klaus? Ultimately it remains a mystery. Throughout his life Klaus had been subjected to personal attacks and misrepresentation by Social Democrats and in their publications could always count on hostile commentary on almost whatever he wrote. Judging by the tenor of the criticism, the animosity may be partly traced to the intense homophobia rampant in these circles, where Klaus's life and novels were considered debauched. The political smear is harder to explain. It had to be evident to anyone that

Klaus was not a communist, and no rational person could think that he was a communist agent. To be sure, he had always insisted – as had Churchill and Roosevelt – that Germany rather than the Soviet Union was the immediate enemy. Such was not the view of zealots like Epstein and Seger or of the FBI. That *Decision* purveyed a communist line could have been refuted by a quick glance at any of the twelve issues. Rational accusations can be rationally answered, irrational ones are irrefutable. And that was the situation Klaus faced.

In an attempt to help his son, Thomas wrote to Francis Biddle whom he vaguely knew. Biddle enquired of the FBI and received a predictable answer, which he did not question. In a preposterous response, he wrote to Thomas saying he had seen 'reports which I would prefer not to discuss – certainly not in a letter . . . Under the circumstances I do not see that there is anything I can do.' In other words he might tell Thomas orally but not put in writing that his son was considered a Russian spy. On reading Biddle's letter, Katia exploded. She saw the 'reports' as wanton character defamation and wondered whether the Gestapo was somehow behind them. Klaus had little doubt that they related to the accusations of his being a communist. But since the judge and the attorney general declined to say, he was in the impossible position of trying to defend himself against he knew not what, asserted by he knew not whom. 'Kafkaesque', that much overused term, was in this case fully apt.

Military officials had no idea what to do with the suspicious Sergeant Mann. On 10 June they decided. Klaus, whose expertise in radios was limited to turning one on and off and fiddling with the station dial, was assigned to Camp Crowder in Missouri as a radio repair specialist. When he went to headquarters to point out that his orders had to be a ridiculous mistake, the attending officer made an obscene gesture, nodded toward the door and barked, 'Get out of here.' Appropriately enough, Klaus was at the time reading – and no doubt drawing some solace from – Evelyn Waugh's *Put Out More Flags*, about similar goings-on in wartime Britain. What followed can be gleaned from a few notes in his diary. 'The "war of nerves" in Ritchie during these last days. Orders, counter-orders, rumours, uncertainty. My idiotic assignment cancelled, reaffirmed, etc. Army life is at once the dullest and the most fantastic affair in the world.' To Katia he wrote that he was officially considered 'misplaced'. And in the view of the commandant of Camp Crowder when he arrived on 13 July that was precisely *le mot juste*.

Travelling through the American Midwest by train had in the past always left Klaus with a sense of cosmic boredom. Now he was living there in a military encampment and from the first moment found himself overwhelmed by this feeling. It was not just the geography. 'The worst thing in army life is not the discipline, the monotony, the lack of privacy', he had written in his diary of 20 June, 'but the terrible *waste of time.*' Daily life was a blank. In the barracks he was surrounded by young recruits who spent their free time half naked, reading comic strips, wagering a month's pay in poker games and bragging about their girlfriends. His only contact with them appears to have been in the ancient role of *notarius civitatis*. Being the sole person in the company with a typewriter and an ability to spell, he obligingly wrote their letters for them.

How did someone as sexually promiscuous as Klaus react in the close company of men generally of the type to whom he was attracted? Evidently he erected a mental barrier. Of course he knew that being caught in flagrante would result in dishonourable discharge or even a stint in the stockade. In any event his diary is void of a single word suggesting that any of them had appeal, much less that he was ever tempted to do anything about it. Indeed, the sole reference to his celibate state was an almost bemused diary comment. 'My own sex life – or complete lack of it, for the past few months – begins to become somewhat alarming.' He dealt with the problem like Onan in the Holy Scriptures. But since he found auto-relief 'monotonous and somehow humiliating' that was not much help.

The result of this sexless, friendless life? 'An intense feeling of loneliness. So far away from everything. Far away – from *what*? There is no place or group or person to whom I belong. I feel more disconnected, uprooted, isolated than ever. The concept of God – however vague, however frightening – is more *real* to me than all human things. That is why everything in the army strikes me as chimerical – like a Kafka nightmare.' The hoped-for talisman had turned out to be a curse.

Paralyzed by sadness and the intense summer heat, Klaus became desperate. 'If my application [for a job in Military Intelligence] should be outright rejected – against all justice and reason – SUICIDE would be indeed the only logical, almost inevitable reaction.' The mood passed.

But not the boredom. So one morning he marched off to headquarters and appealed for some sort of work – *anything* – to occupy his time. His commanders were sympathetic, but what could they do? Eventually one of them had an idea. Klaus – he who had over the years written novels, dramas, biographies, autobiographies, reviews and essays – was charged to write nothing less than 'A History of the 825th Signal Repair Service'. And, as if that were not enough of a challenge, he was also invited to contribute articles to the unit's newspaper, *Camp Crowder Message*. Since the intellectual pressure of all that was less than overwhelming, he was left with infinite amounts of time to read. He ransacked the camp library and begged books from friends. In a few weeks he went through Benvenuto Cellini's autobiography, a biography of Rupert Brooke and new novels by Noël Coward, Ernest Hemingway and Evelyn Waugh. Of it all what meant most was Proust, which he read in Scott Moncrieff's famous translation. Yet what really kept him going was a new novel of his own. For hours his mind was occupied sketching out a plot and inventing dialogue. It was the only positive thing in his life. By early August he had drafted a first chapter.

What about his military training? Strange to say, at times he almost enjoyed it. On occasion he even found it humorous and once in a while was actually proud of his performance. Mornings began with a daily gas mask drill. This was scary. With the mask on he felt as though he was suffocating. But then he had a further concern, which he expressed to Katia. 'What do you do if your nose itches? What a dilemma in case of a veritable gas attack.' Bayonet training, the supreme test of an ability to be blood-thirsty, was scarier still. Your adversary may be a straw dummy but psychologically you had to envisage sinking your bayonet into another human being's guts. Guns were more impersonal, and when it came to target practice he was proud of the fact that he exceeded his own modest expectations. That was not saying much since he never qualified – the consequence of technical incompetence or a subconscious pacifist hangover? The high – or low – point was the infiltration course. 'Crawling on muddy ground (100 yards) under machine gun fire (live ammunition). Barbed wire. Explosions. Quite an experience. Rather enjoyed it.' In a way it was an existential moment in his life, 'this creeping reptile-like, through the Missouri mire'. He asked himself how he would respond if the rifle bullets were being fired by Japanese or Nazis. 'I, for one, wanted to know if I can take it all right.' Now he knew. 'After this well-staged and instructive "dress rehearsal", I am more eager than ever to see the show proper and to play my little part in it.'

Learning to hate the enemy was not part of the curriculum. But while Klaus admired the anti-militarism of Americans, he was appalled at their continued lack of understanding of what the conflict was about. 'The war is generally considered a gigantic nuisance with which one has to cope, somehow. This country would be doomed if it were not for its colossal strength and vast dimensions. From its very size and power result both the unshakable self-assurance and the fundamental good nature of its people. (Contrast to France.)'

All in all Klaus was fond of Americans in the mass and his diary makes repeated references to their casual, easy friendliness. A two-day train journey from the east coast to Missouri was almost a session in applied sociology. Everything caught his attention, or, rather, everyone did. Above all he marvelled at how quickly people made friends. After watching a boy and a girl, two soldiers, two old women and several businessmen, he found it impossible to make out whether they had known one another for years or had just met thirty minutes ago. He quickly fell in with the mood and chatted for a long time with several black women. Their hats, their dresses, the expressions on their faces, their conversations intrigued him. Since the train was crowded, he offered one of them his seat for several hours. He teased a little girl and she teased him back. He learned a lot about Americans during his trip. But this very fascination showed how foreign he still felt. Only once, though, did he admit to a twinge of nostalgia. 'Homesick for Europe. Tired of this country. (Maybe the result of reading Proust. Europe at its best. But shall I find it again?)'

Following the fiasco of his naturalization in Baltimore, Klaus's security investigation became active and now shifted to California, focusing on the whole Mann family. This complicated matters, however, since Thomas himself had for some time been suspected of being – in the FBI's wonderful way with words – 'docile to any plans of the communists'. So on being interrogated at his home in Pacific Palisades, he had to defend not only his son but also himself. Both he and Klaus 'had the same democratic ideals', he patiently explained, and while Klaus 'was liberal-minded, he had never evidenced any radical tendencies'. Two days later Katia was questioned – a wife and mother in the grotesque position of having to vouch for the integrity of her husband and her son. So benighted was the agent that 'Katia' was a name that was quite beyond him to pronounce or spell and in his report he christened her 'Catherine'. Patiently she explained that Klaus was 'quite like his father' and his father was a stalwart democrat. As for political suspicions she pointed out, for example, that her son's book on the anti-communist André Gide had been roundly cursed by the communist *Daily Worker*. The investigation did not neglect neighbours and family friends. Based on their comments, the Military Intelligence agent commented – rather as though Klaus was a racehorse – that 'Subject came from a fine family, sound stock and his home life had been excellent'. The agent was assured that Klaus had never said or done anything 'un-American'. The exile novelist Bruno Frank added that Klaus was 'a capable writer, clever psychologist with high character and abilities'. Yet even though by mid-June Military Intelligence was developing a picture of 'Subject' different from that of the FBI, he was still denied a clearance.

In mid-July Klaus was given leave and went to visit his parents. A few days after arriving, he received a letter from a fellow writer and old friend, Eugene McCown, saying he had heard that Klaus was being denied naturalization and a security clearance because of his 'premature anti-fascism'. The precise nature of this crime was not spelled out but it presumably related to being anti-Nazi prior to America's entry into the war. That finally did it. Though slow to anger, Klaus was so furious he sent a telegram to Francis Biddle appealing for an audience. The attorney general referred him to the head of the Immigration Service in Philadelphia. Immediately Klaus crossed the country in a ghastly, six-day journey on a slow, over-crowded train. The diary for 17 August records the result – 'Harrison greets me with the most cordial courtesy. Yet he remains non-committal and I am only half-satisfied.' At Harrison's suggestion he trundled on to Baltimore to see the immigration authorities dealing with his case. There he was told that his file had been forwarded to Kansas City, presumably because it was near Camp Crowder.

'Things begin to move,' Klaus wrote optimistically in his diary on 30 August. He decided to force the issue by volunteering to be interrogated by the Counter Intelligence Corps. The questions concentrated on his sex life. 'He asked me the most peculiar questions', Klaus remarked later of the interviewing officer. 'Is it true that I ever claimed (in a conversation with a lady "back East") that there is no vice I did not used to practice?' Far from being intimidated, he faced the agent down and fought fire not with fire but with water, blithely drenching the accusations with buckets of exculpatory claims. Stories of perversion were, he said, 'slanderous, fantastic and false rumors'. Some of these were spread by Nazi propagandists, some were based on his novel about Alexander the Great and some grew out of his father's novella *The Blood of the Walsungs*. He swore he 'had never engaged in any sex practices other than those normal to a young unmarried man, who was more or less sowing his wild oats'. The syphilis infection followed a romp in bed with a prostitute he had picked up on the street – which was in a way true. 'I had no idea Klaus could lie so well', Golo said many years later when shown a transcript of an interrogation. It could be argued, though, that Klaus's testimony was not so much lies as casuistry. He merely said he had not engaged in perverted sex. Since he did not consider homosexuality perverted, he had not lied.

The homosexual issue was in any case a red herring. When conscription was introduced in 1940 homosexuals and blacks were rejected as unsuitable for service. But by 1942 the armed services needed to take men in, not to keep them out. So blacks were inducted and unless a person was 'blatantly homosexual' – a ballet dancer was specified as an example – he was normally accepted. In Klaus's case a steadfast denial was sufficient.

Early in September a Military Intelligence agent wrote up the concluding report. One kudos followed another. 'Subject is highly intelligent and possesses a wonderful command of the English language.' 'Loyal, trustworthy, honest, discreet, persevering, choosy in his friends.' 'Well-behaved, anti-Nazi, extremely democratic, liberal in ideas, not communist.' And finally, 'This agent is of the opinion that citizenship should be allowed Subject.' In a remarkable volte-face the FBI endorsed the conclusion. 'This Agent is of the opinion that Subject would be very useful in combat propaganda and unless adverse information other than that contained in previous investigations is found, citizenship should be allowed to Subject.'

The weather at Camp Crowder on 25 September was glorious and Klaus was among the unnumbered confirmands waiting on the parade ground for the swearing-in ceremony. For the unlucky Klaus nothing was ever simple. When the government official arrived from Kansas City to administer the oath of allegiance, it was discovered that his name was not on the list. Restrained panic, unrestrained confusion, telegrams, phone calls. Finally all was straightened out and the ceremony began. The commandant called upon the men to be brave soldiers, the chaplain prayed to his God that they would be effective killers and Klaus – five years to the day after arriving in the United States for good – became a citizen. Even that was not quite the end of the story. In a final touch of ubuesque surrealism, the FBI's investigation was not formally concluded until 10 August 1956, seven years after 'Subject' had died.

The first thing Klaus did after his investiture was to apply for immediate transfer to a military intelligence unit in the European theatre of operations to serve in any capacity. The second was to proceed with a plan for an auction of autographs. This ingenious and for once brilliantly successful scheme was to put up for sale signed photos, manuscripts and books by well-known public figures. The proceeds would be used to purchase war bonds. Probably his commanding officers found the idea bizarre but were fond of Klaus and let him go ahead. Thanks to his extraordinary range of contacts and brute nerve, he sent out over a hundred requests – to people he knew, including alumni of *Decision* such as Somerset Maugham, Franz Werfel, Upton Sinclair, Lotte Lehmann, Albert Einstein, and to people he knew less well or who were even complete strangers, such as Wendell Willkie, William Shirer, Pearl Buck, Hedy Lamarr and Greta Garbo.

The auction was held on 9 October at the home of the president of the University of Missouri at Kansas City and the entire collection was bought for $1,400,000 by the director of an insurance company, who donated it to the university. The event was reported in the national press, making it as far as the *New York Times*. To celebrate, there was a reception at the home of the university president and a lunch at which Klaus was seated next to General Eisenhower's brother. 'I was forced to be charming from four in the afternoon until midnight', he complained. What did he think when comparing the amazing proceeds of the auction, so easily earned, with the paltry $20,000 he had needed to keep *Decision* going?

Klaus's direct superior, Colonel Pratt, was so impressed by the success of the sale that he was moved to write to Thomas saying that Klaus would be greatly missed when he went overseas. In a handwritten postscript he said he had read – virtually studied – *The Turning Point*, and as a result felt he actually knew the Mann family. Thomas was enormously pleased by the letter and noted in his diary that Klaus's service had been so outstanding his superiors had written to praise him.

Camp Crowder was a large base, with forty-seven thousand transient troops and an adjacent camp for fifteen thousand prisoners of war, some Italian but mostly Germans. In early November, still awaiting travel orders, Klaus was given permission to visit the German contingent. Wearing an American army uniform among German soldiers left him feeling odd – 'rather dreamlike, half amusing, half embarrassing'. His account of the day is fascinating for reasons he was unaware of. 'The Nazi boys seem extremely pleased with their present plight; everything is spick and span – barracks, P.X., mess hall, where we have luncheon. Their snappy discipline and some-what servile politeness appeals greatly to American officers – especially Major Judkins, in charge of the camp. When the prisoners marched by, he said – in the presence of a prisoner who understands English – "They are the best outfit in this whole post." One of the boys is painting his portrait in oils.'

Had he pondered the sight of Judkins having his portrait painted by a German trooper, Klaus might have had some inkling that there was some-thing fishy going on. Small wonder the prisoners were well-disciplined and content. Under Judkins's sympathetic eye and generous treatment, Nazi Wehrmacht thugs ran the camp through intimidation and threats. What was dangerous about Judkins's attitude was that it typified the sympathy towards Germans of many American commanders. Even in the midst of a brutal war, they saw members of the Wehrmacht and the SS not as wanton killers and mass-murderers but as clean, neat, efficient, well-disciplined soldiers. To the colonel Judkinses and millions of Americans, the war itself still seemed far away and the destruction and suffering already wrought upon Europe by the Wehrmacht left remarkably little impression. It was a state of mind that Klaus had been railing against for years and was to bedevil the military occupation to come.

During most of the month of November, Thomas and Katia had been travelling around the northeast coast of the United States, where Thomas gave a series of lectures and attended a rancorous meeting of German exiles, some of whom wanted him to be head of a German government in exile. On their way back to Pacific Palisades, they stopped in Kansas City to see Klaus before he left for overseas. Erika also arrived that day and so there was a small family reunion at the home of the university president. Eventually the time came for Klaus to say goodbye to his parents. In a rather emotional moment Thomas wished him farewell. That night, in one of the most moving entries in his entire diary, Klaus recorded, 'Saying goodbye, he embraces me – which had never happened before.'

On December 4 he received his orders and ten days later shipped out to an embarkation camp on the East Coast. Just before leaving the base he wrote a final entry in his diary. 'It is time I close these notes and pack this book with other superfluous things into a box which will go to Pacific Palisades and probably will be lost. The six months at Camp Crowder weren't so bad on the whole. The first three or four weeks were bitter – empty and dismal, haunted by the suicide obsession. But then things gradually picked up. Col. Pratt was indeed very good to me. I would have been lost without him . . . For what Tomski gave me, during the past two years, was only pain. It seems that I am going to get the kind of work and adventure I want. We are going to win this war before long. It will be not without interest to watch further developments.'

CHAPTER 11

German Problem Children
1944–45

Travel as a non-com on a troop transport in wartime must rank as one of life's less pleasant experiences, especially if you are crossing the North Atlantic in early winter on the *USS General Anderson*. 'Horrible, a real nightmare, the worst thing I have ever experienced in the army or anywhere else', Klaus wrote to Katia on 15 January, two weeks after arriving in Casablanca. Eight thousand soldiers on a boat designed for three thousand, with half the space reserved for officers. The bunks – hammocks in fact – were in the bowels of the boat, where there was electric light only during the day. To be able to read, he stood, book in hand, in the latrine, surrounded by his fellow sweating, swearing, seasick hoplites. There he celebrated – or rather survived – Christmas and New Year's Day. Details of the GI chow were too unspeakable to be mentioned.

Once back in the Old World, he could scarcely wait to get to the front. But yet again there was a glitch in his orders and yet again his unit moved on without him. For three weeks he lived in a tent, freezing in the cold Saharan nights, without anything to do. 'WAITING: the soldier's main occupation', he complained to his diary. Fortunately the whole of Casablanca lay just beyond the perimeter of the base and there he spent many hours, intrigued by the exotic combination of French and Moroccan sights, colours and smells. Otherwise he whiled away the time drafting a short story on a rickety typewriter in the Red Cross office. Eventually his assignment was approved and he travelled in extreme discomfort to Algiers and on to Tunis. There he had hoped to find André Gide, who had fled from France a year or so earlier. His hero, he learned, had gone underground in Algeria.

Not until 11 February did he finally sail to Sicily. Then, proceeding on to the mainland, he was assigned to the Fifth Army and ended up near the battlefront a week later. The ferocious combat at Monte Cassino was then under way and left his parents terribly anxious. Assuming as much, Klaus wrote to Katia on 17 February, '*There is absolutely no reason to worry about me. I am quite safe* – much safer, indeed, than you are when you drive to Beverly Hills and don't make a full stop before crossing Sunset Boulevard.' After that he uncharacteristically fell out of touch. 'We have had hardly any news from Italy', Thomas complained to Heinrich on 24 March. For reasons of military security, Klaus did not comment in his letters or his diary on the course of the fighting. But there are hints that he was aware that the Allied campaign was a botch, both in strategy and tactics. Although Naples had fallen on 1 October, as a result of indecision, compulsive caution and bad morale, the American army did not reach Rome – eighty miles distant – until the following June. After that it was the same story as Allied forces stumbled and crept north.

Klaus had assumed that his work in the Psychological Warfare Branch would prove interesting and give him at least a minimal feeling of participation in the defeat of the Third Reich. The art of breaking down enemy morale has been traced as far back as Cyrus the Great and is said to have been perfected by Tamerlane and the Mongols, who used severed human heads in large quantities – a pile of ninety thousand in one case – to intimidate their opponents. But over the centuries techniques had softened. Instead of lobbing dead heads over the front line, Klaus's unit tossed leaflets appealing to the German troops to recognize that the war was lost and it was only smart to desert. To intensify the temptation, a few cigarettes were attached in order to suggest the luxury of life on the other side of the battlefield. Through interrogation of deserters he was to find weak points in Wehrmacht morale. Battle fatigue, for instance, he discovered to be stronger with older soldiers, lower ranks and Austrians. So he wrote flyers to exploit this sentiment. But did he accomplish anything? Always the cynic, he doubted it. His diary records his frustration: 'boring, rather lonely life', 'not given any work to do', 'good idea for a leaflet, but who really cares', 'rewrite speech but will probably not be used'.

Living conditions hardly compensated. He was bunkered in a tent that was freezing in the winter, stifling in the summer and flooded when it rained, which was often. He 'dined' on survival rations. Four months passed before he slept in a bed. He was bombed and shelled. Still, he counted himself better off than men directly on the front line and rarely complained. In fact, in letters to friends and family he tried to be reassuring. 'It is strange and exciting to be in Europe again, under such extraordinary circumstances', he remarked to Hermann Kesten. 'Yet I wish the whole mess were over at last and I could return to my hotel room and my desk, and write about the war, instead of participating in it.' He signed the letter, 'Incorrigibly yours'. And to his mother he wrote, 'Did my last letter sound somewhat gloomy, by any chance? One should never write letters if one happens to be in a bad mood.'

By mid-April Klaus was in fact in a filthy mood. It rained incessantly, mud was ankle deep, he had toothache, was lonely and, worst of all, felt useless. The only entertainment was seeing nearby Vesuvius belching ever-more threating amounts of fire and smoke. On 18 March, while he was watching with fascination, it exploded and in no time destroyed several towns and, for the second time in two millennia, reached Pompeii, causing serious damage. For the author of *Der Vulkan*, here was a visible manifestation of nature imitating art. A month later he imitated nature, exploding in such frustration with his work that he went to headquarters to plead for something more consequential. 'Not very satisfactory' was the result.

It was not all gloom and boredom. Klaus was intrigued by the wild surrealism of life at the time – brutal fighting on the front line while just a few miles behind it everything went on almost as in peacetime. Not long after arriving near the front line, for example, he attended a performance of *Cavalleria Rusticana* at the Naples Opera and in the days that followed he explored Pompeii and Herculaneum. For all his complaints of loneliness, he had an impressive array of interesting Italian friends and acquaintances. One of them was Sforzino Sforza, son of Carlo, Count Sforza. The Sforzas were one of the great noble families of Italy. Count Sforza had been the Italian foreign minister after the First World War, but immediately quit when Mussolini came to power. Like the Manns, the Sforzas found their lives uprooted, lost their property – in the Sforzas' case an immense fortune – and in 1926 went into political exile. Klaus and Sforzino had met in Toulon in 1933. Sforzino was then sixteen and, according to the Count, he looked up to Klaus almost as though he were an older brother. In 1943 they met again, both now in uniform and both at Camp Ritchie, where they occasionally peeled potatoes together in the kitchen. One of the earliest Italian exiles to return, Count Sforza arrived in November 1943 and was appointed a minister in the first postwar provisional government. Sforzino eventually became his private secretary.

At the first opportunity Klaus hired a car, at what was for him consider-able expense, to travel to Naples to find Sforzino. In the months that followed the two became close companions. Sforzino introduced him to his Italian friends, one of them Benedetto Croce, the distinguished philoso-pher who was now briefly a government minister. On 22 April Sforzino took Klaus to Sorrento to meet the great man. 'I spent a stimulating weekend with Sforzino and the Croces – just the day after the formation of the new government', as he wrote to Katia. He described the very Italianate scene. 'The house seemed to be constantly swarming with people whose identities are completely unknown to the hosts – young British lieutenants from neighbouring rest camps, American military government officers, Italian generals covered with decorations, Neapolitan politicians, ladies with dogs and children, foreign diplomats.' Klaus could not have but marvelled at the contrast to the serene life on San Remo Drive in Pacific Palisades. Throughout the summer he continued to see the Sforzas as well as Elena Croce, the eldest daughter, and her husband, the historian Raimondo Craveri. Together they went on occasional outings in the Alban Hills. He even wrote an article about the two families which was published in *Town and Country*.

Within a few months he came to know some of the leading cultural figures in Italy. One was Alberto Moravia, whom Klaus found a bit of a curmudgeon. Another was Ignazio Silone. Klaus knew him as a contributor to *Die Sammlung* and with whom he had cordial relations. Silone had gone into political exile in Switzerland in 1930 and returned to Italy in 1944. Klaus felt a special affinity with him. 'Abroad he might be considered Italian, but not here . . . Bitter is exile. Still bitterer is the return.' He came to be particularly fond of the surrealist painter Leonor Fini and they spent several afternoons together in the countryside outside Rome. She included him in her social circle and painted his portrait. From the acting world he made friends with Anna Magnani. And he came almost to idolize Aurel Milloss, director of the ballet of the Rome Opera.

Klaus could not have been more delighted than when a number of old friends suddenly materialized. One was the irrepressibly exuberant Jack von Ripper. He was now Lieutenant Ripper and a war hero decorated for his amazing exploits in the Austrian underground. There were also new companions. One of the closest was Hans Busch, the son of the noted conductor, Fritz, who had fled from Germany in 1933. Hans was a dramaturge and impresario at the operas in Naples and Rome and supplied Klaus with tickets to performances. It is clear, just from a few of the names mentioned in his diary, that Klaus enjoyed the company of non-Americans, found them more interesting and was far closer to them than to anyone in the army.

With the fall of Rome on 4 June and Florence on 15 July, the flow of prisoners and deserters steadily swelled – as many as ten thousand were taken in a two-week period. Klaus interrogated them for militarily useful information. In this person-to-person contact he at last found interesting work. The cull included generals and privates, Nazis and anti-Nazis, sophisticates and louts. Some comprehended nothing and refused to believe Germany would ever be defeated. He concluded that German soldiers would battle on, not because they were forced to but because war and Hitler were part of the natural order of things. And they believed Goebbels when he said that the end of the Third Reich would be a catastrophe not only for Germans but for all Europeans.

One day a prisoner appeared who immediately stood out from the others. He was Hans Reiser, a twenty-five-year-old actor from Munich. Hans was a survivor of the anti-Nazi 'White Rose' student group at Munich University. As Klaus wrote to Erika, 'Even in our circle, I have scarcely ever heard such fulminating words of condemnation, of fury . . . I stared at him, as he spoke – the fervent look, the shining forehead, the defiantly strong chin. I thought, "Are there many like you?"' Hans had fought at Stalingrad and, when transferred to the Italian front, was determined to desert at the first opportunity.

Klaus immediately fell for him, not only politically but emotionally, and after a second meeting commented in his diary on 28 June, 'Happier than I have been since – when?' So taken was he that when Reiser was moved to another prison, he searched all the jails in Rome to find him. Yet he knew there was no hope of a relationship then or even after the war. Hans was engaged to a Munich actress and, as Klaus remarked to Katia at the time, 'One allows oneself, once in a great while, to indulge in emotional delusions – which are so beautiful and comforting as long as they last.' Katia found these words rather alarming, afraid he risked jeopardizing his military career. He wrote to reassure her. 'As for "*la Grande Illusion*", to which you refer in your letter – there is, alas, no reason to be worried; not in the sense you may have had in mind. The illusion started under peculiar circumstances, never materialized and is not likely to do so, for the time being . . . This, in itself, would of course be a rather saddening experience; but, first, there are still certain hopes (if only of a rather vague nature) for future fulfillments. And, besides, the last convulsions of Nazism are so absorbingly interesting that it seems somewhat difficult to concentrate on anything else.'

Work was now becoming steadily more gruelling. On some days Klaus interrogated more than thirty prisoners. For a time he was fascinated by many of the stories he heard and gradually formed a picture of what life had been like during the nearly twelve years of Nazism. For every Hans Reiser there were dozens of others who exasperated him by expounding their unshakable belief in Hitler. As late as the end of June, when he conducted an informal poll, he found that when asked, 'Do you have confidence in the Führer?' thirteen out of twenty-five still unhesitatingly replied 'Yes'. As he commented, 'Always the same formula, the same lacrimonious tone. "I can't do anything about it. Orders from above, orders from higher authority, and still higher authority. Orders from the Führer." In this way the issue of guilt is settled.' According to another theme popular in the Wehrmacht, the Allies were making a big mistake. The enemy was not Hitler but Stalin and, once the Russians reached Germany's eastern border, the Allies would come to their senses, make a separate peace and join Hitler in a war against the Soviet Union.

By August Klaus concluded from his interrogations that morale in the Wehrmacht had noticeably declined following the 20 July plot against Hitler and the military defeats on every front. He warned his headquarters not to expect any consequences on the battlefield, however. 'The army is too well disciplined ever to revolt. German soldiers are too much used to taking orders . . . It has already become part of their character.' He pointed out that there were additional reasons the Wehrmacht was fighting so tenaciously. Some soldiers said they feared a bloodbath if their country was defeated. Others were convinced Hitler's much-rumoured *Geheimwaffe* – the V-1 and V-2 rockets – would in the end save the day. There were a few who realized the war was lost and wanted only to survive, but they found it extremely difficult to desert; opportunities were relatively rare and failure was fatal. The commanding general of the Wehrmacht in Italy, the brutal Albert Kesselring, ordered that any soldier who attempted to desert would be hanged from the nearest tree. He later boasted that, as a result of his threat, he never saw a single dangling corpse. Had Allied commanders made a similar threat, the trees would have been festooned with cadavers. The military stalemate, the missed opportunities, battle fatigue and poor leadership had a disastrous effect on morale. British and American soldiers deserted, certainly not in droves but in alarming numbers, living on the run, disappearing into large cities, working as farmhands or even being 'adopted' by Italian families.

In this unreal world Klaus compiled his reports for Fifth Army headquarters. He later drew on these in writing a number of articles – 'The Conquerors', 'Reunion Far from Vienna', 'My Former Countrymen', 'Notes on the Re-education of the Germans', 'Writing about the War' and 'Observations on Being a War Prisoner'. Few of them ever got beyond typescript during his lifetime. Only three minor ones were published – 'Tragedia Sul', about German soldiers in Italy, appeared in *Nuovo Mondo*; 'Hölderlin in the Barracks' in the *Saturday Review of Literature* and 'My Old Countrymen' in the American army daily, *Stars and Stripes*.

The truth was that for the first time in his life Klaus lacked the impulse to get down to serious work. He admitted as much to Carson McCullers in a letter on 23 March. 'I feel like writing something myself, and to make something of the many impressions and experiences I've had during the past 15 months – especially since I went overseas. But I am afraid I won't be able to do so, not for the duration plus six months. For it is strangely difficult to concentrate on writing, under the circumstances.' In a letter to his father six months later, he sounded an equally pessimistic tone. 'As for my own lyre, it is getting rusty. In fact, I don't even know what kind of book I shall write, if and when I am again free to indulge in such luxurious occupations as the writing of books. I am afraid this War is no good from a cynically literary point of view. Everything written about this War is second-rate, or purely journalistic. There is nothing inspiring about this War; it is not a mission but a duty – as that clever chap, [Arthur] Koestler, put it.'

By autumn the routine, boring nature of his job had become unbearable. Rarely did anything bring him more than passing joy. Nothing excited or even interested him for very long. It took only a rainy day to leave him depressed. Klaus had joined the army as a way out of a dead end in his life but now found himself in another. He was feeling almost as much a prisoner as the Germans he interrogated. He pondered ways of escape. He sounded out the American Information Service and the American Embassy. Another idea was to apply for a Guggenheim Fellowship to finance a book on the European cultural scene at the end of the war. In the interim, with the support of his superiors he asked to be released from his army unit and transferred to the Psychological Warfare Branch as a civilian with officer rank. His request was turned down. In frustration, on 17 September he sent a letter to Robert Sherwood, who had been a member of the board of editorial advisors of *Decision* and was now President Roosevelt's speechwriter. 'The melancholy fact remains', Klaus wrote, 'that I feel almost completely wasted here and have felt that way ever since my arrival in Italy about eight months ago. Whatever contribution I might have been able to offer has been consistently *not* used.'

In the meantime he had asked his father to write to Elmer Davis, head of the Office of War Information in Washington. Davis replied directly to Klaus. His words were shocking. 'It is our view at present that our work in Germany could best be conducted by men who had no intimate contact with prewar controversies and politics.' In clear text, the criminals were to run the prison and émigrés and anti-Nazis were to be disqualified from any role in building a postwar Germany. That assertion was followed by an equally outrageous corollary, 'You and all members of your family are so well known that, while your talents would undoubtedly be of great value, I am inclined to think it would be difficult for the German people to disassociate your private standing and your official position with a government agency.' In other words, good Nazis were in effect to be allowed to decide who would administer the American Zone of Occupation. Specifically, all members of the Mann family were to be excluded from taking any part in constructing a new German republic. And that is what eventually came to pass.

A few months after that Klaus was asked by the editor of *Stars and Stripes* to write an article addressing the question, 'How do men like yourself, of German birth and, until recently, of German citizenship, feel fighting against former countrymen?' Speaking for himself, his family and thousands of other exiles, Klaus replied, 'We had failed twice in our historical duty. We had not succeeded in preventing Nazism in Germany and our voices had been too weak to arouse world public opinion to the imminence of the Nazi danger. Now we have the opportunity to make good, to a certain extent, our previous failures.'

Well before the end of the war Klaus was becoming disillusioned by the course of political events. The death of Roosevelt on 12 April had been a devastating blow. To Katia he wrote, 'Never before has the death of any public figure left me with such an intense feeling of bitter, personal loss.' He added, 'Victory doesn't seem to be quite the right thing under these circumstances.' Thomas was even more stricken, seeing it as an evil omen for his own personal relationship with the United States. 'An epoch has ended and the America we came to no longer exists.' For both father and son the great mediator between Churchill and Stalin was no longer there.

Klaus's admiration for the British prime minister was fading fast. In Italy Churchill had not only vetoed Count Sforza as foreign minister of a new Italian government but was also doing his best to preserve a fatally compromised monarchy. Even before then Klaus had been taken aback when Churchill visited Fifth Army headquarters, where he set off a ceremonial cannon and joyously claimed to have hit the target. For Klaus, nothing touched a more sensitive nerve than violence. Fooling around with an instrument of destruction and death, even in jest, was to him no joke. 'He is certainly not a man of peace.' In Greece Churchill followed an even more reactionary course, backing the king and German collaborators in a horrible civil war. With good reason Klaus complained to Katia on 6 December, 'I am rather depressed about the political goings-on in Europe – Poland, Belgium, Greece, Italy. It's too bad for words.' When, a few months later, the Labour Party in Britain won the national election, he wrote in his diary, 'The first encouraging development since the end of war.'

Of course what was uppermost on Klaus's mind was the shape of postwar Germany. How was the country to be reconstructed when a majority of Germans had no sense of responsibility for the horrors that the Third Reich had visited upon the rest of Europe and upon itself? How should a postwar democratic political culture be developed? How much of the job could be done by the German people themselves? How could a nation of criminals and madmen revert to being a nation of *Dichter und Denker*? The 'German puzzle' had plagued Klaus all his life. Now he struggled to solve it. The resulting essay he entitled 'Notes about the Re-education of the Germans'.

His starting point, influenced by his interrogations, was stark. 'We have to accept and face the fact that most Germans are Nazis.' The reason the German people were fighting to the last was not only out of sense of obedience and fear of foreign occupation but also because 'they are unable to conceive a world without Hitler and without war. The vast majority of the German people prove this every day by their dogged and idiotic loyalty to the criminal ruling gang.' Klaus knew what he was talking about – unlike the German colony back in New York, who talked a lot but knew little of what was going on. Klaus had them in mind when he wrote, 'Yet some exiled German politicians and publicists insist that the Germans have actually nothing to do with Hitler and should be treated with the utmost delicacy and respect, as soon as Hitler is gone.' Among those Klaus was thinking of were certain influential New York émigrés – among them the theologian Paul Tillich and the writer Hubertus zu Löwenstein – who staunchly maintained that Nazism was a doctrine imposed on a German people who had never fallen for it. This was to become a central issue for postwar Germany and no one was quicker to identify the problem than Klaus.

In his view Germans were collectively responsible for the atrocities of National Socialism. But to what extent and in what way? And how could this moral perversion be cured? Of course there was 'the other Germany' just as there were 'decent Germans' who were anti-Nazi. In reality, the vast majority were loyal to Hitler. Only in recognizing that fact could a sick German society hope to be healed. This was more important than physical

rebuilding, urgent though that was. He went on to write, with great presci-
ence, 'I wager that it will take Germans little time to overcome postwar
chaos. They hate anarchy and being an orderly and hard-working people
will get economic life going in no time. Where they will need help is in
the psychological and moral sphere.' Re-education had to be the first step.
Teachers in schools and universities would have to be carefully vetted, the
press as well. The basic elements of democracy had never been deeply
rooted. Now they had to be learned.

He was not without hope, however. In an unpublished essay, 'The
German Problem Children', he wrote, 'If we believed in the innate and
incurable meanness of a German child, we should therewith accept the
Nazi doctrine of an inferior race.' He went on, 'If education has proved such
a formidable weapon in the hands of the Nazis, why should we not try to
use it as well? If it was possible to indoctrinate German youth with the
slogans of Nazism, why should not an effort be made to familiarize "Hitler's
children" with the principles and purposes of democracy?' 'Our moral
teaching will not be complete unless we succeed in convincing German
youth – through our deeds even more than through our arguments – that
our way of life is preferable to the Nazi way of life and that our ideas are
right and Hitler's ideas are wrong.' None of the writings of this period were
published until forty years after the war.

By the end of 1944 Klaus found that interrogating prisoners and writing
propaganda leaflets had become unbearable. In the first week of January he
was given several days leave and went immediately to Rome to see Major
John Neville, Mediterranean bureau chief of *Stars and Stripes*, to ask for a
job. Klaus proposed to remain in the army but to be assigned to the paper
as a reporter. Having already contributed a number of articles, he was well
known and his proposal was accepted. It took six weeks to get the necessary
authorizations but finally on 19 February he started work. Rather than
following major military and political developments, he was to operate as a
roving freelance reporter.

It was an ideal arrangement. The paper had a correspondent who knew
German and European affairs better than almost anyone else, and Klaus
was free to travel wherever he wanted and write on whatever he pleased.
Stars and Stripes did not have the prestige of a great metropolitan daily
but it was effectively the sole paper in the war zone and had an assured

readership of tens of thousands of soldiers. The months that followed were undoubtedly the happiest of his time in the army.

The articles flowed. He wrote about what was of interest to him personally, to be sure, but the topics were those that he, almost alone among the newspaper staff, had the sophisticated background to address. One of these was 'The Last War of the Junkers', about the declining days of the reactionary groups that had put Hitler in power. Another, 'Over the Rhine to Valhalla', elucidated the significance of the Rhine in German thought and literature. There followed an interview with Count Sforza and two essays, 'Why Are the Germans Still Fighting?' and 'The Last Days of Hitler and Co'. The articles did not shun controversy. 'Field Marshal Kesselring' exploded the myth, firmly held by top Allied commanders at the time, that he was an honourable soldier. With equal imagination and daring he even ventured into the Vatican and had several interviews with Monsignor Ludwig Kaas, the highly controversial head of the (Catholic) Centre Party, which had supported Hitler's ascent to power in 1933. He also had his say about von Papen and Ribbentrop, Hitler and Mussolini. Taken together, his articles during that spring and summer constitute a valuable historical account of that chaotic time.

By now it was the end of April. The Third Reich was in its final agony. 'It's good to know that the great nightmare is over at last', Klaus wrote to Katia on 28 April. 'By the time you receive this note, the European part of the Second World War will already be history.' And so finally he could return to Germany. Did he wish to? Was it safe? Six months earlier both Erika and Katia had warned him that any member of the Mann family who showed his face in Germany risked being shot on sight. Klaus considered this a bit of a joke. 'I'd better be careful and never go out without a pistol and a handsome bodyguard', he jested to Katia. While he claimed he had mixed feelings about going back, there was never the slightest doubt about it. As he remarked to her, 'I couldn't even say that I completely dislike the idea, although there is something slightly gruesome about it. But on the other hand, it's not without a certain sinister fascination.'

Klaus left Rome at seven in the morning on 5 May, two days before the official surrender document was to be signed at Reims. Suddenly he found himself in places – Bolzano, Trento, Innsbruck, Berchtesgaden, Obersalzburg and Hitler's lair, the Berghof – which he never dreamed he would live to see. It was at Innsbruck that he first entered the late Grossdeutsches Reich. Did he come as a liberator or an occupier? He did not know; the Austrians did not know. There were those who certainly did know. They were the Poles, Dutch, Russians, French and Italians from concentration camps and forced labour camps who were wildly celebrating their freedom. When he reached the Berghof on the following day he discovered that American and French soldiers, in a drunken orgy of plundering, had in two days stripped Hitler's retreat, along with its wine cellar, bare. They left a squalid wreck which Klaus found beautifully symbolic. 'These ruins, one somehow feels', he wrote in *Stars and Stripes*, 'ought to be preserved just as they are – with Allied flags, torn Nibelung heroes, broken bottles and all – as a telling monument to the crushing defeat and fall of the Nazi regime.'

On 10 May he reached Munich. 'I thought it would be bad', he wrote to his father, 'but it was far worse. The destruction is beyond description. Munich is dead; the city exists no more. What was once the most beautiful city in Germany has been transformed into a gigantic cemetery. In the entire centre, without exaggeration, not a single building has survived. Only with difficulty could I find my way through streets I once knew very well. Was this homecoming?'

Then he headed for Poschinger Strasse. Fully a year before, Klaus had envisaged the scene of his return, writing to Katia of the moment 'when I shall requisition personally good old Poschi – throwing out, with the utmost brutality, its present inhabitants and moving right into my old room'. Now on the way there, he recalled reading that the residential area of cities had been largely spared and hoped that his old home would be as he had left it twelve years and two months before. Passing Bruno Walter's house, he was encouraged when he saw that it was perfectly intact, as was Ricki Hallgarten's. And so he confidently imagined the moment of his arrival. The ensconced Nazi official would come to the door and he would say, 'I give you two-and-a-half minutes to get out.'

When he got there, he found neither a Nazi official nor even a door. The handsome family villa was little more than a shell. He later heard that Himmler himself had briefly lived there and after that a succession of Gestapo families. Between 1938 and 1940 it was a centre of Lebensborn, an organization that operated what can best be described as whorehouse-maternity homes for the breeding of pure Aryan children. Toward the end of the war the place had been wrecked. 'Our poor, mutilated, polluted house!' Klaus wrote to his father a few days later. 'The discovery about the SS baby factory established in our home seems to be correct . . . The SS occupied the house during the first years after our departure . . . The inside looks, however, as if several families had lived there . . . The only thing I found unchanged downstairs was the fireplace in the lobby . . . Most of the interior is altogether destroyed, but the outside structure has remained fairly well intact. We could reconstruct the place, if we cared to do so . . . I thought it would be impossible to get up in the upper floors. Just before leaving, however, I discovered that the balcony in front of my room was occupied by a girl – a bombed-out steno-typist, as I found out, who had no other place to stay and had therefore taken shelter in the ruined building.'

The young woman, twenty-five or twenty-six, was typical of millions of Germans. Three times she had been bombed out and in the last raid had witnessed her sister-in-law being burned alive. Her fiancé had died in a Russian prison camp, one brother fell at Stalingrad, another had lost both legs in battle, her parents died following a bombing. She had no relatives, no job, no money, no place to live. 'But you have to survive somehow and have a little bit of luck', she told Klaus. 'Take the balcony, for example; finding that was a great stroke of luck.' Klaus noticed that she had done her best to make it comfortable, furnishing it with a chair, an alarm clock and a small table on which she had placed a bowl of fresh flowers. When he asked if she knew the identity of the original owner, she understood it had belonged to a writer, perhaps a Jew, who had died a miserable death. She invited him to spend the night with her – 'it is so *gemütlich* here' – and appeared rather hurt when he said he had to go.

Standing next to the wreckage of the very room where he had written his early works, Klaus suddenly found the scene unbearable. In an article written a short time later and appropriately entitled 'You Can't Go Home Again', he vented his feelings. 'The sense of estrangement and profound perplexity which I had already experienced in the ruined streets overcame me again, almost intolerably intensified. To look at these broken walls and empty windows was like facing a sinister caricature of my own past. I made haste to get out.' The scene haunted him and he later drew on it to draft a short story, 'The House of Hollberg', about an American soldier of German descent who returns to his family's former residence and learns some surprising things about it.

It is scarcely likely that Thomas and Katia would ever have wanted to live there, though Thomas wrote somewhat ambiguously to his brother Viktor in December 1945, 'Had a real house in Munich been waiting for us, it would have something heartwarming about it.' On their first visit to Munich after the war, in October 1949, he and Katia decided not to go to see it. But on returning in September 1952, they could not resist. 'Moved and pensive' was his laconic diary comment. A year later he instructed that the plot should be sold. A reproduction of the house was later constructed on the site. The government gave him a token restitution payment.

The Mann family home was symbolic of Klaus's view of Germany itself – it could not be patched up but had to be torn down and replaced. He emphatically warned his father in a letter on 16 May, 'I feel now more definitely than ever that it would be a very grave mistake on your part to return to this country and play any kind of political role here. Not that I believe you were harboring any projects or aspirations of this kind. But just in case any tempting proposition should ever be made to you (which seems hardly probable, for the time being), my little advice is that you remain impervious, adamant. Conditions here are too sad. All your efforts to improve them would be hopelessly wasted. In the end you would be blamed for the country's well-deserved, inevitable misery. More likely than not, you would be assassinated. It will take years or decades to reconstruct these cities. This deplorable, terrible nation will remain physically and morally mutilated, crippled, for generations to come. You will contribute much more to the slow process of Germany's spiritual rehabilitation if you conclude your life-work somewhere between Pacific Palisades and Küsnacht, than you would by accepting any hopeless and thankless political mission or position. You would know what I mean if you had seen the ruins of Munich with me. But I am sure you know anyway.'

The following day Klaus went to Dachau, the site of the first concentration camp, opened in March 1933. Before the end of the war people outside Germany had little or no idea of the vast archipelago of such camps, much less the existence of killing factories. What he now found was a horror equalling in human wreckage what Munich was in physical ruins. He was soon to learn that Dachau was almost a resort compared with some of the others. From there he had to hurry to Augsburg to participate in an interview by some twenty other journalists of one of the founders of concentration camps, Hermann Göring. It was a moment he never anticipated. Author meets Mephisto. The Reichsmarschall was by turns defiant and pathetic. He knew nothing of concentration camps, of course; that was all Himmler's doing, as were all the other abominations. At the time there was still uncertainty whether Hitler was in fact dead or had fled. When Klaus posed the question, Göring replied that there was no doubt about it. In his report for *Stars and Stripes* Klaus wrote, 'His ugly hands trembled a little as they kept twisting a pair of elegant grey gloves. Obviously he was exceedingly nervous; the self-assurance of his gait and speech was altogether forced. He did not succeed in hiding his embarrassment and dejection . . . He is far from being a half-crazy clown . . . He is shrewd, hard-boiled and calculating . . . He is conciliatory, moderate, and yet avoids being undignified and too deferential.'

Several months later Erika was the sole woman in a group of journalists who visited the prison-hotel in Luxemburg where Göring and other major war criminals were held prior to the Nuremberg trials. After they left, he asked the identity of 'the woman' and became very agitated when told who she was. He was sorry he hadn't met her, he said, so he could have made clear that he would have handled 'the Mann case' in an entirely different way. Thomas Mann would have fitted into the Third Reich perfectly.

Klaus's next destination was Prague. He arrived on 19 May, a mere two days after President Beneš had made his triumphal return from exile in London. Even so, when Klaus contacted his office, he was immediately invited to call – the first foreign journalist to do so – and they conversed for a full hour in the same office where the two had met eight years earlier. The report Klaus wrote about their conversation, withal very discreet, nonetheless conveyed a scarcely veiled unease on the president's part. Not surprisingly, his remarks centred on the intentions of the Soviet Union. Beneš's main point, to which he returned again and again, was that the relationship between East and West was crucial. 'Everything depends on that – for our country, for the continent, for mankind.' Could his country maintain its unity, Klaus asked? Beneš did not much like the question and admitted that there were problems with the Slovaks. But these would be solved once the economy got going. And, since the nation's industrial plant was essentially undamaged, the outlook was promising. The democratic political structure was also intact and would have the support of the Russians. 'The Kremlin keeps its word', he assured Klaus – or perhaps he was trying to assure himself. 'I have no reason to doubt the good will of our Russian friends.' As for the Germans, he said, they were acting true to form – none had been Nazis and none knew of any atrocities and everyone had a non-Aryan grandmother.

In Klaus's diary for the same day was a simple entry. 'Evening. Goebbels's propagandist exposed.' More dramatic was the *New York Times* headline of the same event: 'Klaus Mann Captures E.L. Delaney, U.S. Traitor.' The fact was that Klaus had met someone in his hotel who bragged that he was now broadcasting in Prague against the Germans, having broadcast German propaganda from Berlin to the United States during the war. Far from admiring the man's 'cleverness' in switching sides, as expected, Klaus became so suspicious he reported him to the Czech police, who promptly arrested him and turned him over to American military authorities. Delaney had in fact been indicted for treason in 1943.

Klaus's primary reason for going to Czechoslovakia was to track down his uncle Heinrich's first wife and their daughter. In 1914 Heinrich had married a Jewish Czech actress, Maria Kanova, known as Mimi, and in 1916 they had a daughter, Goschi. The couple divorced in 1930 and after the German annexation of Czechoslovakia in March 1939 had lost contact. On 22 May Klaus left Prague to visit the nearby concentration camp at Theresienstadt in an attempt to find the two women. What he witnessed – and later described in two articles in *Stars and Stripes* – left him even more shaken than the sights he had seen at Dachau. With considerable effort he learned of the two women's whereabouts. Once again he confronted a human tragedy all too typical of the time. Several years earlier, as his aunt was about to be shipped to Auschwitz, Goschi was taken from her. Her screams were evidently so shattering she was allowed to stay but suffered a stroke that permanently crippled the left side of her body and contorted the muscles of her face.

Klaus immediately cabled his uncle and then wrote him a long letter. 'I have seen Goschi and Mimi in Prague. Goschi is all right. Of course she has been having a pretty terrible time during the six years of Nazi occupation

– being racially mixed and, what is worse, your daughter . . . Mimi's case is much graver. She has passed the last three or four years at a terrible place called Theresienstadt . . . She must have suffered a lot . . . I could hardly recognize her at first. Some kind of nervous stroke has paralyzed one of her legs and arms – affecting also her face, half of which is constantly twisted . . . She is really in sad condition. Yet the fact that she has survived is miraculous in itself. Mimi and Goschi are completely penniless and have no resources. They are lacking not only in cash but in other necessities, especially clothes. I have left some money with them but it won't last long. Mimi is very worried. I am sure you can write to them. But don't write in German! It's an unpopular language.' On the same day he wrote to Katia asking her to send a package of food and clothing. 'They have absolutely niente.'

After visiting Theresienstadt and meeting two survivors, Klaus wrote in *Stars and Stripes*, 'Every German mother should be told this story. Every German should know about these things. If they all knew, the better ones among them might subscribe to those candid, repentant words I have seen written with chalk over the front of one of Munich's most famous monuments: "concentration camps of Dachau, Velden, Buchenwald! I am ashamed that I am a German".'

On his way back to Germany on 28 May, Klaus went to Bad Ischl – in the good old *k.und k.* days the favourite summer residence of Emperor Franz Josef – where he sought out Franz Lehár, who had spent every summer there for forty-two years. Living on a street named for him, he was not difficult to find. Lehar, who greeted Klaus warmly, was dressed in a Tyrolean outfit and might have stepped right out of one of his operettas. He enjoyed being interviewed, though whenever questions touched on Hitler or the Nazis he was uneasy. When Klaus referred to Hitler's infatuation with *The Merry Wives of Windsor*, he became very agitated. 'Ja, ja. That was Hitler's favourite operetta. But that's not my fault, is it?' He pointed out he was popular everywhere, including on Broadway, and had nothing to thank the Nazis for. After that he insisted, 'No politics please . . . Politics are dirty and I don't like to talk about dirty things.'

Another composer who hated to discuss dirty things – and in fact does not appear to have made their acquaintance – was Richard Strauss, whom Klaus went to see at his beautiful villa at Garmisch. Immediately on display were some of the personal traits for which the composer was famous – his geniality and naïveté, his egotism and amorality. All his life he had cared only about his art and the money that flowed from it – plus skat, of course. From the beginning to the end of the Third Reich, he had gone along with the regime without deigning to join anything so lowbrow as the Nazi party.

For an hour or so the three of them – Curt Riess, a fellow reporter, had gone along – sat in the garden chatting. Klaus gained the impression that the composer could have lived in a land of a hundred Hitlers, providing no one bothered him personally. On one occasion, not long before the end of the war, Nazi authorities had actually tried to interfere by telling him to put up several bombed out families in his nineteen-room villa. Even now Strauss could scarcely contain his indigation. 'Imagine that! Strangers here in *my* house!' In the end the issue was referred to Hitler, who decided not to insist. Strauss did not think much of Hitler, however, because Hitler did not think much of his operas. The most recent, *Die Liebe der Danae*, he simply ignored.

Klaus asked the composer what he thought, now that the war was over, of his old friend Hans Frank, the infamous governor of Nazi Poland and administrator of Auschwitz, who a short time later was hanged for crimes against humanity. 'Fine man. Very cultivated. He admired my operas.' Baldur von Schirach, the Nazi governor of Vienna? Another fine gent. He had arranged for Strauss and his family to live comfortably in Vienna to escape the bombing of Munich. Asked whether he had ever considered fleeing, he found the question so odd he did not at first quite grasp it. But why should he have left? Leave a country with eighty opera houses? When Klaus interjected that there *had* been eighty opera houses, Strauss did not catch the point. The war had passed him by. He finally conceded that had the food situation become desperate, he would have gone to Switzerland. By now Klaus could stand no more and brought the interview to a close. Amiable to the last, the old man invited his guests to stay for a meal. Klaus declined. As they left, Strauss offered each of them a signed photograph. Riess accepted. 'I don't collect photos', Klaus said. The composer looked askance and shrugged. As Klaus later commented, 'If it hadn't been for my appreciation of his musical genius, I might have told him.' In any case he was not sure whether he could ever again enjoy his operas.

Strauss was no friend of Thomas Mann. A few weeks after Hitler had come to power, the composer was one of a group of cultural grandees who had in effect hounded him out of Germany by publishing a petition accusing him of disloyalty to Richard Wagner and therefore the Vaterland. So Klaus had decided to identify himself simply as an American army correspondent. His report appeared on 29 May with the title 'Music Master Richard Strauss Found Nazis Not Such Bad People'. It was picked up by the international press and created quite a stir outside Germany, for a time casting a dark shadow on the composer's reputation. Naturally Strauss was infuriated, even though he had condemned himself out of his own mouth. He drafted a letter to Thomas but decided not to send it – unfortunately, since Thomas's reply would no doubt have been a masterpiece.

More shocking still – downright scandalous in fact – was Klaus's meeting with another unrepentant. In fact, 'still Nazi and still proud' could have been her motto. As he reported, 'Finally I have met an admirer of Adolf Hitler in Germany. After having talked to hundreds of persons who claimed to be anti-Nazi, I met a woman who admitted with remarkable frankness her devotion to the defunct Führer.' She was Winifred Wagner, owner-manager of the Bayreuth Festival. '"I know what you are going to ask me," she said with a bland, innocent smile. "You would like to find out whether there had been a romance between the Führer and me. Well, I am going to disappoint you. I never had an affair with him nor had he ever proposed to me or otherwise suggested that he had any intention of making me Mrs. Hitler. If you've heard any rumours about the Führer having been in love with me, that's all idle gossip."' There is no reason to think that Klaus had heard such stories, and in any case he would no doubt have found them too grotesque to credit. Shamelessly, Winifred plunged ahead. 'I liked him because he was always the most chivalrous man I've ever met. He had that typically Austrian charm, you know, and he had a perfectly delightful sense of humor.' Long before now Klaus must have felt that here was a case of mistaken identity. But she was defiant. 'And what a connoisseur he was in all artistic and music matters! He was generous, too. Out of his own pocket he contributed 100,000 marks to every new festival production.'

Winifred's fantastic words troubled few, if any, German readers of Klaus's article and, of course, meant nothing to the American military. So what was a scoop – a unique, on-the-record acknowledgement by one of

Germany's most prominent cultural figures of her undiminished admiration for Hitler – went unnoticed. A generation passed before, in 1975, she repeated these views before a German television audience. Then her comments created a national and international uproar.

At the time Klaus believed that Winifred merely said openly what other Germans thought privately. It took only his initial visit to Munich to show him that the physical and, even more, the moral damage far transcended anything he had imagined. As he commented to his father, 'The German people don't understand that their present calamity is the direct, inevitable consequence of what the German nation, as a collective body, has done to the world during the past five years. Nor do they understand that they were wrong in electing and supporting such a terrorist regime, and that it would have been their duty as civilized human beings to protest against its outrages.' He wrote up his experiences in a long article for *Stars and Stripes* on 13 May under the title 'The Job Ahead in Germany'. Today it stands as a document illuminating the German state of mind at the end of the war.

But if Winifred Wagner articulated what most Germans thought in 1945, there were those few for whom Karl Jaspers spoke, as he did in a long interview with Klaus on 17 June. An unrepentant democrat with a Jewish wife, the two had lived under the constant risk of being dispatched to a concentration camp. For the moment when the Gestapo came for them, they had kept aside vials of poison. A distinguished professor of philosophy and psychology at Heidelberg, Jaspers had been forced to retire in 1937. The following year his books were banned. Not a single professor stood by him. '1940 was the most terrible year', he told Klaus. 'My depression increased with every new German victory. And I was so alone! All my acquaintances seemed overjoyed as our armies invaded one European country after another. There was no one in whom I could confide my true feelings.'

Jaspers said he was not proud of having survived. In a speech given when the university reopened, he condemned himself and those like him for failing to raise an open protest when Jews were rounded up and taken away. 'That we are alive is our guilt.' To this Klaus commented, 'There you have a real, reliable anti-Nazi. There are others of his kind – not many, but at least a few thousand of them, scattered all over the Allied-occupied

Reich.' Yet Klaus did not exempt him from the collective responsibility for his nation. 'After what the Germans, as a collective body, have done, no German individual, however innocent or worthy he may be, is permitted to claim anything as "his moral or political 'right' ".'

As he travelled around Germany Klaus wondered what had happened to his friends. He gave a partial answer in a long letter to one of them, Eva Herrmann, who was back in Los Angeles. 'Almost every day that I live in this mutilated and fractured postwar Europe, I am surprised by some new horror story. From Amsterdam I learn that my friend Walter Landauer was beaten to death. Querido and his wife were deported to Poland. The old couple, both well over seventy, died. We don't want to know how. A girl I was a friend of at the Odenwald school had her head smashed with an axe and was then beheaded. Also executed was my friend Christa Hatvany-Winsloe – you knew her, didn't you? – she of the French resistance. I feel really wretched about her, the dear old thing. Yesterday I met here my dear old friend Mopsa Sternheim. Where had she been? In Ravensbrück, the camp for women. For eighteen months she was there, following horrible days in a torture chamber of the Paris Gestapo. She had been in the French resistance and for that the Germans had smashed in all her teeth. But she can still laugh – or can laugh once again, if without teeth for the moment. That is how strong she is! Eighteen months in hell. Who would know how to smile after that? I have almost forgotten myself, even though I was never in Ravensbrück.'

Some other old friends had prospered and at the end of the war continued to do so. One was Erich Ebermayer, a film script writer. Though not an avid Nazi, he had been an avid opportunist who had lost no time in turning his back on Klaus in 1933. Although at risk as a homosexual, he could count on the protection of several high-placed family relations in the party, as well as Göring and Goebbels, who liked his sappy films. In fact he earned so much from this sentimental froth he was able to buy a small schloss not far from Bayreuth, in the town of Kaibitz. As soon as the war was over, he was appointed mayor. Considering himself a martyr and 'inner-émigré', he wrote to Klaus saying he could see no reason why they could not take up where they had left off in 1933. Klaus could see a reason. 'There are many things I want to discuss with you – but not in a letter', he replied. 'I wouldn't know where to start or with what to begin. Don't forget

that we have been living in two different worlds for the past twelve years . . .
I don't say that it will be impossible for us to understand each other again,
but I am afraid it may turn out to be more difficult than your letter seems
to suggest. Well, let's try!' But neither side seems to have tried. After the war
Ebermayer defended Winifred Wagner and Emmy Göring in their denazification trials – he was also by profession a lawyer – and wrote biographies
of Magda Goebbels and Emmy Göring and books in praise of Bayreuth and
Winifred Wagner.

No one was more eager to meet Klaus than one of his oldest friends,
Wilhelm Süskind – he who had taunted Klaus for leaving Germany in 1933,
who considered him stupid not to have supported the Third Reich, who
had praised the book-burnings in which Klaus's own works were consumed
and who had himself taken on the editorship of an important literary publication within weeks of Hitler's coming to power and turned it into a Nazi
journal. Süskind's later career was another parable of life in those days. In
1943, in the land of the death camps, Goebbels appointed him literary
editor of both the *Krakauer Zeitung* and *Das Reich*, a relatively highbrow
weekly. Come the end of the war, he was immediately taken on by the
Süddeutsche Zeitung, an important Munich daily, as a correspondent and
later as editor. That he had been an ardent Nazi propagandist troubled
neither the American occupation authorities nor journalists nor Bavarian
readers. For twelve years newspaper writers had been Nazis; how could
they be any different now?

Süskind's outrageousness reached its height when he attended the
Nuremberg trials for his paper and ran into Erika and Golo, also there as
reporters. As Golo descrbed the scene, 'Süskind walked up to Erika with
open arms. She, in her military uniform looking like a war goddess, turned
her back on him.' He then went to Golo and said, 'For the most part people
forget that he [Thomas] did not really emigrate. He simply happened to
be outside Germany when these things happened!' Most Germans, he
explained, felt that bygones should be bygones. 'He believed I really wanted
to hear this', Golo commented. 'But how can we talk to people of this sort?'

It was, of course, impossible. 'What can you say? What can you do?' as
Klaus wrote to his father. 'They say we are not in a position to judge. They
have suffered, they have run risks, they have desperately tried to save at
least certain vestiges of the great German tradition, they have made as few

compromises as possible, they belonged to a secret, always endangered circle of non-Nazified intellectuals.' He went on, 'All this may be so; in any case, so far I have refused to see Süskind. It's all very confusing and somewhat depressing, even though fascinating.'

Klaus never could bring himself to see either Ebermayer or Süskind. For Süskind he had contempt but, forgiving to a fault, he eventually wrote him several friendly letters. Still, he never fell for the exculpatory claims of those Germans who said they had passed the dozen years of the Third Reich in a state of 'inner emigration', having been anti-Nazi *in petto* all along. Süskind never gave up trying to conciliate the Mann family. As late as 1955 he wrote a letter to Erika on her fiftieth birthday. 'I am no one's judge', she responded, 'but one thing I am sure of and that is that our paths have separated forever.'

After going into exile Erika had come to detest Germans and detested them for the rest of her life. 'As you know Germans are hopeless', she wrote to Klaus on 5 January 1945. Those who knew her well – Monika for one, Sybille Bedford for another – all agreed that she was a powerful hater. In Sybille's words, 'Erika could hate, and she hated the Germans. She felt passionately about things. For a time during the war she was in favor of castrating all German men. And she wanted revenge – Klaus was entirely different. Erika could not forgive.' An old friend of both, Thea Sternheim, commented similarly in her diary after running into Klaus during one of his visits to Paris. 'I was sitting at dinner in a bistro when suddenly a young man in uniform came in. On recognizing him I shouted, "Klaus". He was a hundred per cent more likeable and lively than his sister Erika. I find him far more engrossed in the German disaster than Erika, and certainly less sensationalist.' Golo agreed. 'To observe his talent, his curiosity – a quality related to his love of life – he seemed to me not only as great as ever but at a peak. He treated his former countrymen individually in a friendly and helpful way, quite unlike his sister. But no misery could make the moralist in him forget what had happened in the past. Of "the Germans" collectively he was pessimistic, at this time and in the years that remained to him.'

Although the war in Europe was over, Klaus went on with his assignment as a roving correspondent for *Stars and Stripes*. Late in June he returned to Rome, where he led a pleasant if rather aimless life. He got

along well with Italians and met and dined with some of the leading cultural figures of the early postwar period. But he was intellectually too lean
and hungry to be content for very long with the city's surpassing beauty, its
softness and somnolence. Then suddenly he was forced to make a decision.
On 16 August the army lowered the voluntary age of discharge to thirty-
eight, qualifying him for immediate release.

In a way it was back to 1933. Little man, what now and where now?
Remain in the army with its security and steady, if modest income? Become
a professional newspaper correspondent? Go back to the United States and
write novels? Stay in Europe? 'Dear old Europe', a phrase that he had used
again and again over the years, made clear where his heart lay. The notion
of settling in Berlin as a *Stars and Stripes* reporter briefly flickered in his
mind. Erika would join him, just as in the far-off days of 1924 when they
lived together in a flat off the Ku'damm. But Berlin was a ghost town and in
any case the fascination of Germany year-zero had already run its course.
Katia was appalled at the very idea, writing on 21 October, 'In principle I
would be very pleased if all of you would get out of that godforsaken and
unholy country.'

Klaus had come to agree. In a postwar edition of *The Turning Point* he
was then working on, he concluded with a melancholy passage. '*You can't
go home again*. It was a great American writer, the late Thomas Wolfe, who
chose this phrase as the title for one of his novels. *You can't go home again*.
These words were in my mind – haunting me like a nostalgic tune, a melancholy leitmotiv – while I was touring occupied Germany, in 1945 and 1946.
Yes, I felt a stranger in my former homeland. There was an abyss separating
me from those who used to be my countrymen. Wherever I went in
Germany, the melancholy tune and nostalgic leitmotiv followed me: YOU
CAN'T GO HOME AGAIN.'

Even though living in Germany was out of the question, the idea of
becoming a newspaper correspondent sat well. In light of his success with
Stars and Stripes, he thought he would stand a good chance. 'Of course, the
great question is whether I'll manage to get myself a job', he wrote to Fritz
Landshoff on 28 July. 'I am not without hope, however, considering the fact
that my recent journalistic work has in general been rather well received
and should have helped in building up my reputation as a smart reporter.'
His optimism soon faded. As he wrote to Katia a few weeks later, 'I have not

managed, so far, to get myself accredited as a regular war correspondent. It is pretty difficult to get such an assignment, as each publication is entitled only to a very limited number of correspondents, and there seem to be no vacancies.'

Being turned down is always a blow to self-confidence, and in this case Klaus was more disappointed than he let on. Looking over his later life, it seems clear that this was the first in a chain of misfortunes that led to disaster. He had been an outstanding journalist, knew his way around Europe, had an inquisitive mind, understood the issues and spoke several languages. Few could claim as much. He might have become a reporter-commentator who would have been a credit to any paper or magazine. But for the Germans he was a pariah's pariah. He had no entrée into the American press world. And he lacked the financial means to freelance. Unappreciated and unwanted, he lost what was probably his last best chance of finding himself and settling into a solid professional life. From now on he was dangerously on his own.

Uppermost in his mind was getting his works, especially *Mephisto* and *The Turning Point,* published in various translations. Otherwise he had only one concrete idea – a book on the state of European culture at the end of the war and the outset of the postwar era. The title was to be 'The New Face of European Culture' and the topic would be developed from discussions with cultural figures throughout Europe, including Germany. It was a fascinating topic and promised to be a fascinating book.

He started his interviews in Rome. Before he knew it, he found himself in the coterie around Roberto Rossellini. The director had just completed his masterpiece, *Roma, città aperta,* and was already thinking of another wartime film, this one about the adventures of American soldiers during the Italian campaign. In the course of their social encounters and lunches together, Klaus and Rossellini impressed one another to the point that on 31 July the director formally asked Klaus to write the script. The movie was to be called *Seven from the USA.*

Klaus was enthusiastic. He was so filled with ideas he started work four days later, even before signing a contract and while still in the army. To Hermann Kesten, he wrote on 11 August, 'Perhaps I will collaborate on an Italian-American film (G.I.'s in Italy), which promises some money and an interesting experience.' The deal was closed on 14 August and specified that

Klaus would be given $2,500. It was not much, but he was willing to accept an exiguous fee in exchange for working with Rossellini on a project he considered artistically important. The Italian press learned of his involvement and was enthusiastic. 'The subject of the film, entitled *Seven Americans*, is being written by Claus [*sic*] Mann, son of Thomas Mann, the famous anti-Nazi German writer in exile in America. The action breathes a sense of profound humanity and above all a profound understanding for our tragedy', reported one paper. Even now, he was 'the son of'.

Two days later he decided, after weeks of thought and on the strength of his film job, to resign from the army. On 22 August he signed the papers and on 29 August was discharged. 'It went all rather fast and painless', he wrote to his mother. His military service was probably the one thing in his life that had made Thomas proud of him, in part no doubt because he knew what courage it took for someone so un-martial to have seen it through and made a decent success of it. 'We were always filled with admiration at how you managed over so many years', Katia wrote on 5 November. But, she went on, it had been 'an unnatural situation' and was now well over. Klaus himself was not so sure. 'Discharged. Uncertainty. Uprootedness. Disgust' was the ambiguous entry in his diary on the day. His army colleagues were all returning to the United States. Should he remain in Europe? 'I stay. Am I making a mistake?' For the first time since joining the army, the horror of homelessness and loneliness stared him in the face.

Klaus's future, personal and professional, was now linked to Rossellini and his next film. The movie evolved into the story, told in six episodes, of the liberation of Italy by American soldiers. It was to be entitled *Paisà* (paisan). Klaus liked the story and, having served in the army, had an excellent feel for the subject. The whole of the original script was his work. But the temperamental differences between an insecure German-American and a bullish Italian, between an introverted writer and a moody film director made frictions inevitable. Trouble broke out when Rossellini called in one of his old scriptwriters, Sergio Amidei, to participate in the project. Klaus's grasp of the theme and the speed at which he translated it into a film text left Amidei feeling overshadowed by an upstart. Klaus found himself being shoved aside and his work, when not trashed entirely, revised beyond recognition. By 15 November he could take no more. In a memo to the producers, themselves no pillars of professional rectitude, he wrote, 'The Italian text of Amidei's new versions which I received last night makes it quite clear that there is no place or function for me in the present setup. What Rossellini wants me to do is to act as Amidei's translator. I refuse to accept this role ... So I have to go. Amidei wins.' As in a bad marriage there were tears and apologies, rows and reconciliations. But it was over. As Klaus commented to Katia on 23 November, 'They are quite too vain and treacherous.'

Rossellini's biographer, Tag Gallagher, explained what had gone wrong. 'Mann wearied Rossellini. He worked with devilish efficiency, dialoging an entire sequence in a single night and his enthusiasm was pesky. In fact Roberto had gotten what he wanted out of him; he didn't want him around when filming started and used Amidei to get rid of him ... Then Roberto got rid of Amidei.' That was not the end of the sad affair. Originally Klaus was to be paid a small honorarium for his work and given screen credit. Rossellini refused to give him either.

Yet again, failure and humiliation. The man of no luck. Rossellini's secretary-translator, Ursula Werber-Starrabba, had come to know Klaus well and was conscious of his desperate disappointment. The two grew quite fond of one another, to the point where Klaus even raised the question of their marrying, a proposition she tactfully fended off. In the evenings they took long walks together in the Villa Borghese when Klaus would unburden himself. He complained that no matter how hard he tried, he never received recognition. 'I am going to give it up; nothing comes out well when I write, and my head isn't in it.' When she asked him to let her see some of his work, he refused. 'He always spoke nervously', she said, 'his inner restlessness was always evident in his speech.' She began to notice that he was popping pills, two or three at a time. When she asked why, he said it was because he could not sleep. She was also aware that frustration and depression infiltrated his sex life as well. The riffraff he went around with left her appalled. No work, no love. She saw it all adding up to self-destruction.

So in a sense Klaus found himself back in spring 1942. One by one doors had closed behind him. The Germany of 1945 was not a Germany he knew or wanted to know. Anyway, the Germans would not have him. Italy never really felt like home and his painful experience with Rossellini inevitably left a bad taste. He could find no place in the American literary scene. Even France seemed somehow disappointing when he visited in July. 'In Paris I was not very happy', he wrote to Katia. 'Everything seemed so different – not at all the way I used to know and like it.' Suddenly he felt himself a stranger everywhere.

Even the literary world that was his home was changing. Existentialism had replaced modernism, surrealism and the other isms. Gide and Cocteau were becoming passé, replaced by Sartre and Camus. Sartre was then the most brilliant star in the intellectual firmament; Camus's *La Peste* ('The Plague') was the literary sensation of the season. In what turned out to be their last meeting, Klaus and Gide discussed all this. Predictably, Gide lamented the passing of the past. He said he considered Camus a nullity and remarked that he accepted Sartre's intellectual stature but not his existentialism. For a few years more France remained the centre of European culture, but Klaus recognized its terminal decline.

After a morning at the famous postwar Picasso retrospective, he visited Cocteau. The meeting was bound to be at the very least tricky. Only someone as naïve as Klaus would have even ventured it. While writing *The Turning Point* in 1942, he had learned of Cocteau's collaboration with the Germans during the occupation. In some of the most brilliant pages in the book, he limned some of Jean's traits. 'He may be a morbid clown, a treacherous freak, and what not. But he is not to be equalled as a phenomenon.' On he went for pages, piling ironic compliment upon ironic compliment. 'He is neither a moralist nor a liar but, primarily and essentially, a performer . . . Can a rope dancer betray his principles? He has none. Neither has Jean Cocteau.' Even that was not enough. 'Cocteau, the embodiment of the lie, says always his whole truth when he lies. Confronted with the alternative to commit either a treacherous or a trivial act, Jean would decide in favour of treachery.' Klaus went on, 'He has the eyes of a hypnotist and the hands of a pickpocket. His smile is that of a cunning infant or an infantile murderer.' And then the final touch, 'His compliance with Nazi barbarism is a melancholy event but was to be foreseen . . . Jean is not a free man but enslaved in a double way – by his vanity and by opium.'

At least some of this must have reached Cocteau. Nonetheless he played by the rules of a civilized European and at their meeting was his usual debonaire self and made not the slightest reference to Klaus's war-time words. It was a pretence, of course. When Klaus transformed *The Turning Point* into *Der Wendepunkt* in 1948, he typically forgave all and apologized for his overwrought criticism. 'For all his vanity, Cocteau is a good friend. Compassionate, ready to help, not without sympathy and warmth.' How little did he know.

Throughout the autumn, once again in Rome, Klaus desperately scrabbled for some type of work. Judging by a very cryptic diary, he apparently sought out the American Information Service and even the American ambassador. He applied for a job with United Press. It was all to no avail. Deep down he would like to have gone back to writing fiction – plays and novels – but even deeper down he suspected he was no longer up to it. His discouragement was no doubt lightened by an extremely active social life – almost every day a lunch, dinner or reception with the likes of Luchino Visconti, Anna Magnani, Giorgio de Chirico, Silone, Moravia, Leonor Fini, Elena Croce, Czesław Miłosz, Mario Praz. What probably meant most to him, however, was being with friends such as Hans Busch and Sforzino Sforza. Of course there was socializing of a different sort – in the parks, where he apparently had a 100 per cent success rate, if also the syphilis that went with it. None of these nocturnal contacts led to satisfying relationships.

It was at this time that his oldest and closest friendship was seriously damaged. After two years of separation, during which they led drastically different lives and had little contact, the old intimacy between the *Dichterkinder* had dissipated. During the war Erika had a more adventurous life as a correspondent for the American weekly *Liberty* and other publications. She also had a new lover, Betty Knox, an American reporter for several London papers. On 12 October, on her way to cover the Nuremberg trials, Erika passed through Rome. The visit went badly. Klaus let her know how hurt he was because she had not kept in touch, and Erika in turn resented his reproof. As she wrote to him on 11 November, 'I am slowly recovering from the sadness you caused me – surely unintentionally.'

On 22 December Klaus left Rome. The Italian adventure was over. He had mixed feelings about the people. 'I hate these Italians!' Ursula recalls him saying after the break with Rossellini. But then he immediately added, 'No, no I also like them.' He headed for Zurich and arrived on

Christmas Day to be with Erika and Betty. It was the first time he had been in Switzerland since the family had left for America in September 1938 and he spent the following weeks visiting old friends. On New Year's Eve he went to a party which he described as 'ghastly' and saw the year out at a gay bar.

CHAPTER 12

The Shadow Falls
1946–47

Despite all the end-of-year disappointments, 1946 appeared promising. Fritz Landshoff had written to say that *The Turning Point* was going into a second printing in Britain and that a Paris publisher intended to bring out a French edition, *Le Tournant*. An Italian translation was already under way. *Heart of Europe* was selling well, he went on, and Querido wanted the manuscript of his proposed book on postwar European culture as soon as possible. Fritz asked Klaus about a German edition of *The Turning Point* and whether he would translate it. The response was, of course, enthusiastic. Nothing was more important to Klaus now than translating his English texts into German, his German into English and seeing them all in print.

There was more. Having had a taste of film-making – however unsuccessful – Klaus now proposed making one of his own. On 23 February he despatched a long letter to Bruno Walter suggesting a collaborative effort on a film about the life of Mozart. He received little encouragement. 'Find idea attractive', Walter cabled back. 'Suggest verbal discussion in Beverly Hills where I shall be from this June to September. Could think of limited cooperation but not before spring 1947.' Sensing the conductor's reserve, Klaus dropped the proposal. Instead he thought about a film of one of his father's novels – not, oddly enough, *Death in Venice*, but *The Magic Mountain*. The projects did not end there. What about a satire on postwar Germany? And a new riff on *Candide*? Perhaps an application to the Guggenheim Foundation, this time for a biography of the late German mystic Jakob Böhme.

In other words, yet another beginning-of-the-year bout of creative hypothermia. Robert Lawrence, an associate of Roberto Rossellini, gave a good description of Klaus in action. 'Klaus was – let's say he was a restless man. He had so many ideas and so much energy . . . I don't think he could sit still for two minutes. He had a cigarette in his mouth perpetually and was in constant movement. You could feel the vibrations of his energy.' This could have been said at almost any time in Klaus's life. Between the conception and the creation, however, falls the shadow. It was now the shadow began to fall.

Since Klaus's diary for 1946 has been lost, the events of this year are difficult to track. The outlines are clear enough, however. Instead of following through with any of his notional projects, he decided to spend the early winter months in Zurich working on a play – his first since 1932. 'What really amuses me now is the idea of writing a very good play', he had commented to Katia some weeks earlier. 'I'll write it in English, and then make a German version. I want it to be produced all over the world. Isn't that a good idea?' The words sounded like an eerie echo of 'I want to be famous', the prayer he raised as a fourteen-year-old. The drama was to be called *Der Siebente Engel* in German and *The Seventh Angel* in English, the title referring to a passage in the Book of Revelations 'from the sounding of the seventh angel's trumpet the world will move relentlessly toward the fulfilment of all the prophecies of the Bible and truth will be revealed'. Klaus saw it as a metaphor for the state of the world after the Second World War. The theme reflected his deepening fear that the postwar world was splitting into two hostile camps that would result in a cataclysm.

While he was working on his play, a newly established English-language newspaper in Rome, the *Rome Daily American*, took him on for several months to report about developments in Austria and Germany. He set out on 13 April, first going to Amsterdam to discuss with Landshoff the prospects for publication of his works in Germany. During his visit he received a cable from Katia saying that Thomas was to undergo very risky lung surgery. 'Departure not urgent', it said, 'but your presence desirable.' As it turned out, he recuperated rapidly. Golo later ventured the opinion that the operation marked a critical event – or non-event – in Klaus's life. Had Thomas died at that point, Golo believed, Klaus would at last have been able to emerge from under his father's shadow and go on to great success. Perhaps subconsciously Golo was to some extent thinking of himself. Years later, after Thomas's death, he declared in a live television interview – to the manifest astonishment of viewers – that he had welcomed his father's death. Only then could his career as a historian take off.

From Amsterdam Klaus went by train to Frankfurt, where he met Erika and Betty and drove with them to Berlin. There he had an experience that shocked him to the core. Like his father, he was disgusted with cultural figures who for twelve years had supported the Nazi regime with their art, had personally profited from it and now acknowledged no complicity with the Nazis, indeed maintained they had actually served culture. He discussed the topic in some detail in an essay, 'Kunst und Politik', using Gustaf Gründgens as an example. It could not have been more apt. The actor, recently released from Russian detention, was to return to the stage in West Berlin on 3 May in a performance of Carl Sternheim's satire *Der Snob*. The public could scarcely wait to see him. Tickets on the black market sold for astronomical prices. The first night was a sensation, the greatest theatrical event in Germany since the early war years. When the curtain went up, Gründgens stood alone on stage while the audience gave him a wild ovation lasting more than five minutes. When it went down for the last time, the stage was awash with flowers and the applause and cheers went on until the police finally closed the theatre.

Two weeks later, when Klaus attended, the audience was just as enthusiastic. Although he subsequently wrote about the event coolly, at the time he could only have been crushed beneath the irony of life. He had given up everything when he fled from Munich in 1933. For a dozen years he had fought Nazism in every way he knew. Now he was homeless, almost penniless and unknown. And there on stage was a triumphant Gründgens. He had served the regime. He had been the darling of its supreme leaders, was prosperous, admired and famous. This was no longer Balzac, it was Shakespeare at his blackest. Did Gründgens see him in the audience? The actor was shortsighted, so probably not. In any case, Klaus would have nothing to do with him. As he wrote in an article, 'Old Acquaintances', in *Town and Country*, his rule was not to meet anyone unless he had been provably anti-Nazi before 8 May 1945. For Klaus there was yet a further drop of acid. At the very time Gründgens was being adulated in his theatre, in another part of Berlin an anti-Nazi film, *The Last Chance,* was being screened in a nearly empty cinema.

So Klaus personally witnessed what he had been hearing. Most Germans had learned little and repented less. They were incapable of acknowledging that they and only they were responsible for the disaster that befell their country and the rest of Europe. A year after the end of the war the moral situation was not better but worse. In an article 'Nazism in Germany Again on the Rise', published in the *Rome Daily American* on 5 June, he commented that 'while the German sickness may not be forever incurable, at the moment a cure is not in sight'. To the question of how many remained Nazis, the answer he most often received was 90 per cent. People believed that life had been better under Hitler, that democracy does not work and that Americans would soon realize their mistake and join Germany in a war against the Soviet Union. A sixteen-year-old student told him that at least 60 per cent of her schoolmates still subscribed to Nazi ideas. Anti-Semitism was rampant. Returning exiles – generally regarded as 'traitors to the fatherland' – related hair-raising stories about their experiences. A professor at Berlin University told him, 'It will take at least a half century for Germans to wipe the moral slate clean.' Klaus turned these newspaper reports into a long article, 'Problem Child of Europe', which was published in *Free World* in July.

By the end of June Klaus's reporting assignment was finished and, though his father's health was restored, he sailed on 2 July from Palermo headed for Pacific Palisades. He was not sure what he would do there and even how long he would stay. But he wanted to write and the California coast would be a hospitable place. A few days after landing in New York he once again travelled by train across America. And once again he was left with a terrible feeling of crushing monotony as he passed through miles and miles of empty space. 'We have just left alcohol-free Kansas and are now in New Mexico – or it is Texas?' he wrote to Hermann Kesten en route. 'What's the difference? The scenery is everywhere equally desolate and flat.' He reached Los Angeles on 27 July 'without concrete plans' and with 'dark premonitions'.

Even though his homecoming marked his first encounter with his father in nearly three years – since those far-off days when they had said farewell in Kansas City – Thomas's diary entry is astringent. '11 o'clock, arrival of

Klaus who remains in my study for a long time.' The further comment, 'Pleasure in seeing him again, and being greeted', was not a reference to his son but to his new dog.

Klaus had arrived in Pacific Palisades just as his father was within five or six months of finishing his new novel, *Doctor Faustus*. For some time Thomas had been turning to Erika for help and advice about his writings and speeches. By now he was dependent on her emotionally and professionally. With no further prospects as a correspondent or lecturer, she decided to make her father her new vocation and moved in with her parents. As Elisabeth remarked to Andrea Weiss, 'She returned home because she had exhausted her career, and so devoted herself to the work of her father.' She now became, in Thomas's own words, his 'secretary, biographer, literary executor, daughter-adjutant'. This caused problems at home. Again in Elisabeth's words, 'Erika was a very powerful personality, a very dominant domineering personality, and I must say that this role that she played in the latter part of her life as the manager of my father was not always quite easy to take for my mother, because she had been used to doing all of that.'

At the end of August Klaus was invited to vacate the family home to make room for Michael and his family. He had not accomplished much during the previous two months, vaguely telling his parents he was translating his play and even more vaguely was looking for work in Hollywood. He left on 28 September for New York, where he lived for the next three months in Lotte Walter's apartment. There he immediately set to work on a German translation of his study on Gide and the English translation of *Der Siebente Engel*. He also proposed writing a book with Christoper Lazare about homosexual life in America. Having published the first gay novel in Germany, Klaus now wanted to do the same in the United States. It was to be called *Windy Night, Rainy Morrow* and would be published under the pseudonym 'Martin Laroche'.

In a précis intended for a publisher, he was frank. 'It is the author's ambition to present the first complete, unbiased picture of a certain aspect of American life neglected or distorted, so far, by American writers.' It went on, 'The homosexual, under present conditions, either develops a guilt complex and a morbid sense of self-castigation or else goes to the other extreme and turns opportunistic, reckless, cynical – ignoring the code of normal morality out of a defiant desire to punish society for its prejudice.' It concluded, 'The book is not to have an explicit message, unless through its dramatic reportage and informal documentation, it happens to convey an insight and intelligent tolerance of a problem as "human" and as misunderstood in our time as adultery was in the days of Hawthorne's *Scarlet Letter*.' It is hardly surprising that the proposal was rejected out of hand by every publisher he ventured to approach. Several years later Gore Vidal, through his connections, managed to get his gay novel *The City and the Pillar* into print, only to set off a huge scandal – for some years the *New York Times* would not allow his name to be mentioned and his books were blacklisted. When Klaus read the novel during one of his flights to Europe, he was not so much scandalized as disappointed. An author's copy sent to Thomas received merely a polite acknowledgement.

Just after New Year's Day 1947 Klaus moved from Lotte Walter's apartment to a place of his own in the Hotel Sevilla on the Upper East Side. To most people a hotel room is hardly a home but, as always, it suited Klaus, who, by and large, could have been content in a monk's cell. Like Papageno, all he required was sleep, food, drink and, if possible, a sex mate. With few possessions and all his meals taken in a restaurant, his way of life reflected the absence of anything solid or settled. Nonetheless the Sevilla became almost a family assembly. Golo moved into his own room there a few weeks later. Whenever Erika came to New York, she checked in. And Monika, who had been cordially asked by her parents to leave Pacific Palisades in 1942, was now living in New York, studying to be a professional pianist. On the side she began to write. Pacific Palisades was appalled. Klaus, however, encouraged her and invited her to work with him on a translation of *The Turning Point*. Still another visitor was Michael, who came from California – on one occasion with his wife Gret and their boys, Fridolin and Anthony. Old friends, too, freely came and went. Tomski was one of them; sometimes he brought along a man whom Klaus referred to as his 'fiancée'. There was no jealousy because there was no feeling, the relationship between the two having dissolved.

By now one of Klaus's best friends was Christopher Lazare. Or perhaps one of the worst. Sometime in 1946 Klaus began taking drugs again. Without a diary for that year it is impossible to know exactly when and why he started. What seems certain is that since April 1938 he had indulged in no more than a rare dose of Benzedrine. Most likely Christopher got him started again and it was from Christopher's doctor, Arno Herz, that he procured his drugs. From now on 'inj 2 D' or 'inj 3 D' or 'inj 4' was almost a refrain in Klaus's diary – 'D' being the abbreviation for Dilaudid, the commercial name for a morphine derivative. There were rare mentions of opium and heroin as well as novolandon, paropervaminoin and several other drugs impossible to identify. Most of the time Klaus injected himself after midnight, sometimes alone and sometimes with Lazare, or even occasionally with Erika and Landshoff. 'With Christopher, inj., D 3 until 5 in the morning', is the diary entry for 8 February. From mid-1947 on, his normally meticulous handwriting in his diary was slovenly, difficult to read at times and the pages themselves were smudged with ink, no doubt under the influence of one drug or another.

Destructive drug addiction was complemented by destructive sex addiction. Klaus did not need David Hume to tell him that reason is the slave of the passions. After a period of abstinence, temptation became too great and, when in Rome toward the end of 1944, he started picking up young men for quick sex from the street or on the Pincio near his pension. Far different were the toughs from the streets of New York. When his diary resumed early in January 1947, he had just met two men named Harold. 'Harold I', as Klaus identified him, was a black from Harlem. A day or two later Klaus sent him packing because he had meanwhile found 'Harold II', a merchant seaman by the name of Harold Fairbanks. Immediately infatuated, Klaus proposed their living together. In his memoirs Christopher Isherwood left a description. 'He was well built (though in danger of fat) and quite good looking. He drank a lot. He could be very amusing or sullen or aggressive or sentimental, switching his moods suddenly and often. When he was drunk and encountered one or more sexy young studs in a bar, his favourite challenge was, "Fuck or fight" – he didn't seem to mind being beaten up, at all.'

Harold II had an unconventional notion of social relations in other ways as well. After four days he vanished without a trace. 'Harold does not show up – depressed', Klaus noted in his diary. A week later he returned but the following week disappeared again. 'Harold gone – worried.' Yet again he reappeared, this time with a young dancer in tow. The *ménage à trois* dissolved in acrimony after a few days. On one occasion Harold took Klaus and another sailor to a bar, where they were, as Klaus cryptically put it, 'thrown out because of Nazi talk'. The relationship rocked along until Harold announced at the end of February that he was going to sea again. Exactly two months later he phoned from Baltimore to ask for the fare to New York, which Klaus promptly wired him. The following day Harold's mother phoned to say that her son would not be coming to New York after all. To console himself Klaus wandered through the streets until he found Jack. The encounter led nowhere, but still later that evening he met Jim, whom he took home for a night of bad sex.

The deeper tragedy is that Klaus's professional life was also out of control. Writing had become so difficult and unpleasant he almost had to force himself to get down to it even for a few hours and then was unhappy with the result. What he had once described as natural and as necessary as breathing was now laboured and almost suffocating. On he struggled with the tiresome business of translating *Gide* and *Der Siebente Engel*. To say that he hated the work would perhaps be going too far, but it bored and wearied him. As always he was conscientious; not a day passed without his toiling bravely on. He began to think either he would finish *Gide* or *Gide* would finish him. He felt so demoralized that he started thinking about death. 'Working very slowly, tediously. Very depressed. Desire to die overwhelming.' Eventually, on 3 July, he could note, underlining every word, *'finished the German translation of my book on Gide – at last'*. What had taken three months to write required sixteen months to translate. Meantime *The Seventh Angel* had become an agony of a different sort. He finished a revised version on 5 February but all his efforts to find a theatre in Zurich or Vienna to stage it failed. No publisher showed any interest.

To be sure, he was the same old Klaus brimming with ideas. They took shape, but then burst like soap bubbles. One of the bubbles was a biography of Baudelaire which he had wanted to do for many years. So he drafted a précis, and on 21 January sent it to one of his publishers, Creative Age. It was rejected within a week. Another old idea was to do an anthology of American poetry. On 18 March he discussed the proposal with Kurt Wolff, who had recently founded Pantheon Books in New York. No interest there. Ten days earlier Klaus thought briefly of taking up the 'Speed' story, along with earlier manuscripts, and reworking them. Nothing more was heard of that. Around the same time he translated 'Une Belle Journée', a story that had appeared in Austria the year before. Apparently he did not even offer it for publication. In mid-April he finished 'Dream America'. It was a clever account of how differently Kafka, Cocteau and Hitler's favourite author, Karl May, viewed the United States. He sent it to *Town and County*, which turned it down. Still another notion was to collaborate with Erika on a book about Germany in the aftermath of the war, to be called *Sphinx without a Secret*. Klaus would draw on his reports for *Stars and Stripes* and the *Rome Daily American*. Erika would adapt some of her own articles and experiences as a war correspondent. Their outline was rejected by every publisher they showed it to.

Although by now he must have felt like an authorial St. Sebastian, Klaus continued to dream up new topics. Literally dream up on one occasion when, according to his diary, he awoke in the morning with an idea for a satire about postwar Germany, to be entitled *Fräulein*. Getting started was a misery. 'Working – still very slow'; 'Working on Fräulein—slow, slow, slow', his diary recorded. Finally on 6 May he wrote the terrible words, 'Dropped sample chapter because I just *can't do it.*' That was the end of *Fräulein* and, as it turned out, almost a pre-announcement of the end of his writing career. In a stark reversal of his early years when he effortlessly succeeded at everything – even if only to create scandal – he asked himself why he should struggle any longer. His published writings were largely disregarded, his manuscripts were rejected, his proposals found no response. His supreme hope of being accepted as an American author had failed.

Part of the problem was that for Americans history always ended two weeks ago, just as the world ends at the shores of the Atlantic and Pacific. A disastrous conflict that had devastated Europe seemed scarcely to have touched the United States. On arriving back after two and a half years' absence in July 1946, Klaus had been shocked to find that the war was almost forgotten and its results were without interest. For these reasons Erika decided to give up her lecturing career. 'No one wants to hear about Europe', she complained to friends. The overall postwar mood was well caught by a character, an ex-GI, in Arthur Miller's 1947 play *All My Sons*. 'And then I came home and there was no meaning in the war here. The whole thing to them was like a kind of bus accident.'

Germans could not ignore Klaus, however. He was a finger in the eye. At the end of the war, praising Thomas Mann was, in narrow cultural and social circles, a mode of vicarious rehabilitation. Disowning Klaus Mann was a way of effacing the past. Pamela Wedekind – who in the 1970s was still wondering whether she and Klaus should have married in 1924 – recalled that after the war no one in Germany wanted to have anything to do with him. Not even an old friend like Süskind was willing to invite him to contribute articles to the *Süddeutsche Zeitung*, she commented. All he got from Germans, she said, was the same old prewar carping about his person and sarcasm about his works. When a number of German authors patronizingly offered to introduce émigrés to the contemporary literary scene, Erika blew up. In a letter to the Berlin daily *Kurier*, she said exile writers had 'no inclination to be introduced to German readers by persons who had not lifted a finger when books were burnt'.

Recognizing that he was as good as washed up both in the German and the American literary worlds, Klaus began lobbying for a job with some publication in the field of international affairs. He saw accreditation as a way of getting hold of a press pass – invaluable in the early postwar period – which would open the way to return to Europe. On 16 April he was hired as a correspondent for *United Nations World* and within a month was on his way. He was not sorry to leave New York. A city he and Erika had adored on first arriving there in October 1927, and for years afterwards, had by now lost its attraction. No longer did it symbolize excitement. It now epitomized rejection. His sex life was unsuccessful, he was hooked on drugs, the local literati did not know who he was and daily life was plagued by loneliness, boredom and disgust. Another door had closed.

On 22 May Klaus for the first time crossed the Atlantic by airplane. Sure of a friendly welcome from the ever-loyal Fritz Landshoff, he landed in Amsterdam, where he had always been happy and now planned to make his home. But before settling in, he went to Zurich for a meeting of PEN International, where the main topic was whether a German PEN club should be re-established. As honorary president of German PEN in exile, Thomas chaired the proceedings. This put him in a delicate position. As recently as 7 September 1945 he had written an outspoken open letter to Walter von Molo, quondam president of the prestigious Prussian Writers' Union, declaring, 'in my eyes any books that could be printed in Germany from 1933 to 1945 are worse than worthless, and I am reluctant to touch them. A stench of blood and disgrace clings to them; they all ought to be pulped.' But now, feeling unencumbered by his noble words and eager to regain his German readership, he backtracked and strongly supported readmission, even suggesting the names of members. Klaus wrote a ten-page commentary on the event – never published – which makes clear that he agreed with the French resistance writer Vercors, and others from formerly occupied countries, that the time had not yet come.

Klaus had rarely been a lucky man, but suddenly fortune seemed to smile. Back in Amsterdam he was rather mysteriously invited to lunch on 11 July by someone unknown to him. Este Aliventi was a wealthy Spanish publisher with lofty intellectual interests and prodigious ambitions. She had an idea to discuss. In a letter to a friend some days later Klaus revealed it. 'I am busy with a rather wonderful magazine project that has been proposed to me. A rich, rather flighty lady wants to establish something really great and make me editor. I have already gotten a little money; nonetheless I don't really believe anything will come of it.' Needless to say, Klaus immediately threw himself into the work with his usual enthusiasm.

The journal, to be called *Synthesis*, was to appear in English, Russian, French and Spanish. Its purpose was to encourage an interchange among disciplines – education and philosophy, religion and economics, science and politics, poetry and sociology. The concept was so grand it was never feasible. Quite when and why it stalled is not clear, but at a lunch on 9 December Klaus pulled out. 'I don't think I want to do it', he wrote in his diary for that day. They had one more meeting, on 30 December. 'Lunch with Aliventi "rather stormy": probably our last.' It was.

Klaus was buffeted not only by failures but even by a form of betrayal. On 16 May a telegram had arrived from his father, then in mid-Atlantic headed for Europe. As Klaus wrote in his diary, 'Good news from the *Queen Elizabeth* – Magician offers co-editorship of Goethe anthology.' The telegram had apparently been inspired by Erika, who hoped to cheer up her brother following his long string of disappointments. She succeeded. And he was delighted. Here at last was a unique, if restrained, sign of his father's confidence. He immediately got down to work and in the following months trawled through Goethe's writings with his customary conscientiousness. When the book appeared a year later his name was not mentioned.

In mid-September Klaus travelled to Paris to see old friends and to try to find a publisher for a French edition of *The Seventh Angel*. He arrived gloomy and ill-tempered. As he wrote to Erika the next day, 'The French *Turning Point* will be out in November, a year and a half late. Similarly *Gide* in England. The German *Turning Point* goes forward. But so what? It no longer gives me any pleasure.' He found Paris itself depressing and likened it to 'Vienna anno 1920', its splendid ministerial buildings constructed to govern an empire that no longer existed. A few friends were still around and renewing old friendships meant a lot to him. The most important was of course Gide, who on 21 September invited him to lunch at his home. It was the first time they had met in two years and Gide spoke very frankly. He told Klaus that his faith in human beings had suffered a grievous blow as a result of his experiences during the German occupation. He went on to say that all the literary buzz in France about Camus and Sartre left him unimpressed. Together they speculated about the buzz on another subject – Gide's prospects of winning that year's Nobel Prize.

Later that afternoon Klaus went to the cinema to see for the first time Rossellini's *Paisà*. To his shock he found that, contrary to the terms of his contract, his name was not listed in the credits. He immediately contacted Bernhard Buchwald, his lawyer and ever-loyal friend in New York, with a view to taking legal action. In the end the film credit was not changed, though internet sites today list him as one of the scriptwriters.

A few days later he called on Cocteau for the first time in a year. Still too innocent to sense that the temperature was well below zero, Klaus later wrote to Hans Feist, 'We are on cordial terms again.' How wrong he was. In fact Cocteau only agreed to see him thinking that he might persuade Thomas – through Klaus – to translate his *La Machine infernale* into German. Klaus promised to intercede with his father in the hope that Cocteau would adapt *The Seventh Angel* for the French stage. In fact Cocteau had forgiven Klaus neither for his adaptation of *Les Enfants terribles* nor for what he had written about his behaviour during the war. The break was total, if silent. A few years later Cocteau and Gründgens met and the two of them had a fine time tearing Klaus and Erika apart. In his diary Cocteau made great fun of Klaus, both as a person and as a writer. Even his death evoked no compassion. 'Poor Klaus ultimately killed himself because he was at the end of a cul-de-sac without direction or escape. Erika lives in Austria. Their drama is a drama of frivolity.'

Certainly Klaus had his bad traits. Frivolity was not among them. It was the complete reverse when it came to his consuming interest – political affairs, and especially the state of Germany. More than two years had passed since the war. Contrary to his hopes, he had found no sign of moral or political renewal. In an interview on 11 November with the north German paper *Nordexpress*, he said as much. 'The only regret the Germans have is losing the war. Never is a word heard from them – as for example sympathy for Poland – only an overwhelming sense of self-pity.' He added that he 'did not feel German in the slightest' and had 'no particular feelings for Germans'. He had as little desire to return to live in Germany as did his parents.

It is not a German trait to speak with such unvarnished frankness and Klaus's words touched a nerve. A twenty-two-year-old reader, Klaus Wust, replied in English. 'Dear Mr Mann, I simply felt obliged to write these lines to you because your statement is right on the whole. We are a small group here fighting to take our German people away from the habit of self-pitying and its attempts of finding foreign scapegoats for its tragedy. Two years can't be sufficient time to change the majority's mind. Do help us. And never do say, it is hopeless.' Klaus was encouraged by the response and was pleased to be invited to meet Wust and his 'Gruppe '47'. Perhaps attitudes were changing after all, among the young at least. He was wrong. Wust wrote to say he had to withdraw the invitation because Klaus's presence would be too controversial.

The refusal to meet, Klaus later said, precisely answered a question he was often asked, 'Why don't you return to Germany?' This was, 'Quite simply, because no one there *wants* me.' And they did not want him, he was convinced, because they would not tolerate any émigré commenting on the country's political affairs. By now three years had passed and he had arrived at the bitter conclusion that Germans were irredeemable. He said as much to Grete Weil, a friend from his long-gone Berlin days, whom he had run into in Amsterdam around that time. Being Jewish, she had gone underground and somehow survived. Now she wanted to return to Germany and Klaus spent a whole evening trying to dissuade her. 'Never did I meet a Jew as filled with hatred', she later told a friend. 'Had I believed in collective guilt, I would have killed myself.'

It was not only Germany that Klaus found worrying. Like his father, he correctly anticipated a lurch to the right in the postwar political mood in the United States. By the summer of 1947 the notorious congressional investigations of the Hollywood film industry had begun and many of the

Manns' close friends and neighbours were being pilloried. The Manns themselves again fell under suspicion. At the end of the year the Library of Congress was denounced as a centre for 'foreign-minded Americans' which, given Thomas's association with the institution, was clearly aimed at him – in fact he had recently given a talk there. Meanwhile Erika's application for American naturalization stalled following an investigation into her sex life and political views. A thoroughly depressed Thomas wrote to Agnes Meyer on 1 December, 'As a German I am naturally inclined to be pessimistic and sometimes I am frightened of having to go through the same miserable experience all over again – if in a somewhat modified version – and from which there would be no place to emigrate – because, where to?' After years of exile and a horrifying war, after the death of fifty million souls, after the defeat of Hitler and Mussolini, the Mann family and those like them had now to worry – as they had been worrying since 30 January 1933 – about how to survive political persecution.

In Washington a lunatic counter-revolution was already devouring the Mann children. Even though Klaus had served in the military for nearly three years and had travelled around Germany as a correspondent for *Stars and Stripes*, even though Erika had worked for the BBC during the Blitz and served as a foreign correspondent for American publications during the war, both of them suddenly found they stood accused once more of being communist agents. 'Someone in Washington does not trust me', Klaus wrote to Hermann Kesten on 1 August. How right he was. A scarcely literate military government memorandum recommended denying him an entry visa into the American Zone of Occupation. Because 'his publication *Decision* advocated Communism for the US and [he is also] alleged to have run a similar publication in Paris, France before World War II. Klaus Mann [is] friendly to numerous US Communists and [is] believed [to be a] member of [a] Front Organization. Erika Mann in 1941 [was] an active Communist and in '45 member [of the] Free German Committee which was planned by Thomas Mann to rule Germany. [The] Committee [was] abolished by the State Dept because [its] membership was in [the] German American League for Culture, Communist since '36. True purpose of Mann's visit to Germany [is] believed [to be] in furtherance of Communist activities.'

Furthering communist activities was the last thing Klaus had in mind. What he hoped to further was European appreciation of American literature, which he had come to admire enormously, and to do this through a lecture tour. In an essay 'Lecturing in Europe on American Literature' he recounted how this came about. 'With most of my old acquaintances belonging to the literary set of Amsterdam, what was the usual subject of our luncheon chats and long nocturnal debates? We would talk shop of course – discussing books, publishers, writers and the stylistic mannerisms, sexual habits and financial conditions of our colleagues in various parts of the world. But nothing seemed to fascinate my Dutch friends as much as what I had to tell them about the trans-Atlantic literary scene. They decided that I was to repeat all my stories for the benefit of a wider circle – which marked the beginning of my career as a lecturer in Europe.'

He started in the Netherlands and was amazed at the extent of interest. 'Groups of students, club women, educators, businessmen, people from all walks of life seemed eager for a bit of first-hand information about "New Faces and Tendencies in American Literature".' Word spread and soon he received invitations to speak in Copenhagen and Stockholm. Fortunately the British military government did not consider him a communist menace and issued a pass allowing him to travel through the British Zone of Germany by train.

When Klaus arrived in Copenhagen on 10 November he was pleased by the warm reception. A press conference had been arranged and his remarks were reported in all the papers the following day. He had been invited by the so-called English Debating Club to discuss the current state of American literature. His talk went over well and was followed by a lively discussion. His second major engagement was another lecture, 'Is There Cultural Life in Germany?' It excited similar interest. But a shadow followed him wherever he went. And so, by popular demand, he had to give what he called 'an improvised talk' answering questions about his father – his health, what was he working on, how he reacted to the attacks on him from Germans. On another occasion the conversation turned to international relations. The predominant mood of the Danes, he found, was one of war-weariness and fear – of 'the Russian danger' and of 'the American war psychosis'. There was also lively interest in 'the problem of Palestine'. It happened that Klaus's forty-first birthday fell during his visit and he was well taken care of by his Danish hosts who arranged a celebratory dinner that evening. From Katia and Erika came a congratulatory telegram. From his father, silence.

Two days later he reached Stockholm, where he was again greeted by interviewers and photographers. Again the following day's papers carried full reports and photos. He spent twelve days there as the guest of his Swedish agent, who had arranged a busy schedule. On the evening of his arrival he gave a reading in German of his father's *Doctor Faustus* to a student group. A few days later a lecture on 'Occupied Germany' was such a success that even Klaus admitted it had gone over well. His principal engagement was a commentary, 'An American Soldier Revisits His Former Homeland', on Swedish radio. This was also highly praised. Klaus decided to extend his visit so he could attend the ceremony for Gide, who had just been awarded the Nobel Prize for Literature. But when the laureate announced he was unable to travel to Stockholm, Klaus immediately left.

He returned to Amsterdam on 4 December. The days that followed were not happy. His diary entry for 7 December is fairly typical. 'Working all day long – without too much enthusiasm . . . Dinner alone at the Café Américain. Walk through the fog. Café. Picked up Joop. Assez gentil. X [sex] Reading the *New Yorker*. Maurice Sachs *Le Sabbat*.' Although he was making some progress with an English translation of *Der fromme Tanz*, he could not break through his writer's block when it came to an article on his visit to Copenhagen. 'Worked on the Danish article with so much disgust I finally decided to drop it.' And on that sombre note the year came to an end. Fritz Landshoff – a Kurvenal, if ever there was one – invited him to spend New Year's Eve with his family. Klaus supplied the champagne.

CHAPTER 13

Todessehnsucht
1948

'Working (very little)' are the first words Klaus wrote in his diary on New Year's Day 1948. 'Working (little)' are the last on the following New Year's Eve. Between the two dates those words became almost a litany, the expression of the agony of someone who senses he is burning out. Yet to read his diary – as brief as it was by then – for the 364 intervening days is to find that he was immensely active. He travelled, wrote essays, articles and book reviews, broadcast, gave lectures and readings as well as translating two of his books into English. And in free moments he visited and dined with a multitude of friends and acquaintances.

For Klaus all that was time-filler, however. Work was writing the novel that would establish him as an important writer. By now he was beginning to fear this was beyond him. If writing is tied to your sense of self-worth, even your identity, but the words do not come, you feel wiped out. 'No choice, no road, no hope' was the way F. Scott Fitzgerald described it after his crack-up. Fitzgerald was famous at twenty-three, washed up at forty and dead at forty-four. Klaus's statistics are almost identical. So, though his days during the last year of his life were full, even successful in their way, they were to him full of nothing.

At the outset of the year excerpts and favourable reviews began to appear of the Swiss edition of his book on Gide, *André Gide: Die Geschichte eines Europäers* ('André Gide: The Story of a European'). The buzz caught the attention of French occupation authorities. Unlike their American and British counterparts – who may never have heard of André Gide or Klaus

Mann – the French were actively promoting cultural programmes in their zone. Lectures by a person of note about an eminent French author were ideal for their purposes. Klaus unexpectedly found himself invited to give a number of talks. If he could no longer write, he could at least speak.

He began on 21 January in Baden-Baden, headquarters of the French Zone military government. There he made three recordings for radio broadcast before going on to Mainz, where the French had established a new university. After several talks and readings, he concluded his visit at the University of Freiburg. The tour had gone well and he was asked to return to Freiburg ten days later to give a lecture before the faculty and students. He later remarked that he had been received by the French 'quite warmly' but by the Germans 'with polite reserve'.

In the period between the two appearances, Klaus travelled to Geneva to give his talk 'New Faces and Tendencies in American Literature' to the Anglo-Genovese Society and some weeks later to the Swiss-American Society in Zurich. The head of a Swiss writers' association, Walter Fabian, was so impressed he invited Klaus to return for a repeat performance before his own group. Klaus agreed, but on the understanding he would not be introduced as the son of Thomas Mann. The event took place on 4 March and Fabian later recalled that the talk was masterful, delivered fluently and without notes. Klaus's diary comment on the enthusiastic response? A simple 'OK'.

Although he could easily fill an auditorium with a public eager to hear what he had to say, his simple 'OK' tells a tale. The two letters signalled that he had become indifferent to whether anyone listened to him and took any interest in what he had to say. There was now a deadness in his life, almost an apathy towards the world. The change had been coming on for some time and those who knew him had a sense that he was leading an almost shadow existence. 'By now at the latest', Kroll commented rather melodramatically, 'the light in his soul seems to have gone out.' Others had a vaguely similar feeling. In early January Klaus ran into Wolfgang Frommel, a poet whom he had known since 1924 and whose work he had occasionally reviewed. Klaus did all the talking and Frommel found that his words seemed almost to come from his subconscious. 'He never spoke about himself but always about others. He looked beleaguered; his face was lined and not pale but grey.' He left Frommel with the impression he almost enjoyed believing himself in decline. During a visit to Vienna around this time, he seemed to another old friend to be 'struggling against demons'. Still another noticed that he looked depressed, drank a lot – without getting drunk – and appeared sunk in his own thoughts and almost never spoke. Yet another considered him a straight-out candidate for suicide.

But it was his friend, the Jewish poet Hermann Hakel, who limned the fullest picture. 'When he spoke he whispered politely, but with his face averted, without looking at the person sitting across from him. He seemed depressed and did not show even the slightest trace of pleasure in life. There was nothing peaceful in his silences.' Hakel went on to say that never before had he seen such a weary young author, 'a person fatigued to such a degree that it nearly seemed he was not there, despite his restless, nervous, weary hands.' He saw Klaus as 'a typical product of the collapse [of Europe]'. Comments in this vein went on and on. Such was Klaus's state of mind when he suddenly found himself an observer of the most critical political event since the end of the war.

Word of the success of his lectures had reached Prague and on 14 February Klaus was surprised to receive an invitation from the Czech Ministry of Information to give talks on American literature. Six days later the communists launched the so-called Prague coup and within a week Czechoslovakia had turned into a communist dictatorship. Klement Gottwald became prime minister; Beneš remained president for a time and then resigned. 'Painfully preoccupied with the Czech crisis and its consequences. *War is now inevitable*', Klaus commented in his diary on 28 February. What to do? As he remarked to a friend, 'Worried by the panicky headlines, I sent a wire to Prague inquiring whether the anti-fascist group still wanted me to come and talk about US writers. Their prompt answer confirmed the original invitation in even more urgent terms. Although my Swiss friends warned me against such a foolhardy venture, I decided to go after all.'

On 7 March Klaus left Zurich and arrived in Prague late that afternoon. Wherever he went, he always had friends and acquaintances to welcome him. On this occasion they were a number of old-time communist writers. The one he saw most of was Jiri Mucha, an author and dramatist who had escaped from Prague in 1939 and served in the RAF during the war. He and

Klaus became good friends and Klaus devoted a great amount of time in the last years of his life to vetting the German translations of his works. He later used Jiri as a model for a character in one of his own stories. It would have amazed him to know that Jiri's real life story was more fantastic than anything he could have dreamed up. In 1950 he was arrested as a Western spy and sentenced to four years hard labour in a uranium mine. On release – perhaps as a condition of it – he was said to have been recruited by Czech secret police to be an agent whose mission was to seduce the wives of foreign diplomats with the intent of blackmailing their husbands, a mission at which he apparently succeeded admirably.

Klaus had been in Prague for only three days when Jan Masaryk, the foreign minister and only non-communist in the cabinet, was reported to have jumped to his death. 'Struck, deeply disturbed by news of Jan Masaryk's suicide', Klaus wrote in his diary. A week later he went to visit his cousin Goschi. His diary records a 'long political discussion with Goschi and her husband', but strangely gives no hint of what they talked about. What is mysterious is that during a major national and international crisis his diary is completely silent about the unfolding events and what he and his friends said about them.

In the face of these dramatic developments Klaus went ahead with his talk 'Political and Cultural Currents in America', which he gave in German. 'Ticklish but OK', he wrote in his diary with his now usual brevity. But it was not at all OK. The discussion that followed turned the occasion into an anti-American revelry. Freedom of the press in the United States was dismissed as 'freedom of misinformation'. Kafka's popularity in America was treated as an unwholesome symptom of decadence, a sign of escapism. Kafka himself was roundly denounced by one person in the audience as a manic-depressive suffering from a virulent persecution complex, whose works appealed 'only to muddle-headed dilettantes and aesthetic snobs'. Since Kafka was one of Klaus's favourite authors, the remark must have stung. In a later essay, 'Europe in Search of a Credo', he saw Masaryk's suicide along with those of Ernst Toller, Virginia Woolf and Stefan Zweig as models of protest and frustration with life.

Immediately after Masaryk's funeral Klaus started writing an article about the question on everyone's mind. Was it suicide or murder? For once Thomas was wiser than his son. He withheld judgement, commenting, when he heard the news, that suicide seemed 'not very likely'. Without any apparent reflection, Klaus accepted the government's statement that it had been a voluntary act. 'I emphatically stress that I am convinced that the rumours of murder are nonsensical and untenable. His death was a deeply bitter disappointment to the Gottwald government. The idea that he was murdered by the communists is on the face of it absurd.' He acknowledged there were those who suspected murder. 'But the most intelligent know that he voluntarily committed suicide.' To clinch his argument, Klaus observed that there were personal factors in Masaryk's life to support this. His mother had been a depressive and for a long time in a sanatorium while his sister was 'hyper-nervous, difficult and melancholy'. He himself was labile and, 'behind a playboy façade', was neurotic, depressed, a heavy drinker and an insomniac.

On 16 March Klaus commented in his diary, 'Finished "The Masaryk Tragedy" – not very satisfied.' With good reason he was not very satisfied. Unintentionally he had produced a propaganda screed and it was certainly the worst piece he ever wrote. He cannot be faulted for getting it wrong. Not until 2002 did an investigation by Czech authorities conclude that Masaryk had in fact been murdered. Klaus's mistake lay in his categorically ruling out murder and ruling it out for ideological reasons. Was he taken in by his communist friends and simply adopted the party line? Did they feed him the purported intimate details of Masaryk's private life? 'There was something depressing about Prague', he remarked, 'but a lot less cata-strophic than as presented by our warmongering press.' And in a speech in The Hague not three weeks later, he commented, 'No occupation (no Soviet troops), no Russian intervention, no terror in the Nazi style (no concentra-tion camps, mass executions, etc.) Party dictatorship, no doubt, with all its unpleasantries.' Unpleasantries? The Third Reich was 'unpleasant'? Had he for the moment fallen into the trap of anti-anti-communism?

Klaus flew to Vienna on 21 March and two days later had a long private meeting with Karl Renner, President of Austria and head of the Austrian Social Democrats. Klaus was deeply impressed by Renner and felt that Austria was recovering better, despite its reputed *Schlamperei*, than the German-Prussians with their discipline. Early that evening he gave his talk on American literature to a large audience, which he described in his diary as 'quite bored'. In reality he was the one who was bored; the event was a great success and he was deluged with phone calls and letters in the days that followed.

Klaus spent two weeks in Vienna and, judging even by the abbreviated entries in his diary, his life on the surface appeared normal, which is to say hyperactive. As always he saw a vast array of people, visiting some of them, dining with others, being invited to drinks, going to the theatre or opera and, as always, reading a book or two each week. His diary for 24 March, the day after his talk, notes, 'Endless telephone calls – answer fan mail – lunch with Loisl Engländer ('Regina') – [gay] baths (Diana Baths) – visited by Eric Krüger, later joined by a friend – inject morphine – 6 p.m. Herz, cocktail party with Otto Basil (publisher of *Plan*, etc) – Zimmer-Lehmann (publisher of *Die Furche*) – people from the American Embassy etc. – late to a PEN club reading by Hans Müller, and later with him, Csokor, Maria Becker, Skoda, the actor, etc.' And so on it went, day after day.

Of course there were the usual twilight revelries. Despite drugs, dissatisfaction with his writing and all his other problems, Klaus's libido remained as buoyant as ever and his diary for February and March, for instance, when he was in Zurich, Prague and Vienna, sounds like a page torn out of Leporello's list. But as always there were frustrations. On one occasion he met 'a nice-looking young fellow, Gustav, who at the last minute runs away'. Two days later it was someone who was too drunk to do anything. Then he looked up his old friend Eric Krüger and took him to an excellent performance of *The Magic Flute*. Eric slept through it all. That was the end of that relationship. Eventually drugs became so serious a problem that on 5 April he checked into a sanatorium in Salzburg for treatment. 'Go to see a doctor about my legs (all enflamed from those rotten injections – evening alone making compresses).' He spent the whole of the next day doing the same.

Continuing his tour, on 7 April Klaus arrived in Munich, which he described as reeking of 'the pestilential stink of hopelessness' and 'moral nihilism' of large German cities. The first person he visited was his uncle Viktor, Thomas's younger brother, who proudly announced that he was busy writing a family history to be called *Wir Waren Fünf* ('We Were Five'). Their meeting was relaxed and friendly and several days later, when Klaus missed the last train to Frankfurt, he returned to spend the night in his apartment. But nothing was more important than tracking down Hans

Reiser. It was quite a search through the still ruined city – first to Hans's mother and then various theatres until finally he found the actor and his girlfriend.

As it turned out, Klaus's most important encounter in Munich was serendipitous. One evening, at what he referred to as 'an American party', he fell into a conversation with Melvin Lasky. Famous for his bravado and peacock ego, Lasky was associated with the CIA in Berlin, where he was essentially an ideological huckster selling anti-communism on the East-West frontier. He was smart enough to realize that anti-communist propaganda would be more effective if it came from the anti-communist left. Klaus, with his name and reputation, was ideal. Lasky offered to work out a programme for him.

On 3 May he flew to Berlin. This was his third postwar visit – after those of September 1945 and May 1946 – and the longest, giving him ten days both to carry out the official programme arranged by Lasky and to see a multitude of old friends. He made several radio broadcasts, gave his lecture on American literature at the America House and spoke about his book on Gide at the Hebbel Theatre. By coincidence the talk on Gide was held on 10 May, the fifteenth anniversary to the day of the book-burning and not far from the very site where both his and Gide's works had been ceremoniously incinerated. The theatre was packed and his remarks were well received. All in all the whole programme was a marked success. The often acerbic *Der Spiegel* welcomed his presence in Berlin and characterized his lectures as 'masterful, brilliant, animated'. Although Klaus would probably never have admitted it, the Berlin engagements reaffirmed that his intellectual powers were undiminished and that he could command a ready audience eager to hear what he had to say.

The message he wanted to convey was that in the postwar, interdependent world, literary isolationism was as passé as political isolationism. 'European-born writers now living in the United States, as American citizens, may contribute their bit to the development of American letters by acting as go-betweens and mediators between the mellow, somewhat weary and problematical culture of the old continent on the one hand and, on the other, the young striving civilization of the new world.' Klaus clearly foresaw that in the postwar era the United States would inevitably be dominant politically, economically and militarily. But he hoped that in literature there would be interchange not domination. He wanted his own work to manifest an international spirit. In the end each side went its own way and – apart from a few publications such as *Der Monat* and *Encounter*, both bankrolled and controlled by the CIA – no exchange ever came about.

The visit to Berlin gave Klaus an opportunity to look for old friends, while old friends, having read in the newspapers that he was to give two talks, did their best to find him. There was no one he was more eager to trace than his old bedmate, Willi, who had enlisted in the SA in 1932. In fact Willi Luschnat had gone into the Wehrmacht, been wounded on the Leningrad front in September 1941 and returned to Berlin to serve in a staff job. Each searched for the other and then suddenly found themselves face to face. They were as fond as ever. One of Klaus's last letters was to Willi.

A banquet was arranged in Klaus's honour and it is easy to imagine the eerie emotions, each person having been to hell and back during the previous fifteen years. There could only be mistrust and some of the encounters were sticky. Klaus was frank. 'I knew I could no longer feel at home with them in their circle', he later wrote in his essay 'Lecturing in Europe on American Literature'. Whenever he met someone, he could not help wondering whether the person had been a loyal Nazi to the very end or even a mass murderer.

It was not all heavy going, though, and years later one of the guests favourably recalled his encounter. 'I mentioned to Klaus that I was experiencing difficulty in finding an adequate German translator for some poems by Constantine Cavafy, a modern Greek poet whose work is studied only by a very small group of scattered readers. Klaus immediately gave me the name and address of a young German poet who lives in exile in Holland who had made some excellent translations of Cavafy. This was typical of Klaus; it is one of the many bits of unbelievably varied information that always made an hour's conversation one of the most profitable and stimulating experiences that a colleague could expect.'

So he gave his talks and interviews and saw friends. But, most important of all, he met Georg Jacobi, an editor at Langenscheid Verlag, and raised the all-important matter of a German publication of *Mephisto*. Jacobi thought well of the idea and they signed a contract. This would mark Klaus's breakthrough into the German literary world.

And poor, mutilated Berlin itself. What did he think of it now? He found he still felt some affection. No talk here of 'the pestilential stink of hopelessness' or 'moral nihilism'. In one of his last articles, a review of Pierre Frédérix's *Mort à Berlin*, he wrote, 'Yes, I loved Berlin and one remains true to one's old loves.' Even the monumental ruins, he thought, were almost treasures, possessing 'a sort of grandeur, a character of tragic pomp'. He added, 'I shall never forget what the English author Stephen Spender said of the German ruins. "Every epoch has its architectural style – baroque, renaissance, gothic, etc. We also have a style – jagged edges, holes, abysses – this is the architectural style of the twentieth century." '

As in 1933, friends sought to persuade him to stay. And as in 1933, Klaus said he could not. The past was more than he could forget or forgive. The tie had been broken forever. In an essay he had written while in Prague several months earlier, 'Ich bin kein Deutscher', Klaus had commented, 'For some fifteen years now I have not been a German. For five years I have been an American. For me returning to Germany is out of the question. But as a citizen of the world and devout internationalist, I can only hope that it will be possible gradually to become engaged in literary work there and establish contact with German intellectuals, especially young people.' When he boarded a plane at Tempelhof airport on 13 May, he left Germany forever. Or, perhaps, Germany had left him forever.

Unable to write and unable to conquer his drug addiction, Klaus decided that he must have a change of scene, return to as much of a home as he had, and be near Erika – Santa Monica. On the night of 14 April he took a KLM flight to New York. There he spent the better part of a week with Monika, Landshoff and other old friends. Among them was Charles Neider, a member of the *Decision* staff and then at the outset of a distinguished writing career. He invited Klaus to dinner and later recorded his impressions of the evening. 'It seemed to me that he was mellowing in some quite beautiful way (he had put on weight and had begun to gray), and that he was, if one could at all apply the phrase to him, at least temporarily at peace with himself. I was pleased and reassured; I fondly and foolishly told myself that out of the agony and brutality of a shattered Berlin, he had captured the germ of some uplifting theme which he had sought and that he himself had miraculously escaped the flames. We escorted him to the street, my wife and I. He the continental figure, the truly international type, like one of

Henry James's better people, the tender, shy, gently renouncing kind, was all attentive to us. We hailed a cab and saw him into it. Out of its gloom he thrust a white hand and a part of his sensitive face. "Au revoir, see you again sometime", he said musically. One felt it in one's guts, his bravery, at such moments, the fugitive inkling of his hidden self – tormented, lonely, at times desperately seeking, and brave. After the cab had gone I said to my wife: "Perhaps we shall never see him again." "I was thinking just that," she replied soberly.'

Erika picked Klaus up at the Los Angeles airport when he arrived on 24 April. More than a year and a half had passed since he was last there and nearly a year since he had seen any of the family. To celebrate there was champagne and, according to Thomas's diary, the day was spent hearing about his travels and 'the problem of Monika'. In the evening he took a walk with Nico, Thomas's new poodle, and returned to listen to a concert on the radio. The next day Bruno and Lotte Walter visited and the conductor marked the homecoming by playing the piano score of the andante of Beethoven's Sixth Symphony. The placidity of the music and the serene, domestic life were not to last.

While in Europe, Klaus had occasionally written to his friend Harold Fairbanks and on arriving in New York had sent him a telegram. No sooner was he back in Los Angeles than Harold phoned from San Francisco to say he had lost his job and was coming to be with him. From the start there were problems. On their first night Harold insisted on going on a bar crawl and, to Klaus's disgust, got roaring drunk. On other occasions Harold corralled a third person to join them and then there were quarrels. On 7 June Harold phoned from the Los Angeles county jail to say he had been locked up. When he arrived there, Klaus found that it was 'quite a messy affair'.

In fact Harold was accused of having had sex with a teenager. It turned out that the kid was a hustler, had been picked up by the police and got off by grassing on men he had been with. The following day Klaus put up a $500 bond and Harold was released. But instead of appearing in court the next day, he disappeared. In reality he had not skipped bail; he was in another jail on suspicion of burglary. The charge was baseless and quickly dropped. Not long afterwards Klaus and Golo ran into him on the beach in Santa Monica, where he apparently spent most of his time. Golo had never seen him before and found him 'good-natured but lacking any education and judging by his appearance a horrible brute'.

In many ways the tableau on the beach illustrated the sexual dilemma that had plagued Klaus all his life. What he most wanted was the companionship of another homosexual man. Occasionally he had found it – with Tomski, Hans Aminoff, Wolfgang Hellmert, Brian Howard and others. But these relationshsips were neither permanent nor satisfactory. So he contented himself with what he found on the street and that was almost always trash. Except for Johnny Fletcher, the connection was purely mercenary. Klaus paid up and then felt guilty. And so it was with Harold. No more was Klaus able to confront or break with him than he had been able to confront or break with all the other Harolds of his past. So he led an incongruous life in which at one moment he might be at a jail with a lawyer arranging bail for a boyfriend and that night attend a dinner party with Bruno Walter, Alma Mahler and Herbert Marcuse.

Sex was not the only problem. Writing was by now an incubus. On arriving in Pacific Palisades he started work on a report about his European lecture tour. Day after day he groaned to his diary. 'Work a little'; 'working (if you can call it that)'; 'worked whole day on Lecturing – how long it takes; is it worth the effort?' Then finally on 26 June, the awful comment, 'working on Lecturing – a torment – why can't I write anymore? What's wrong with me??' Four days later, after a further struggle, 'Am I through? Can't I write anymore??' And then, in perhaps his saddest letter – to Peter Viereck, the American historian – he remarked, 'I find it increasingly difficult to write and to live (which means almost a pleonasm as the two terms, *life* and *work*, are practically tantamount to me). There are moments when I feel almost incapable of facing the world's mess and my personal mess any longer. I am planning to deal with the issue of suicide in my next novel – which will be more tedious and more painful but somehow more honourable than actually doing it.'

He was again shooting drugs – morphine, antropine and a variety of others, identified only by an initial in his diary. Because of the morphine he could scarcely write and because of the antropine he could scarcely read. This was an especially acute problem at the time because he was trying to study *The Magic Mountain*. There was active discussion of making a film out of it, and Klaus hoped that he and Erika could help produce the script.

It was now that he took what was for him the daring step of leaving the family home and living on his own. He bought a car and learned, more or less, to drive it. To go with his car he rented a small apartment on Amalfi Drive. As soon as he moved in, however, the thought of living alone was unbearable. So he decided to invite Harold to be with him. The first night was disastrous. Harold wandered off and returned at five in the morning with an old bum who collapsed going up the stairs. Klaus still desperately hoped the arrangement would work. And for a short time it did. 'Life with Harold – pleasant and peaceful on the whole', he wrote in his diary on 7 July. It was not to last; the next day Harold got himself in trouble and vanished.

It was more than Klaus could stand. That night he disconnected the hose from the gas stove and began inhaling the fumes. A neighbour smelled the odour, broke into the apartment and discovered Klaus, who then ran to the bathroom, locked the door and cut his wrists. He was taken by ambulance to the Santa Monica hospital. A very cranky Katia arrived around one in the morning and stayed for several hours. A not much less choleric Erika appeared later. The family considered 'the episode' a huge nuisance. Thomas was too appalled to care – or, rather, did care and was furious. Four years before, Heinrich's wife, Nelly Kröger, had killed herself. In Thomas's eyes Nelly was hopelessly vulgar and what she did was hopelessly vulgar. Now, when he learned of his son's suicide attempt, Monika heard him say in disgust, 'Das macht die Kröger' (that is the sort of thing a Kröger does – the exact equivalent of the famous final line in *Hedda Gabler*, 'Proper people don't do such things.'

To Theodor Adorno, the émigré philosopher-musicologist, Thomas wrote, 'I am somewhat angry with him for wanting to do that to his mother. She is understanding about everything – and so am I. That spoiled him. The situation remains dangerous. My two sisters committed suicide, and Klaus has much of the elder sister in him. The impulse is present in him and is favoured by all the surrounding circumstances – except that he has a parental home he can always rely on, although naturally he does not want to be dependent on it. It is a good sign that he curses the publicity that followed the incident on the grounds that this makes it so hard to start over again.'

To Thomas's mortification, 'the publicity' was broadcast in the international press. The compassion Klaus did not obtain from his family he received in cards, telegrams, letters and phone calls from friends and even strangers around the world. Upton Sinclair was one of the first. 'My dear Klaus: Don't do it! You have written fine books and you can do a most important job in helping to interpret Europe to America and vice versa.' Willi wrote in a similar vein from Berlin. 'You can still achieve a lot, don't ever forget that. You can even create and be happy. Some day you will find your way.' Lora Lumsden, a rather fanciful German-Jewish writer, also tried to be encouraging. 'How more than sad it makes one feel that so brilliant a writer should so suffer. Please do get better, so that you may go on writing still finer books.' Even the manager of a hotel in Zurich, where Klaus had once stayed, sent him a letter. 'Your Gide biography had such an outstanding reception that it is impossible to escape the conviction that you still have much to say to the world.' Tomski waited three weeks to get in touch and then tried to be lighthearted. 'Suicide, as I once wrote in that unpublished article, never pays. I hope by now you are out of the melancholy woods and any thoughts of such nonsense are out of your mind.' By no means was Klaus out of the melancholy woods. In his diary on 16 July, he commented, 'And I still would *love* to be dead.'

Klaus's cuts were so superficial he was able to leave the clinic in the morning and go swimming in the afternoon. Erika collected his things from the apartment and, since the Mann household was full – Monika as well as Michael and his family were staying there – she arranged for him to go to Bruno Walter's home, where she herself was living. Klaus spent the first evening there reading Oscar Wilde's *De Profundis* – just the thing for someone in his moral condition. Harold showed up the next morning, but not until two days later did Thomas traverse the meagre distance to his neighbour's house to talk to his son.

In the meantime Friedrich Hacker had been there. Hacker was a thirty-four-year-old Freudian psychiatrist and émigré from Vienna whom Klaus had by chance met at a dinner party several days earlier. Now they talked for a long time. In a letter written years later to Fredric Kroll, Hacker discussed Klaus's case frankly. 'Obviously his whole personality formation and psychodynamics were decisively determined by his relationship to his father.' He went on. 'He frankly conceded that he was suspicious of psychiatrists and what they had to offer . . . We had become great friends; he rather freely discussed all his current problems with me which were mostly concerned with current homosexual relationships and getting out of certain complications that had arisen in connections with them. Particularly also as a result of these involvements, he was often tense, anxious and quite depressed. What I found in him more explicit than anyone I have known before or after, was a kind of romanticized longing for death – "Todessehnsucht". To him death seemed not only nirvana but blessed paradise, the surcease of all earthly worries and the attainment of a kind of constant, even ebbing and flowing but never ceasing serenity, which he of course never was able to achieve in his life.'

Golo later criticized Hacker for seeming to have written Klaus off by telling him, 'In nine months you will do it again.' On learning this, Hacker responded, 'I had been very blunt with him in regard to his prognosis because I felt that as long as he considered death . . . as a positive goal to be accomplished as a crowning glory, we did not have much chance to keep him alive. He enthusiastically agreed and gave the impression that he hardly could wait until he could enter this new, more glorious phase.' Yet in a later television interview Hacker said he believed that if Klaus had outlived his father, he would have been liberated from his overbearing presence and thoughts of suicide would have fallen away – Golo's view exactly.

During the following several weeks Klaus toiled away, unhappily answering 'melancholy fan mail' and even more unhappily translating *The Turning Point*. For a time things took a sudden turn for the better when he was asked to do a German translation of Anita Loos's Broadway hit, *Happy Birthday*. He immediately took to the idea – certain lines must have spoken to him, such as, 'Oh, I want so much to be loved. By everyone!!!' Thanks to a little help with the more arcane passages from his eternal admirer, Hans Feist, he finished the job in two weeks. It was a remarkable achievement yet not one that mended his battered self-confidence.

Klaus's relationship with Harold had by now evolved into equal parts sex, rows and forgiveness, all equally intense. During one of the conciliatory cycles, the two decided to live together at the El Kanan Hotel in Santa Monica. But nothing changed. 'Around 3 a.m. Harold comes back with a sailor – blow-up – I leave the house and walk the streets for several hours.' That was the entry, written in French, presumably so Harold could not understand it, for 8 August. The following one reads, 'Harold's birthday – fight and reconciliation.'

Greatly complicating matters, Christopher Isherwood also lived at the El Kanan and was also strongly attracted to Harold. In his memoirs Christopher described what he observed. 'On the surface, as always, Klaus was bright, witty and seemingly interested in what was going on in the world around him. He had a lot of courage and he tended to keep the melancholic side of his nature hidden. I don't think that he got much moral support from any of his love affairs. Certainly not from Harold Fairbanks, who was fond of him no doubt but much too unstable to be able to take a lasting interest in other people's problems.' He went on to write – in the third person – 'I am sure Klaus's realistic pessimism convinced him that there was no future in their relationship. He did however make a scene on one occasion when he found Harold drinking with Christopher in Christopher's room late at night. Christopher and Harold weren't, in fact, doing anything sexual, but Christopher rather wanted to go to bed with him and Harold realized this and would probably have said yes if Klaus hadn't shown up.' Klaus's diary comments, 'Quarrel with Harold who has been drinking with Christopher – more angry words, more tears.'

Klaus could take no more. He decided to go to live in Amsterdam. The day before he had received a telegram from Landshoff saying that Querido, now re-established in Europe, was expanding and needed editorial help. In a typically kind gesture, Fritz invited him to be a reader. Klaus needed only overnight to think it over. Was it the old appeal of Amsterdam? Was he fed up with Harold and Christopher? Or was he once more on the run? Probably all three.

Less than two weeks later, on 15 August, he flew from Los Angeles to New York, where he checked into the Bedford for five days. There he polished his translation of *Happy Birthday*, visited gay baths, had drinks and dinner with Curtiss and spent every evening with Christopher Lazare, who once again got him back on drugs – this time for good. He also took the occasion to visit his publisher, Allen, Towne and Heath, and to talk to David Ewen, a founder of the firm, who handed him a pile of reviews of *Pathetic Symphony*, which had finally been published. Inevitably the comments were mixed, or as Klaus noted in his diary, 'some rather nice, others annoying'. Thirty years later Ewen still remembered their meeting that day. 'I found him to be an inordinately unhappy man; I cannot remember him smiling. I think he carried the burden of being Thomas Mann's son too heavily, from some casual remarks he made.'

After a cancelled night flight, Klaus left New York early on the morning of 21 August. He had taken care to book a window seat, to the unmistakable displeasure of the person who was assigned the aisle seat next to him. The peeved neighbour, he noticed, spent his time reading the funny papers and showed no inclination to talk. Gradually he came to look familiar; in fact he rather looked like Allen Dulles. So Klaus ventured to ask him whether he was perhaps the author of a book on the German resistance. He replied he was his brother. Instantly Klaus jumped in and said, 'So you are our future secretary of state.' Among John Foster Dulles's many talents, charm was not one. The future secretary of state decided to move to another seat. He was, as Klaus wrote to Katia and Erika, a pill.

Landshoff met Klaus at the airport and drove him to a pleasant accommodation behind the Rijksmuseum. Fritz and his wife Rini did all they could to encourage him in the weeks that followed and more often than not had him to dinner. To all appearances his life continued, for better or worse, to run along the usual course. He read a great deal, wrote scores of letters, saw friends and above all laboured on with his translation of *The Turning Point*. Judging by the abbreviated notes in his diary, he seemed to exist rather than live. There was no joy in his life. Fritz alone kept him on an even keel.

It is difficult to make out how much Klaus did for Querido, or what he was expected to do. Fritz probably had little more in mind than giving him a place to settle while he convalesced psychologically. And probably Klaus did more than he said in his ever sparer diary notes. There he merely mentions writing the odd press release – on the history of the firm or on a forthcoming book – and looking over an occasional manuscript. Even so he learned something about Querido's operations and the problems of the book trade as it tried to re-establish itself while Europe was still recovering from the war.

Translating and revising *The Turning Point* continued to be an agony – '6 ½ pages, that's all!' (28 August). 'Worked (if you can call it that.)' (18 September). 'Slow, slow, slow – in spite of inj. (3 No). Thinking of death, craving it, waiting, hoping for it every hour of this long tedious day' (29 September). On 25 October he finished the translation of 'Chapter 10: Exile' and immediately started work on the last one, 'Volcano'. Despite his depression, on he went day after day, week after week. With slightly less pain he completed his essay 'Lecturing in Europe on American Literature', which was published by *Vogue* in December.

In the meantime, Rolf Italiaander, a dubious Dutch-German journalist, had appeared at Klaus's Querido office and invited him to give his talk on American literature in Hamburg. To prepare the ground, *Die Welt*, one of Germany's leading dailies, would publish a few extracts from *Der Wendepunkt*. In the end nothing came of the proposal to speak, but the extracts appeared on 28 October. Those two book reviews, the short story 'Une belle journée' and the essay 'Contemporary German Literature' were the sum total of Klaus's postwar publication in Germany during his lifetime.

It was not that he was unwilling to be published in Germany, but invitations never came. A pleading letter to Melvin Lasky offering to contribute to *Der Monat*, which he edited, is painful to read. 'I was pleased to see Golo mentioned as one of your future contributors. But what about me? I am just doing a piece for *Tomorrow* about "the ordeal of European intellectuals" which might fit into that series of essays you announced in connection with the Sartre piece. Or would you rather like a fragment from my autobiographic book, *The Turning Point*, the German version of which I am just concluding? Or a letter from Amsterdam. Or what else. Let me know.' Apparently Lasky did not reply.

Nothing is so boring as a succession of sunny days, Goethe is supposed to have said. The claim is one Klaus would have been among the last to vouch for. Scarcely was his life settling down into its normal pattern of trials, tribulations and *Todessehnsucht* when, from an unexpected direction, came a pernicious attack. On 22 October there appeared in the Munich weekly *Echo der Woche* an article headlined, 'Erika Mann as Stalin's Agent – Stalin's Fifth Column at Work'. It was written by the chief editor, Harry Schulze-Wilde, in response to a radio broadcast in the United States in which Erika spoke in favour of doing a deal with the Russians over Berlin – this was the time of the blockade – in order to avoid a possible war. 'I don't think there are enough German democrats in Berlin to be worthy to fight over, actually.' Although Klaus made no comment on the topic, Wilde linked him with his sister as a 'salon Bolshevik'. More than salon, in fact. Not only had he been the paid guest of the communist government of

Czechoslovakia, he had also recently been invited to Berlin by a communist writers' group in East Germany. Together, Erika and he were doing Stalin's work by preparing the way for a communist takeover of Germany.

Harry was a notorious journalist, renowned for inventing stories devoid of fact. Character defamation was a specialty. But why Klaus? The two had met in Amsterdam in January 1936 – had even had sex together – but evidently had had no further contact. The ensuing controversy was as boring as it was absurd. Suffice to say Klaus defended himself in a letter to the paper and threatened legal action. And, suffice to say, Wilde replied by descending into petty insult and calling upon his readers to chime in with their opinions on 'the Erika and Klaus Mann case'. The smear campaign was picked up by other newspapers and spread throughout West Germany. Action by Klaus and Erika to sue Wilde for slander was blocked by American occupation authorities. Twenty-five years later Wilde was still pursuing his vendetta. Klaus may not have been strictly speaking a communist but he was, as he phrased it, 'in effect a communist agent'.

For the Manns the incident had two results. On the one hand it reinforced the sentiment in Germany against Erika and Klaus. On the other it deepened Erika's loathing of Germans and convinced Klaus he would forever be rejected in Germany, an object of defamation and derision when not ignored.

As if that were not torment enough, on 10 November the sky fell in. Or, as he wrote cryptically in his diary on that day, 'The "overcoat" affair turning unpleasant. Talks with Mr Jacoby; to Meyer (lawyer). Decide to leave.' Klaus had always taken risks with his pickups and was lucky to have been beaten up only once – in Toulon in May 1936 – and occasionally to have had small amounts of money or clothing stolen. On arriving in Amsterdam he had in no time found Henk, Herbert, Joop, Jaap, 'Belgian boy', 'soldier' and several others. Jaap he used as a messenger. But he was a thief; he not only stole two pairs of Klaus's trousers but the overcoats of a number of residents at the pension. There were stories of blackmail by Jaap and hints of underage sex, though that is unlikely given the sort of men Klaus habitually sought out.

In a letter to Katia, written in London three days later, Klaus was only slightly more specific about why he had decided to leave. 'Aren't you surprised? I rather am, too. It came a bit suddenly. I am on my way to New York. In Amsterdam a rather annoying and potentially dangerous situation suddenly came out of the blue, something not entirely dissimilar to what happened to Harold in California . . . I was not inclined to run a risk. Incidentally nothing unpleasant ever occurred – and probably never would. But not only a lawyer but also a local friend advised me to be careful. . . . So why take chances?'

Klaus flew to New York on 18 November, the day of his forty-second birthday, a fact unnoted in his diary. He was anything but welcome to his family. When he telephoned Katia, he must have got an earful, or, as he gently phrased it in his diary, 'She does not sound very enthusiastic'. Even less 'enthusiastic' was Erika. Her patience was now at an end. She was furious that he had not stayed in London or gone to Italy and suspected him of returning primarily to see Harold. But she had her own problems, and when Klaus arrived in Los Angeles he found his sister in terrible shape. For some years she and Bruno Walter had secretly been pursuing a torrid love affair which, after Elsa's death in 1945, Erika hoped would end in marriage. Instead, not long before Klaus's arrival she suffered a shattering blow when Walter ended the affair, telling her that from now on he wanted their relationship to be based on 'a natural, that is, fatherly basis'. In fact he had found another. Erika was so stunned she broke off all contact and sank into a black depression. By now poor Katia was exasperated with her as well. As she wrote to Klaus, 'My God, how can one be so hell-bent on the unfaithful old man? . . . It should have stayed platonic after all.' Eventually, at two in the morning on 27 December, Erika worked herself into a minor heart attack.

There was an old-fashioned German Christmas at Pacific Palisades that year. On Christmas Eve a tree was trimmed and for Christmas Day Katia had found a goose for a proper German dinner. A photo of the family at table would not have shown many smiling faces, however. Thomas was in a black mood, feeling ill and convinced that the political situation in the United States and Europe was headed for disaster. Erika was disconsolate and silent. Klaus was sunk in his longing for death. Monika was morose, weeping, sulking. Heinrich was wretched, ill and impoverished. As usual it was up to Katia to draw on all her boundless tact and effervescence to inject some joy into the occasion.

New Year's Eve was the last time the whole family, albeit minus Elisabeth, was together. Michael and Gret came down from Berkeley with Frido and

Toni. Golo brought his latest companion, Anthony. Erika had recovered sufficiently to play recordings of light-hearted Noël Coward songs. Katia's twin brother, Klaus Pringsheim, accompanied Michael in performances of old Italian and French music. And Thomas amused the family by reading articles from the Austrian press blaming every ill that had befallen Germany and Austria since 8 May 1945 on Thomas and Klaus Mann.

CHAPTER 14

Death in Cannes
1949

It rained almost ceaselessly in Cannes throughout April and May. Because the Riviera is normally bright and colourful, grey weather there seems somehow greyer than anywhere else. A dreary, monochrome sky fades into a dreary, monochrome sea so that the horizon disappears. Dreary, monochrome buildings float on dreary, monochrome abandoned streets. Inevitably the scene infiltrates the mood. 'Rain – the weather being about as miserable as my moral and physical state', Klaus wrote in his diary on 3 May. In the days that followed, the depression, both meteorological and psychological, dragged on.

Finally, on the night of 20 May the sky cleared. Klaus had a date at the Zanzi-Bar, behind the Croisette – by coincidence a bar that he and Erika had visited eighteen years earlier when writing their book on the Riviera. The next day he was found lying on his bed unconscious and was taken to a hospital, where he died. 'The longing for death pursued him as a relentless assassin pursues his victim.' Were these words, which Klaus had pronounced at a memorial for Ricki Hallgarten in 1932, now true of himself? Had the assassin caught him at last? 'Il n'y a qu'un problème philosophique vraiment sérieux: c'est le suicide.' Hamlet said this first but less concisely than Camus. To be or not to be was the central question that had always confronted Klaus. Was his lifeless body the answer?

The story of his last five months is simply told. On New Year's Day 1949 he wrote in large letters at the top of his diary, 'I am not going to continue these notes. I do not wish to survive this year.' But he had made statements like that many times. Was the inscription intended to challenge death? Or was he teasing it? Golo recalled that day. 'I see him still, in the pajamas that he liked to wear until noon, and can still sense the mood, the nameless sadness.'

Yet the diary, now nothing more than a small pocket calendar with a few scribbled names and words, is singularly free of morbid comments. Writing, tedious as it was and as slow as it went, progressed. He struggled with his revision and translation of *The Turning Point*, now *Der Wendepunkt*, and to his enormous relief finally finished it on 13 February. For three days he reviewed and corrected the text and then sent it off to Fritz Landshoff in Amsterdam for publication by Querido. 'Out of *Turning Point*, which is 366 pages, has emerged *Der Wendepunkt* with 675 pages!!' he remarked to a friend. He was not dissatisfied with the result, and he was right not to be. Many consider it his best book. In time it became a European classic.

A week or two later he began work on what was to be his final important essay, 'Europe's Search for a New Credo'. It turned out to be his *Weltabschiedswerk* and was an appropriately apocalyptic farewell. He argued that Europe had been in decline since 1918, to the point that it had become nothing more than an impotent observer of world affairs and its intellectuals and thinkers unheard voices. What was to be done? One response would be to follow the proposal of a student he had met in Uppsala – a mass suicide of European intellectuals as a protest against being crushed between 'American money' and 'Russian fanaticism'. This course Klaus rejected. 'One doesn't commit suicide for politics, unless one is a politician', one of the characters in *The Last Day* says. Despite this emphatic repudiation, the notion of mass suicide has often been attributed not to the Swedish student but to Klaus.

The Last Day was the title of a novel Klaus began outlining during the previous autumn. It was essentially about the dilemmas facing European intellectuals in a world increasingly divided into hostile ideological blocs. The story, which takes place in Berlin, was to be about the last day in the lives of an American writer on the Western side and a communist author in the East. The American wants to mobilize his countrymen against the rising threat of fanatical right-wing anti-communism in the United States. He fails and commits suicide. The German in the Russian sector can no longer bear living under the communist regime. He decides to flee to the

West but is killed in a car accident as he crosses the border. The hopelessness in the story reflected not only the hopelessness in Klaus's life but also the hopelessness of East–West relations. He worked up an elaborate sketch of the plot but the words of the narrative would not come. There were only fragments of text by the time of his own last day.

Klaus's writing career had now run its course. It was an impressive achievement. It is, altogether, a unique record of the catastrophic first half of the twentieth century, told in both fiction and non-fiction. His political commentary and analysis have brilliantly stood the test of time and provide source material for scholars and students of those years. His works remain in print in various European countries and his plays are performed in the theatre and on television in Germany.

An intriguing question is what Thomas really thought of Klaus's writing. With each new important work he wrote to his son praising it in general terms. But, as Klaus once commented, he sent similar pseudo-friendly letters to total stangers whose books interested him not at all. At least once he went on record with his assessment of his son's work. It was in a letter to Hermann Hesse – and because it was private and written after Klaus's death, there is no reason to doubt that here was a frank evaluation. He commented, 'He was outstandingly talented. Not only *Gide* but also *Tchaikovsky* are very good books and his *Vulkan* – leaving aside relationships that he could have handled better – is perhaps the best émigré novel.' That was it. One can see why he disliked the autobiographies, was pained by the plays and hated the early novels. But did he ever even read any of the essays and political commentaries?

The sunny winter days in Pacific Palisades appeared to relax Klaus, and when Erika returned from a skiing holiday in late February she was pleasantly surprised to see how well he looked. As a book junky he had read piles of books, and as a compulsive letter-writer he had given considerable time to his prolific correspondence. In the afternoons there was always the enjoyment of walking Thomas's poodle. And for entertainment of sorts the remnants of the German refugee colony came occasionally to dinner. When Lotte Walter was wed on 8 February, he was flattered to be asked to be best man. Bruno Walter had not seen him since his suicide attempt in July and now was struck by 'his relaxed, happy mood'. For whatever reason there was apparently no prowling at night, so for once his life was uncomplicated by sexual misadventure. The relationship with Harold was finished. Erika's suspicion that Klaus had returned to California primarily to be with him proved false. Klaus visited him at his work camp on 16 January but did not see him again until he was released on 12 February. After that they met only a few times and then usually in the company of Christopher Isherwood.

Despite his miserable experience with Rossellini, Klaus still dreamed of participating in the production of a film. Having dropped the idea of a life of Mozart, he now proposed writing a script with Isherwood about Han van Meegeren, the notorious Dutch forger of famous Dutch paintings, some of which he sold to Nazi bigwigs. While living in Amsterdam Klaus had been fascinated by the story and, after a visit to the painter, wrote 'The Double Life of Han van Meegeren', which was published in Denmark and in New York by *Town and Country*. Isherwood appeared willing to join in, but when he finally managed to meet with one of the moguls of MGM, he was turned down. Another idea he remained keen on was to film *The Magic Mountain*. Thomas had in fact sold the rights. But in the end Hollywood rejected that too.

It was bad luck. Had either project gone forward and had Klaus been one of the scriptwriters, he would have been bound to stay in California. Instead, he made what turned out to be the worst mistake of his life. As Thomas wrote to his brother Victor on 11 March, 'In a few weeks Klaus wants to go to Europe – that is, back to the South of France to work.' When Golo heard of this, he confronted Klaus. He pointed out that Thomas, Katia and Erika were going to Europe on 16 April and would not return until the end of the summer. He would be alone in the house – Pacific Palisades was a perfect place to write and he could invite friends to stay. Klaus did not reply.

In a way the silence is not surprising. Despite their long intimacy, the brothers by now had little to say to one another. To be sure, Klaus was the only member of the family Golo had ever been close to – he disliked his father, mistrusted his mother and in his memoirs scarcely mentions his sisters and other brother. But, for all their affection and mutual regard, their characters were fundamentally different and they had led entirely different lives. On political issues they generally saw eye to eye but they disagreed on how to respond. Perhaps the contrast can be illustrated in one sentence.

After the war Golo said that, while he had chosen to leave Germany in 1933, he did not judge those who chose to stay. To Klaus such moral and political indifference was inconceivable. Now, in the growing anti-communist hysteria of the United States, Golo stood passively by. This was impossible for Klaus and the gulf between them became insurmountable.

At least twice during this period, on 17 and 19 March, Klaus, Thomas and Erika had long evening discussions about political developments. There is no record of what they talked about, but letters give the gist. One topic was the state of Germany. To alembasize the exchanges into two sentences, Klaus declared that his personal experiences left him 'anti-German in the good old Uncle Heinrich sense'. To which his father replied, 'I approve of all the punishment inflicted on the race God has smitten.' Sentiments like these when made public prompted Bertolt Brecht's famous riposte, 'The Nobel Prize Winner Thomas Mann gives the Americans and English the right to chastise the whole German population for the crimes of the Hitler regime.'

The three Manns were even more deeply worried by American foreign policy. The Nato treaty, just announced, they saw as a holy alliance against Russia and a humiliating subordination of Europe to American interests. Europeans were being bought off by the Marshall Plan, then armed, demeaned and made dependent. The result was bound to be a ruinous arms race that risked leading to a nuclear war. Their fears reached the public when Thomas openly protested against the American government's efforts to sabotage a Cultural and Scientific Conference for World Peace about to be convened in New York. For this he was rewarded by having his photo published in *Life* magazine, along with that of Einstein and some twenty-five others, under a heading 'dupes and fellow travellers of communism'.

Klaus felt political climate the way others feel heat and cold. The political environment was an existential element in his personal life. No other single issue so occupied and preoccupied him as an overpowering fear of war. From the moment Hitler rose to power it was an ever-present, almost irrational obsession. Was the United States headed in the same direction? That is what frightened him. It also frightened Albert Einstein. 'Intellectual intolerance, political inquisition and declining legal security – all this in the name of an alleged state of emergency,' he declared in a radio talk. 'This is how it started in Germany.' Thomas went so far as to say he hated the joint heads of the House Un-American Activities Committee as much as he had hated Hitler. Erika was being harassed by the FBI over her application for citizenship. In the novel he was working on around this time, he wrote, 'Oh America, my dreamland – my lost dream.' In this atmosphere he parted from his family. 'Take leave of Klaus, who is flying to New York, Amsterdam and southern France to work. The dog is sad,' Thomas wrote in his diary.

From this time on Klaus was never again settled for more than a matter of days or weeks. On 20 March he flew to New York where he saw old friends and had a long talk with Bernard Buchwald, who had handled legal matters for *Decision* and now was doing his best to squeeze out of Roberto Rossellini the money owed to Klaus for *Paisà*. In the end he got a derisory $1,750, and that only after Klaus's death.

Two days later Klaus flew on to Amsterdam. While he was there Thomas finally had to reach a decision on whether to go back to Germany. He had been offered awards in Munich and Frankfurt. The issue had stirred up a family row. Erika was so determined never to set foot on German soil, she adamantly refused to accompany her father if he went. In early March, while Klaus was still at Pacific Palisades, there had been such a ruckus at dinner that she stormed out of the room. 'Her irrational grief over the possibility of my visit to Munich', Thomas wrote in his diary. 'Desultory conversation with my sons over the question. Irritating and troublesome on account of Erika.' Klaus had sided with his sister and now, on 27 March, sent his father a telegram. 'Everything considered, in your place I would NOT go to Munich . . . Out of a sense of filial duty, I again advise you against it.' Thomas replied, 'I am *very grateful* to you for your letter, which is certainly right.' Right Klaus may have been, but in the end Thomas chose to go. The decision was very typical of him. On the one hand he was deeply bitter about the way the Germans had undone the denazification programme, allowing Nazis to remain active in public life. On the other he was congenitally unable to resist the flattery of being given an honour, even at the cost of being used as an instrument of political rehabilitation.

After a few days Klaus went on to Paris for his fourth and final visit. He saw his publisher, his agent and his old friend Mopsa Sternheim who, as often in the past, supplied him with 'stuff', their euphemism for morphine.

He also met James Baldwin, who was just at the outset of his literary career. Disillusioned by prejudice against blacks and homosexuals, Baldwin had abandoned the United States and settled in Marseilles, where Klaus visited him a number of times. Finally, on 5 April Klaus reached the Riviera at Cagnes-sur-Mer. His diary for that day reads, '? (not so good)'. The following day, '? (and tried it again)'. The cryptic note may well have been a reference to the effect of Mopsa's 'stuff' – a concoction that, judging by the result, was tainted. On 10 April he moved into the Pavillon Madrid in Cannes, a small pension run by a Latvian-Russian countess, Lilly Medem. Room 555 there was not quite the twelve-hundredth room of the verses he wrote in 1931, but it was to be the last.

Throughout his life Klaus had been blessed with many good and loyal friends, people who had both respect and affection for him. None was to prove more affectionate and more faithful than someone who now entered – or re-entered – his life. This was Doris von Schönthan, a coeval journalist and photographer, who looked like she had stepped out of a Kirchner painting. She and Klaus had met during their wild days in Berlin in 1930, and his diaries at the time are filled with references to their friendship. She had fled when Hitler came to power and the two did not meet again until 1935, by which time she had married Bruno von Salomon, a communist journalist. The couple went underground in 1940 but she and Klaus somehow maintained contact and, when he arrived on the Riviera, Doris, now living in Cannes, was the first person he looked up. Her own circumstances were extremely difficult but she was quick to realize that Klaus was deeply depressed. A mutual friend described the relationship that developed as being like that of 'two freezing animals clinging to one another to stay warm'. She gave him a degree of stability, offered him encouragement and lent him money, although she had very little. So that he would not be alone for a whole day, more often than not she, or she and Bruno, had lunch or dinner with him. Together she and Klaus occasionally went to a bar or the casino, where he usually lost money.

The problem was he had no money to lose. He already owed 10,000 francs to Doris alone and was soon to owe the countess for his room rent. By now it must have been painfully clear to him that, from a financial angle alone, it had been a great mistake to have come to live in such a costly place as the Riviera. His only income, apart from his mother's monthly stipend, was nothing more solid than an aleatory chance of royalties from Querido. From the first day expenses and income diverged. His desperation is evident in the scraps of scribbled calculations among his surviving papers, as well as in his correspondence with Landshoff. On 20 April his diary reads, 'Letter to Fritz – SOS cry for money.' A few days later he received the reply. 'Oh, Klaus – dear, dear friend – how I would like to free you from your worries and leave you free for your novel.' Unfortunately he had to point out that the financial situation was tough both for Querido and for himself and there was not much he could do to help. But he assured Klaus that something would eventually be worked out. Klaus was not so sure and became deeply depressed. 'Feeling low, low, low – completely knocked out, unable to do anything.'

Despite all this, daily life proceeded more or less on its usual course. As always he read whenever he had a free moment – during these weeks, among other books were Norman Mailer's *The Naked and the Dead* ('Yes, it's quite a book!'), Gore Vidal's *The City and the Pillar* ('*not* a good book') and Elizabeth Bowen's *The Heat of the Day* ('how beautifully written'). And of course he laboured on. Sometimes even with success. An essay-review of Jean Cocteau's *Lettre aux Américains* he completed on 19 April in little more than two weeks. But he was making little or no progress on his novel. 'Started in all earnestness *The Last Day* – Chapter 1 (how often written) – 3 pages.' Three days later, 'It's no good – has to be started all over again.' For a time he had thought Mopsa's 'stuff' would help. On 16 April he had commented in his diary, 'Late at night notes for novel (quite exciting with help from –)' and the day after, 'late at night, novel notes, in a euphoric state'. But then he decided the 'stuff' was ruining him. 'Another bad, sleepy day – I know why – has to be changed.' That was on 23 April. A week later, 'Rien – unable even to read (consuming large quantities) – il faut en finir'. As he admitted to Erika, 'It is a very strong schnapps, a few drops is enough. It has a very soporific effect, so not the thing to be taken before a party or similar occasion but rather in minimal doses before going to bed.'

Doris came to his rescue by persuading him to go for treatment at Clinique St Luc in Nice. He was there for ten days and returned to Pavillon Madrid on 15 May. According to Golo, it subsequently became clear from tests at the clinic that Klaus had in effect been poisoned by the morphine concoction he had brought with him from Paris. On returning to Cannes, he took one final tiny dose and then decided to remove temptation. 'Letter to Mops (return the rest of the stuff – or most of it).' Waiting for him at the pension was a package of medication sent from New York by Robert Klopstock, the doctor who had treated him in Budapest at the time of his breakdown in 1935, to help deal with withdrawal symptoms.

While at St Luc, Klaus suffered a devastating shock. Georg Jacobi, the editor at Langenscheidt, sent a weasel-worded letter saying that his firm would not after all carry out its contract to bring out *Mephisto*. In West Germany, he wrote, 'it would be difficult to publish *Mephisto* since Herr Gründgens occupies a very significant position here. It might have been possible in Berlin but here in the West to take a step like this would not be at all easy.' This was not the first time the book had been rejected. A year earlier Klaus had approached the Munich publisher Desch Verlag and was told, 'Too risky. Gustaf is again on top.' Here was the stuff of drama, and Ariane Mnouchkine's famous dramatization of *Mephisto* in 1979 opens with a narrator quoting the text of the letters.

In an embittered reply on 12 May – the very day *Der Spiegel* brought out a friendly cover article on Gründgens – Klaus wrote, 'Your letter is price-less. To publish a novel – that means to you "to take action". In your opinion in the case of *Mephisto* this action would be "not at all easy" and must therefore now be brought to an end. Why? Because Herr Gründgens "occu-pies a very significant position here". That I call logic! And civil courage. And honouring a contract. I do not know what I find more perplexing: the baseness of your attitude or the naïveté on which it is based. Gründgens is successful, why bring out a book which could appear to be directed against him? Just no risks. Stand on the side of power. Swim with the current. You know where that leads – to concentration camps which no one wants to hear about later.' To Klaus the rejections and the reason for them simply proved what he had concluded several years earlier when interrogating Wehrmacht prisoners – that Nazism was so deeply embedded in the German psyche that no one, publishers or whoever, had the courage to think independently.

Even now, despite all his problems and disappointments, Klaus did not lose his zest for writing. Sometime during the month he made a complete inventory of his work between 1939 and 1948 and then outlined a plan for the next ten years. 'The beginning decade, 1949–58 (if it has to be). *The Last Day* (English and German). A homosexual novel, a historical novel (Greek? Jeanne d'Arc?), three successful plays (one sordid, morbid, sexy, bold and tragic; one in a lighter vein – maybe an historical comedy); one fantastic maybe utopian or with ghosts. A booklet on Picasso, illustrated. A quasi-philosophical monograph, a travel book (Far East, China and India), articles (but not too many), collected works in German and English.' And the list continued.

More immediately he thought of drawing on his experiences at the Clinique St. Luc as material for fictional treatment. He sketched out some of the text of a short story and decided to call it 'The Cage'. What survives suggests that it would have been a sad and ironic tale, in the spirit of *The Magic Mountain*. Next he wanted to translate Elizabeth Bowen's book into German. But hovering over everything was *The Last Day*, and here he was getting nowhere. Or at least not beyond deciding on a dedication. It was to be a passage from St Luke from the New Testament, 'For whosoever shall save his life shall lose it; but whosoever shall lose his life, the same shall find it.'

When he returned to the Pavillon Madrid he was more deeply in debt than ever. Now he owed money not only to the countess and Doris but also to the clinic. 'Stupidly I am in a horrible financial situation', he wrote to Erika. 'This means that I am stuck in a foreign country without cash. You can imagine how irritating that is.' At the last minute a cheque arrived from *Tomorrow* for his 'Europe's Search for a New Credo', which made it possible to pay at least some of his overdue bill at the pension. But that left him still in arrears and with nothing to live on.

By chance Klaus now learned that Gide was in a clinic in Nice and on 15 May sent him a wire proposing to meet. 'Regrets but not in condition to receive you', came the response. Gide was genuinely in poor shape, but his reply may have seemed like cold rejection. Suddenly there was some cheering news, though. Michael, accompanied by Monika, was on a tour of Europe as a solo violist and would pass through Cannes in a day or two. A visit by a brother and sister offered just the sort of comforting presence Klaus needed. Erika later commented, 'In his final letters there emerged a deep "sense of family" which I never before knew.' When the boat arrived, however, only those passengers were permitted to disembark whose final destination was Cannes. The letdown after the happy anticipation hit him hard.

On 19 May the bad weather at Cannes reached its climax with a cloudburst accompanied by thunder, lightning and hail. Despite the din, Klaus completed the German version of his Cocteau article and that evening he accompanied Doris to a Chopin concert, which he enjoyed. The next morning was given over to writing letters. One was to Hermann Kesten. 'My spies, snoops, bloodhounds and agents bring me the rumour that you are thinking of coming to France "in June". Is there any truth to it? And when in June would it be likely? And where in France? It would be charmant to have you here. I shall be in Cannes to the end of June. It is good to be back again on our coast – only that unfortunately it is *always* raining, really raining nonstop. It gets you down. The next little station on my programme is Austria. . . . I am trying to concentrate on my next book but there are always petty things to be taken care of.'

The other letter was to Katia and Erika, then on their way to Sweden, where Thomas was to give two speeches. 'Dearest mom and sis', it began, and went on to thank them for their recent letters. 'I appreciate that, in the midst of all these festivities, you had a little time for a sickly hermit. Here it mostly continues to rain, except when it hails, storms, and thunders. Never was there a May like this. It was also distressing that it proved impossible to meet Bibi and Mönnle.' He went on to complain about the difficulties with his international money transfers, his desperate financial situation and the frustrations with Querido in getting *Der Wendepunkt* in print. 'Nothing pleasant then? Oh yes. I am reasonably well; I am trying to write – only trifles for the moment, but soon I will get down to work on the novel.' He then quoted Jacobi's letter on *Mephisto* and added, 'Now if you please. He certainly won't be flattered by my response. WHEN DO YOU PLAN TO BE IN AUSTRIA? Where? Maybe I could meet you there – sometime around 29 June. My friend Mucha (whose novel I spent evenings in Pacific Palisades correcting) cordially invited me to Prague. Maybe we could go there together, Erika – in a car, with Knox?'

That afternoon he walked with Doris to the post office to mail his letters and then went to a photographer's shop to pick up pictures that had been taken of him just before he entered the clinic in Nice. After that nothing more is known of his movements. His diary had a simple entry, '10 Louis

(Zanzi-Bar)'. The rendezvous was with someone he had met several days earlier and spent the night with. There is no way of knowing whether they were together on this occasion or even whether Klaus went to the bar. At some point he put a 'do not disturb' sign on the door and locked it. Around noon the following day a *femme de ménage* found his door locked and notified Countess Medem who, at some risk, climbed from the balcony of a neighbouring room, looked in the window and saw Klaus's inert body. He was taken to the Clinique Lutétia, where doctors struggled unsuccessfully to save him. He died at around six in the evening. The following day a Nice daily, *Le Patriote,* stated that in his room medicine bottles had been found with the name of the medication scratched out. This rumour was contradicted by the rival *Nice-Matin,* which claimed that only a book lay open on a table by his side. Police authorities refused any comment and their report was routinely destroyed some years later.

When Thomas, Katia and Erika reached the Grand Hotel in Stockholm that evening, a message was awaiting them. 'On arrival at hotel terrible shock', Thomas noted in his diary. 'Telegram that Klaus lies in the clinic in Cannes in desperate condition.' It had been sent by Doris, who soon afterwards phoned to say that Klaus was dead. 'Long communion in bitter sorrow', Thomas commented. In fact he was furious. Once again he was brought into embarrassment by his infernal son – and from the grave, no less. Through the night the three debated whether to attend the funeral. From afar, Golo advised against it and at length they agreed. Thomas would remain to give his lecture 'Goethe and Democracy' in Uppsala and Stockholm and later Copenhagen and Zurich, but forgo any social engagements. Two days later, however, he attended a cocktail party given by the French ambassador. Even so, there were problems. Would it not be awkward to be giving rarefied lectures when one's son was not yet cold in the ground? And would audiences not be asking themselves about the circumstances of his sudden death?

So Thomas issued a statement saying that Klaus had died of a heart attack and that is what the international press reported. When rumours began to circulate that he had taken his own life, Thomas put out a new story. His son had accidentally died of tainted sleeping pills purchased from a drugstore in New York – or, as he wrote in his diary, 'the poison he received from the idiotic Klopstock'. Any account was better than a messy suicide that could reflect badly on himself. Once the press reported that Klaus had killed himself, exculpation became the order of the day. After that, within the family, the subject was for evermore taboo.

In death Klaus at last achieved what he had always sought. In the words of the sub-headline of the *New York Times*'s obituary, 'Won Recognition on His Own.'

At three thirty in the afternoon on 24 May, a beautiful spring day on the Riviera, Klaus was buried in a distant grave at the Le Grand-Jas. Would he have found it irony or mockery that to reach the site mourners had to follow the Path of Farewell, traverse the intersection of the Path of Sleep and the Path of Peace, then proceed up the Path of Silence to the Path of Rest? Doris and Bruno, along with eight or ten others, mostly newspaper reporters, were there. On the coffin lay a spray of flowers with a note, '*témoignage de l'affliction d'un père au souvenir de son "fils bien-aimé"*'. At the last minute Michael, having interrupted his concert tour, arrived and played a largo by Benedetto Marcello on his viola. The work was well chosen, not mournful but conveying a sense of quiet acceptance and peace at last. Apart from the viola, it was the funeral that Klaus had said seven years before that he wanted – 'no speeches, please! no music! no flowers! no lies'. Afterwards Michael went to the Pavillon Madrid and collected his belongings. With money from Thomas he paid all the bills, which amounted to 132,000 francs.

Klaus had plenty of reasons to want to end his life – writing going badly, financially bust, addicted to morphine, lonely beyond words, pained by a political world moving in a direction that was opposed to everything he believed in. He feared a repetition of the thirties. He was afraid of a war. In Germany he was being hounded as a Russian spy and no publisher would bring out his works. People like Gründgens prospered – he had just been invited to the Edinburgh Festival to give his *Faust* performance that had so impressed Hermann Göring – while Klaus suffered an increasing sense of decline, rejection and failure. Erika – his emotional centre, rock, anchor and ultimate friend – even she had fallen away.

And, all too obviously, there was the overwhelming presence of Thomas. 'All I have written has been about you. I only poured out in it what I could not pour out on your breast. It was a deliberately *prolonged* farewell to you, a farewell imposed by you, though I determined its course.' Klaus Mann?

No, Franz Kafka in a letter explaining to *his* father how he had tried but failed to win his trust. Franz's father was a businessman. Klaus's father-problem was infinitely more difficult. Throughout his life he had to bear the odium of 'Ah, you are also a writer?'

Klaus feared he was jinxed. After 1933 every accomplishment – *Kind dieser Zeit, Die Sammlung, Mephisto, Der Vulkan, Decision, The Turning Point, Paisà, Synthesis, Der Wendepunkt* – dissolved into failure, and every aspiration – a role in journalism, a career as a film scriptwriter, an accepted figure of American letters, a welcome figure in postwar Germany, an intermediary between American and European writers, a solid relationship with another man – was disappointed. 'A man of no luck? Get him out of my sight!' Both Frederick the Great and Napoleon are supposed to have uttered words to this effect. A person could have judgement, talent and experience but if he had no luck, he and all he did would be doomed. Klaus had judgement, talent, experience and a dozen other outstanding traits, but no luck. More and more he was plagued by a feeling of frustration and hopelessness. What deserved to have been success after success dissolved into failure after failure. The future seemed to promise only the same.

And so it has been taken for granted that he believed he had come to the end of the road and deliberately took his life by overdosing on sleeping tablets. From feeling hopeless to killing yourself is a big jump. Yet without any evident examination of the circumstances of his death, biographers have simply assumed he deliberately made the leap. Suicide was the inevitable conclusion of a lifelong obsession with death.

But what about this obsession? When Klaus came to write *Kind dieser Zeit* in 1932, he traced it back to his eighth year, when he nearly died of appendicitis. 'Its shadow', he believed, remained lodged in his subconscious, marking him for evermore. And indeed, death is the dark theme that runs through his fiction, his diary and his life. Mahler's *Kindertotenlieder* that he loved so much could have been the background music to his biography.

Klaus's notion of death was strangely ambiguous, however. His diary entries over the years make clear that for him death was an idealized state of existence, not the extinction of life but the reverse, a transfiguration into a blissful state of consciousness. It is revealing that he once likened it to the sense of serenity that followed taking a drug. After his discussion with Klaus, Friedrich Hacker described this as a romanticized longing for a paradise free of cares, a world of tranquillity, a state of nirvana. There was always something not quite serious about it, though. Marcel Reich Ranicki also sensed this and remarked that in his flirtation with death, Klaus 'seems to be winking at us'. More poetically, in the words of Keats's ode, he was 'half in love with easeful death'. But only half.

All that said, was he not a suicide in waiting? After all, had he not for years played Russian roulette? Even on the occasions when he fired a loaded chamber, however, the cartridge was a dud. That is to say, the pill-taking, the wrist-slashing were too dilettantish to have been intended to be fatal. It is telling that Hacker considered the most serious episode, that in Santa Monica – and by extension all the others – as 'a suicidal gesture'. Interestingly, Klaus had used exactly the same term seventeen years earlier. In February 1931 he published an essay in the *Vossische Zeitung* about friends who had killed themselves. How enviable it was, he wrote, 'to make the most noble and uncompromising of all gestures'. Yet in the end the question 'whether to give up the fight or fight on had to be answered in favour of life'. On learning of Ernst Toller's death, he had exclaimed, 'I will not do it. It is too gruesome.'

References in his diary to suicide and death make clear that there was a wall between them. 'I am planning to deal with the issue of suicide in my next novel – which will be more tedious and more painful but somehow more honourable than actually doing it.' So, for example, he had written to Peter Viereck. And later on he specifically rejected the Swedish student's idea of a mass suicide of intellectuals. Suicide may have been admirable for others but not for himself.

Death would come when it would come. He would be its object, not its agent. 'I await my death like a child awaiting a vacation.' This is a typical diary entry. Death was 'a state to be gratefully accepted'. 'I ask myself, practically every hour of the day, whether DEATH, which is so close to my heart, will not be kind enough to take me to itself.' Even so, there were times when he hoped that death would be thoughtful enough to wait until he had finished whatever he was working on at the time. Once he went further. 'It may be most timely, just now, to debunk the romanticism of suicide. Under the circumstances the impatience for death seems as nonsensical as fear of it. Why accelerate its coming?'

Klaus was in bad shape, it is true, but he had faced and survived hard times before. It is the paradox of his life that despite the disappointments, humiliations, misadventures, ever-present thoughts of death and desperate loneliness that besieged him from early youth, he had the guts to go right on living and writing. This inner strength is all the more remarkable in view of his acute lack of self-confidence, a psychological debility that originated in his relationship with his father and was reinforced by sexual rejection. Looking over the whole of his life, a truly heroic courage emerges as his outstanding trait. His strength was as the strength of ten.

There is no concrete evidence Klaus intended to kill himself that night. It is not known what he ingested or how much. He may have swallowed sleeping tablets and/or Klopstock's medication for withdrawal symptoms and/or whatever remained of Mopsa's 'stuff'. Any combination might have had an entirely unintended toxic effect. It is possible he went to the Zanzi-Bar, drank a lot and, on returning to his room, was careless about what and how much he took.

And what was an overdose in his case? For years he had been a sleeping pill junky. In her last letter, Erika cautioned him about 'chewing all those sleeping pills without interruption'. After long addiction to various drugs and cigarettes, his body may well have been too weak to survive what would not have been fatal to another person. In commenting on his death, the psychiatrist Harald Neumann wrote, 'Any irregularly nourished body, weakened by decades of chronic cigarette smoking and especially the misuse of drugs of various sorts would be unable to tolerate an entirely normal dose of sleeping tablets intended to induce sleep. In the case of Klaus Mann the conclusion is as good as inescapable that death was the result of an accidental poisoning with sleeping tablets.'

Had he been really serious about ending his life would he not have done something instant and decisive – shot a hole in his heart like his friend Ricki, or hanged himself like Ernst Toller, or drowned himself like his admired Virgina Woolf? He had his models.

Klaus was never deceptive. It is impossible to see in his final correspondence with Katia and Erika or with Hermann Kesten the slightest hint of a plan to commit suicide a few hours later. Quite the contrary. He was clearly looking forward to travelling with Erika to Prague to see Jiri Mucha who, a short time previously, had begged him to visit. Moreover, he had just outlined a long-term schedule of writing projects. And, what had undoubt-edly meant a great deal to him, he signed contracts late in April with two publishers, Querido in Amsterdam and Duell, Sloan and Pierce in New York, for *The Last Day*. He had a lot to live for.

Golo himself doubted the idea that his brother had deliberately over-dosed. 'He had evidently planned nothing for the day of 21 May; what he planned was to work and to travel.' Erika also had difficulty believing he had taken his life. As she wrote to Pamela Wedekind, 'In Cannes we searched everywhere for farewell letters, for some "final word". But I am absolutely certain that *nothing*, no scrap of paper, no greeting, *absolutely* nothing was to be found.' Since then no document, letter or testimony has come to light to support the suicide theory.

Did Klaus at last find the peace for which he had always longed? From the grave he gave his answer and it was the final, appropriately ambiguous words of *Der Wendepunkt*. There would be no peace until the end and even then there would still be a question mark. '*Ruhe gibt es nicht, bis zum Schluss. Und dann? Auch am Schluss steht noch ein Fragezeichen.*'

Epilogue

As in the final pages of a mystery novel, the main characters were now unmasked. Thomas was exposed – or had exposed himself – as an unforgiving, uncomprehending, hate-filled father. To his diary he confided, 'My inward sympathy is with the mother's heart and with Erika. He should not have done this to them . . . The hurtful, ugly, cruel inconsideration and irresponsibility.' To his brother Heinrich, he wrote, 'These are sad days. Katia sighs heavily, and it pains me to see Erika always in tears. She is abandoned, has lost her companion, whom she always tried to keep clutched to her side. It is hard to understand how he could do this to her. How deranged he must have been in that moment!' There was more still. Klaus was not just cruel and crazy, he was also close to worthless as a human being. 'Despite all the support and love . . . he made himself incapable of any feelings of faithfulness, consideration or gratitude.' Golo commented later, 'For this remark I can never forgive him.'

In comments to those outside the family Thomas offered various explanations for his son's death. To some he protested that suicide was in his genes since his two sisters, Carla and Julia, had killed themselves. To others he portrayed his son as a victim of the times, somone who lost his balance in 1933 and now found the world moving in a direction in opposition to all his hopes since then. Whatever the reason, his personal relationship with his son certainly had nothing to do with it.

Katia mourned but survived the blow surprisingly well. She saw it as inevitable and perhaps thought it was best over for everyone's sake. As she wrote to Heinrich, 'It was necessary to be prepared for it constantly, and I was.' On returning to Zurich from the Scandinavian lecture tour, Klaus's grieving parents were not so grief-stricken as to miss a performance of *Der Rosenkavalier* at the Zurich Opera. Hacker, who happened to be in Zurich at the time and at the opera that evening, was shocked to see them there and in good humour. 'To my great surprise, I noticed in the next box, Thomas and Katia, who greeted me in an extremely friendly fashion. In the interval, I went over to their box, not exactly knowing what to do because it did not seem to be a fitting place and occasion to offer condolences. Thomas Mann took me to the back of the box, shook my hand, touched my shoulder in a kind of half embrace and thanked me with a sort of naïve heartiness though nevertheless with complete poise for everything I had done for Klaus. I was rather apologetic, regretting my failure. Thomas Mann thanked me again and said, "We both did our best for him".' Thomas's diary makes no mention of the encounter. Already Klaus was vanishing from his father's mind, almost never again referred to in his diary or correspondence.

Golo, who was then teaching at Claremont College in California, kept his feelings of grief well under control. 'I was certainly deeply moved, but no more than that', he said in his memoirs. 'The next morning I taught my classes as usual.' Monika lamented the death of her only friend in the family. But, as Katia said, it was 'worst of all for poor Erika'. Years later Elisabeth told Andrea Weiss, 'When Klaus died, she was totally, totally heartbroken. I mean that it was unbearable for her, that loss. That hit her harder than anything else in her life.' As a result of the blow, she seemed to rediscover her old feelings. 'We were a part of each other', she wrote to a friend, 'so much so that my existence is unthinkable without him.' And to Pamela Wedekind, from the far-off days of *Anja und Esther*, she admitted, 'How I shall live, I don't yet know; I only know that I have to.'

Christopher Lazare never forgave Erika and her parents for refusing to attend the funeral. Curtiss proved true to character. Interviewed years later, he passed off the death with icy indifference. 'Well, everyone must die sooner or later.' Brian Howard composed a poem and sent it to Erika, who responded, 'The poem you wrote for Klaus has an optimistic ring, all sorrow notwithstanding, and is full of conviction that a future lies ahead in which men may live together in peace and brotherly unity. Did you ever really believe that? I am sure that such a mirage swam before your eyes, like a Fata Morgana when, during those brief moments on Germany's highest mountain, you thought of your dead friend, Klaus, your "German brother" and all of the dreams you dreamt with him.'

Erika spent the rest of her life tending Klaus's literary estate. Within a few days of his death, she travelled to Amsterdam to see Landshoff about getting *Der Wendepunkt* published as quickly as possible. Then, on 9 June, she flew to Cannes, where she ordered a gravestone inscribed with Klaus's words from St Luke and collected the immense trove of drafts and notes, including the outline and opening pages of *The Last Day*, which had been left in his room. She could only have been horrified by what she saw. Much of it was the scrawlings of someone broken in spirit, in torment, in agony, a lost soul.

The story of Erika's struggle to get her brother's writings published in Germany reveals a lot about the political mood in the early postwar period. For all but a few Germans, such as Karl Jaspers, the Third Reich was an 'episode', now over and best forgotten. No one wanted to hear about it, much less be taunted and shamed by an émigré. So Klaus's works caused a tremendous scandal.

The opening skirmish was over *Der Wendepunkt*. In 1948 Querido and Bermann merged. As a result of Landshoff's increasing ill health Bermann ran the firm his way. His way was to sell books and that meant selling books German readers wanted; they did not want books that rubbed their noses in the smelly past. When Landshoff gave him the rights to Anne Frank's diary, for example, he refused to publish it. He was equally adamant about Klaus's works. For three years Thomas, no doubt at Erika's insistence, prodded him. Just as insistently he refused to budge, giving one excuse after another. The exchanges became increasingly testy, and it was not until 1952 that Bermann relented. Before publication Erika intervened and deleted or altered a number of passages about Gründgens.

The big battle was over *Mephisto*. Although it had been published in Amsterdam by Querido in 1936, West Germans had to wait forty-five years before being permitted to read it – and even then only after the most disgraceful legal-literary scandal in postwar Germany. Publishers who considered bringing it out not long after Klaus's death backed off when warned that Gründgens would take action, and no one doubted that the courts – populated with judges of the Third Reich – would back him. Not until 1956 did it find a publisher and then one in East Germany. In no time it appeared throughout Eastern Europe and the Soviet Union, and was eventually translated into some twenty languages. A few copies made their way illegally across the border into West Germany – sometimes bartered by East Germans for food, clothing and other items unavailable in the East. In 1963 Gründgens died from an overdose of sleeping tablets. The following year a small Munich house, Nymphenburger Verlag, announced plans to bring out the book. Immediately Peter Gründgens-Gorski, the actor's companion and adopted son, filed suit to prevent this on the grounds that it was not a legitimate novel but a work of character defamation. Various levels of the West German courts ruled in his favour. In 1971 the case finally reached the Federal Constitutional Court, the German supreme court, which supported the ban with the notorious words, 'The general public is not interested in being given a false picture of the theatre world after 1933 from the point of view of an émigré.'

So matters stood for ten years. Then Rowohlt Verlag decided to call the court's bluff. Without any announcement or publicity, it published the text on 3 January 1981, fully thirty-six years after the war. The initial printing of thirty thousand copies sold out within a few days and a reprint in three hundred thousand copies within three months, a historically unprecedented figure in postwar German publishing. Eventually nearly a million copies were sold. Around the same time the novel was being adapted for theatre – Ariane Mnouchkine was the first to do so – and then film. The movie, by the Hungarian director István Szabó, won an Academy Award as best foreign movie of 1981 and the prize at Cannes for the best screenplay. In an Italianate solution to German legal sclerosis, the courts maintained the fiction of a legal ban but no longer enforced it. In any case, by the end of the 1960s the political ice jam was breaking up and what had been taboo was now accepted. Not only were Klaus's novels printed and his plays performed but also collections of his essays and letters were issued, so that eventually all his important writings were in print. Through their publication he achieved posthumously what he had sought from the time he left Poschinger Strasse in 1933 – to rescue German culture from Nazi desecration. And in that way he finally succeeded in realizing his deepest, lifelong wish – to be judged as himself and not as 'the son'.

After Klaus's death the Manns continued to be unhappy, each in his or her peculiar way. Thomas, relieved by the disappearance of his embarrassing eldest son, went on writing, travelling and collecting honours. His twilight years were anything but serene, however. Health problems became more frequent and troublesome. Writing went slowly. And he was driven to the limits of despair by the sight of handsome young men. 'Close to a desire for death because I can no longer endure the longing', he complained to his diary in August 1950.

In a less personal way he was equally tormented by fear arising out of an increasingly frigid Cold War, which intensified with the conflict in Korea. Like Klaus in his last years, he was obsessed by fear of war. In a speech to be delivered to the Library of Congress in spring 1950, he remarked on 'the mindless hysteria' driving American foreign policy. The event was, of course, cancelled. Discussions around this time to rearm Germany horrified him and he joined Einstein and others in condemning the proposal. On 1 February 1951 the *New York Times* mentioned him in the same breath as the communist American singer-actor Paul Robeson. The mere association was enough to send his publisher, Alfred Knopf, into a tizzy. Book sales were at risk. In a sickening near-replay of the Bermann-*Die Sammlung* affair of 1933, he virtually commanded Thomas to deny any connection with the demon singer. By now even respectable newspapers were suggesting he was a communist dupe. One of them commented, 'With amazing consistency he continues to back every Stalinist organization that carries the word peace in it.' A congressman from California described him as 'one of the world's foremost apologists for Stalin and Co'. The mood reached the point where Thomas saw similarities to that in Germany in the years just before Hitler came to power. Eventually he began feeling ashamed to travel with an American passport. 'I am more and more disgusted with this country', he wrote in his diary. He and Katia liked Pacific Palisades, their house and the California climate. But finally the political climate was too much and in the autumn of 1952 they moved back to Switzerland and eventually found a house in Kilchberg, near Zurich.

For a time Thomas found the mood in West Germany scarcely better. He himself was widely considered anti-German and criticized for refusing to return and live there – and even for having stayed outside the country during the Third Reich. But in time there was a measure of reconciliation.

From official circles awards, prizes, honours of every sort rained down upon him, the tribute for exculpation. None came from the West German government, however. He had done the unforgivable. He had refused to recognize the cultural division of Germany and had even participated in several cultural events in the Eastern Zone and accepted several prestigious awards. To Konrad Adenauer, whose favourite author was Agatha Christie, he was anathema. On his eightieth birthday, on 6 June 1955, Thomas was deluged with tributes from just about everywhere in the world except West Germany. Only two days before his death did Adenauer relent and allow him to receive the country's highest honour, Pour le Mérite. He died on 12 August 1955.

In the years after Klaus's death, Katia's life went on as before. She ran the household with her usual efficiency and served as Thomas's escort as he travelled around Europe. But she looked on passively as Erika became the dominant influence on Thomas's professional affairs. Following his death, she, Erika, Golo and young Frido lived unhappily together in the Kilchberg house, which Frido later described as 'more and more a depressing and oppressive museum'. He added, 'There never was any frank talk in the family. Depression, drugs, homosexuality, the suicide of Klaus – all that was taboo.'

As time passed, loneliness overtook Katia as her brothers, to whom she was closely attached, and good friends died. Like most seniors, she had difficulty accepting her decline and her insistence on driving her car well into old age led to rancorous feuds with the Swiss traffic police.

In conjunction with her ninetieth birthday in 1973, Katia reluctantly agreed to answer questions posed by Michael and the author Elisabeth Plessen. The text was published in 1974 as *Meine ungeschriebenen Memoiren*. It was widely praised for her random reminiscences. But her most interesting remark came at the end of the interview. 'I just wanted to say that I was never able to do what I wanted to do.' By the time of Michael's funeral in 1977, there were clear signs of encroaching dementia. She died at the age of ninety-seven in April 1980.

It is doubtful Erika was ever really happy after Klaus's death. Her own life became steadily more difficult. In investigating her application for American citizenship, the FBI was increasingly intrusive. She was harried as a lesbian and suspected of being a communist, even a Russian agent. In disgust she withdrew her request in December 1950. As the anti-communist delirium in the United States grew, she pressed her parents to return to Europe and then organized the move. Any notion of settling in Germany, however, she rigorously quashed. To the end of her days she loathed the German people and never forgave the fact that the country was not seriously denazified.

Even before Klaus's death, Erika had turned her father into a literary corporation with herself as chief executive officer. After his death she took charge of his literary legacy, editing manuscripts, translating texts and even supervising film versions of his novels. In 1965 she wrote a hagiography, *Das letzte Jahr. Bericht über meinen Vater*, published in English as *The Last Year of Thomas Mann. A Revealing Memoir by His Daughter*. Between 1961 and 1965 she also edited and published her father's letters, editing that was criticized by Monika and Golo as well as by literary critics for its tendentious omissions.

Following Thomas's death, Erika's health steadily deteriorated. Suffering from migraines, insomnia and arthritis, among other ailments, she drank a great deal and became addicted to various painkillers and barbiturates. The combination at times left her so blotto that Katia often had to help her up the steps to her room at night. She got along with no one in the family and had next to no friends. She died, a tragic figure, in August 1969 in the cantonal hospital in Zurich.

Golo was content at Claremont College – he later said his years there were the happiest in his life, despite his 'painfully stupid' students – and remained there until 1958, when he returned to Germany to take a position at Münster University. To avoid any comparisons with his father, he had waited until Thomas died before launching himself as a serous writer. In 1958 he had a manuscript ready; it was *Deutsche Geschichte des 19. und 20. Jahrhunderts* (published as *German History Since 1789*) and it made him a celebrity. In 1971, to even greater success, he published a somewhat unorthodox biography of Albrecht von Wallenstein, the famous commander during the Thirty Years War. In 1986 his memoirs appeared. By then he had achieved the status of national guru, dispensing his wisdom in newspapers and on television while making himself increasingly controversial. Over the years he became an avid collector both of prestigious honours and prizes as well of prominent political and social figures. He could count among his friends Chancellor Adenauer, President Heuss, Chancellor Brandt, Bavarian Minister-President Franz Josef Strauss and even such surviving members of the old aristocracy as Princess Margaret von Hessen und bei Rhein.

Yet in the end it all turned to ashes. In the background he could hear the mockery of his elder brother and sister – they would have been as unlikely to accept an honour as to have been offered one. 'Erika and Klaus, once so brilliant and superior to me', he wrote in his diary. 'What a miserable end they both came to. Now I am at the height of my success, such as they never achieved. NO satisfaction. SADDENING.' When asked by the *Frankfurter Allgemeine* in 1980 what he would liked to have been in life, he responded, 'Someone who is happier than me.' He later went even further, saying that he would have been better off had he at birth been accidentally exchanged with a baby from a 'normal, healthy family'.

Golo's personal life had always been troubled by depression, recessiveness and anxiety. The death of his father gave him a sense of liberation, but even then he was taunted by recurrent dreams in which Thomas poked him with a needle. His homosexuality posed a lifelong problem. It was at Salem in 1923 when he was fourteen that he had realized he was gay. He later said he considered this to be the greatest misfortune of his life. Over the years he had many casual male friendships but they lasted only briefly. In 1955 he fell in love with a thirty-years-younger pharmacist, Hans Beck, whom he adopted in 1972. Beck, who in the meantime had married and had two children, died in 1986. Only a few days before his own death did Golo publicly acknowledge in a TV interview that he was homosexual. 'I did not fall in love often. I kept it to myself, perhaps that was a mistake. Also, it was forbidden, even in America [discretion] was necessary' – an astonishing thing to say considering that Klaus had exposed himself publicly and fearlessly seventy years earlier.

In his later years Golo was increasingly hostile to other family members, including Katia and Michael and even Gret and Frido. As Frido told it, 'When Golo adopted Hans Beck, he turned to my mother with a face contorted with hatred and said, "I am doing this only so that none of you inherits anything from me".' Frido himself had thought that Golo loved him as a child, only eventually to find he secretly despised him. Family squabbling went on to the last, with an ugly dispute over Monika's estate.

Golo was living with Ingrid Beck, Hans's widow, when he died in April 1994, a few days after his eighty-fifth birthday. Even from the grave he continued to feud. Although he wished to be buried in Kilchberg, to dissociate himself from other family members he insisted on being interred alone, outside the Mann gravesite. He further left explicit instructions that no family member should be present at his burial ceremony, instructions that Elisabeth and Frido ignored.

With Klaus's death Monika lost a good friend. All her life, when not disliked and disparaged, she was at best tolerated by the others in the family. Her parents had dumped her in Salem when she was fourteen and after that saw as little of her as possible. In later life she had difficulty getting settled, living at times with her unwilling parents, at times with Michael and at times on her own. In November 1942 she moved into an apartment in New York, where she continued to study piano with the intent of being a concert pianist. Several years later she decided to become a writer and in time was profilic, contributing to several important newspapers and a variety of magazines for the rest of her life.

Homesick for Europe, Monika decided in September 1952 to return there and resided at various places in Italy during the next thirty-five years. In 1955, while living in Capri, she met the love of her life. Antonio Spedaro was – to the bemused scorn of her family – a fisherman. Not long afterward she published her memoir, *Vergangenes und Gegenwärtiges* ('Past and Present'). Even now, with all of her children approaching their twilight years, Katia could not resist dispatching a nasty letter. 'Of all the children you were the most remote and what in this book is said about him [Thomas] – which is not very much – arises out of your fantasy.' When Antonio died in December 1985, Monika went to Zurich and stayed with Golo at the family home at Kilchberg. While there she met Ingrid Beck, who visited Golo from time to time, and the two became friendly. When she and Golo found they could not live together, she went to stay with Ingrid in Leverkusen in the Ruhr. There she died in March 1992.

By the time of Klaus's death, the pan-Europeanism that Elisabeth picked up from her eldest brother in 1930 had been reinforced by the work of her husband. Borgese was one of the key figures in the writing of the 1948 constitution of the Union of World Federalists. Elisabeth was equally idealistic and equally committed – and more successful than her husband. Being front-staged by a woman, even if his wife, was too much for an old-fashioned macho Italian male, and the couple came to the point of divorce. When Borgese was offered a professorship in Italy, he and Elisabeth, along with their two daugthers, Angelica and Domenica, moved to Europe and settled in Fiesole. He died soon afterward, making Elisabeth a widow at thirty-four. Her independence had the effect of releasing a Klaus-like surge of intellectual energy – as a writer, of course. She wrote short stories, novels and essays; she translated; she became an active feminist. Eventually she also established a liaison with Corrado Tumiati, a writer, journalist and poet, also considerably older than she. They were both devoted to literature and art. In 1964, however, her political idealism took hold again and she became an associate of the Center for the Study of Democratic Institutions, an influential think tank in Santa Barbara, California. When Tumiati died in 1967 she moved there.

In that year she met Arvid Pardo, Maltese ambassador to the UN, who became famous as 'Father of the Law of the Sea Conference'. There followed a brief romance. When the Club of Rome was founded in 1968 she was the sole female member. Through these years Elisabeth was writing both novels and short stories as well as books and articles on the place of women. In 1978 she accepted an offer to be professor of International Law of the Sea at the University of Halifax in Nova Scotia. She not only threw herself into the work but even used her royalties from her father's estate to support it. In February 2002 she went skiing in St. Moritz, where she died of a heart attack. Asked in an interview not long before her death whether she was the only one of the children who had had a happy life and who was eventually reconciled with the family, Elisabeth thought for a long time and finally said, 'Yes.'

On arriving in the United States in 1940, Michael and Gret had settled in California but at a sufficient distance from Pacific Palisades to avoid contact with Thomas. Michael continued his musical studies and in 1942 joined the San Francisco Symphony as a violist. In 1949 he left the orchestra and performed, with some success, as a soloist on a tour of the United States and Europe. It was then that he attended Klaus's burial. In 1951 he performed in duo recitals with the pianist Yaltah Menuhin until his violent temper got the better of him and he struck her. In 1953 he went on a world tour as a solo violist.

Two years after Thomas's death Michael decided to give up his music career, telling friends that music was great as a pastime but not as a profession. Aged forty he enrolled at Harvard and, after receiving his doctorate in German literature in 1961, he joined the German literature department at Berkeley. No doubt to work through his love-hate relationship with his father, he made Thomas's writings the centre of his interest. On the one hundredth anniversary of his father's birth, he gave a series of talks about him and his novels in the United States and Europe. Like all the Manns, he wrote – works on Schiller and Heine as well as on music.

Golo said Michael was 'the only he-man in the family'; he loved sailing, fishing, flying and women. His home life, however, was a disaster. On one occasion his temper flared and he slugged Gret in the face in front of the children. Both parents had less than no interest in the two boys. At fourteen Frido was hived off to live with his grandparents. Thomas almost idolized him and portrayed him in *Doctor Faustus*, as the young Nepomuk Schneidewein. In an interview in April 2008, Frido said of his father, 'Although there were occasional shows of affection, he went to almost absurd lengths to keep his distance from my brother and me. That went so far as to leave nothing to my brother and me in his will.' (In the same interview Frido said he felt more sympathetic to Klaus than to any other member of the family.) In October 1963 Michael and Gret adopted Raju, an orphan from India, and made her the beneficiary of their estate.

In 1975 Michael read his father's still unpublished diary and found the entry of 28 September 1918 revealing that he was undesired by his parents and was born only because an abortion would have endangered Katia's life. The effect was devastating. After that he was indifferent as to whether he lived or died. On New Year's Day 1977 he was found dead from an overdose of alcohol and barbiturates. Since he had been indulging in both for some time and had repeatedly been delivered to a hospital to be resuscitated, it was not clear whether the death was accidental. Queried later by a newspaper reporter whether he thought his father had commited suicide, Frido replied, 'I don't think he deliberately took a double dose.' Asked about the strange death of his mother – who was found drowned in her swimming pool, her face covered with cat scratches – he responded, 'Her death will always remain obscure.'

As Frido summed up Michael's life, 'My father's trauma – one that he never got over – was that as a child and teenager he felt totally rejected by his father. He was the object of silence, discipline, disparagement and rage. The result was a vicious circle. Being helpless, his only refuge was to act in a way that provoked even further anger. And then he had to witness that his father absolutely adored and loved me.'

And Frido himself? His life was one of trying to come out from under the crushing burden of the Mann curse. At twenty he had a nervous break-down, feared he was going mad, experienced a sense of rebirth through religious conversion and eventually, and no doubt appropriately, became a psychoanalyst. For twenty years he refused to read a word written by his grandfather. 'I wanted to escape from his shadow and the embrace of the overwhelming family influence.' When his grandfather died? 'The ever-present black cloud that had been following me was suddenly no longer there. For the first time I felt free.'

Notes

Abbreviations

TP – *The Turning Point*
KZ – *Kind dieser Zeit*
BA – *Briefe und Antworten: 1922–1949*
W – *Der Wendepunkt*

Chapter 1: First Writings 1906–24

p. 5	'Where does the story begin?'	*TP*, ix.
	'. . . not as a meeting . . .'	*TP*, xvii.
	'I married only . . .'	Uwe Naumann, ed., *Die Kinder der Manns: Ein Familienalbum*, 28.
p. 7	'My husband and I . . .'	Katia Mann, *Meine ungeschriebenen Memoiren*, 56.
	'You never liked me . . .'	Golo Mann, *Erinnerungen und Gedanken*, 213.
	'Mielein minds you . . .'	*TP*, 9.
	'I could go to her . . .'	Uwe Naumann, ed., *'Ruhe gibt es nicht, bis zum Schluss': Klaus Mann (1906–1949)*, 33–4.
	'To enter his study . . .'	*TP*, 7–8.
	'We almost always . . .'	Golo Mann, *Erinnerungen*, 48.
p. 8	'From the very . . .'	Naumann, ed., *Die Kinder der Manns*, 53.
	'I didn't really know him.'	Jeffrey Meyers, 'Family Memoirs of Thomas Mann', *Virginia Quarterly Review*, Winter 1999.
	'It was as though I . . .'	*Die Manns: Ein Jahrhundertroman* (film)
	'I never spoke to him . . .'	Ibid.
p. 9	'He has his little . . .'	*TP*, 7.
	'he rose up and . . .'	Fredric Kroll, *Der Tod in Cannes*, 605.
	'Use the tip . . .'	*TP*, 7.
	'You can never tell . . .'	Kroll, *Der Tod in Cannes*, 605.
	'Sometimes our house . . .'	*TP*, 127.
p. 10	'Without you . . .'	*KZ*, 83.
	'He played and . . .'	*TP*, 70–1.
	'What a wretched . . .'	Golo Mann, *Erinnerungen*, 362.

p. 11	'Erika and I belonged . . .'	*TP*, 54.
	'I had a melancholy . . .'	Television interview.
	'For none of the . . .'	Ronald Hayman, *Thomas Mann: A Biography*, 303.
p. 12	'During his formative . . .'	Quoted in Meyers, 'Family Memoirs'.
p. 13	'Whenever I think . . .'	*KZ*, 13.
	'We children . . .'	*TP*, 65.
p. 14	'The deadly ecstasies . . .'	*TP*, 40.
	'Klaus almost died . . .'	*TP*, 34.
	'I believe it was . . .'	*KZ*, 42–3.
	'This wartime father . . .'	*TP*, 38.
p. 15	'Even the most exciting . . .'	*TP*, 54.
	'Mann, Klaus has neither . . .'	Uwe Naumann, ed., *'Ruhe gibt es nicht'*, 37.
p. 16	'the intrinsic law . . .'	*TP*, 34.
	'completely uninterested in . . .'	*KZ*, 97ff.
	'Elmar had silky-smooth . . .'	*KZ*, 115.
p. 17	'If *that* is spring! . . .'	*KZ*, 121.
	'School can destroy . . .'	Hayman, *Thomas Mann*, 104.
p. 19	'Naturally all of us . . .'	Naumann, ed., *Die Kinder der Manns*, 77.
	'Revolution! . . .'	*TP*, 43.
	'One of them . . .'	*KZ*, 68.
p. 20	'We liked them . . .'	*KZ*, 85.
	'With the same enthusiasm . . .'	*KZ*, 87.
	'On his own . . .'	*Berliner Beiträge*, 17.
p. 21	'The story of this . . .'	*KZ*, 93–4.
	'had read it . . .'	*KZ*, 93.
	'I don't know how many . . .'	*TP*, 58.
p. 22	'Eissi has sent . . .'	Letter, 11 July 1920.
	'tactlessness that only . . .'	*KZ*, 87.
	'Where did I put . . .'	Golo Mann, 'Erinnerungen an meinen Bruder Klaus', *BA*, 636.
	'It is almost incredible . . .'	*KZ*, 91.
	'Night falls . . .'	*TP*, 61.
p. 23	'It looked as though . . .'	*TP*, 75.
	'In the midst . . .'	*TP*, 81.
p. 24	'a school for very talented . . .'	Peter T. Hoffer, *Klaus Mann*, 29.
	'It was in my fifteenth . . .'	5 May 1936.
	'I love you . . .'	*TP*, 84.
	'I don't belong here . . .'	12 June 1923, *BA*, 15.
p. 25	'Among all the . . .'	*KZ*, 158.
p. 26	'Sodom and . . .'	*TP*, 86–7.
	'It was a flop . . .'	*KZ*, 156.
	'Why should we be . . .'	*Treffpunkt im Unendlichen*.
p. 27	'Perversion is good . . .'	*KZ*, 170.
	'With a patience I . . .'	*KZ*, 171.
	'Too young . . .'	*KZ*, 181.
	'poet, alchemist . . .'	*TP*, 97–8.
p. 28	'We could hardly deviate . . .'	*TP*, 81.
	'I can see it . . .'	*TP*, 106.

Chapter 2: First Scandals 1924–28

p. 29	'Yes, I had a job . . .'	*TP*, 105.
	'I could not help . . .'	*TP*, 105.
	'I was smart . . .'	*TP*, 104.

p. 30 'Everything seemed . . .'	*TP*, 104.
'It is doubtful . . .'	Marcel Reich-Ranicki, *Thomas Mann and His Family*, 164.
p. 31 'I read young . . .'	Letter, 7 May 1925.
'Go ahead, young friend . . .'	*TP*, 113.
p. 32 'The first day in Paris . . .'	Klaus Mann, *Die neuen Eltern*, 44.
'treated with the . . .'	*TP*, 111.
'the blare and stink . . .'	*TP*, 111.
'half ballet-school . . .'	*TP*, 107.
p. 33 'Dismal silence . . .'	*TP*, 108.
'Prolific and hostile . . .'	Peter Gay, *Weimar Culture*, 110.
p. 34 'Ten horses . . .'	Klaus Harpprecht, *Thomas Mann: Eine Biographie*, 565.
'In Klaus Mann the younger . . .'	Naumann, ed., *'Ruhe gibt es nicht'*, 55.
p. 35 'The flamboyance . . .'	*TP*, 125.
'He never seemed . . .'	*TP*, 126.
'This time it had . . .'	*TP*, 114.
p. 37 'Klaus did not conceal . . .'	Harpprecht, *Thomas Mann*, 569.
'Sometimes I was perplexed . . .'	*TP*, 121.
'My relations with . . .'	*W*, 231.
p. 38 'The encounter . . .'	*TP*, 198.
'He gave me . . .'	*TP*, 198.
p. 39 '. . . the very vocabulary. . .'	*TP*, 197.
'Liquor provokes . . .'	*TP*, 175.
'Undoubtedly he is . . .'	*TP*, 175.
'young, handsome . . .'	*TP*, 181.
p. 40 'I knew his books . . .'	*W*, 229.
'Never will I . . .'	*W*, 230–1.
'Paris was swarming . . .'	*TP*, 119.
p. 41 'We Europeans . . .'	'Heute und Morgen', in Klaus Mann, *Die neuen Eltern*.
'We were booed . . .'	*TP*, 124.
p. 42 'A convention of . . .'	12 November 1933.
'Klaus sprained his . . .'	Reich-Ranicki, *Thomas Mann and His Family*, 165.
'You simply must . . .'	*BA*, 77.
p. 43 'It looked as if . . .'	Donald Friede, *The Mechanical Angel*, 31.
p. 44 'From the very beginning . . .'	*TP*, 132.
'a callous system . . .'	*TP*, 135.
p. 45 'kept in that luxurious . . .'	*TP*, 153.
p. 46 'It was a rich . . .'	*TP*, 153.
'A journey around . . .'	*TP*, 163.
'My fundamental error . . .'	*TP*, 169.

Chapter 3: First Drugs 1929–32

p. 47 'I must write . . .'	Kroll, *Der Tod in Cannes*, 601.
'The very act of . . .'	*TP*, 309.
p. 48 'The more contact . . .'	*KZ*, 195.
'. . . a shoddy halo . . .'	*TP*, 124.
'The whole world . . .'	*TP*, 125.
p. 49 'I am afraid . . .'	*TP*, 163.
p. 50 'A centrifugal force . . .'	*TP*, 172.
'Never shall I . . .'	*TP*, 193.

p. 51 'Effects of cocaine . . .'   16 June 1932.
    'the effects of morphine . . .'   27 January 1932.
    'I read a bit . . .'   16 January 1932.
    'Injected euka . . .'   5 September 1934.
    'the different things . . .'   Letter to Erich Katzenstein, quoted in *BA*, 235.
p. 52 'I ruined . . .'   *TP*, 118.
    'I recall rooms . . .'   *TP*, 172.
    'Twelve hundredth . . .'   *Querschnitt*, 11 July 1931, in Naumann, ed., *Die Kinder der Manns*, 102.
    'My life was not . . .'   *TP*, 172.
p. 53 'Were Klaus Mann not . . .'   15 November 1930.
p. 55 'Recently I read . . .'   *Neue Rundschau*, May 1933.
p. 56 'I sensed the innermost . . .'   *TP*, 247.
    'We were very . . .'   Marie-Jaqueline Lancaster, *Brian Howard: Portrait of a Failure*, 193.
    'I have made . . .'   Ibid., 191.
p. 57 '. . . my find of . . .'   Ibid., 197.
    '. . . probably the first . . .' Ibid., 193.
    'The father-son conflict . . .'   *TP*, 172.
p. 58 'The son admired . . .'   Reich-Ranicki, *Thomas Mann and His Family*, 166.
    'Klaus Mann's book . . .'   Count Harry Kessler, *Aus den Tagebüchern 1918–1937*, 328.
p. 59 'It's a pity . . .'   *TP*, 249.
    'It was lots of fun . . .'   *TP*, 251.
    'Out of selfishness . . .'   *TP*, 250–1.
    'Death, which once . . .'   Klaus Mann, *Prüfungen: Schriften zur Literatur*, 360.
p. 60 'He said it . . .'   Letter to Eva Herrmann, 1 December 1932, *BA*, 81–2.
    'I have lost . . .'   *TP*, 247–8.
    'He shot himself . . .'   *TP*, 249.
    '. . . with what bitter . . .'   Reich-Ranicki, *Thomas Mann and His Family*, 162.

Chapter 4: Fleeing Hitler 1933

p. 63 'Never before nor . . .'   *TP*, 61.
    'I might have been . . .'   *TP*, 238.
p. 64 'Anyone who was . . .'   *Die neuen Eltern*, 306.
    '. . . gets things done . . .'   *TP*, 234.
    'As for myself . . .'   *TP*, 235.
    'More and more . . .'   *TP*, 233.
p. 65 'Hitler – after all . . .'   *TP*, 233–4.
    'They are going to be . . .'   *TP*, 240.
    'Horrifying victory . . .'   25 April 1932.
    'The Mann family . . .'   Naumann, ed., *Die Kinder der Manns*, 104.
    'Extremely serious . . .'   5 April 1932.
    'It was a most . . .'   *TP*, 236.
p. 66 'My mistake was . . .'   *TP*, 237.
    'Though they may . . .'   Hayman, *Thomas Mann*, 398.
    'Conditions in Berlin . . .'   7 March 1933.
p. 67 'The essential reason . . .'   *TP*, 267.
    '*bad* advice'   14 May 1933.

p. 68 'It is difficult . . .'	Golo Mann, *Thomas Mann: Memories of My Father*, 12–13.
p. 69 'To give up your . . .'	TP, 267.
'It was a tedious . . .'	TP, 268.
p. 70 'If you know of . . .'	30 March 1933, Monacensia.
'Cast your expressive . . .'	27 April 1933, *BA*, 87.
p. 71 'Yesterday all my . . .'	11 May 1933.
'What could bring you . . .'	Letter to Gottfried Benn, in Klaus Mann, *Zahnärzte und Kunstler: Aufsatze, Reden, Kritiken 1933–1936.*
p. 72 'Klaus would be justly . . .'	Fredric Kroll, *Repräsentant des Exils 1933–1937*, 36.
p. 73 'I don't have the strength . . .'	Golo Mann, *Erinnerungen*, 484.
'could cause the . . .'	Kroll, *Repräsentant des Exils*, 35.
'Letters reached me . . .'	TP, 267.
p. 74 'Could you not at least . . .'	BA, 116–17.
'There is a wall of . . .'	5 August 1933, *BA*, 688–9.
p. 75 'Throughout the day . . .'	5 July 1933.
p. 77 'Another visit . . .'	4 June 1933.
p. 78 'Klaus never lived . . .'	Golo Mann, 'Erinnerungen an meinen Bruder Klaus', *BA*, 643.
'One does not entrust . . .'	21 August 1933, *BA*, 122–4.
p. 79 'If anyone lacks . . .'	Hayman, *Thomas Mann*, 407.
p. 80 'Must confirm . . .'	Harpprecht, *Thomas Mann*, 774.
'Long letter from . . .'	15 September 1933.
'What is at issue . . .'	15 September 1933, in *BA*, 134–5.
p. 81 'The communist and Jewish . . .'	*Die neue Literatur*, November 1933.
'There is currently . . .'	Naumann, *Klaus Mann*, 61.
p. 82 'Tea in the little . . .'	23 September 1933.
p. 83 'Klaus did not ever . . .'	Television interview, 13 May 1999, Andrea Weiss, *In the Shadow of the Magic Mountain*, 123.
'Here was the . . .'	Harpprecht, *Thomas Mann*, 777.
'. . . producing culture . . .'	7 September 1945 to Walter von Molo, in Richard and Clara Winston, *Letters of Thomas Mann*, 478ff.
p. 84 'Dinner with . . .'	31 October 1933.

Chapter 5: Homosexualities 1934–35

p. 85 'Thoughts of death . . .'	15 January 1934.
p. 86 'I wrote the novel . . .'	W, 332.
p. 87 'content with the literary echo . . . *Neue Zürcher Zeitung* . . .'	21 October 1934.
'It really angers . . .'	3 September 1934.
'I am not angry . . .'	20 December 1934.
'And so it begins . . .'	13 February 1934.
'Nothing good is . . .'	18 February 1934.
p. 88 'information that Thomas . . .'	Kroll, *Der Tod in Cannes*, 185–6.
'I have no passport . . .'	17 June 1934, *BA*, 187.
p. 89 '*Under no circumstances* . . .'	Letter, 26 October 1934, Kroll, *Der Tod in Cannes*, 290.
'That is our bitterest . . .'	15 January 1935.

p. 91	'I have a somewhat . . .'	Christopher Isherwood, *Christopher and His Kind*, 206.
	'I didn't see her . . .'	Humphrey Carpenter, *W.H. Auden*, 177.
	'WOLFGANG'S DEATH . . .'	28 May 1934.
p. 92	'How powerful are the . . .'	15 February 1936.
	'The WAR comes . . .'	17 March 1935.
	'Will it be followed . . .'	6 April 1935.
	'Hitler does not want . . .'	27 July 1934.
p. 93	'He was the perfect . . .'	Quoted in Nicole Schaenzler, *Klaus Mann: Die Biographie*, 307.
	'. . . whispered platitudes . . .'	*TP*, 286.
p. 94	'the essential triviality . . .'	*TP*, 286.
	'. . . the high-minded . . .'	*TP*, 284.
	'I could never . . .'	*TP*, 287.
	'Root out homosexuality . . .'	Klaus Mann, 'Homosexualität und Fascismus', in *Zahnärzte und Künstler*, 235–6.
p. 96	'But I am glad I wrote . . .'	Letter to Franz Goldstein, 30 December 1934.
	'. . . problematic.'	Harpprecht, *Thomas Mann*, 814; Thomas Mann, diary 1934, 592.
	'Never again will . . .'	17 December 1934.
	'I would not want . . .'	23 December 1934.
	'The reunion.'	30 August 1934.
p. 97	'Yes, it has come . . .'	18 March 1934.
	'I look without hope . . .'	28 November 1934.
	'It is of course insane . . .'	11 March 1935.
	'Our threatened lives . . .'	23 November 1935.
	'First two movements . . .'	7 January 1934.
p. 98	'She sings *gloriously* . . .'	11 April 1936.
	'Obviously I know . . .'	*TP*, 283.
	'I wrote his story . . .'	*TP*, 283.
	'Even if there were . . .'	*W*, 333.
p. 99	'The particular form . . .'	*W*, 333.
p. 100	'He was an émigré . . .'	*W*, 334.
	'Most of it was certainly . . .'	*Symphonie Pathétique.*
p. 101	'friendly reserve . . .'	Harpprecht, *Thomas Mann*, 869.
p. 102	'Once it is done . . .'	2 March 1935.
	'the most corrupt and . . .'	*TP*, 304.
p. 103	'Desperately sad'	7 May 1934.
	'*Unbelievably* sad'	31 October 1934.
	'The whole day . . .'	24 January 1934.
	'Dreamed about being . . .'	3 May 1934.
	'A chloroform mask . . .'	4 July 1935.
	'a young, blond Nazi . . .'	13 January 1934.
	'Hitler visited me . . .'	13 January 1934.
p. 104	'Took heroin . . .'	18 March 1934.
	'Just a mild . . .'	28 November 1934.
	'No doctor can . . .'	13 November 1935, *BA*, 235.
	'Evening. *Screamed* . . .'	25 November 1935.
p. 105	'The Kleist of my . . .'	*W*, 112.

Chapter 6: Lecturing to Americans 1936–37

| p. 107 | 'You should write . . .' | 15 November 1935, *BA*, 236–9. |

p. 108 'Mephisto will be . . .'	15 April 1936.
p. 109 'Old enmity . . .'	23 April 1937.
p. 110 'This book is not about . . .'	'Kein Schlüsselroman', in *Zahnärzte und Künstler*, 405.
'I visualize my . . .'	*TP*, 282.
'As an example . . .'	Ibid., 335.
p. 111 'If I told you . . .'	Letter, 12 April 1933, quoted in Hayman, *Thomas Mann*, 405–6.
p. 112 'I could cry . . .'	1 April 1935.
p. 113 'I read her . . .'	19 January 1936.
'. . . be in your presence . . .'	Letter, 19 January 1936, in Harpprecht, *Thomas Mann*, 876–7.
'A long letter from . . .'	22 January 1936.
'Urgently request . . .'	26 January 1936, in *BA*, 243.
p. 114 'You are, apart . . .'	Harpprecht, *Thomas Mann*, 878.
p. 115 'Nothing would have . . .'	11 May 1936.
'But of course before . . .'	16 August 1936.
p. 116 'I ask myself . . .'	8 October 1936.
'This sadness . . .'	23 November 1936.
p. 117 'A boundless feeling . . .'	10 January 1937.
p. 118 'I again feel very . . .'	25 February 1937.
p. 119 'The boy is . . .'	7 June 1937.
'. . . irritated with members . . .'	31 March 1937.
'Naturally Klaus . . .'	Golo Mann, 'Erinnerungen an meinen Bruder Klaus', in *BA*, 632.
'What hurt Klaus . . .'	Kroll, *Der Tod in Cannes*, 611.
p. 120 'Excited to do . . .'	14 March 1937.
'His prodigious castles . . .'	*TP*, 306.
'The material . . .'	17 March 1937.
'One promenade . . .'	*TP*, 301.
p. 121 'A right melancholy . . .'	27 May 1937.
'A pleasure that . . .'	29 May 1937.
p. 122 'In the foreseeable . . .'	7 June 1937, in *BA*, 305–6.
'You have seen . . .'	Quoted in ibid., 10 June 1937.
'I pay no . . .'	Ibid.
'The luck and . . .'	19 May 1937.
'. . . still very happy . . .'	16 June 1937.
'Shall I love . . .'	28 May 1937.
p. 123 'I was happy . . .'	*TP*, 306.
'Sad about . . .'	24 November 1937.
p. 124 'Now I have it.'	31 March 1937.
'Slight depression . . .'	29 June 1937.
'I like this . . .'	30 July 1937.
p. 125 '*Vergittertes Fenster* is . . .'	Hoffer, *Klaus Mann*, 98.
'*he* already loves . . .'	7 September 1937.

Chapter 7: Stalin's Agent 1938–39

p. 128 'The events of the . . .'	12 March 1938.
'LIFE – my work . . .'	12–14 March 1938.
p. 129 '*What should we do?* . . .'	18 March 1938.
'It appears highly . . .'	30 March 1938.
p. 130 'I do not think . . .'	1 April 1938.

'total collapse . . .'	3 April 1938.
'Binswanger wants to . . .'	8 April 1938.
p. 131 'I do not know . . .'	Golo Mann, 'Erinnerungen an meinen Bruder Klaus', *BA*, 640.
'Discussion of the family . . .'	9 April 1938.
'What we teach . . .'	*TP*, 225.
'Drugs. I use . . .'	21 April 1938.
'I didn't breathe . . .'	28 April 1938.
'We both wanted to . . .'	*TP*, 310.
p. 132 'I don't really want . . .'	21 June 1938.
'We made friends . . .'	*TP*, 312.
p. 133 'I didn't have . . .'	Ibid.
'How remarkably . . .'	26 July 1938.
'Writing is the . . .'	3 August 1938.
p. 134 'A series of . . .'	25 August 1938.
'Very old, almost . . .'	28 August 1938.
'Deep despondency . . .'	5 September 1938.
p. 135 'The cold sacrifice . . .'	22 September 1938.
'The dilemma which . . .'	22 March 1942.
p. 136 '*Profound political depression* . . .'	30 September 1938.
p. 137 'un petit sauvage . . .'	12 November 1938.
'And then suddenly . . .'	15 November 1938.
'Anything German . . .'	20 November 1938.
p. 138 'Not without danger . . .'	4 January 1939.
'Suddenly think of . . .'	4 May 1936.
p. 140 'In practically no other . . .'	Naumann, ed., '*Ruhe gibt es nicht*', 229.
'Neither effort was . . .'	*TP*, 309–10.
p. 141 '. . . with emotion and . . .'	*BA*, 389.
'Your letter which . . .'	*BA*, 391–2.
'a barbaric gentleman . . .'	4 May 1939.
p. 142 'I see everything . . .'	21 May 1939.
'He *needed* fame . . .'	23 May 1939.
'Practically everybody who . . .'	*W*, 377.
p. 144 'I scarcely dare . . .'	6 June 1939.
p. 145 'Not a true . . .'	12 April 1939.
'Both are . . .'	7 April 1939.
'young British leftists . . .'	21 April 1939.
p. 146 'Between Auden and . . .'	19 June 1939.
'Writers understand nothing . . .'	19 June 1939.
'For example, Heinrich . . .'	Fredric Kroll, *Trauma Amerika 1937–1942*, 196.
p. 147 'We all felt . . .'	3 September 1939.
'These Americans . . .'	25 August 1939.
p. 148 'Why don't Americans know . . .'	15 October 1939.
'Everything very, very . . .'	20 October 1939.
'Even the type of . . .'	*TP*, 309.
p. 149 'Is that the price . . .'	18 November 1939.
'The end of a . . .'	18 November 1939.
p. 145 'No, I didn't know . . .'	Naumann, ed., *Die Kinder der Manns*, 162.

Chapter 8: Farewell to Germany 1940–41

p. 151 'How about an author . . .'	*TP*, 351.
'The innermost substance . . .'	Ibid.

p. 152	'The writer must not . . .'	Ibid.
	'The last thing I . . .'	22 February 1940.
p. 153	'I have a few . . .'	19 September 1940.
	'To be honest . . .'	15 March 1940.
	'Let them all go . . .'	19 September 1940.
p. 154	'Exile has reached an . . .'	3 March 1940.
	'Eventually I will be . . .'	27 December 1940.
	'Again and again . . .'	22 September 1940.
	'Cute little scoundrel . . .'	17 January 1940.
p. 155	'The character of Speed . . .'	10 September 1940.
	'It makes you literally . . .'	18 June 1940.
p. 156	'*Hours* of doubt . . .'	Kroll, *Trauma Amerika*, 262–3.
	'Desperate cries for . . .'	*TP*, 331.
p. 157	'I never really . . .'	13 October 1940.
	'I tried to explain . . .'	Christopher Isherwood, *Diaries: Volume One, 1939–1960*, 8 July 1940.
p. 158	'Long conversation with . . .'	15 July 1940; *TP*, 331–2.
	'Klaus looks very . . .'	Isherwood, *Diaries: Volume One*, 8 July 1940.
	'the strength of the . . .'	Carpenter, *W.H. Auden,* 308.
p. 159	'Erika Mann does not . . .'	Ibid., 307.
	'I would never have . . .'	Christopher Isherwood, *Diaries: Volume Three, 1970–1983*, 27 June 1981.
	'Once again stubborn . . .'	30 May 1940.
p. 160	'We see each other . . .'	Kroll, *Trauma Amerika*, 262.
	'It all took place . . .'	Monika Mann, *Vergangenes und Gegenwärtiges*, 76ff.
p. 161	'Chamberlain is more . . .'	9 January 1941.
	'It is impossible . . .'	Kroll, *Trauma Amerika*, 232.
p. 162	'If America allows Hitler . . .'	18 June 1940.
	'From America *nothing* . . .'	Thomas Mann, diary 1940–43, 104.
	'The more dramatic and imminent . . .'	'Unsere Bewährungspflicht' in *Zweimal Deutschland*, 17.
	'Yes, political-literary . . .'	Letter, 31 December 1939, *BA*, 409.
	'Erika did not . . .'	26 December 1940.
p. 163	'I felt a sense of . . .'	14 October 1940; *TP*, 396.
p. 164	'Tea with the Huxleys . . .'	*TP*, 332–3.
	'Went to see Noël . . .'	29 November 1940.
	'The nicest person . . .'	10 November 1940.
	'the strange house . . .'	8 October 1940.
p. 165	'George in a . . .'	8 October 1940.
p. 166	'What a weird set-up . . .'	17 November 1940.
	'Klaus and Erika . . .'	Janet Flanner, *Janet Flanner's World: Uncollected Writings 1932–1975*, 182.
p. 167	'You should be proud . . .'	25 September 1942.
	'I miss you . . .'	15 May 1945.
	'You are brilliantly gifted . . .'	23 March 1944.
	'a passionate friendship . . .'	Robert Greenfield, *Dreamer's Journey: The Life and Writings of Frederic Prokosch*, 158.
	'I went there . . .'	*TP*, 150.
	'I liked Klaus . . .'	Frederic Prokosch, *Voices: A Memoir*, 130.
p. 168	'Sometimes I would like . . .'	Quoted in Kroll, *Trauma Amerika*, 401–2.
p. 169	'Worn out and . . .'	*TP*, 330.
p. 170	'Amazingly it materializes . . .'	*TP*, 338.
	'I had scarcely believed . . .'	*TP*, 339.

p. 171 'Some friends keep warning . . .'	25 September 1940.
'It seems to me . . .'	Kroll, *Trauma Amerika*, 284.
p. 172 'I work at least . . .'	Quoted in Naumann, *Klaus Mann*, 110.
'Klaus goes to all . . .'	Frankenberg, Colby College Archive.
'He spoke too fast . . .'	Plant, 'Eine persönliche Erinnerung an Klaus Mann', in Kroll, *Trauma Amerika*, 298–9.
p. 173 'How cruel and capricious . . .'	TP, 344.
p. 174 'Social gatherings are . . .'	Letter, 23 May 1941.
'I felt very strongly . . .'	Kroll, *Trauma Amerika*, 288.
'The Mephistophelian old pimp . . .'	Ibid.
'I am afraid . . .'	'Last Decision', Monacensia.
p. 175 'When I think of all . . .'	Richard Winston, *An Exceptional Friendship: The Correspondence of Thomas Mann and Erich Kahler*, 101.
p. 176 '*Rien à faire* . . .'	Letter, 29 December 1941, Klaus Mann Archive.

Chapter 9: A New Identity 1942

p. 177 'I have invested more . . .'	TP, 356.
p. 178 'If a venture of this . . .'	TP, 333.
p. 179 'I don't know what . . .'	Michael Shelden, *Friends of Promise: Cyril Connolly and the World of Horizon*, 86.
p. 181 'I am left alone . . .'	22 September 1940.
'Nothing happened . . .'	30 January 1941.
'There was this . . .'	30 May 1940.
'He tells me . . .'	8 October 1940.
'he wanted to see . . .'	6 September 1940.
p. 182 'I shall not forget . . .'	8 June 1942.
'I really care . . .'	18 June 1942.
'He is – and remains . . .'	21 June 1942.
'appalling, drunk . . .'	8 March 1942.
'How inadequate . . .'	31 May 1942.
'Better today than . . .'	9 June 1942.
p. 183 'Tomski's romance . . .'	21 June 1942.
'Yes, I am afraid . . .'	25 June 1942.
'For the first time in . . .'	TP, 362.
'Yes, I want to . . .'	TP, 363.
p. 184 'It would be difficult . . .'	8 June 1942.
'I am impatient to . . .'	31 May 1942.
'very active agents . . .'	Alexander Stephan, *Im Visier des FBI*, 99–100.
p. 185 'Klaus Mann, Erika Mann Auden . . .'	Ibid., 86–7; Kroll, *Trauma Amerika*, 374.
p. 186 'it was an open secret . . .'	Kroll, *Trauma Amerika*, 339.
'subject occupies . . .'	Stephan, *Im Visier des FBI*, 89–90.
p. 187 'at 12:32 p.m. at which time . . .'	Ibid., 90.
'stated that Klaus Mann . . .'	Ibid., 89.
'advised that there was . . .'	Kroll, *Trauma Amerika*, 375–6.
p. 188 'I don't want to lie . . .'	18 August 1942.
'To tell the truth . . .'	1 August 1942.
p. 189 'I am not interested in . . .'	18 August 1941.
'Shall I ever live . . .'	3 March 1942.
p. 190 'To keep things in perspective . . .'	Harpprecht, *Thomas Mann*, 1284.

p. 191	'Ill. Monday and Tuesday . . .'	Kroll, *Trauma Amerika*, 380.
	'If I have to make up . . .'	'The Last Decision', in *Zweimal Deutschland*.
p. 192	'YOUR DEAR ONES . . .'	*BA*, 486.
	'The N.Y. Times . . .'	Kroll, *Trauma Amerika*, 391–2.
p. 193	'It is an unusually . . .'	Letter, 2 October 1942, *BA*, 487–9.
	'6 months will pass . . .'	6 October 1942.
p. 194	' "Encouraging", he told . . .'	6 October 1942.
	'I consider it . . .'	22 October 1942.
	'I feel like an actor . . .'	Ibid.
	'Passed the morning . . .'	24 October 1942.
	'Realizing I am . . .'	Ibid.
p. 195	'This is obviously . . .'	Ibid.
	'no speeches, please . . .'	Ibid.
	'After having sobbed . . .'	26 October 1942.

Chapter 10: 'Misplaced' 1943

p. 198	'Don't think you . . .'	Kroll, *Der Tod in Cannes*, 10.
p. 199	'for two reasons . . .'	*BA*, 501–2.
	'It don't make no . . .'	Kroll, *Der Tod in Cannes*, 14.
	'I don't give a damn . . .'	Ibid., 13–14.
p. 200	'The drills are especially . . .'	Letter, 14 February 1943, *BA*, 498.
	'irregular in his . . .'	Kroll, *Der Tod in Cannes*, 14.
	'I am certainly not . . .'	*W*, 440–2.
p. 201	'So that your mind . . .'	*BA*, 506.
p. 202	'. . . our relationship is . . .'	4 June 1934, Johannes Schmidinger, *Wo freilich ich ganz daheim sein werde*, 193.
	'. . . a confused mixture . . .'	24 May 1948, ibid.
p. 203	'I have suffered bitterly . . .'	Winston, *An Exceptional Friendship*, 422–4.
	'Only since I have lived . . .'	*W*, 440–2 (the notes were incorporated in a letter to Erika, 14 February 1943).
p. 204	'You are a Jew . . .'	5 June 1943.
	'They have taught me . . .'	Kroll, *Der Tod in Cannes*, 23.
p. 205	'[Seger] considers Klaus . . .'	FBI report, 31 May 1943, in Kroll, *Der Tod in Cannes*, 34.
	'He knew Subject . . .'	Ibid., 35.
p. 206	'He is pro-communist . . .'	Ibid., 32.
	'. . . had engaged in all . . .'	Ibid., 35.
p. 207	'reports which I . . .'	8 July 1943, ibid., 37.
	'The "war of nerves" . . .'	11 June 1943.
p. 208	'The worst thing . . .'	20 June 1943.
	'My own sex life . . .'	11 October 1943.
	'An intense feeling . . .'	13 June 1943.
	'If my application . . .'	1 July 1943.
p. 209	'Crawling on muddy . . .'	28 September 1943.
p. 210	'. . . docile to any . . .'	Stephan, *Im Visier des FBI*, 95.
	'had the same democratic . . .'	Ibid., 95.
p. 211	'a capable writer . . .'	Ibid., 96.
	'He asked me the most . . .'	Ibid., 93.
p. 212	'Subject is highly intelligent . . .'	Ibid., 93–4.
	'This agent is . . .'	Ibid.
p. 213	'I was forced to be . . .'	11 October 1943.
p. 214	'The Nazi boys seem . . .'	7 November 1943.

p. 215	'Saying goodbye . . .'	3 December 1943.
	'It is time I close these . . .'	8 December 1943.

Chapter 11: German Problem Children 1944–45

p. 216	'Horrible, a real . . .'	*W*, 453.
	'WAITING . . .'	13 January 1944.
p. 217	*'There is absolutely . . .'*	Kroll, *Der Tod in Cannes*, 89.
	'boring, rather lonely . . .'	9–12 April 1944.
p. 218	'It is strange and . . .'	1 March 1944, *BA*, 523.
	'Did my last letter . . .'	26 April 1944, Kroll, *Der Tod in Cannes*, 94.
p. 219	'I spent a stimulating . . .'	26 April 1944.
	'Abroad he might be . . .'	Kroll, *Der Tod in Cannes*, 146.
p. 220	'Even in our circle . . .'	Ibid., 105.
p. 221	'One allows oneself . . .'	28 June 1944, ibid., 107.
	'As for "la *Grande Illusion*" . . .'	31 July 1944, ibid., 108.
	'The army is too well . . .'	Ibid., 111.
p. 222	'As for my own lyre . . .'	13 October 1944, *BA*, 529.
p. 223	'The melancholy fact . . .'	17 September 1944, Kroll, *Der Tod in Cannes*, 118.
	'It is our view . . .'	18 September 1944, ibid., 121.
p. 224	'We had failed . . .'	Quoted in *Auf verlorenem Posten*, 138ff.
	'Never before has . . .'	28 April 1944, Kroll, *Der Tod in Cannes*, 149.
	'He is certainly . . .'	Ibid., 126.
p. 225	'The first encouraging . . .'	27 July 1944.
	'We have to accept . . .'	*Auf verlorenem Posten*, 138–52.
p. 226	'If we believed . . .'	Unpublished essay, Kroll, *Der Tod in Cannes*, 112–13.
p. 227	'I'd better be careful . . .'	Letter, 23 July 1944, Kroll, ibid., 123.
	'I couldn't even . . .'	Letter, 1 September 1944, Kroll, ibid., 125.
p. 228	'These ruins . . .'	*Stars and Stripes*, Kroll, ibid., 155.
	'I thought it would . . .'	Letter to Thomas Mann, 16 May 1945; *Stars and Stripes*, 20 May 1945.
	'when I shall requisition . . .'	28 June 1945, Kroll, *Der Tod in Cannes*, 155.
p. 229	'Our poor mutilated . . .'	16 May 1945, *BA*, 536.
	'But you have to . . .'	*W*, 481.
	'The sense of . . .'	*Stars and Stripes*, 20 May 1945.
p. 230	'Had a real house . . .'	15 December 1945; Winston, *Letters of Thomas Mann*, vol. 2, 491.
	'I feel now . . .'	16 May 1945, *BA* 540.
p. 231	'Everything depends . . .'	*W*, 494–5.
p. 233	'I have seen Goschi . . .'	Letter, 24 May 1945, *BA*, 541–2.
	'Every German mother . . .'	*Auf verlorenem Posten*, 234.
	'Ja, ja. That was Hitler's . . .'	*Stars and Stripes*, 8 June 1945.
p. 234	'Imagine that! . . .'	Ibid., 29 May 1945.
p. 235	'Finally I have met . . .'	Ibid., 29 May 1945.
p. 237	'There you have a real . . .'	Ibid., 17 June 1945.
	'Almost every day . . .'	Letter, 1 July 1945.
p. 238	'There are many things . . .'	Letter, 21 July 1945, *BA*, 543.
	'Süskind walked up . . .'	Harpprecht, *Thomas Mann*, 1534.
p. 239	'What can you say?'	Letter, 16 May 1945.
	'I am no one's judge . . .'	Erika Mann, *BA, 1949–1950*; Kroll, *Der Tod in Cannes*, 278.
	'As you know . . .'	Letter, 5 January 1945.

'Erika could hate . . .'   Video interview.
'I was sitting at dinner . . .'   Kroll, *Der Tod in Cannes*, 180.
'To observe his . . .'   Ibid., 178.
p. 240 'In principle I would . . .'   Letter, 21 October 1945, Kroll, *Der Tod in Cannes*, 196.

'You can't go home . . .'   TP, 367, 372.
p. 241 'I have not managed . . .'   Letter, 17 August 1945, Kroll, *Der Tod in Cannes*, 196.

p. 242 'The subject of the film . . .' Ibid., 186.
'It went all rather fast . . .'   Letter, 30 September 1945, Kroll, *Der Tod in Cannes*, 209.

'Discharged . . .'   29 August 1945.
'I stay . . .'   30 August 1945.
p. 243 'The Italian text . . .'   Kroll, *Der Tod in Cannes*, 215.
'Mann wearied Rossellini . . .'   Tag Gallagher, *The Adventures of Roberto Rossellini*, 183.

'I am going to give . . .'   Kroll, Ibid., 218.
p. 244 'In Paris I was not . . .'   Letter, 15 July 1945, Kroll, ibid., 178.
'He may be a . . .'   TP, 175.
p. 245 'For all his vanity . . .'   W, 221.
'I am slowly recovering . . .'   Letter, 11 November 1945, Kroll, *Der Tod in Cannes*, 211.

Chapter 12: The Shadow Falls 1946–47

p. 247 'Find idea attractive . . .'   BA, 553.
p. 248 'Klaus was – let's say . . .' Weiss, *In the Shadow*, 220.
'What really amuses . . .'   Letter, 19 December 1945.
'Departure not urgent . . .'   Cable, 18 April 1946, BA 554.
p. 250 'We have just left . . .'   Letter, 25 July 1946, BA, 559.
p. 251 '11 o'clock, arrival . . .'   27 July 1946.
'She returned home . . .'   Weiss, *In the Shadow*, 225.
'It is the author's . . .'   Kroll, *Der Tod in Cannes*, 273–4.
p. 253 'He was well-built . . .'   Christopher Isherwood, *Lost Years: A Memoir, 1945–1951*, 155.

'Harold does not . . .'   13 January 1947.
'Harold gone . . .'   21 January 1947.
p. 254 'working very slowly . . .'   28 June 1947.
p. 255 'No one wants . . .'   Kroll, *Der Tod in Cannes*, 313.
p. 256 'In my eyes any book . . .'   Winston, *An Exceptional Friendship*, 481.
p. 257 'I am busy with a . . .'   Kroll, *Der Tod in Cannes*, 304.
p. 258 'The French *Turning* . . .'   Ibid., 314.
'We are on cordial terms . . .'   Letter, 2 October 1947.
'Poor Klaus ultimately . . .'   Cocteau, *Le passé défini, 1951–1952*.
p. 259 'Dear Mr Mann . . .'   Kroll, *Der Tod in Cannes*, 362–3.
'Never did I meet . . .'   *Berliner Beiträge*, 46.
p. 260 '. . . his publication *Decision* . . .' Office of Military Government memo of 2 July 1947, Kroll, *Der Tod in Cannes*, 303.

Chapter 13: *Todessehnsucht* 1948

p. 263 'By now . . .'   Kroll, *Der Tod in Cannes*, 375.
p. 264 'He never spoke . . .'   Ibid., 358.

p. 265 'When he spoke ...'	Ibid., 377.
'Worried by ...'	Ibid., 368.
p. 266 'Struck, deeply ...'	10 March 1948.
'Ticklish but OK ...'	17 March 1948.
p. 267 'I emphatically ...'	'Die Tragödie Jan Masaryk', in *Auf verlorenem Posten*, 469ff.
'No occupation ...'	Kroll, *Der Tod in Cannes*, 373.
p. 270 'European-born writers ...'	Ibid., 389–90.
p. 271 'I mentioned to Klaus ...'	Ibid., 391.
'I shall never ...'	Ibid., 401.
'For some fifteen ...'	*Auf verlorenem Posten*, 467.
p. 272 'It seemed to me that ...'	Kroll, *Der Tod in Cannes*, 402.
p. 274 'I find it increasingly ...'	*Klaus Mann: zum Gedächtnis*, 168.
p. 275 'I am somewhat angry ...'	Letter, 12 July 1948.
'My dear Klaus ...'	12 July 1948, *BA*, 584.
'You can still achieve ...'	Kroll, *Der Tod in Cannes*, 418.
'How more than sad ...'	Ibid., 416.
'Your Gide biography ...'	Ibid.
'Suicide, as I once ...'	Ibid., 415.
p. 276 'Obviously his whole ...'	Ibid., 413.
'I had been very blunt ...'	14 January 1982, ibid.
p. 277 'On the surface, as ...'	Isherwood, *Lost Years*, 156.
'Quarrel with Harold ...'	3 August 1948.
p. 278 'I found him to be an ...'	Letter, 25 January 1978, Kroll, *Der Tod in Cannes*, 427.
'So you are ...'	Letter, 23 August 1948.
p. 279 '6 ½ pages ...'	28 August 1948.
'Worked (if you can) ...'	18 September 1948.
'Slow. Slow, slow ...'	29 September 1948.
'I was pleased to see ...'	27 October 1948.
p. 280 'he was *in effect* ...'	Kroll, *Der Tod in Cannes*, 453.
p. 281 'Aren't you surprised? ...'	13 November 1948.

Chapter 14: Death in Cannes 1949

p. 283 'The longing for death ...'	Reich-Ranicki, *Thomas Mann and His Family*, 174.
p. 284 'I see him still ...'	Kroll, *Der Tod in Cannes*, 459.
'Out of *Turning Point* ...'	Ibid., 462.
'One doesn't commit suicide ...'	Ibid., 595.
p. 285 'his relaxed, happy mood'	*Klaus Mann: zum Gedächtnis*.
p. 287 'Intellectual intolerance ...'	Anthony Heilbut, *Exiled in Paradise: German Refugee Artists and Intellectuals in America from the 1930s to the Present*, 386.
p. 288 'Oh America, my dreamland ...'	Kroll, *Trauma Amerika*, 403.
'Everything considered ...'	*BA*, 607–8.
p. 289 '... two freezing animals ...'	Kroll, *Der Tod in Cannes*, 510.
p. 290 'Oh, Klaus-dear ...'	Letter, 29 April 1949.
'Feeling, low, low ...'	29 April 1949.
'Started in all ...'	24 April 1949.
'It is a very strong ...'	Letter to Erika, 4 May 1949, *BA*, 613.
p. 291 'Letter to Mops ...'	17 May 1949.
'it would be difficult ...'	Letter, 5 May 1949, *BA*, 798.
'Too risky ...'	Kroll, *Der Tod in Cannes*, 515.
'Your letter is priceless ...'	12 May 1949, *BA*, 614.

p. 292 'Stupidly I am in . . .'   Letter, 4 May 1949, *BA*, 613.
        'Regrets but not . . .'   Kroll, *Der Tod in Cannes*, 519.
        'In his final letters . . .'   Erika Mann, *BA*, 105.
p. 293 'My spies, snoops . . .'   *BA*, 623–4.
        'Dearest mom . . .'   *BA*, 624–6.
p. 297 '. . . suicidal gesture . . .'   Kroll, *Der Tod in Cannes*, 413.
        'I will not do it . . .'   22 May 1939.
        'I am planning . . .'   *Klaus Mann: zum Gedächtnis.*
        'I await my death . . .'   21 May 1939.
        'I ask myself . . .'   8 October 1936.
        'It may be most . . .'   14 March 1942.
p. 298 '. . . chewing all those sleeping 15 May 1949, Erika Mann, *BA*.
            pills . . .'
        'Any irregularly nourished . . .'   Harald Neumann, *Klaus Mann: Eine
                                               Psychobiographie*, 157.
p. 299 'He had evidently . . .'   Kroll, *Der Tod in Cannes*, 535.
        'In Cannes we searched . . .'   Letter, 27 July 1949.

Epilogue

p. 300 'My inward sympathy . . .'   22 May 1949.
        'These are sad days . . .'   Letter, 26 May 1949, Hans Wysling, ed.,
                                               *Letters of Heinrich and Thomas Mann,
                                               1900–1949*, 260–1.
        'For this remark . . .'   *Die Manns* (television film).
p. 301 'It was necessary to be . . .'   Letter, 24 May 1949, Wysling, ed., *Letters*, 260.
        'To my great surprise . . .'   14 January 1982, Kroll, *Der Tod in Cannes*,
                                               555–6.
        'worst of all for . . .'   Weiss, *In the Shadow*, 244.
        'When Klaus died . . .'   Ibid., 247.
        'We were a part of each other . . .' 17 June 1949, Erika Mann, *BA*, 261.
        'How I shall live . . .'   16 June 1949, *BA*, 260.
        'The poem you wrote . . .'   Lancaster, *Brian Howard*, 300.
p. 303 'The general public . . .'   Naumann, ed., *Die Kinder der Manns*, 86.
p. 304 'With amazing consistency . . .'   Hayman, *Thomas Mann*, 583.
        'I am more and . . .'   Ibid., 577.
p. 305 'more and more depressing . . .'   Interview with *Die Welt am Sonntag*, 27 April
                                               2008.
p. 307 'Erika and Klaus . . .'   12 January 1972.
        'I am doing this . . .'   Interview with *Die Welt am Sonntag*, 27 April
                                               2008.
        'When Golo adopted . . .'   Ibid.
p. 310 'Although there were . . .'   Ibid.
        'I don't think he . . .'   Ibid.
        'My father's trauma . . .'   Ibid.
p. 311 'I wanted to escape from . . .'   Ibid.

Bibliography

Principal Works

Vor dem Leben (1925)
Anja und Esther (1925)
Der fromme Tanz (1926)
Kindernovella (1926)
Revue zu Vieren (1926)
Heute und Morgen (1927)
Rundherum (co-authored with Erika Mann) (1929)
Gegenüber von China (1929)
Alexander (1929)
Geschwister (1930)
Das Buch von der Riviera (co-authored with Erika Mann) (1931)
Treffpunkt im Unendlichen (1932)
Kind dieser Zeit (1932)
Athen (1932)
Symphonie Pathétique: A Tchaikovsky Novel (1935)
Mephisto (1936)
Vergittertes Fenster (1937)
Der Vulkan (1939)
Escape to Life (co-authored with Erika Mann) (1939)
The Other Germany (co-authored with Erika Mann) (1940)
The Turning Point: Thirty-five Years in This Century (1942)
André Gide and the Crisis of Modern Thought (1943)
Heart of Europe: An Anthology of Creative Writing in Europe 1920–1940 (co-edited with Hermann Kesten) (1943)
Der siebente Engel (1946)
Pathetic Symphony: A Novel about Tchaikovsky (1948)
André Gide: Die Geschichte eines Europäers (1948)
Der Wendepunkt: Ein Lebensbericht (1952)

Filmography

Films about Klaus Mann

Treffpunkt im Unendlichen – documentary film by Heinrich Breloer (1983)
Bitter ist die Verbannung, bitterer noch die Heimkehr – documentary film by Bart van Esch (1998)
Dichtung und Wirklichkeit: Klaus Manns Mephisto – documentary film by Veronika Vogel (1998)
Escape to Life – documentary film by Andrea Weiss and Wieland Speck (2000)
Die Manns: Ein Jahrhundertroman (2002)
Das kleine Europa (2004)

Television films of Klaus Mann's works

Treffpunkt im Unendlichen (1983)
Flucht in den Norden (1986)
Der Vulkan (1996)

Index